MANAGEMENT, WORK AND ORGANISATIONS

Series editors: **Gibson Burrell**, The Management Centre, University of Leicester
Mick Marchington, Manchester Business School
Paul Thompson, Department of Human Resource Management, University of Strathclyde

This series of new textbooks covers the areas of human resource management, employee relations, organisational behaviour and related business and management fields. Each text has been specially commissioned to be written by leading experts in a clear and accessible way. The books contain serious and challenging material, take an analytical rather than prescriptive approach and are particularly suitable for use by students with no prior specialist knowledge.

The series is relevant for many business and management courses, including MBA and post-experience courses, specialist masters and postgraduate diplomas, professional courses and final-year undergraduate courses. These texts have become essential reading at business and management schools worldwide.

Published

Paul Blyton and Peter Turnbull **The Dynamics of Employee Relations** (3rd edn)
Sharon C. Bolton **Emotion Management in the Workplace**
Sharon C. Bolton and Maeve Houlihan **Searching for the Human in Human Resource Management**
Peter Boxall and John Purcell **Strategy and Human Resource Management**
J. Martin Corbett **Critical Cases in Organisational Behaviour**
Keith Grint **Leadership**
Irena Grugulis **Skills, Training and Human Resource Development**
Damian Hodgson and Svetlana Cicmil **Making Projects Critical**
Marek Korczynski **Human Resource Management in Service Work**
Karen Legge **Human Resource Management**: anniversary edition
Helen Rainbird (ed.) **Training in the Workplace**
Jill Rubery and Damian Grimshaw **The Organisation of Employment**
Harry Scarbrough (ed.) **The Management of Expertise**
Hugh Scullion and Margaret Linehan **International Human Resource Management**
Adrian Wilkinson, Mick Marchington, Tom Redman and Ed Snape **Managing With Total Quality Management**
Colin C. Williams **Rethinking the Future of Work**
Diana Winstanley and Jean Woodall (eds) **Ethical Issues in Contemporary Human Resource Management**

For more information on titles in the Series please go to www.palgrave.com/busines/mwo

Invitation to authors
The Series Editors welcome proposals for new books within the Management, Work and Organisations series. These should be sent to Paul Thompson (p.thompson@strath.ac.uk) at the Dept of HRM, Strathclyde Business School, University of Strathclyde, 50 Richmond St Glasgow G1 1XT

Series Standing Order

If you would like to receive future titles in this series as they are published, you can make use of our standing order facility. To place a standing order please contact your bookseller or, in case of difficulty, write to us at the address below with your name and address and the name of the series. Please state with which title you wish to begin your standing order.

Customer Services Department, Macmillan Distribution Ltd
Houndmills, Basingstoke, Hampshire RG21 6XS, England

Other books by Sharon C. Bolton

Emotion Management in the Workplace

Dimensions of Dignity at Work

Searching for the human in human resource management

Theory, practice and workplace contexts

Edited by

Sharon C. Bolton and Maeve Houlihan

Selection and editorial matter © Sharon C. Bolton and Maeve Houlihan 2007
Individual chapters © contributors

All rights reserved. No reproduction, copy or transmission of this
publication may be made without written permission.

No paragraph of this publication may be reproduced, copied or transmitted
save with written permission or in accordance with the provisions of the
Copyright, Designs and Patents Act 1988, or under the terms of any licence
permitting limited copying issued by the Copyright Licensing Agency,
90 Tottenham Court Road, London W1T 4LP.

Any person who does any unauthorised act in relation to this publication
may be liable to criminal prosecution and civil claims for damages.

The authors have asserted their rights to be identified
as the authors of this work in accordance with the Copyright,
Designs and Patents Act 1988.

First published 2007 by
PALGRAVE MACMILLAN
Houndmills, Basingstoke, Hampshire RG21 6XS and
175 Fifth Avenue, New York, N.Y. 10010
Companies and representatives throughout the world

PALGRAVE MACMILLAN is the global academic imprint of the Palgrave
Macmillan division of St. Martin's Press, LLC and of Palgrave Macmillan Ltd.
Macmillan® is a registered trademark in the United States, United Kingdom
and other countries. Palgrave is a registered trademark in the European
Union and other countries.

ISBN-13: 978-0-230-01935-5 paperback
ISBN-10: 0-230-01935-8 paperback

This book is printed on paper suitable for recycling and made from fully
managed and sustained forest sources. Logging, pulping and manufacturing
processes are expected to conform to the environmental regulations of the
country of origin.

A catalogue record for this book is available from the British Library.

A catalog record for this book is available from the Library of Congress.

10   9   8   7   6   5   4   3   2   1
16   15   14   13   12   11   10   09   08   07

Printed and bound in China

The main content of Chapter 12 is Copyright (c) Polly Toynbee. From *Hard
Work: Life in Low-pay Britain* published in 2003 by Bloomsbury. Reproduced
by permission of the author c/o Rogers, Coleridge & White Ltd., 20 Powis
Mews, London W11 1JN.

To our families, whose special role in our lives means never having to search very far for the H.

Contents

Acknowledgements

The idea for this book was born during one of many long phone calls between Preston and Dublin . . . or was it on a long walk and pub supper in Dalkey? Or might it have been at an Academy of Management conference in New Orleans? Or perhaps during dinner at an International Labour Process gathering in Glasgow? It is the joy of a friendship and a vibrant working partnership that it is sometimes difficult to pinpoint the exact moment when conversations become ideas, and ideas become actions. We have enjoyed the putting together of this book, more and more so with each step as searching for the H has come to life through dialogues with each of the contributors. The arguments you will find on the following pages give voice and clarity to passions so many of us feel arising from our ongoing work with and study of contemporary work organisations, and their relationship with society. We hope you will join in this dialogue, whether to enlarge upon it or add counterpoint, so as to ultimately build a growing and urgent search for and affirmation of the human side of contemporary organisations, that like our own search, sees ideas move from eclectic words into practical action.

Eclectic words can do only limited justice to the warm thanks we owe to each of the authors who so graciously and enthusiastically responded to our proposals, prompts and, indeed it has been said, at times 'bossy' timelines. We are proud to have your work in this book, and deeply appreciative of your involvement in this project. We are pleased to be able to feature a chapter from Polly Toynbee's classic *Hard Work: Life in Low-pay Britain* and thank Polly, and Michael Baskhar at Rogers, Coleridge and White for their speedy and wholehearted help with copyright permissions. We are also grateful to Rosemary Batt, Professor of Women and Work, Cornell University, for her wonderful support of the symposium 'Searching for the H' at the Academy of Management, Atlanta, in August 2006. A special 'thank you' goes to Gemma

Wibberley at Lancaster for her diligent editorial assistance and to Ursula Gavin, Lee Ann Tutton and all at Palgrave Macmillan for their great support and enthusiasm for the project. And of course we thank our families, friends and colleagues for their continual support and interest in what we do as well as their patience with the long silences, short tempers and occasionally absent presence which our humanity sometimes proffers. You have our heartfelt gratitude.

SCB and MH

Notes on contributors

Sharon Bolton is Professor of Organisational Analysis in the Department of Management at Strathclyde Business School. Sharon moved to Strathclyde University in March 2007. Prior to this she spent six years in the Department of Organisation, Work and Technology at Lancaster University Management School and her first academic position was as Simon Marks Research Fellow in the Department of Sociology, University of Manchester. She completed her PhD in May 1999 in the Department of Behaviour in Organisations, University of Lancaster. In her previous life, Sharon worked as a Senior Administrator in the public and private sectors. Her research interests include the emotional labour process, public sector management, the nursing and teaching labour process, gender and the professions and dignity in and at work in a moral economy. Sharon continually searches for the H and is pleased to say she often finds it in her gorgeous sons, partner, family and special friends and colleagues.

Jane Bryson is a senior lecturer in the Victoria Management School at Victoria University of Wellington, New Zealand. She has taught in HRM, industrial relations, organisation development and public management since embarking on a full-time academic career in 1999. Prior to this she worked as an organisational psychologist and consultant in New Zealand, Australia and the UK, and as a HR Manager in the public sector. Her doctorate in Psychology, completed in 1997, examined the tensions inherent between professional values and managerial imperatives in the health sector. She remains fascinated by managers and professionals, and issues connecting institutional, organisational and individual influences on behaviour. She is currently leading part of a project exploring influences on the development of human capability in New Zealand workplaces. Jane is also Associate Fellow of the ESRC Centre on Skills, Knowledge and Organisational Performance (SKOPE) in the United Kingdom.

Rick Delbridge is Professor of Organizational Analysis at Cardiff Business School and Senior Fellow of the ESRC/EPSRC Advanced Institute of Management Research. His research interests include work organisation, employment relations and the organisation and management of innovation. He is the author of *Life on the Line in Contemporary Manufacturing* and co-author of *The Exceptional Manager*. He is an associate editor of *Organization* and co-editor of the Routledge book series *Studies in Employment Relations*.

Steve Fleetwood is a keen cyclist, runner and fell walker. If he has any energy left, he teaches Employment Relations in the Department of Organisation, Work and Technology at Lancaster University Management School, and has published several articles on philosophy of science, political economy, labour markets and Human Resource Management. A new book, *The Performance of HR: Towards a New Meta Theory,* jointly authored with Anthony Hesketh, is to be published later in 2007 by Cambridge University Press.

Irena Grugulis is Professor of Employment Studies and head of the human resource management and organisational behaviour group at Bradford University School of Management. She has researched and written on numerous aspects of skills and training including the nature of skill, links to productivity, soft skills and emotional labour, Investors in People and NVQs. Her work has been funded by the ESRC, EPSRC and EU. Current projects include an exploration of skills in the film and television industry and employment and productivity in retailing. She is author of *Skills, Training and HRD* (2007) and has co-edited *The Skills that Matter* (2004) and *Customer Service* (2001). She is currently the Debates and Controversies editor of *Work, Employment and Society*.

Gerard Hanlon works at Queen Mary, University of London. He has been employed by a wide variety of Universities throughout the UK and made redundant by one or two. In this HRM-driven world of work he agrees with Ronald Reagan's comment 'It's true hard work never killed anybody, but I figure, why take the chance?' Unfortunately, he also believes that increasingly only American presidents and the like can get away with such a position.

Maeve Houlihan works at UCD Business Schools, University College Dublin, Ireland. Having a background in Industrial Relations and Human Resources, and following a Masters in Organisation Studies, she began lecturing at UCD in 1993. Maeve completed doctoral studies at Lancaster University's Department of Organisation, Work and Technology where her PhD involved a participant ethnographic study of the experience of working and managing in call centres. She may have sold you an insurance policy during that time. Maeve returned to UCD in 2000, where she coordinates the Masters in Management and Organisation Studies at the Smurfit School of Business and leads the undergraduate OB teaching team. Her research and publications focus on contemporary working lives, management practices, and their links with society, and current projects include the Ireland Study for the Global Call Centre Project and the UCD Egalitarian World Initiative.

Sarah Jenkins is a Lecturer in HRM at Cardiff Business School, Cardiff University. She earned her doctorate in Sociology from Northumbria University based on her research on gender relations and employment restructuring within six organisations in the North East of England. Sarah moved to Cardiff Business School as an ESRC-funded researcher to map the transformation of work at Royal Mail (with Miguel Martinez Lucio and Mike Noon). Her current research (with Hazel Conley at UWE) centres on changes in the teaching profession with specific interest in issues of emotional management. She is a member of Cardiff Business School's Organisational Research Group and has a broad range of research interests relating to the nature and content of, and employee responses to, workplace change. In addition, Sarah specialises in teaching contemporary issues in work and employment and qualitative research methods.

Marek Korczynski is Professor of Sociology of Work at Loughborough University Business School. He received his Doctorate from Warwick University. His research interests centre on social theory and work, the sociology of service work, and on the relationship between music and work. Among his books are *Human Resource Management in Service Work* (2002) and *Social Theory at Work* (2006, edited with Paul Edwards and Randy Hodson).

Karen Legge is Professor in Organisational Behaviour, Warwick Business School. Until 2003 Karen was joint editor of the *Journal of Management Studies* and has also served on numerous editorial boards including *British Journal of Industrial Relations, Gender, Work and Organization, Human*

Resource Management Journal, Industrial Relations and *Organization and Philosophy of Management.* Karen's research interests lie in the area of applying postmodern organisation theory to HRM, change management, development of learning organisations and organisational ethics. She has published widely in these areas, a well-known publication being *HRM: Rhetorics and Realities* (1995), a new, updated edition of which (The Anniversary Edition) appeared in 2005.

Joe O'Mahoney is a Lecturer in Organisation Studies at Cardiff Business School, University of Cardiff. He completed his BA in Ancient History at Oxford University in 1995 and his MA and PhD at Warwick Business School shortly after. After a few years in management consulting, specialising in organisational design, he decided he missed the good life too much and returned to academia. His research interests focus on the philosophy of identity, management consulting and anxiety at work. As well as his current position in Cardiff, Joe has also taught at Lancaster, Aston and Warwick Business Schools.

Martin Parker works at Leicester University School of Management, having previously been employed at Staffordshire and Keele. He mostly writes about politics, culture and ethics. Recent books include *Against Management* (2002), *For Business Ethics* (with Jones and ten Bos, 2005), and *The Dictionary of Alternatives* (with Fournier and Reedy, 2007). Some people claim he does Critical Management Studies, but he is not quite certain what that means.

Andrew Sayer is Professor of Social Theory and Political Economy in the Department of Sociology, Lancaster University, UK. His books include *Microcircuits of Capital* (with K.J. Morgan, 1988), *Method in Social Science* (1992), *The New Social Economy* (with R.A. Walker, 1992), *Radical Political Economy: A Critique* (1995), *Realism and Social Science* (2000) and *The Moral Significance of Class* (2005). He is currently working on 'moral economy' and a critique of social science's treatment of values in everyday life and in its own research. Other interests include making music, cycling, walking, having a life.

Paul Thompson is Professor of Organisational Analysis and Head of Department of Human Resource Management in the Business School at the University of Strathclyde. Amongst his recent publications are *Organizational Misbehaviour* (1999, with Stephen Ackroyd) and *A Handbook of Work and Organization* for Oxford University Press (co-edited with Stephen Ackroyd,

Pam Tolbert and Rose Batt, 2004). His research interests focus on skill and work organisation, control and resistance, organisational restructuring and changing political economy. He is an editor of two Palgrave Series – *Management, Work and Organization* and *Critical Perspectives on Work and Organization*.

Polly Toynbee is a Guardian columnist and broadcaster and was formerly the BBC's social affairs editor. Books include *Hard Work: Life in Low-pay Britain, Did Things Get Better? An Audit of the Labour Government* (with David Walker), *Hospital, Lost Children, The Way We Live Now* and *A Working Life.* She has won National Press Awards and was *What the Papers Say* columnist of the year. She lives in Lambeth and has four children.

Fiona Wilson is Professor of Organisational Behaviour in the School of Business and Management at the University of Glasgow. Her research interests span all areas of Organisational Behaviour and Work. She has published in a very wide range of journals including *Administrative Science Quarterly, Organization Studies, Organization, Human Relations, Sociology* and the *British Journal of Management.* She has also authored two books – *Organizational Behaviour and Work* and *Organizational Behaviour and Gender.*

1

Beginning the search for the H in HRM

Sharon C. Bolton and Maeve Houlihan

Introduction

The genesis of this book lies in some perennial questions concerning what is it to be human, what is the relationship between people and work, and what is the fundamental conception of human relationships embedded in the practice of Human Resource Management (HRM). We are not alone in asking such questions. Indeed, a growing literature bears testament to the fact that HRM has failed to deliver on many of its early promises and been unsuccessful in its attempts to achieve status as either a strategic partner or an employee champion. Within the field of HRM, desperate attempts to legitimise its own existence have led to an ever more economic approach, with greater and greater emphasis on providing empirical links between people management techniques and company performance. Turning to workplace contexts, whilst the 'soft' rhetoric of people as an organisation's greatest asset is universally maintained, here too, as the contributions in this book will testify, observation of practice indicates that 'people' figure largely as part of a balance sheet equation. Practitioners, prescriptive writers and critical commentators have, in various ways, noted the hard edge to the notion of human in HRM, and yet within these commentaries we find little illumination on the missing human. In sum, we suggest that in HR theory, practice, and in the workplace experience, though people appear to be of central concern, the rich, warm and unpredictable faces of humanity are all too clearly absent.

We aim to address the issue of the missing human in HRM by taking a fresh look at the Human in relation to society and organisations. Looking through a social lens, our approach situates people at the heart of how society

1

works and puts forward a 'thick' understanding of human relations (Sayer, 2005). People, in modern society, are not only economically dependent on the contributions made by others but also emotionally and psychologically dependent, just as organisations depend on the very humanity of their human resources, in all sorts of unacknowledged ways – a mutual reciprocality. Yet, despite this mutuality, we suggest that when employment relations are primarily conceived in economic terms, the 'thick' nature of human relations is reduced to a 'thin' veneer. Thinning relations can be observed most acutely in the contemporary practices of 'hard' HRM: the polarisation of skills, and occupational restructuring through work routinisation, lean staffing, contracting, agency work, casualisation and outsourcing; but it can also be found among the recesses of 'soft' HRM: individualisation, flexibility, strong culture management, and the many dimensions of the HR cycle.

The missing H is most clearly represented in the fact that, over the past twenty years, despite economic growth in most developed countries, rather than better jobs and better work, we have seen increases in job dissatisfaction, work intensification, hours worked, job insecurity and economic and social inequality (Ackroyd *et al.*, 2005, p. 12; Ehrenreich, 2001; Taylor, 2002; Toynbee, 2003). Rather than empowering people, the legacy of HRM as it is currently practised is to create a structured dependency for employees and citizens. While the market and economy go from strength to strength, it seems that the employees' lot improves, only (and not always) in economic terms, and that instead the focus of satisfaction has migrated from work (production) to consumption.

In making this argument, we would clearly state that we are not harking after a sentimental humanised past, a return to an earlier era of Human Relations arguments, or a revolutionary turn. We recognise and acknowledge that capitalism exists, and as managers, employees, organisations, consumers, we are all thoroughly involved in the powerful logic of accumulation which traps us in a cycle of produce, consume– produce, consume. This is not going to change. However, in contrast to the economically defined world of the organisation, we must remind ourselves that human relations are socially embedded, multi-dimensional and deeply reciprocal. Human behaviour is complex, various, flawed, but also agential, choosing, knowledgeable, development-oriented, and ethically and morally skilled. Management prescription recognises this, and strives to harness it through a rule-based order, and impose organisational-based feeling, acting and performance standards. What this prescription appears not to understand is that social life has its own moral order, and when it is moved into the economic sphere, and stripped away from its social embeddedness, it becomes distorted. Spontaneous judgements and moral acts become 'crowded' by instrumentalisation and codification; this in itself does not wholly suppress moral order, but it does ignore the strengths and opportunities within it.

Searching for the H in human resource management

From Personnel Management to HRM, Strategic HRM, High Commitment Management, and the latest incarnation, the Management of Human Capital, the management of people has traversed a long and winding road in search of prescription for how to best configure and harvest people skills and abilities in the organisation. How do contemporary debates and practices within HRM reflect on the notion of the human and human relations?

Mainstream functionalist HRM theory and practice optically indicates the centrality of the person: witness Pfeffer's (1996) boldly titled *Competitive Advantage Through People*. However, despite language to the contrary, contemporary accounts (Appelbaum *et al.*, 2000; DTI, 2004; Leary-Joyce, 2004; Pfeffer, 1996; Schuler and Jackson, 2005)) reference a specifically 'thin' form of human relations. In the Strategic HRM literature, a prescriptive 'bundle' of strategies and policies – strategic recruitment, team organising, flexibility, strategic performance management, performance-related pay, training and development, knowledge management, 'empowerment' initiatives – foreground the individual, though they rarely discuss people per se (MacDuffie, 1995; Ulrich and Beatty, 2001; Ulrich and Brockbank, 2005). It would seem that the unitarist frame of reference underpinning mainstream HRM is directed towards the desired outcomes of the organisation, apparently to the exclusion of the individual needs and values of the employee.

HRM practice is theorised as having diverged along two lines – Hard (The Michigan School) and Soft (the 'Harvard' Model). However it is true to say that the distinction between the two has weakened in veracity as contemporary HR practice typically deploys elements of both hard and soft models (Storey, 2001). These, in combination, are fundamentally driven by the goal to achieve both the control and consent of employees that are 'both dependable and disposable (Hyman, 1987, p. 43)' (quoted in Legge, 2005b, p. 225). Both models clearly involve a very narrow view of the employee as a potential source of sustained competitive advantage.

In simple terms, hard HRM prioritises rational profit maximising and views the employee as a 'headcount resource' (Legge, 2005b, p. 223), thereby lending itself to core–periphery models and the management of costs through routinising, delayering and outsourcing (Collins and Porras, 2002; Hammer and Champy, 2004; Kotter and Cohen, 2002). Simultaneously, occupational restructuring and automation through technology has simplified and eradicated the craft and quality of many occupations, further increasing the tendency to job displacement. In small contrast, soft HRM places a higher value on the human resource as a valued asset, and foregrounds their proactive capacity, motivation and commitment based on a unitarist view of reciprocal obligations and mutuality (Barney, 1991; Pedler *et al.*, 1997; Senge, 2006). Soft HR purports to treat the individual as a whole, with attention to stress, well-being, and family needs, but the underlying instrumental exchange orientation casts these initiatives simply as more effective methods of motivation and control. In a similar vein, a variety of 'people'-oriented cultural management practices under the moniker of HCM (high commitment management) are used both to manage difficult motivational contexts, and to (hopefully) heighten employee commitment to and identification with the organisation so that employees might act flexibly and exercise their initiative towards organisational ends. Such feeling-oriented practices include, for example, structured career development plans, involvement initiatives such as quality forums and self-managing teams, and/or the creation of 'fun' and attractive places to work (Leary-Joyce, 2004; Peters and Schrage, 1999; Reeves, 2001; *The Sunday Times*, 2006). However though all these routes indicate a more plural approach, fieldwork amply demonstrates that the hard and soft aspects of HRM are analytically inseparable as in combination they have a tendency to rupture with tensions due to the fundamental economic goal at their core (Delbridge, 1998; Houlihan, 2002; Strangleman and Roberts, 1999).

Despite its intuitive appeal, the conjoining of people management with business strategy in Strategic HRM suffers from a number of problematic underpinning assumptions. Notably, it assumes a very simplistic, one-dimensional view of human nature. It assumes that human resource strategy can be managed in a planned way, and shaped to fit the business strategy, counter to the insights that strategy is emergent and messy (Mintzberg and Walters, 1985), and neglects the numerous stakeholders to, and societal, historical, cultural, institutional and even financial influences on, strategic direction (Legge, 2005b, p. 227). Moreover, as Legge points out, it particularly downplays the psychological contracts between the organisation and employee, and where these might diverge. By viewing the employee as an individual resource unit to be optimally configured and managed, these practices conceptually divorce employees from their social context – that is, other relations, other shaping forces and other commitments (even within the workplace). In sum, contemporary HRM practice, and the theory that

┌───┐

What sorts of humanity does HRM address?

• Bring us your emotional labour and intelligence though not your emotional needs
• Bring us your ideas though not your objections
• Bring us your creativity though not your misbehaviour
• Bring us your loyalty, so long as we need you
• Work to our codes and procedures, but remain flexible
• Bring us your motivation though make it work related
• Be a team member, though we will manage you as an individual
• Develop, but on our terms, and towards our goals
• Listen and communicate, but don't have human conflicts, and we won't listen to you in the same way

Figure 1.1 'The HRM Contract'

informs it, is based on a thin view of mutuality that we somewhat acerbically characterise as 'the HRM contract' (Figure 1.1).

This review gives pause for thought about the degree to which Strategic HRM is truly directed at 'releasing the untapped reserves of "human resourcefulness"' (Keenoy, 1990). More immediately, we might ask: how effective has functionalist HRM proved at delivering on its promises? Roundly criticised from the business perspective for failing to deliver on '20 years of hopeful rhetoric' and a lack of strategic leadership (Hammonds, 2005), HRM also appears to fail to do what it says it does in terms of the business bottom line; despite many optimistic claims to the contrary (Guest, 1997, 2000; Huselid, 1995). Coming from a resolutely bottom-line focus, Hammonds berates HR for its focus on efficiency over value, administration over strategic leadership, processes over results, and for chasing defensive homogenisation and policy uniformity over flexible support of individual achievement. While coming at it from a rather different perspective than Hammond, we would share his contention that HR promotes short-termist cost efficiency rather than long-term value, and delivers limitation rather than human resourcefulness. As a partner to the business goals, HRM is espoused to deliver strategic strengths in the human resources, yet the evidence from the field is that HR goals become short term, instrumental, and fail to navigate the complex multiple, and necessarily contradictory, demands of its various stakeholders.

The critical response

Human Resource Management's attempts to manage employees in ever more inventive ways and the push towards normative controls involving the management of values and feelings have, unsurprisingly, elicited various critical responses over a number of years. There are those who, whilst apparently supporting the legitimacy of HRM and its human-centred practices, question some of the claims regarding its 'soft' focus and recognise how the logic of the market permeates and undermines its practices (Boxall and Purcell, 2003; Bratton and Gold, 2004; Guest, 1990; Sparrow and Marchington, 1998; Storey, 2001). However, rather than human agency, a narrow and somewhat functionalist understanding of the H in HRM seems to prevail at the heart of these analyses. Other writers have questioned the legitimacy of HRM and the gap between its rhetorics and realities (Caldwell, 2003; Guest and King, 2004; Keenoy, 1990; Legge, 2005a; Noon and Blyton, 2002; Watson, 2000). Such accounts question HRM prescription whilst accepting the active role of human agency in either supporting or resisting various control attempts and in doing so they provide valuable insight into the potential failings (for employees and organisations) of various HR practices (Callaghan and Thompson, 2002; Delbridge, 1998; Grugulis et al., 2000; Korczynski, 2002).

However, from within the critical schools, another very particular and rather bleak understanding of human agency – the 'disciplined worker thesis' – has evolved into a dominant voice on HRM, its role in society, and its effects. Emerging from a broader base and trend in cultural theory, this view contends that the pressures of modern life induce the routinisation of all that it is to be human (Anderson and Mullen, 1998; Bryman, 1999; Cremin, 2003; Meštrović, 1997; Ritzer, 2004). And so the argument goes, in the unreliable, fragmented conditions of consumer capitalism the world of production offers a stable platform where identities can be confirmed and people can take their rightful place in the world of consumption (Rose, 1999). Thus, for this view, the new source of control is the imperative of the free market and the related culture industry, as both producers and consumers willingly collaborate in their own exploitation and 'personalities' are saturated with the 'culture of enterprise' (Cremin, 2003; du Gay, 1996). For this group of thinkers, it has almost become a taken-for-granted base of analysis that 'if industrial capitalism was all about demoralisation, contemporary society is much more about the production of synthetic or instrumental morality' (Fevre, 2003, p. 8). Such an approach has impacted upon an understanding of HRM as a powerful tool of normative control that represents the much bigger forces of 'demoralisation' at work. HRM is seen to discursively produce a new form of 'manufactured morality' that makes up humanity in different ways (Casey, 1995; Deetz, 1998; du Gay, 1996; Fleming and Spicer, 2003; McKinlay and Starkey; 1997; Scott, 1994; Sewell, 2005; Townley, 1994; Wilmott, 1993).

Unfortunately, in its articulation of the death of the social, the disciplined worker thesis produces an image of emotionally anorexic social actors, leading to a veritable 'asphyxiation by society' (Archer, 2000, p. 18) that downplays the varying responses available to employees. In presenting the constitution of the enterprising self as an 'accomplished fact' (Fournier and Grey, 1999, p. 107), such interpretations unwisely underestimate the interconnectedness of social ties and, hence, people's abilities in manoeuvring, manipulating or simply enduring various life situations. In effect, the disciplined worker thesis is blind to the human capacity to continually comply, evade, re-interpret or merely survive management practice. We find these arguments excessive in their bleakness and dubious in their blindness to human agency, and so suggest that if we search a little harder we can find humanity and avenues for restored possibility.

Being human: HRM and the employment relationship

What we want to offer is an analysis that includes humanity – that is, social actors who are capable of moral commitment, who are involved with society *and* whose activities take place within multiple and layered frameworks of action. Humans have an unquestionable sense of being situated within a web of obligations, commitments, and 'moral sentiments'; factors that make up community (Sayer, 2005). They calibrate and monitor their behaviour in order to maintain social order but to also create and sustain human bonds (Goffman, 1961). Relationships, including the employment relationship, are formed and broken but relationships are a vital and necessary part of a stable social order. Indeed it has long been recognised that organisations rely on the co-operation of people in the organisation, with colleagues, with management, with customers – though the conceptualisation and recognition of that connection and cooperation varies greatly. Ample empirical evidence suggests that it is human connection that oils both the social and the economic wheels of organisational life (Bolton and Boyd, 2003; Bolton and Houlihan, 2005; Callaghan and Thompson, 2002; Korczynski, 2003). This phenomenon is exemplified by people's behaviour at work as their actions continually cross boundaries between the formal and informal – gaining pleasure (and sometimes pain) from interaction with others. It is thus that we argue work-based relations have economic, but also social consequences.

And yes, of course, organisations are not blind to this. Much of the prescriptive HRM literature assumes a need for connection in their 'soft' practices of culture, empowerment, team work, etc. Unlike previous approaches to people management, but building on human relations approaches, HRM recognises the potential in the irrationality of humanity.

Whereas the raw edges of humanity were once firmly excluded from organisational life, HRM *appears to* invite humanity in and celebrate it as a source of creativity, energy and commitment. And one can only think that this is a welcome divergence from management prescription that assumed *homo economicus* in the shape of theories X and Y and pathologised leakages of feelings (Mayo, 1946; McGregor, 1960). HRM's apparent celebration of the human invites a description of their recognition of the employment relationship as 'thick'; involving recognition, respect, trust and, perhaps most importantly, reciprocal obligation. Of course, there will always be dishonesty, disinterest, conflict and contradiction; some may say this is an inherent part of any employment relationship, but a *thick* employment relationship is more likely to encourage accommodation rather than conflict and produce what Andrew Sayer describes as an 'ethical surplus':

> As long as the employment contract lasts, the moral expectations and commitments are likely to spill beyond what is contractually defined. (2005, p. 89)

To foster and nurture 'thick' employment relationships appears to make both economic and moral sense; committed workers, increased performance, reservoirs of goodwill and gift relations that can be drawn upon at times of economic necessity. This is certainly the picture portrayed by the advocates of HRM practice. So why do we not see more evidence of the thick employment relationship in action? The most obvious answer might be that, unfortunately, in a market economy it is almost obligatory for companies to exploit the 'ethical surplus' and treat their employees instrumentally (Sayer, 2005; Thompson, 2003). However, this is to assume that an ethical surplus has been produced and that HRM does indeed create the conditions in which thick employment relationships might flourish. We would suggest that this is not the case for two reasons: first, economic considerations override ambitious schemes to humanise HRM; for instance, flexibility translates into insecurity and excessive hours; appraisal focused on development is superseded by concerns with short-term performativity and the suppression of human instincts to help a customer, do a quality job, forgo a sale on ethical grounds or other such measures of humanity that the *Resource* in Human Resource Management overrides and squeezes out. Second, HRM bases its practice on an impoverished model of humanity (Archer, 2000). Despite HRM warmly welcoming humanity into the organisation, it has its very own house rules – feelings, emotions etc are confined to different spheres of economic action and in doing so are rationalised. HRM does this with such ease because it holds onto the functionalist's (Unitarist) conception of humanity. The complexities of humanity are never recognised and employees are conceptualised as a passive, one-dimensional resource entirely disembedded from the social realm. Human connectivity is squeezed and moulded into certain shapes that can be monitored, controlled and utilised as another factor of production, i.e., coaching sessions, 'fun at work' days, 'team players', etc. The combination of economic priority and instrumental action directed toward a narrow conception of humanity creates not a 'thick' employment relationship but a 'thin' one and *homo economicus* is apparent in all of its forms. Nevertheless, though some forms of the human relationship (such as dimensions of the employment relationship) may be overridden by economic demands some moral concerns remain – though, unfortunately, this may exist mainly rhetorically in HR prescription, it does exist in other forms in the shape of calls for corporate social responsibility and trade union activity and the simple forming of social bonds between people at work.

Searching for the human in contemporary HR practice

How then is the human faring in day-to-day practice on the HRM frontline? We have acknowledged that the language of people-centredness pervades HR practice, as it does HR theory. A quick look around flags numerous examples of best practice HR management, from the national standard for human resource development's evocative moniker 'Excellence Through People' to the High Commitment Practices of Google, Mircrosoft, eBay, Dell and many more firms internationally lauded for HR best practice. The 'top places to work for' lists (Great Place to Work Institute, 2006; *The Sunday Times*, 2006) emphasise that people are at the heart of their success, and flag creative initiatives around fun, development and flexibility. This introductory chapter is not the place for a deeper analysis of these practices; however, while acknowledging that humanistic HRM practices are widely to be found, the following questions must be considered:

- WHAT: Is there a choice for diverse needs? Who defines these needs?
- WHO: Who gets to avail of them? Is it all employees, or merely some?
- WHAT IF: When it comes to competing interests: who prevails?
- WHERE and WHEN: Does human-centred practice prevail when it comes to choices between economic and human interests, and at the level of Board and strategic decision making?
- WHY: What precisely are organisations' views of humanity?

These questions tend to reveal the fact that behind soft HRM initiatives lies an economic instrumentality whereby their deployment is conditional on their contribution to the bottom line. Organisationally, the economic imperative sets in train a cycle of undelivered promises whereby resources are not harvested either strategically or socially, leaving the organisation and HR in a constant search for new recipes for improvement. It eases the way for waste, errors, and lost checks and balances, at its worst, organisational silence, injustices, and opportunistic corporate misbehaviour. All have societal consequences. By managing the employment relationship solely in economic terms, humanity is 'squeezed', and the resource is never seen in its full light.

Putting the H back in?

By looking beyond models of market society and *homo economicus* we reintroduce humanity to the analysis of the employment relationship, and restore attention to Aristotle's notion of the collective as an arena for human flourishing. We can envisage the embedded nature of economic relationships and their reliance on human connectivity and community. Shifting the gaze from *thin* to *thick* conceptualisations of the employment relationship enables a better understanding of the complex and various motivations that lie behind people's actions. This in turn lends much support for a re-worked HRM model of developed, empowered and involved employees – reflexive, thinking, creative and value-bringing agents. This is more than current models of HRM bring, with their basis in unproblematic, one-dimensional characters. It is also much more then the manufactured morality suggested by contemporary critical writers. It is a model that involves reciprocal obligation – rights and responsibilities – recognition of multiple (and sometimes contradictory) motivations and autonomy and trust – an employment relationship that is recognised for its reliance and embeddedness in the political economy: the employment relationship as a *thick* human relationship. However, to escape the 'soft-headed attitude' often attributed to such calls and avoid being 'lost in the humanistic forest' (McGuire *et al.*, 2005), we have to recognise the irrevocable drive of the market; the logic of capitalism that overrides concerns for human relationships and forces labour into quantifiable units.

The aim of the book is to highlight the missing H and to create a forum where the dynamics that arise when the management of people is structured predominantly or exclusively as an economic relationship can be debated constructively. Our goal is to open up space for reflection and debate about the impacts of HRM on people and society. At a time of growing prosperity in first-world economies, we feel it is pertinent to ask: what about the Human in Human Resource Management?

Searching for the H: theory, practice and workplace contexts

Throughout the book, contributors argue that although the employment relationship has both social and economic elements, evidence from the contemporary workplace indicates the (increasing) economisation and instrumentalising of that relationship and the de-prioritisation of social and non-economic needs. Collectively, we argue that a solely economic orientation to the employment relationship erodes the human resource by individualising and narrowing both organisational and interpersonal relationships. Organised into three parts, the book explores theory, practice and context. Setting the scene, Andrew Sayer's is the first chapter in the theory part. Andrew adopts a 'moral economy' approach in order to emphasise the socially embedded nature of economic activity and the complex and multi-faceted activity of humanity. He asks 'what it is to be human?' and sets out a plea that in analysing organisational life we should not treat people as cultural dopes and neither should we ignore organisations as goal-centred institutions. To do so is to potentially damage both employee and organisational well-being. Steve Fleetwood also adds to our theoretical understanding of the missing human in his review of the nature of theory that informs our understanding of various approaches to HRM and the methodological underpinnings of studies that claim to empirically 'prove' the HR and performance link. Drawing on critical realism, Steve questions how an approach that is methodologically incapable of capturing the essence of human activity in organisations can ever assess how HR practice might impact upon an organisation's economic performance. In Chapter 4, Irena Grugulis explores the nature of skill and how we might better understand contemporary forms of employment that draw on human capacities for emotion and knowledge work. Irena reminds us that humanity and work might be a complex and sensitive topic but that this should not mean it can be evaded or side-lined. Irena goes on to link humanity with the notion of 'decent work' and consider what humanising and humanised workplaces might look like. Concluding the theory part, Paul Thompson contends that the normative and strategic dimensions of HRM are underpinned by notions of human capital that attempt to measure and remodel employees into valuable organisational assets that under the direction of High Commitment Work Practices can and will produce shareholder value. However, Paul highlights the tensions that arise when capital markets create conditions that squeeze the human out of human capital.

Our second part continues the search for the Human, this time in HR Practice. Opening the theme, Marek Korczynski examines the 'enchanting' illusion of menus of choice within the HR cycle, and asks critical questions about who defines the choices, and what might be missing. Marek's analysis highlights not only the fallacy of choice, but the enactment of individualisation processes through HRM, and the masking of power and its operation in the workplace. For him, this obscuring of power is fundamental in making the workplace less human, and his arguments serve as a sharp reappraisal of HR activities such as training, stress management and coaching. Karen Legge, in Chapter 7, further explores the question of what it means to be human and what is required for a fulfilling life, and turns her analysis to contemporary flexibility practices ranging from empowerment to temporary contracts and outsourcing. Karen offers a rigorous analysis of the evolution of flexibility, concentrating on its tensions and contradictions and she judiciously reflects on the prognosis for flexibility and humanistic practices under contemporary capitalism. In Chapter 8, Martin Parker pens a provocative challenge to the selectivity of truth within HRM practice, and in particular, the question of corporate citizenship. Offering a characteristically wry perspective, he illuminates the potential for employees, in parallel with citizens of the state, to turn the citizen-oriented language of HRM (with its talk of family, shared mission, strong cultures and corporate citizenship behaviour) on its head and, perchance, to 'have it their way'. In doing so, Martin offers a dynamic, and we believe, far from Utopian, agenda for practical radicalism. In the following chapter, Fiona Wilson turns her attention to organisational diversity, and asks just how human, or indeed effective, is the HRM practice of diversity management? Fiona does this by reviewing the evidence and statistics on diversity representation and the wide gap between policy and practice, and by dialoguing with the curious contradiction that diversity practices seem at once to celebrate but also to squash 'difference', by operating both with and without 'regard for persons'. Her recommendation is that the emphasis on the business case for diversity management needs to be foreshadowed by a search for the human benefits of diversity-centeredness. Jane Bryson, in Chapter 10, adds a fresh perspective to current thinking on human resource development, noting how insular and prescriptive much HRD writing tends to be. Jane draws on the Nobel Prize-winning work of Amartya Sen whose fluent and passionate writing on human capability has much to offer current HRD thinking. For Sen, and for Jane, there is a responsibility to create enabling environments, and to put human development and freedom to achieve at the heart of the (organisational) worlds we create. As Jane argues, it is time for HRD managers to 'lift their eyes to purpose and principles' if they are not to remain slaves to short-term cycles of organisational performance, with little or no real impact.

Our third and final part turns from theory and practice, to give voice to workers and the workplace experience. This part seeks to re-examine a variety of specific organisational contexts as indications of the extent to which the H is missing in action on the ground. Here we see most clearly the sharp divide between rhetoric and reality. Opening the part with Chapter 11, Sarah Jenkins and Rick Delbridge offer a valuable review of some key field studies in a range of 'high performance' factory settings. Their work maps the experience of HRM initiatives at the coalface, and offers troubling conclusions: not only are 'high performance work systems' failing in their promises – underscored by a narrow, self-interested understanding of what people want, look for, and are motivated by – but these same systems, and their fractured enactment, are producing significant disconnections in employee interests, identities and relations. Thus they fail to contribute to, and at times even undermine, the very performance and employee outcomes they set out to achieve. Sarah and Rick are incisive in their examination of the evidence and offer a great deal of food for thought for the HR practitioner, and in pointing to the disconnections within systems of capital, they also remind us that the causes and solutions to these challenges are far from simple and linear. Firmly putting the employee back into a social context, they conclude by reinforcing the necessity to engage with humans in all their knowing, agential and social complexity, rather than rely on a thin and, ultimately, misleading proxy. Chapter 12 draws on a writer that has influenced us both. Polly Toynbee has long been a provocateur and writer of conscience in the British media, and here we are delighted to include a section from her 2003 book *Hard Work: Life in Low-pay Britain*, to observe through Polly's eyes as she joins the ranks of careworkers who offer their emotion work to elderly and incapacitated residents in nursing homes everywhere. In this account we see for ourselves just how much is exchanged for so little, underscoring the irony of an economic view of employee exchange. Polly's accounts richly convey the humanity in human resources, and put people, both as clients and carers, firmly in our gaze. Grasping this understanding, it is hard to imagine how work and workers can ever be seen in solely economic terms. This is followed in Chapter 13 by an examination of our own of frontline customer service work in call centres. Here, we articulate the ways in which codification and scripting of interaction seems to squeeze humanity out of the customer–employee interaction, and yet, how, through the voices of customer service representatives, humanity and the deeply social interaction order bubble at the surface nevertheless. We ask why the customer and the employee are constructed so as to divorce human connection, and offer some of the consequences that result. In

Chapter 13, Gerard Hanlon examines the state of the professions, and charts the growing marketisation, quantification of performance, and reliance of immaterial labour within these contexts. Drawing extensively on Marxist critique to examine the labour process and the contradictions produced by the juxtaposition of freedom and control within HRM, Gerry persuasively speculates that HRM may in fact be redundant. He offers a picture of a growing trend mirrored across an ever-greater variety of work contexts, and asks challenging questions about the direction in which we are heading. Far from being idealistically or polemically argued, Gerry situates this perspective in an analysis of capitalism's contradictory reliance on driving down human resource costs on one hand, and depending on the spending power of these same 'resources' as consumers on the other. In our final chapter, Joe O'Mahoney turns his attention to an often-neglected life form in the analysis of work and organisations – the consultant. Looking at the consultant from a rare perspective as human, and through the lens of Joe's own participant observation in the work, we learn just how fraught this role really is. Joe describes the pains of consulting life and the tensions it absorbs with rich humanity, and on this journey offers a deeper understanding of the fragile worlds that create some of the HRM tensions this book evaluates.

All in all, this tour of the theory, practice and context of HRM presents a chorus of voices that would firmly reinsert the human in organisational life, and pause to ponder the causes and consequences of its absence. We hope you will join us in this debate, whether to amplify or offer counterpoint, but ultimately to search for, find, and insist upon the human as the focal point of organisational life.

References

Ackroyd, S., Batt, R., Thompson, P. and Tolbert, P. (2005) (eds), *The Oxford Handbook of Work and Organisation*, London: Oxford Press.

Anderson, D. and Mullen, P. (1998) *Faking It: The Sentimentalisation of Modern Society*, London: The Social Affairs Unit.

Appelbaum, E., Bailey, T., Berg, P. and Kalleberg, A.I. (2000) *Manufacturing Advantage: Why High-Performance Work Systems Pay Off*, Ithaca: Cornell University Press.

Archer, M. (2000) *Being Human: The Problem of Agency*, Cambridge: Cambridge University Press.

Barney, G. (1991) 'Firm Resources and Sustained Competitive Advantage', *Journal of Management*, 17:11, 99–120.

Bolton, S. and Boyd, C. (2003) 'Trolley Dolly or Skilled Emotion Manager?', *Work, Employment and Society*, 17:2, 289–308.

Bolton, S. and Houlihan, M. (2005) 'The (Mis)representation of Customer Service', *Work, Employment and Society*, 19:4, 685–703.

Boxall, P. and Purcell, J. (2003). *Strategy and Human Resource Management*, London: Palgrave.

Bratton, J. and Gold, J. (2004) *Human Resource Management* (4th Edition), London: Palgrave Macmillan.

Bryman, A. (1999) 'The Disneyization of Society', *The Sociological Review*, 47, 26–47.

Caldwell, R. (2003) 'The Changing Role of Personnel Managers: Old Ambiguities, New Uncertainties', *Journal of Management Studies*, 40: 4, 983–1005.

Callaghan, G. and Thompson, P. (2002) 'We Recruit Attitude: The Selection and Shaping of Routine Call Centre Labour', *Journal Management Studies*, 39:2, 233–53.

Casey, C. (1995) *Work, Self and Society: After Industrialisation*, London: Routledge.

Collins, J. and Porras, J. (2002) *Built to Last: Successful Habits of Visionary Companies*, New York: Harper Business.

Cremin, C. (2003) 'Self-starters, Can-doers and Mobile Phoneys: Situations Vacant Column and the Personality Culture in Employment', *Sociological Review*, 51:1, 109–28.

Deetz, S. (1998) 'Discursive Formations, Strategized Subordination and Self-Surveillance' in McKinlay, A. and Starkey, K. (eds), *Foucault, Management and Organisation Theory*, London: Sage Publications.

Delbridge, R. (1998) *Life on the Line*, Oxford University Press: Oxford.

Department of Trade and Industry (2004) 'Best Companies: Best Practice', sourced at http://www.dti.gov.uk/bestpractice%20URN%2004/813 www.dti.gov.uk/bestpractice URN 04/813.

du Gay, P. (1996) *Consumption and Identity at Work*, London: Sage.

Ehrenreich, B. (2001) *Nickel and Dimed: Undercover in Low-Wage USA*, London: Granta Books.

Fevre, R. (2003) *A New Sociology of Economic Behaviour*, London: Sage.

Fleming, P. and Spicer, A. (2003) 'Working at a Cynical Distance: Implications for Power, Subjectivity and Resistance', *Organisation*, 10:1, 157–79.

Fournier, V. and Grey, C. (1999) 'Too Much, Too Little and Too Often: A Critique of du Gay's Analysis of Enterprise', *Organisation*, 6:1, 107–28.

Goffman, E. (1961) *Encounters*, New York: The Bobbs-Merrill Company Ltd.

Great Places to Work Institute (2006) http://www.greatplacetowork.com/best/list-bestusa.htm.

Grugulis, I., Dundon, T. and Wilkinson, A. (2000) 'Cultural Control and the Culture Manager: Employment Practices in a Consultancy', *Work, Employment and Society*, 14:1, 97–116.

Guest, D. (1990) 'Human Resource Management and the American Dream', *Journal of Management Studies*, 27:4, 378–97.

Guest, D. (1997) 'Human Resource Management and Performance', *International Journal Human Resource Management*, 8, 263–76.

Guest, D. (2000) 'Piece by Piece', *People Management*, 20 July, 26–30.

Guest, D. and King, Z. (2004) 'Power, Innovation and Problem-Solving: The Personnel Managers' Three Steps to Heaven?', *Journal of Management Studies*, 41:3, 401–25.

Hammer, M. and Champy, J. (2004) *Re-engineering the Corporation: A Manifesto for Business Revolution*, London: Harper Collins.

Hammonds, K. (2005) 'Why We Hate HR', *Fast Company*, 97, August, 40.

Houlihan, M. (2002) 'Tensions and Variations in Call Centre Management Strategies', *Human Resource Management Journal*, 12:4, 67–86.

Huselid, M. (1995) 'The Impact of Human Resource Management Practices on Turnover, Productivity and Corporate Financial Performance', *Academy of Management Journal*, 38, 635–72.

Hyman, R. (1987) 'Strategy or Structure? Capital, Labour and Control', *Work, Employment and Society*, 1:1, 25–55.

Keenoy, T. (1990) 'HRM: A Case of the Wolf in Sheep's Clothing?', *Personnel Review*, 19:2, 3–9.

Korczynski, M. (2002) *HRM in the Service Sector*, London: Palgrave.

Korczynski, M. (2003) 'Communities of Coping: Collective Emotional Labour in Service Roles', *Organisation*, 10:1, 55–79.

Kotter, J. and Cohen, D. (2002) *Heart of Change*, Harvard: Harvard Business School Press.

Leary-Joyce, J. (2004) 'Becoming an Employer of Choice. Making Your Organisation a Place Where Great People Want To Do Great Work', London: CIPD.

Legge, K. (2005a) *Human Resource Management: Rhetorics and Realities*, Basingstoke: Macmillan.

Legge, K. (2005b) 'Human Resource Management' in Ackroyd, S., Batt, R., Thompson, P. and Tolbert, P. (eds), *The Oxford Handbook of Work and Organisation*, Oxford: Oxford Press.

MacDuffie, J.P. (1995) 'Human Resource Bundles and Manufacturing Performance: Organisational Logic and Flexible Production Systems in the World Auto Industry', *Industrial and Labour Relations Review*, 48:2, 197–221.

Mayo, E. (1946) *Human Problems of an Industrial Civilisation*, New York: Macmillan.

McGregor, D. (1960) *The Human Side of Enterprise*, New York: Harper and Row.

McGuire, D., Cross, C. and O'Donnell, D. (2005) 'Why Humanistic Approaches to HRD Won't Work', *Human Resource Development Quarterly*, 16:1, 131–2.

McKinlay, A. and Starkey, K. (eds) (1997) *Foucault, Management and Organisation*, London: Sage.

Meštrović, S.G. (1997) *Postemotional Society*, London: Sage.

Mintzberg, H. and Walters, J.A. (1985) 'Of Strategies, Deliberate and Emergent', *Strategic Management Journal*, 6: 257–72.

Noon, M. and Blyton, P. (2002) *The Realities of Work*, London: Palgrave.

Pedler, M., Burgoyne, J. and Boydell, T. (1997) *The Learning Company: A Strategy for Sustainable Development* (2nd Edition), London: McGraw-Hill.

Peters, T. and Schrage, M. (1999) *Serious Play: How the World's Best Companies Stimulate to Innovate*, Boston: Harvard Business School Press.

Pfeffer, J. (1996) *Competitive Advantage Through People*, Boston: Harvard Business School Press.

Reeves, R. (2001) *Happy Mondays: Putting the Pleasure Back into Work*, London: Momentum.

Ritzer, G. (2004) *Enchanting a Disenchanted World*, California: Pine Forge Press.

Rose, N. (1999) *Governing the Soul: The Shaping of the Private Self*, London: Free Association Books.

Sayer, A. (2005) 'Approaching Moral Economy' in Stehr, N., Henning, C. and Weiler, B. (eds), *The Moralisation of the Markets*, New York: Transaction Books.

Schuler, R.S. and Jackson, S.E. (2005) *Managing Human Resources Through Strategic Partnerships*, Mason, Ohio: South Western Publishing Company.

Scott, A. (1994) *Willing Slaves?: British Workers under Human Resource Management*, Cambridge: Cambridge University Press.

Senge. P. (2006) *The Fifth Discipline*, New York: Random House.

Sewell, G. (2005) 'Nice Work? Rethinking Managerial Control in an Era of Knowledge Work', *Organisation*, 12:5, 685–704.

Sparrow, P. and Marchington, M. (1998) *Human Resource Management: The New Agenda*, Harlow: Prentice Hall.

Storey, J. (2001) *Human Resource Management – A Critical Text* (2nd Edition), London: Thomson Learning.

Strangleman, T. and Roberts, I. (1999) 'Looking Through the Window of Opportunity: The Cultural Cleansing of Workplace Identity', *Sociology*, 33:1, 47–67.

Taylor, R. (2002) *Britain's World of Work – Myths and Realities*, Economic and Social Research Council. www.esrctoday.co.uk.

The Sunday Times (2006) *The Sunday Times 100 Best Companies to Work For* (2006), published with the Sunday Times, 5 March, London.

Thompson, P. (2003) 'Disconnected Capitalism: Or, Why Employers Can't Keep Their Side of the Bargain', *Work, Employment and Society*, 17:2, 359–78.

Townley, B. (1994) *Reframing Human Resource Management*, London: Sage.

Toynbee, P. (2003) *Hard Work: Life in Low-Pay Britain*, London: Bloomsbury.

Ulrich, D. and Beatty, D. (2001) 'From Partners to Players: Extending the HR playing Field', *Human Resource Management*, 40:4, 293–300.

Ulrich, D. and Brockbank, W. (2005) 'Role Call', *People Management*, 16th June: 25–28.

Watson, T. (2000) *In Search of Management*. London: Thomson Learning.

Willmott, H. (1993) 'Strength is Ignorance, Slavery is Freedom: Managing Culture in Modern Organisations', *Journal of Management Studies*, 30:4, 515–52.

part **I**

Searching for the
human in HR theory

2

Moral economy and employment

Andrew Sayer

Introduction

The Orwellian overtones of 'Human Resource Management' reflect a widely noted tension or contradiction between the dominant instrumental goals of organisations and the diverse needs, interests, concerns and commitments of workers as human beings, which tend to resist instrumentalisation. Clearly, to take the human seriously, we have to go beyond treating people as resources to be managed. HRM may, at least at the level of rhetoric, be an improvement on earlier forms of personnel management, in that it purports to acknowledge the possibility of workers being proactive rather than passive tools of management, but it remains an inherently instrumental, indeed manipulative, way of approaching social relations and behaviour towards others.

To think critically about HRM is, or should be, to address the relationship between the qualities of people – indeed, what it is to be human – and the qualities of organisations. To do this we need to avoid reducing people to mere products of discourses and the organisations in which they work – hence depicting them as 'cultural dopes', 'blank slates' or beings who can be socially constructed in any way imaginable. We also cannot afford to ignore the special character of organisations as hierarchical and instrumental institutions pursuing highly specific goals. We also need to take account of the embedding of both employees and organisations in a wider field of social relations among equals and unequals.

The approach which I adopt here might be called one of 'moral economy', that is, an approach to economic life which examines and evaluates the way in

21

which it is structured by norms regarding people's rights and responsibilities, and how it both relies upon and influences their motivations, character and moral or ethical dispositions (Sayer, 2000, 2005). (I shall use the terms 'moral' and 'ethical' interchangeably henceforth.) Since all economies are influenced by moral sentiments about what is good and proper and structured by norms regarding rights and responsibilities, not only pre- or non-capitalist economies, but all economies are moral economies. The moral sentiments include ideas about what kinds of rewards people should receive for working, what kind of working conditions should be allowed, what kinds of welfare support should be provided and who should be responsible for it, whether creditors should expect interest, and so on. The most important rights and responsibilities tend to be those defined by property rights, and of course these are a major source of economic and political power. All of these can take many forms, and it is a mistake to regard contemporary, local forms as universal.

To highlight the dependence of economic practices on such matters is definitely not to give approval to all that is seen by lay people as ethical within economic life; on the contrary, the point is to evaluate existing economic life and what is seen as justifiable in relation to it. This involves a particular interpretation of morality or ethics, as being concerned with relations with, and behaviours towards, others that have implications for their well-being. Well-being, in turn, is seen as not merely a subjective matter, but one reflecting the objective capacities that people have for flourishing or suffering. When we describe something as human or humane we often mean that it is in some way conducive to well-being and in keeping with our capacities for flourishing. In this respect, as we shall see, the approach has an Aristotelian aspect. By elaborating these capacities for flourishing and what fits or does not fit with them, we can assist critical thinking about HRM. In many ways this differs strikingly from dominant sociological and Foucauldian approaches, although I shall argue that these too have their strengths, if suitably qualified.

Human Resource Management aims to influence the motivations and behaviours of employees in ways which help organisations achieve their goals. For their members, economic organisations are important 'moral arenas': given the amount of time people spend in them, how they are treated within them matters a great deal. The nature of the work, payments systems, employment conditions, social relationships, and norms and ethos of the organisation tend to influence their motivations, moral sentiments, and characteristic behaviours. They may encourage workers to be collegial or selfish, disaffected or committed, relaxed or driven, and so on. HRM tries to manipulate these influences so that, for example, employees do not merely passively comply with managerial directives but become proactively committed to the organisation.

In this chapter I will elaborate on these matters, beginning with some theoretical ground-clearing concerning how moral economic, sociological and post-structuralist approaches deal with the way in which social contexts – such as organisations – affect people and their well-being. I will then discuss how the instrumental character of organisations – the way they are overwhelmingly geared to achieving their own, very specific goals – affects employees who, as people, have multiple, diverse concerns and goals in life. I will then comment on the importance of variety and discretion in work tasks for well-being, and the relationships between individual motivation and the desire for recognition and esteem. Finally, I will illustrate how the hierarchical nature of organisations and the inequalities they reproduce affect well-being, and conclude.

Theoretical preliminaries

To approach the subject of the human in HRM we need to consider a few points about different theoretical approaches, for these shape how we think about both people and organisations. In particular, while sociological and post-structuralist approaches have useful insights to contribute, particularly about the social embedding of economic practices and the role of disciplinary power, our moral economy approach shows them to be unable to confront either how employees are managed or what is problematic about this.

The first point I want to make is one that is both obvious and yet strangely ignored in much recent social science. This is that people are needy beings, indeed having a range of different needs, and they are capable of flourishing or suffering according to whether they can meet those needs. These needs are not merely for resources but for access to ways of living – or 'functionings' as Sen and Nussbaum term them – that enable them not merely to exist but to flourish (Sen, 1999; Nussbaum, 2000). If they are to flourish they need not only material resources, security, good living conditions and access to opportunities ('the social bases of respect') but to be treated in certain ways by others so that they have some control over their own circumstances and can be involved in relationships and practices where they can gain respect and self-respect, and friendship. They need recognition and the possibility of participating in social life on a par with others, through having 'the social bases of self-respect and non-humiliation' (Nussbaum, 2006, p. 77). The particular forms those functionings take may be culturally shaped and specific, but broad categories such as those just mentioned appear to be universal.

The second and more complex set of points concern how people are shaped by their social circumstances. The qualities, dispositions and tendencies which we loosely term human require particular social circumstances to develop, and the imprint of those circumstances, particularly those of early life, tend to be lasting.[1] Human beings have a remarkable capacity for social and cultural variation, so that they come to think, act and live in radically different ways at different places and times. Any process of management has to respond to this. But at the same time not just anything can be socialised. (One cannot socialise a lump of rock, for example). It is precisely our human needs, capacities and vulnerabilities, including our psychological needs and susceptibilities, that enable us to be socialised or 'subjectified'. We are not merely influenced by others and economically dependent on them, but psychologically in need of their recognition. Dispositions, interests, concerns and motivations are of course strongly related to prevailing culture and discourse but there are also some common cross-cultural features as well as cultural differences. Were it not for these similarities, there would be no consistency in the way people in similar situations are influenced by them. For example, it is because people have things in common as well as differences that within a given organisation, there is some pattern to the way people are influenced by the organisational contexts, including management practices.

I make this point because in recent years there has been a strong reaction – indeed, I would argue an over-reaction – particularly in post-structuralist approaches, to 'essentialist' approaches that attribute particular characteristics to people, as human beings.[2] There is indeed a danger of mistaking what are products of particular local forms of socialisation for universal human properties, but as I have indicated, a capacity for social and cultural variation is itself a universal feature of human beings.[3] We must have a certain *susceptibility* to different social influences. For example, to the extent that 'naming and shaming' can be effective in influencing people, this indicates that we are the kind of beings who, at least to some degree, need approval by others. Further, if we were to assume that there were no human qualities, no general capacities for flourishing or suffering, then it is hard to see how we could argue that management practices could benefit or harm anyone.

In recent years, it has become common to acknowledge how actors and economic practices are influenced by their particular social situation by describing them as 'socially-embedded', that is embedded in webs of social relations and norms. While many have found the metaphor of embedding useful, it can become a bland sociological point lacking any acknowledgement of how this makes a difference and why it matters, because sociology so often abstracts from the capacity of people to flourish or suffer. The embedding could be that of a supportive network, a status hierarchy or the calculated intimidation of a protection racket: it's all embedding. To understand how different kinds of embedding make a difference to people in ways that matter, we have to treat them as more than cultural dopes and acknowledge their vulnerabilities and capacities. Actors are not merely differently socialised but affected for better or worse according to the impact on those properties. Again, we are not merely embedded in and strongly influenced by social relations; we *need* them, as social beings who are psychologically, socially and economically dependent on others. If we were not needy social beings, what others did would be largely a matter of indifference. In addition, although norms are a very important element of any social system, they are not simply arbitrary conventions or ways of doing things; some of them have major implications for actors' well-being, and indeed moral norms are distinguished from mere etiquette or convention by the seriousness of their implications for actors' well-being (Midgley, 1972).

Although less bland, and offering more concepts for organisational studies, post-structuralist, specifically Foucauldian, approaches have some similar deficiencies. They emphasise 'subjectification' and disciplinary power and hence the ways in which organisations, through both discursive and material means, 'construct' and discipline workers and inculcate appropriate behaviours (Foucault, 1977). Through measurement, calculation and normalisation, discursive constructions, and regulation of the spacing and timing of individuals and their actions, 'docile bodies' internalising discipline through 'care of the self' are produced – indeed by such means, particular kinds of subject are produced.[4] For example, when we read an organisation's guidelines for employees on criteria used in appraisal and promotion we can get a sense of its ideal employee. Such discourses are not only used by management to monitor, calculate and normalise but they and other forms of disciplinary power invite employees to use the same criteria and descriptions with reference to themselves when engaging with management. At first employees may use organisational discourse knowingly and even ironically, but where it is pervasive and coupled with multiple other forms of disciplinary power and inducement, it can gradually become second nature, so they come to comply with it, perhaps willingly, and think of themselves in the prescribed way. They may become organisation men and women. Thus power can be constructive – in the sense of constructing and shaping people and what they do – as well as destructive or constraining.

Such approaches have many strengths and insights, particularly with regard to the 'micro-physics' of power, but they also have some serious deficiencies, stemming from their extraordinary one-sidedness and their avoidance of any assessment of how power affects well-being. We surely need to know if the particular constructions of people and practices produced by disciplinary power are good or bad for them. This is not purely a matter of value-judgement but of empirical assessment. Not just anything can be passed off as well-being; stress-related illnesses do not constitute flourishing, whereas training workers so that they can carry out skilled tasks is more likely to empower them and contribute to their well-being, other things being equal.

To be sure, Foucault argued that where there is power there is resistance (Foucault, 1979), but quite *why* anyone would want to resist is unclear, for the approach treats them as mere ciphers or products of disciplinary power. If they do resist it is apparently not because they have any particular reasons or principles, or because they are suffering, for conceding such possibilities runs against the anti-humanist and anti-essentialist assumptions of the approach, which have difficulty in acknowledging any powers of subjects that are irreducible to external influence and involve actors thinking for themselves.

Actors may resist in order to increase their own power, but it would be naïve to imagine that all resistance is reducible to the desire for power. Some forms of resistance may be about principles and be ethically based and even involve self-sacrifice in support of others. For example, individual employees may have a sense of justice which leads them to moderate their own demands in recognition of the greater demands and needs of others. Researchers who deny this and claim that all actions and knowledge claims are driven by the desire for power need to be challenged as to whether they could apply this to themselves: do they argue and act as they do simply because they think it's the best way of augmenting their power or because they think those arguments and actions are justified and right. If they choose the former, we can disregard their arguments because they are not even put forward as true; if they choose the latter then we know their claim that power is the only motive cannot be right. Complementing this deficiency is the characteristic poststructuralist ('crypto-normative') refusal of evaluative judgement regarding whether particular forms of power are problematic, despite their dystopian portrayal of the social world. A ruthless manager could learn much from post-structuralist approaches without ever encountering any reasons in that literature why employees should not be subject to (and subjects of) disciplinary power. It simply evades the issue of whether there might be anything harmful – or indeed beneficial – about the practices it analyses. But without that judgement, we have accounts which are not only short on evaluation, but short on description; if we have no idea from a description of a practice whether it is empowering or repressive, then it's a pretty uninformative description.[5]

This tendency to treat well-being as if it were merely subjective and beyond the scope of evidence and reason is combined in both post-structuralism and sociological accounts of embedding with a sociological imperialism which does not want to concede any territory to psychology. Many sociologists, and especially post-structuralists, may baulk at the invocation of human properties because of their tendency, noted by Margaret Archer, to evacuate the human body of biological and psychological properties and fill it with 'social foam', for fear of being accused of 'essentialism' (Archer, 2000, p. 317). Changing the metaphor, we are not blank slates on which anything social can be written.

The general theoretical problem – common more widely in sociology and cultural studies – is a one-sided account of socialisation or subjectification, or more simply 'social shaping', which overlooks the fact that for something to be shaped it must have particular susceptibilities and resistances which enable it to be shaped. That which has no resistance and no susceptibility cannot be shaped or moulded. It is thanks to our human powers,[6] as needy beings capable of flourishing and suffering, needing both autonomy and the support and recognition of others, that we can be socially shaped and enculturated in so many ways. There is no contradiction here in acknowledging these human capacities while noting the remarkable diversity of cultures and social life, for the latter presuppose the former: not just anything can be socially shaped or culturally variable. We must have specific properties such that we can be so shaped. While the extent to which organisations do mould and control people – for better or worse – is striking, perhaps alarming, it is both enabled and limited by features of people some of which can exist independently of the organisation. They are not simply innate, of course, but depend on earlier socialisation in the individual's development, though this in turn is naturally constrained and enabled. Any account of organisational life must, if it is not to mystify, acknowledge these capacities and dependencies.

As Aristotelians argue, we become good or bad by *doing* good or bad: the new manager who puts on an authoritarian persona is likely gradually to *become* authoritarian. While this implies that people are agents having some responsibility for their character and behaviour, it is also acknowledged that different social contexts tend to encourage or deter specific kinds of virtues and vices; thus a lack of rules regarding equal distribution of scarce resources is likely to encourage competitive, selfish behaviour, and equal power is likely to encourage equal respect among people rather than domination, condescension and deference. (The language of virtues and vices may sound old-fashioned but they are things we readily identify in evaluating people as generous, public-spirited, respectful, friendly, courageous, timid, rude, selfish, macho, abrasive, etc. Virtues are generally those kinds of habits of behaviour which are conducive to the well-being of both self and others, and vices those which are not.) This differs from post-structuralist accounts of 'subjectification'[7] in implying that some forms of social shaping (and disciplinary power) are conducive to well-being or flourishing and some not.

Instrumentalism and organisations

As Karen Legge notes, many observers and researchers have emphasised how the supposedly human(e) character of HRM conflicts with its instrumental role in promoting the goals of the organisation (Legge, 2005). However, there are many kinds of instrumental behaviour in organisations and it is important to understand the differences and relationships between them, and in turn, their relationships to *non*-instrumental behaviour.

First, there is the instrumentality of work itself. Work may or may not be intrinsically satisfying, but from a normative point of view this is secondary to the job of providing goods or services. Work – particularly within a division of labour – just is a means to an external end in terms of its function. Thus the point of education is not the job satisfaction of the teacher but the education of the pupil; the health of the patient is more important than the job satisfaction of the nurse; the point of cleaning is cleanliness, not the welfare of the cleaner. No matter how desirable job satisfaction and quality may be, it is not the reason for the existence, or the end, of economic work, whether capitalist or non-capitalist, paid or unpaid.[8] Secondly, employing organisations instrumentalise employees; employees are not hired out of respect or compassion for them but for their usefulness as a means to the ends of the organisation. In not-for-profit organisations these ends are use-values, whether goods or services. In for-profit organisations, these use-values are themselves instrumentalised as means to the end of making profit. Fourthly, to a significant but variable extent, employees' motivations are themselves instrumental, though generally in relation to different goals from those of their employers. However, much behaviour at work is not instrumental but done for its own sake, though this need not coincide with the employer's interest.

The ends of organisations are relatively narrowly defined because they occupy particular places in the social division of labour, and produce specific goods or services. In capitalist organisations, profit may be made by various means, but they tend to be dedicated to particular use-values because each requires specialist know-how and investment. The work-roles of many employees tend to be still more specialised, by virtue of having particular occupations within detailed divisions of labour, carrying out tasks that are just a partial contribution towards the production of particular commodities or use-values, such as button-hole maker, receptionist, or dental nurse.[9] By comparison, the needs and ends of workers as people are 'thick' or multiple, embracing not merely physical survival or economic necessities but the circumstances, commitments,[10] relationships and activities that constitute a flourishing and worthwhile life, such as health, security and safety, caring and being cared for, involvement in activities with others, having some autonomy, recognition and friendship, scope for relaxation, and so on. While to some extent, people may be able to satisfy many of these with little effort, they also generally require some monitoring and balancing and this involves a kind of practical reason that is different from formal and instrumental reason, for it involves an assessment – albeit limited and fallible – of the many different elements that are important for their well-being (Nussbaum, 2000).[11] Individuals' motives are therefore typically mixed, not only because of the competing demands of self-interest and others, but also because of these different aspects of well-being.

The pressures to instrumentalise all activities within an economic organisation for its own ends lead to attempts to reduce employees' actions and concerns at work to just those which are functional for meeting those ends. While this may be largely achieved in some kinds of work – particularly highly deskilled, machine or computer-paced work – it tends to be resisted to some degree by workers, precisely because it is dysfunctional from the point of view of their own well-being, not least their psychological well-being. Any serious attempt to consider the human implications of employment needs an approach which addresses the diversity and complexity of needs and concerns that people have, and not merely as workers. As people, workers are also likely to socialise or compete with others, pursue their self-interest, seek fulfilment, respect and esteem, form attachments and commitments to others and sometimes to their work, become concerned about fairness and about the ethos and politics of the organisation, get distracted, bored or inspired, worry about their families and other relationships, become ill or get pregnant, and generally allow life to intrude on work. They may also want to do their job well, and not let their work mates and customers or clients down, though their ideas about good quality work might differ from their employers'. They are not autistic rational economic individuals, single-mindedly pursuing their self-interest; indeed any employer would be foolish to employ such a person, as they would lack any sense of responsibility towards and for others. Hence, the multi-dimensional interests and concerns of employees' tend repeatedly to spill over the frames that employers try to impose in order to confine them to particular purposes, and in ways that can either further or limit their organisations' success. The greater the competitive pressures on organisations, the more each one is likely to try to 'purify' its activities of all non-functional elements and instrumentalise its members' faculties for its own ends. The problems that result stem not only from the instrumental nature of organisations' activities but from the narrowness of the ends to which they are directed compared to the multiple ends of the people they employ. At the same time, as consumers or taxpayers, we want workers to get on with the work which we are paying for and to do it well, but where employers misread workers' mixed motivations, needs and concerns or try to suppress or instrumentalise them for their own ends, they risk 'crowding out' behaviour which, whether intentionally or unintentionally, may actually be also functional for the organisation.

Daily life, in general, frequently poses moral dilemmas for individuals, particularly where there are competing demands on them, such as the demands of workers' families and those of their employers and workmates. Although people may cope more or less well with these tensions, the relative vulnerability of workers in depending on their jobs for their income is likely to make them respond to these dilemmas differently from how they would if they were not dependent in this way. Of course workers may neglect families and friends for other reasons – excessive ambition or, in the case of male workers, sexism, for example – but the structural context of dependence is itself problematic not only because of the economic insecurity and inequality but also because it prevents us valuing and attending to the needs of others appropriately.

Variety and self-actualisation

Doing a variety of different things and developing our abilities and skills to do them is not only instrumentally useful but also tends to be satisfying and enabling in itself, especially where we feel that the activities are worthwhile. This is sometimes termed 'self-actualisation' or 'being all we can be'. As Aristotelians argue, flourishing consists in cultivating a *range* of different virtues, relationships, activities or 'excellences'. Conversely, as Smith (1759)[12] and Marx (1975) argued, and subsequent empirical research has confirmed, confinement of workers to simple, repetitive tasks has a debilitating effect on their cognitive powers that reduces their ability to function effectively outside their paid work (Murphy, 1993). This diversity of potentials and needs is central to what it is to be human. As Marx put it, we are '*in need of* a totality of human vital human expression' (Marx, 1975, p. 356, emphasis in original). Similarly, according to the capabilities approach, itself influenced by Aristotle, the extent to which people are able to enjoy these functionings, or doings and beings that are valued, is a measure of development and well-being (Sen, 1999). The design of jobs is generally, of course, an intentional act of management. A truly human form of management would seek to design jobs involving varied and interesting tasks rather than tedious and repetitive ones.

Recognition and motivation

As I have indicated, individuals' motives and valuations are generally mixed and complex, but a major concern is *recognition*, in terms of the respect, esteem and approval of others. As Adam Smith argued in his *Theory of Moral Sentiments*, people continually seek the approval of others, and regulate their behaviour in terms of the views of imagined or real others; ostracisation or contempt have serious consequences for their well-being (Smith, 1759). We generally need recognition from others if we are to flourish; indeed lack of recognition often prompts loss of self-esteem and motivation. Workers in low paid and low-status jobs who experience disrespect and racism often complain more about these than their pay; they know when they agree to take on the job that the pay will be low and tolerate it because there are no better alternatives, but they do not expect to be disrespected (Wills, 2006).

Although the 'politics of recognition' is a novel term, covering struggles for recognition of identities, particular ethnicity and sexuality, and often contrasted to the politics of distribution of economic resources (Fraser, 1999), the struggle for recognition of moral worth is much older. As E.P. Thompson showed, many struggles in modern history which were ostensibly about distribution of income and wealth were also driven by a demand by subordinated groups for respect (Thompson, 1963). Distribution of resources is one way in which respect and esteem are signalled. It's common in organisations for employees to feel upset if a colleague within their own rank is promoted above them if they think s/he does not deserve it. The resentment and sense of injustice is generally less about the difference in pay – which is in any case often minor – but the difference in valuation of their worth and competence which the decision signals.[13] Furthermore, recognition is confirmed or contradicted through the distribution of resources and working conditions; the official rhetoric of an organisation may be that all employees are recognised and valued equally, but if they have very different levels of pay and terms and conditions of employment, then what is espoused is contradicted by deeds.

Recognition is of two kinds: first, unconditional recognition of people as persons; and secondly recognition which is conditional on their character, behaviour and performance (Taylor, 1994). (Thus, for example, as a lecturer I am supposed to give unconditional recognition to students as people, but when it comes to assessing their work my recognition is conditional on their performance.) The influence of conditional recognition on motivation is complex. Although having the esteem and approval of others is important, people generally want to deserve that esteem, and they are likely to feel uncomfortable about receiving undeserved esteem, and resentful about others who they feel do not deserve the esteem they get. Insofar as economic rewards are interpreted by actors as evidence of esteem, in a capitalist society this is only weakly related to performance or merit because such rewards depend heavily on power and scarcity (e.g. CEOs pay themselves huge incomes, not because they deserve them, but *because they can*). However, as Smith (1759) argued, individuals often do something not because it will bring them praise or esteem, but because they think it is the right thing to do, because the job needs doing, because they do not want to let others down, and so on, even if it does not bring them approval or reward. Sometimes they do things which they think are right, even though it brings disapproval from others; customer service workers may diverge from their official script and procedures if they think keeping to it would be unethical, even though it may bring them disapproval from management. To be sure, they are likely to feel that they deserve praise or reward for doing what they believe to be the right thing, indeed all the more because they are not doing it merely for the praise, and they may become disaffected if repeated virtuous behaviour goes unnoticed, particularly if others are rewarded for less. It is also possible that workers may sometimes diverge from the rules merely to make life more comfortable for themselves of course, but not always. In other words, while it is always necessary to be sceptical about professed motives, scepticism is not the same thing as cynicism; the most cynical explanation is not always the best, and we should be sceptical about cynical explanations too. Furthermore, recognition is not the only source of satisfaction and self-esteem in work; those fortunate enough to do work that is skilled, demanding and interesting can enjoy the 'internal goods' or satisfactions and achievements of that work itself, though again, achieving such internal goods is likely also to bring them the 'external goods' of recognition too (MacIntyre, 1981).

That people do not work merely for pay is fundamental to understanding motivation in the workplace (Frey, 1997). Sophisticated managers may recognise these characteristics and attempt to treat employees respectfully and provide opportunities for the provision of conditional recognition or esteem, although the instrumental and hierarchical, unequal nature of economic organisations means that this can only be partly realised. When all is said and done, the workers are employed because they are functional for the organisation, not because they are intrinsically worthy.

Geoffrey Brennan and Philip Pettit argue that in addition to the invisible hand of market forces and the visible hand of management directive, there is also an 'intangible hand' which influences employees' behaviour through the granting of esteem and dis-esteem (Brennan and Pettit, 2004). However, like Smith, they acknowledge that workers do not merely work well because it brings them esteem, but because they think it's the right thing to do; they want to be the proper objects of esteem. If they do a bad job, they may feel a sense of shame even if no one else notices. This is an important form of self-regulation. They also tend to want to be treated in a way which signals that they have autonomy and are trusted to work well independently of managerial control and esteem. To be immediately rewarded – either in money or expressions of esteem – for each small good act would be demeaning – like rewarding a dog with a biscuit for obeying a command. By contrast, if managers express esteem for or otherwise reward good conduct over a longer period, then this is more likely to be seen as recognition of a person's *good character*, and not merely from having carried out a particular task well. This can also signal that the management acknowledges that in the specific kinds of work that the individual does, he or she knows better than the management what is needed. Creating a distance between the good behaviour and the granting of conditional recognition is therefore likely to be both better appreciated and more effective. In other words, ways of granting recognition which are seen as rewarding rather than controlling are likely to motivate workers best. These considerations also help explain why many forms of audit and work monitoring are dysfunctional.

Of course, it is more in keeping with the spirit of capitalism that incentivisation is equated with financial rewards, most obviously in the form of performance-related pay. Where employers misread workers' motivations or try to instrumentalise them for their own ends they run the risk of crowding out behaviour which, whether intentionally or unintentionally, is functional for the firm. To treat an employee's actions as purely motivated by the expectation of reward is to reduce virtue to instrumental action for the purposes of exchange. Consequently, they may feel somewhat demeaned by such treatment and become more cynical and instrumental as a result. Of course, the point of employment for employees *is* to get an income, and some will be happy to be treated as if this were their only motivation. Piece-work, and working on commission are common in some kinds of employment – usually ones where either there are no significant intrinsic job satisfactions, or else ones that are not consistent with the goals of the organisation and hence need to be controlled externally; some workers may be motivated by these. However, the immediate rewards in terms of pay and recognition are not necessarily the only motivations for many workers, and for some, they may play a secondary role.

Similar arguments apply to 'good citizenship'. This is important both for the functional success of organisations and for workplace morale. It involves civility and supporting some kind of social life at work, willingness to help colleagues, being flexible and volunteering to do things which support the public good, such as helping to cover for someone who has been off sick, or sitting on a committee. Employees may do these things, at least in part, in order to 'get on', but they can also do them because they feel that such things are the right thing to do. (Some may not have to think about whether to do them, for, through repeated practice, they have developed a habit of behaving in this benevolent and public-spirited way.) If these acts are not equally shared within a workplace, it is likely to cause resentment towards those who free-ride on them. If management tries to encourage them by giving specific payments or benefits to individuals for carrying them out, it is again likely to have a 'crowding-out' effect on that behaviour because it is then likely to be seen as an exchange rather than something that's right and good to do anyway, and those who have been public-spirited in the past are likely to resent those who now will only do what they did for rewards. Self-interested instrumentalism may then drive out duty and benevolence.

The HRM goal of cultivating workers who are proactive and 'committed' rather than merely passive and compliant is in tension with the overriding capitalist requirement of profitability, at least unless the workers are committed to that very goal. Even if they are committed to such a goal, there is no clear relation between their self-interest and its achievement; for example, firms may become more profitable by reducing their workforce and intensifying work. To be committed to something, be it a cause, or a person or group, is to treat it as an end in itself, not merely as a means to an end (Archer, 2000). Often workers are committed to their fellow workers, clients and the service being provided, rather than to making profit or meeting managerial targets. For workers to be committed to the goals of an organisation which, because of its hierarchical structure and the competitive pressures upon it, cannot reciprocate by being equally committed to its employees, could be said to indicate a kind of gullibility; loyalty is simply misplaced in the ruthless, instrumental world of capitalist organisations.

Hierarchy, inequality and domination

Organisations which depend on the employment relation are fundamentally unequal, not merely in that they have internal hierarchies of power, but because their workers generally have no alternative but to seek employment and are dependent on it for their economic security. (There are of course usually other employers too but real labour markets are highly segmented by skill and other characteristics and localised, and jobs of particular kinds only become available intermittently; employers generally have more alternatives and security.) Contractual equality therefore conceals inequalities of resources and options and is therefore quite compatible with domination. Even in non-capitalist organisations, this asymmetry obtains. Employees' scope for action is also constrained and enabled according to their relative position in the organisation. The structure of relationships between individuals within the organisation tends to reflect their different volumes and mixes of economic, social, cultural and educational capital, indeed position within the organisation tends to reflect position within the wider social field, the two being causally related (Bourdieu, 2005). Position within these fields of unequal relations affects not only pay and security but a broad range of circumstances relevant to well-being, including matters of recognition, respect and self-respect. As a result of this, even where positions in organisational hierarchies reflect difference in some kind of merit, access to opportunities to achieve that merit in the world outside are unequal so that the occupancy of those positions tends to reflect those inequalities, according to the lottery of natal class and gender. Organisations may imagine themselves to be meritocratic, but they do not exist on a level playing field. Capitalist organisations depend on inequalities for their very existence, as Marx noted; they also take advantage of wider social inequalities in designing their labour recruitment policies – increasingly, now of course, on an international scale; and they are major reproducers of inequalities in society, simply by differentiating pay and conditions for different groups of workers.

Inequalities reproduced within organisations have systematically damaging effects on people's well-being. This is most evident in health inequalities, where as Michael Marmot shows, life expectancy and health vary remarkably closely with occupational and class hierarchies (Marmot, 2004; see also Wilkinson, 2006). Significantly, Marmot argues that the most likely cause of this is not merely diet but the tendency of stress – particularly the stress of being under pressure while lacking the power and discretion to reduce or resist it – to increase as one moves down workplace hierarchies.

Inequalities within organisations also produce different possibilities for achievement, recognition and dignity. We especially value recognition where it comes from others we respect. To be disrespected by someone we do not respect, is less problematic. Within groups of people who are equal in power and status, conditional recognition can be given freely, and it can be accepted as such – as freely given rather than obligatory, and hence as sincere. But where there are inequalities these relationships of recognition get distorted; workers have to worry about what their managers think about them, regardless of whether they respect them and what they actually think of them, for fear of losing their jobs. It therefore implies a measure of obligatory, hence insincere, deference, which can be demeaning. As Robert Jackall's celebrated study of managers in U.S. corporations shows, economic organisations are typically sites where instrumentalism, dissembling and strategising vie with commitment and the pursuit of integrity, often with the former winning (Jackall, 1988). Those who strategise and manoeuvre for their own advantage, including making insincere expressions of deference to superiors, may succeed, though if they do it too transparently they may risk attracting contempt. Equally, those who never put their beliefs 'on the line' by opposing the dominant, whatever the situation, are likely to be seen as lacking the courage of their convictions, or having no convictions or commitments and hence lacking character. Maintaining integrity in the face of pressures to bend is a prime source of respect and self-respect but it is accompanied by the fear of the contempt and shame which rejection would bring, and more dramatically by the fear of losing one's job in capitalist organisations unrestrained by strong labour organisation and law. It is also common for actors in some positions to try to win respect and self-respect by taking on challenges; although success may bring approval, equally, failure may bring disesteem and possibly shame. Nevertheless, they may feel that unless they take such risks, they will achieve little respect (Harré, 1979).

The critique of HRM must take account of the way in which these complex motivations play out in the context of the internal inequalities of organisation. HRM seeks to produce motivated, proactive employees, yet it does so in a context that is likely to cause problems for them if workers have an ethical approach to their work and work relationships.

Finally, a basic feature of any humane organisation is respect for workers' dignity, but again this is in tension with the instrumental and unequal character of organisations. Dignity at work requires workers to be treated as ends in themselves, to be allowed some autonomy, to be trusted, to be sure that their vulnerability and dependence will not be taken advantage of (for example, through bullying and harassment, or unreasonable demands), to be taken seriously and listened to, and as far as possible, not to have to do tasks which are undignified (Sayer, 2007). Well-placed workers generally do not have to worry about their dignity, but it is a commonly voiced concern of workers in subaltern positions, where the nature of the work and the way they are treated by superiors or customers tends to undermine it. On top of these consequences of the instrumental and class character of organisations, threats to workers' dignity often take sexist or racist forms.

Conclusion

This chapter has attempted to give some indication of the complexity of workers' motivations and concerns, and the often-inept attempts of management to motivate them to work effectively. In order to assess HRM in relation to what is or is not conducive to the well-being of employees and good quality work I argued first that we have to acknowledge that the influence of work cultures and arrangements can only be understood by acknowledging certain functionings or beings and doings that people need to flourish. This involved making a stab at identifying what it is to be human and hence what humane treatment involves. Hypotheses about the elements of this humanity inevitably hover between empirical claims and aspirations precisely because of the nature of needs and concerns: we have them but whether we can meet, satisfy and take care of them depends on our circumstances and actions. For example, security and respectful treatment are things people need and aspire to, but they don't always get them.

Anti-humanist approaches that refuse to acknowledge the existence of universal needs or functionings required for people to flourish leave us without any means for either explaining how organisational practices like HRM affect actors or assessing them critically: if there are no human characteristics to be harmed or benefited, then a critical management studies is reduced to academic criticism of other research rather than criticism of the object. The attraction of an Aristotelian, moral economy approach is that on the one hand it acknowledges the importance of socialisation in shaping people and their dispositions (virtues and vices), while on the other hand recognising that we have certain needs and proclivities towards flourishing or suffering according to how we are able to live. As people, employees have multiple needs and concerns which fit uneasily alongside the narrow and instrumental priorities of the organisation. The need for recognition and participation on a par with others is a condition of flourishing that is in tension with the instrumental and unequal character of organisations, especially capitalist ones subject to the pressure of competition and the upheavals of market forces. Although their motivations are influenced by the characteristics of the organisation for which they work, employees' concerns and interests go beyond it, and attempts to narrow these down to those which can be manipulated to suit the organisation are likely to damage employee morale and well-being and be counterproductive for organisations.

Notes

1. Bourdieu argued that the particular positions in which people grow up and live within the social field, be subordinate or dominant, shape their dispositions so that they are generally attuned to those positions. The structures of dispositions which Bourdieu termed the habitus tend to be durable, but they can be changed gradually if actors' positions change (Bourdieu, 2000).
2. For a critique of these tendencies, see Sayer (2000, Chapter 4).
3. That some other higher animals also exhibit some cultural variation in no way contradicts this point. Universal human properties don't have to be unique.
4. I am deliberately combining approaches from different periods of Foucault's work here.
5. In identifying needs and flourishing and suffering the distinction between description and evaluation collapses.
6. Some of these appear to be unique to humans (e.g. the ability to reflect upon our ends and their worth – or 'strong evaluation', as Charles Taylor terms it) and others (e.g. the ability to develop cultural variations in behaviour) are found in certain other species.
7. Or indeed from Bourdieu's account of the formation of the habitus, although this can be rectified (Bourdieu, 2000; Sayer, 2005).
8. This is an implicit challenge to Marxism's valuation of labour as an end in itself (see O'Neill, 1998).
9. This is also commonly referred to as the 'manufacturing' or 'technical' division of labour, though it occurs in service production too.
10. Commitments differ from preferences and goals not only in strength and durability but in that, the means for meeting commitments have generally to be consistent with the ends, whereas they do not for mere preferences and goals. Thus, meeting a

commitment to one's workmates cannot be achieved by means that do not exemplify that very commitment, whereas anything that increases profitability (within the constraints of legal and other prevailing norms) will do.

11. It also different from the communicative reason emphasised by Habermas (Habermas, 1986).

12. 'The man whose whole life is spent in performing a few simple operations, of which the effects too are, perhaps, always the same, or very nearly the same, has no occasion to exert his understanding, or to exercise his invention in finding out expedients for removing difficulties which never occur. He naturally loses, therefore, the habit of such exertion, and generally becomes as stupid and ignorant as it is possible for a human creature to become. The torpor of his mind renders him not only incapable of relishing or bearing a part in any rational conversation, but of conceiving of any generous, noble, or tender sentiment, and consequently of forming any just judgement concerning many even of the ordinary duties of private life.' (Smith, 1776, pt. III, Art. II, pp. 302–303). Smith also realised that differences in abilities were 'not upon many occasions so much the cause, as the effect of the division of labour'. (Smith, 1776, Book1, chII, p. 19).

13. That they may feel disesteemed even if a colleague merely gets given a newer, nicer bit of office furniture and they do not, shows just how sensitive people are to how they are valued within an organisation.

References

Archer, M. (2000) *Being Human*, Cambridge: Cambridge University Press.

Bourdieu, P. (2000) *Pascalian Meditations*, Cambridge: Polity.

Bourdieu, P. (2005) *The Social Structure of the Economy*, Cambridge: Polity.

Brennan, G. and Pettit, P. (2004) *The Economy of Esteem*, Oxford: Oxford University Press.

Foucault, M. (1977) *Discipline and Punish*, London: Penguin.

Foucault, M. (1979) *The History of Sexuality*, London: Penguin.

Fraser, N. (1999) 'Social justice in the age of identity politics: redistribution, recognition and participation' in Ray, L.J. and Sayer, A. (eds) *Culture and Economy after the Cultural Turn*, London: Sage, 53–75.

Frey, B. (1997) *Not Just for the Money: An Economic Theory of Personal Motivation*, Cheltenham: Edward Elgar.

Habermas, J. (1986) *The Theory of Communicative Action, Vol. 1*, Cambridge: Polity.

Harré, R. (1979) *Social Being*, Oxford: Blackwell.

Jackall, R. (1988) *Moral Mazes*, Oxford: Oxford University Press.

Legge, K. (2005) *Human Resources Management: Rhetorics and Realities*, Anniversary edn: Basingstoke: Palgrave.

MacIntyre, A. (1981) *After Virtue: A Study in Moral Theory*, London: Duckworth.

Marmot, M. (2004) *Status Syndrome*, New York, NY: Henry Holt.

Marx, K. (1975) *Early Writings*, Harmondsworth: Penguin.

Midgley, M. (1972) 'Is "moral" a dirty word?', *Philosophy*, XLVII, 181, 206–228.

Murphy, J.B. (1993) *The Moral Economy of Labor*, New Haven: Yale University Press.

Nussbaum, M.C. (2000) *Women and Human Development*, Cambridge: Cambridge University Press.

Nussbaum, M.C. (2006) *Frontiers of Justice*, Cambridge, MA: Belknap, Harvard University Press.

O'Neill, J. (1998) *The Market: Ethics, Knowledge and Politics*, London: Routledge.

Sayer, A. (2000) *Realism and Social Science*, London: Sage.

Sayer, A. (2005) *The Moral Significance of Class*, Cambridge: Cambridge University Press.

Sayer, A. (2007) 'What dignity at work means', in Bolton, S.C. (ed.) *Dimensions of Dignity at Work*, London: Butterworth Heineman.

Sen, A. (1999) *Development as Freedom*, Oxford: Oxford University Press.

Smith, A. (1759, 1984) *The Theory of Moral Sentiments*, Indianapolis: Liberty Fund.

Taylor, C. (1994), 'The politics of recognition', in Gutmann, A. (ed.) *Multi-culturalism: Examining the Politics of Recognition*, Princetown, NJ: Princetown University Press.

Thompson, E.P. (1963) *The Making of the English Working Class*, London: Harmondsworth.

Wilkinson, R.G. (2006) *The Impact of Inequality*, London: Routledge.

Wills, J. (2006) Talk given to the Transformations of Socio-Economy Workshop, University of Essex, 10–11 July.

3

Searching for the human in empirical research on the HRM–organisational performance link: a meta-theoretical approach

Steve Fleetwood

Introduction

Ever since pioneering work by the likes of Arthur (1994), MacDuffie (1995) and Huselid (1995), a growing army of academics have sought to demonstrate the existence of an empirical link between an organisation's HRM practices and its performance.[1] Whilst these studies vary in the industries and firms they investigate, the independent and dependent variables used and the types of data collected, they share a common *meta-theoretical* approach, that is, an approach to the philosophy of science, methodology, ontology, epistemology and notions of causality. This approach can be sketched as follows: HRM practices and organisational performance are quantified and empirical data generated. Statistical techniques (typically regression, analysis of variance, correlation, structural equation modelling and factor analysis) are then employed on these data to test hypotheses to the effect that certain bundles of HRM practices, under certain conditions, lead to increased organisational performance. In the literature on the HRM–Performance link, this meta-theoretical approach appears to be accepted (almost) entirely without question.

There is, however, something missing in this approach: *the human*. There is no analysis of the human beings, the people, the workers and managers who actually do the day-to-day things in the workplace that influence organisational performance. Indeed, not only is the human missing, I will argue that the meta-theoretical approach currently dominating the research,

41

actually prevents an analysis of the human, for two reasons. First, to *explain* anything requires a theory or theories. To explain what humans do in the workplace requires a theory or theories of *the human* in the workplace. Whilst the meta-theory used in research on the HRM–Performance link generates theoretical statements that deliver predictions, these statements do not deliver explanations, leaving the research without an explanation of *the human* in the workplace. Second, whenever a theory is constructed or invoked, a method or a research technique is employed, or a practical intervention is taken, *presuppositions* are necessarily made – even if they are implicit. Looking closely at research on the HRM–Performance link reveals that the conception of *the human* presupposed by this meta-theory is implausible.

This chapter, then, stands out from the other chapters in the collection, in the sense that it deals entirely with matters of meta-theory. Whilst I suspect many will find this a rather dry subject, the fact is, we all have meta-theoretical commitments, and sooner or later, it does us good to reflect upon those that we hold, and indeed on those held by others.

The chapter opens by adopting a *critical realist*[2] perspective, and working its way through a series of concepts, specifically: the deductive method, ontology, epistemology, events and their regularities and closed systems. Part II introduces two notions of causality and two types of explanation, paving the way, in Part III, to explain the lack of explanation. The final part demonstrates why the concept of *the human* presupposed by this meta-theory is implausible. The conclusion considers the possibility that theory, and hence explanation, lie buried within the expansive literature.

Teasing out the meta-theoretical presuppositions

Whilst we tend not to reflect upon meta-theory, the fact is that mathematical techniques such as regression equations make specific ontological, epistemological and methodological presuppositions. The following section will demonstrate that if the social world (ontology) is reduced to atomistic, observed events, then knowledge (epistemology) is reduced to (trying to) identify event regularities, and methodology is reduced to engineering closed systems so that event regularities can be presented in the form of functional relations – or derivatives such as regression equations. This is not an easy set of propositions, so allow me to proceed step by step.

The dominant method used in empirical research in general, and the HRM–Performance link in particular, appears to be some (unspecified) variant or combination of the covering law model, deductive nomological model, inductive-statistical model, or hypothetico-deductive method. Following Lawson (1997, 2004). I refer to this variant as the *deductive method* or simply *deductivism*. From this perspective to 'explain' something is to make a prediction as a deduction from a set of initial conditions, assumptions, axioms, and law(s) or some other regular pattern of events. Deductivism involves the following steps:

(a) Laws or theories about a phenomenon
(b) Statements about initial conditions
(c) The phenomenon is 'explained' and predicted as a deduction from (a) and (b).

And in the context of the HRM–Performance link, we might say something like:

(a) HRM practices are regularly conjoined and statistically associated with increased organisational performance (laws or theories)
(b) These HRM practices consist of work teams and a performance-related pay scheme
(c) Increased organisational performance is 'explained' and predicted as a deduction from (a) and (b)
(d) Theories or laws are often tested via their predictions.

This last point (d) is important. Research on the HRM–Performance link is preoccupied with what is referred to variously as testing the prediction, testing the hypothesis, testing the theory, testing the model, testing the model's predictions, finding the predictors of their dependent variable and so on. The terminology varies and, it must be said, is highly ambiguous, but the practice is well known. In what follows I will refer (where possible) to *testing the hypotheses*.

Ontology, epistemology, event regularities and closed systems

Events are the building blocks of empirical research: they are the things researchers observe and collect data on. An event might, for example, be: the introduction of team working; the existence of a union; the duration of a training programme; an increase in productivity or some such. If and when these events are observed, recorded, counted or measured (or approximated by proxy measures) in terms of some quantity they become variables. Quantified events become *variables*.

Presupposed here is a certain ontology. Because the ontology consists of what can be observed it is an ontology of atomistic, observed *events*; because these objects are confined to observation the ontology is *empirical*; and because these objects are thought to exist independently of our identification of them, it is *realist*. The presupposed ontology is, therefore, *empirical realist*.

What about epistemological presuppositions? If *particular* knowledge is gained through observing atomistic events, then *general*, including *scientific*, knowledge is only available if these events manifest themselves in some kind of pattern: a flux of totally arbitrary events would not result in knowledge of any kind. Scientific knowledge is, therefore, reliant upon the existence and ubiquity of *event regularities* or *constant conjunctions of events*. This is an important claim so let us spend some time unpacking it.

From the deductivist perspective, to observe two (or more) events simply occurring is not very illuminating whereas to observe two events occurring in *regular succession*, such that whenever event *x* occurs, event *y* regularly accompanies it, is illuminating. To observe a firm introducing HR practices, whilst also observing increases in productivity is not very illuminating. To observe that the introduction of an HR practice regularly occurs with increases in productivity such that whenever this HR practice is introduced, productivity regularly increases, is illuminating. Furthermore, from the deductivist perspective, when these events are quantified and become variables, a whole range of statistical techniques become available to establish properties about the nature of their association. We can explore what regularly happens to the magnitude of the independent variable when the magnitude of the independent variable (or variables) changes, or is introduced. *It is vital to understand that predictions and hypotheses are rendered intelligible only by presupposing the ubiquity of regularities between events.*

For example, in one of the defining, and now widely cited papers in the field, Huselid's (1995, p. 670) first hypothesis states that: 'Systems of High Performance Work Practices will diminish employee turnover and increase productivity and corporate financial performance.' His statement is intelligible on the grounds that in the firms he surveyed, systems of High Performance Work Practices *regularly* diminished employee turnover and increased productivity and corporate financial performance.

Henceforth, I will generalise and style regularities between events as 'whenever event *x* then event *y*' or 'whenever event $x_1 \ldots x_n$ then event *y*'. The fact that Becker *et al.* come extremely close to using this terminology is highly indicative that I am not pursuing a straw person:

Ideally, you will develop a measurement system that lets you answer questions such as, how much will we have to change x in order to achieve our target in y? To illustrate, if you increase training by 20 percent, how much will that change employee performance and, ultimately, unit performance? (Becker *et al.*, 2001, p. 110)

Regularities between events are more often expressed as functional relations, $y = f(x)$ or $y = f(x_1 \ldots x_n)$. It is very important to note that events and their regularities are the basis upon which any mathematical or econometric specification is derived.

Whilst event regularities are extremely important for the deductive method, there is a snag: they only occur in very specific systems, in *closed systems*. Systems are closed when they are characterised by event regularities and, by extension, *open* when they lack such regularity. Events are constantly conjoined in the sense that for every event y, there exists a set of events $x_1, x_2, \ldots x_n$, such that y and $x_1, x_2, \ldots x_n$ are regularly conjoined.[3] A hi-fi system, for example, is a closed system because a change in the volume control is regularly conjoined with a change in volume. A labour market, by contrast, is an open system because a change in wage rates is not constantly conjoined with a change in the demand for, and supply of, labour. Wage rates may rise and sometimes the demand for labour decreases, sometimes it increases, and sometimes it remains unchanged. In the social world, there appear to be few, if any, closed systems (on labour markets and closed systems, see Fleetwood, 2006).

Whilst I could take any of the hundreds of empirical studies as an example, I choose a paper by Laursen (2002, p. 145) because it has the merit of being exceptionally clear about his regression equation – which incidentally is a good example of a stochastically closed system:

$$A_i = a_s \text{SECT}_i + d_s \text{SIZE}_i + u_s \text{LINK}_i + h_s \text{HRMS}_i + e_{ij}$$

Control variables SECT, SIZE and LINK denote the industrial sector, firm size and degree of vertical integration respectively. Dependent variable A_i denotes the firms' ability to innovate. HRMS_i is one combined independent variable expressing the HRM practices associated with performance-related pay (PPAY), delegation of decision rights (DRESP), and team work (TEAM). HRMS_i actually measures the variable denoting how large a share of the firm's workforce is engaged in:

- Interdisciplinary working groups [TEAM 1]
- Quality circles [TEAM 2]

- Planned job rotation [TEAM 3]
- Integration of functions (e.g., sales, production/services, finance) [TEAM 4]
- Delegation of responsibility [DRESP]
- Performance-related Pay [PPAY].

Lauren's model is a (stochastically) closed system in the sense that (after controlling for firm size and vertical integration) the firm's ability to innovate is hypothesised to be constantly conjoined with performance-related pay, delegation of decision rights, and team work.

To summarise, if the social world (ontology) is reduced to atomistic, observed events, then knowledge (epistemology) is reduced to (trying to) identify event regularities, and methodology is reduced to engineering closed systems so that event regularities can be presented in the form of functional relations – or derivatives such as regression equations. Driving the inferential machinery in the deductive method is the presupposition of event regularities which makes possible the deduction or prediction of some events from other event(s). Without regularities between events, that is to say without closed systems, no deduction or prediction is possible.

In parentheses, note it might be possible to maintain a commitment to the systemic openness of the social world, refuse the temptation to impose artificial closure, and yet still be able to pass comment on likely future implications of our actions. We can make what we refer to as *tendential predictions* (Fleetwood and Hesketh, 2006). It is, however, vital not to (mis)interpret tendencies as 'rough and ready' event regularities, or as probabilistic event regularities. Rather, tendencies, as expressions of causal powers can be unconnected to the actual events they govern. The power of gunpowder to explode can be unconnected to events like the actual exploding of gunpowder and the can power remains unexercised even when it does not manifest itself (Fleetwood, 2001). I will return to this below when discussing the powers of human beings. If our research of some phenomenon is sufficiently advanced to the extent that we have a theory, and an explanation, then we have an understanding of the structures and the agents who are enabled and constrained by these structures, and the tendencies this process generates. To the extent that we understand these tendencies (and, of course, countertendencies) we can make claims about the likelihood of an action succeeding. We hesitate to call this a prediction because the term is now so entwined in positivist discourse that it is almost impossible to untangle it and give it another meaning. Nonetheless, it is a prediction of some kind, albeit heavily qualified despite the fact that it is devoid of claims about magnitude and sign.

Causality and explanation

Another important presupposition of deductivism is causality. If the ontology is one of observed atomistic events, then causality cannot be conceived in terms of anything other than a regularity between these events. The cause of event *y* can only be sought in terms of some prior event *x*. This notion of causality is often referred to as 'Humean' causality because it derives from the work of David Hume.[4]

Whilst causality is important for deductivism, it is important to note that *only causality as regularity, Humean causality*, is used. Consider a very well-known example from the HRM–Performance literature.

> To estimate the practical significance of the impact of High Performance Work Practices on productivity, I next calculated the impact of a one-standard deviation increase in each practice scale on . . . net sales . . . The findings indicate that each one-standard-deviation increase raises sales an average of $ 27,044 per employee. (Huselid, 1995, p. 658)

Let me proceed carefully here. It is true that Huselid does not *actually* claim anything about causality here, Humean or otherwise. He does not actually claim that the introduction of certain HPWP's *causes* the increase in sales. And Huselid is not alone. To the best of my knowledge, none of the research on the HRM–Performance link makes specific claims about causality – in fact, many papers point to the problem of reverse causality. Yet if Humean causality is *not* implied in this research, if researchers are *not* claiming that their findings demonstrate that the introduction of HRM practices cause improved organisational performance, then these studies have no practical significance. Huselid does, however, add that his figures 'suggest that firms can indeed obtain substantial financial benefits from investing in the practices studied here' (Huselid, 1995, p. 667) which comes as close to making a causal claim as possible without actually using the term 'causal'.

In addition to Humean causality, there is also something I call *complex* causality. These two notions of causality 'map' onto two notions of explanation. For ease of exposition, allow me to explicate this with examples from the physical world first, and then introduce examples from HRM.

> *Humean causality* refers to a situation where the cause of an event is assumed to be the event(s) that preceded it. The cause of the lamp's illumination, for example, is merely the finger that flicked the light switch.
>
> *Complex causality* refers to a situation where the cause of an event is not assumed to be the event(s) that preceded it, but rather is the wider conflux of interacting causal phenomena. The cause of the lamp's illumination, for example, is the

nature of the glass, the gas, the filament, the wire, the switch, the plug, the electricity, as well as the finger that flicked the switch.

It is extremely important to note that Humean causality does not become complex causality simply by allowing several causal factors into the analysis, which would, for example, mean simply extending the regression equation to allow for more independent variables. Let us, now, link these two types of causality to two types of explanation.

Humean causality and emaciated explanation

Giving a causal history, or account, of a phenomenon, and hence explaining it, could be interpreted to mean giving information about the event(s) that preceded the phenomenon. That is, explanation could be based upon Humean causality. If and when causality is reduced to Humean causality, then explanation is reduced merely to giving information about a succession of events and becomes, thereby, emaciated. The explanation of the lamp's illumination simply requires information to the effect that 'a finger flicked a switch'. Any further information about the finger, the switch, or anything else, adds no more information than is necessary and is, therefore, superfluous. If this information can be said to constitute an explanation at all, then it is a very *emaciated* one. Indeed most of us would not even recognise this as a *bona fide* explanation, because it would simply leave us asking, yet receiving no answer to the question, Why?

Complex causality and robust explanation

Giving a causal history of a phenomenon, and hence explaining it, could be interpreted to mean giving information about the underlying mechanisms and structures, along with (if we are dealing with social phenomena) the human agency that reproduces and transforms these mechanisms and structures. That is, explanation could be based upon complex causality. If and when causality is complex, then explanation cannot be reduced merely to giving information about a succession of events but rather requires information about the wider conflux of interacting causal phenomena beyond that captured even by sophisticated statistical techniques. Information about the nature of the glass, the gas, the filament, the wire, the switch, the plug, the electricity, as well as the finger that flicked the switch all add to the richness of the explanation and are, therefore, not superfluous but absolutely necessary. There is little doubt that most of us would recognise this information immediately as constituting a very rich, or robust, explanation as it would (at the very least go some way to) answering the question: Why?

One of the alleged HR practices influencing organisational performance is teamwork. Indeed, most of the studies have a variable or variables designed to measure the impact of team working. I use this example to elaborate upon the notions of causality and explanation just mentioned, but in the context not only of the social world, but also of the workplace.

If and when causality is *Humean*, then explanation is emaciated because it is reduced merely to giving information about a succession of events. The explanation of the increase in productivity simply requires information about the prior event, namely that *team working was introduced*. Any further information adds no more information than is strictly necessary to establish (Humean) causality, and is, therefore, superfluous. If this information can be said to constitute an explanation at all, then it is a very emaciated one.

If and when causality is *complex*, then explanation is irreducible merely to giving information about a succession of events. A robust explanation of the increase in productivity requires two kinds of information. First, it requires, what might be called, *hermeneutic* information. That is, information relating to the way the relevant agents (e.g. workers, union members, managers) interpret, understand, make sense of, the workplace and initiate action. Second, a robust explanation requires information about a significant (but not infinite) set of interacting causal phenomena through which agents initiate this action. This might, for example, include information on: the social, political, economic and spatial environment of the industry and/or the firm; the industrial relations system; the composition of the team; the nature of the new jobs, tasks and skills (if any); the relationship between team members; the line managers and corporate strategy; the nature of control in the firm; the nature of any synergies (or dis-synergies) created by the interaction of these causal phenomena; and so on.

Clearly, this list is not exhaustive and, furthermore, each of these causal phenomena could be broken down into its sub-components as we try to provide more detailed information.[5] Needless to say, a great deal of this information will be irreducibly qualitative. All this information adds to the richness of the explanation and is not superfluous but absolutely necessary. There is little doubt that most of us would recognise this information immediately as constituting a robust explanation because it would (at least to some degree) answer the question: Why?[6]

It is important, here, to note that whilst complex causality is the kind of causality we seek, because it generates robust explanations, this form of causality *cannot* be accommodated via functional relations or regression equations. Whilst there are several reasons for this, I mention only three here. First, because a great deal of the information that would be uncovered would be qualitative, perhaps hermeneutic, in nature and, thereby, impossible to quantify – at least impossible to quantify meaningfully.[7] Second, because complex causality involves *irregularity* and open systems, yet as I noted earlier, functional relations and regression equations are examples of regularity and closed systems. Ignoring the control variables, Lauren's regression equation (above) states:

$$A = f(\text{TEAM 1, TEAM 2, TEAM3, TEAM 4, DRESP and PPAY}).$$

The presupposition here is that the independent variables are regularly conjoined with the dependent variable such that whenever team working, delegation of responsibility and performance-related pay occur, then the firm's ability to innovate increases. If this were the case, then an organisation could simply implement team working, delegation of responsibility and performance-related pay and expect to see an increase in its ability to innovative. No HR managers would, of course, expect this kind of mechanical transplantation to work, because they intuitively realise that the workplace is not a closed, but an open, system (Fleetwood and Hesketh, 2007).

Third, causality *cannot* be accommodated via regression equations because a work team is best conceived of as an entity with *powers*. A regression equation deals only with observed events, and hence with the *manifestation of powers*. An unexercised power would not manifest itself in an observable event and would not, therefore, find its way into empirical data and hence into a regression equation. Perhaps it is time to elaborate a little on the notion of powers, not only to show how they cannot be mathematised, but also because this introduces notions of *the human* that cannot be treated in this way also.

Human powers

Powers are possessed by humans, and in this context, workers, in virtue of their biological, physiological, psychological and social make-up – although it is important to note that these levels are irreducible to one another so we cannot simply reduce social behaviour to biology. Unlike most animals, humans do not just execute genetically pre-programmed tasks; they conceive these tasks first – although there may be a complex and recursive process between conception and execution. The power of conception is of crucial importance here because it consists of the powers of *imagination, ingenuity* and *creativity* that conceived of the Pyramids, the Guggenheim, the cart, the MIR space station, surgical tools – and nuclear weapons. These same powers of *imagination, ingenuity* and *creativity* are, of course, also exercised in the conception of less grandiose endeavours such as finding better ways of producing a rivet, writing a programme or engaging in a telephone conversation. HRM practices such as team working, total quality management, quality circles, *kaisen*, along with schemes to increase employee participation and empower employees, are designed to unleash and harness the powers of imagination, ingenuity, and creativity that workers bring with them to the work place. If workers did not have these powers, of course, there would be no point whatsoever in even contemplating HRM. The fact (and it probably is) that these HRM practices have not succeeded in unlocking workers' powers does not mean they do not exist: something could be counteracting these powers.

Understood in this way, working is the key activity that differentiates *the human* from other animals and becomes the key activity that defines us as human beings, makes us what we are, expresses our human essence. Working, understood in this way, is not an activity that we necessarily have to be cajoled or coerced or bribed into doing: it is something that we just do because it is part of what we are. If this is true, then human beings not only possess powers for imaginative, ingenious and creative work, they also possess powers for self-motivated, self-directed work. If, for example, a work-team possesses powers for things like creative, imaginative, ingenious, self motivated action, then these powers can only be observed, recorded and transposed into variables, *if and when they are actually exercised*. Even countervailing causal phenomena may deflect or prevent the exercises of these powers. Although a non-manifesting power is real, it would not find its way into a functional relation or regression equation.

Armed with a reasonable grasp of meta-theory I am finally in a position to explain the lack of theory, and hence lack of explanation, that afflicts empirical research on the HRM–Performance link.

Explaining the lack of theory and explanation

Before trying to understand why theory is lacking, it is necessary to have some idea of what a theory is. Whetten offers a good general definition.

[A] complete theory must contain [the following] essential elements ... (i) *What*. Which factors (variables, constructs, concepts) logically should be considered as part of the explanation ... (ii) *How*. Having identified a set of factors, the researchers next question is, How are they related ... (iii) *Why*. What are the underlying psychological, economic or social dynamics that justify the selection of factors and the proposed causal relationships? To summarize thus far: What and How describe; only Why explains. What and How provide a framework for interpreting patterns ... in our empirical observations. This is an important distinction because data, whether quantitative or qualitative, characterize; theory supplies the explanation for the characteristics. (Whetten, 1989, pp. 490–491, numbers added)[8]

There appears to be a vague expectation that a theory is two-dimensional: it has a predictive and an explanatory dimension.

- *The predictive dimension of theory* consists of constructions that deliver predictions in terms of relations between events. When theory predicts, it does so by asking 'What' and 'How' questions. As Whetten (1989, p. 491) puts it: 'Combining Hows and Whats produces the typical model, from which testable propositions can be derived.'
- *The explanatory dimension of theory* consists of constructions that deliver understanding, a specific form of which is explanation. When theory explains, it does so by asking 'Why' questions and answering them by delving into the underlying dynamics.

Recall that explanation and causality can be connected and then note two things. First, the predictive dimension is characterised by (a) *Humean* causality and (b) *emaciated* explanation. Second, the explanatory dimension is characterised by (a_1) *complex* causality and (b_1) *robust* explanation. Unfortunately whilst research on the HRM–Performance link is overwhelmingly preoccupied with prediction, it can only sustain Humean causality and emaciated explanation. Moreover, the emaciation of the explanatory dimension is not accidental, but is a necessary corollary of the deductive method.

And here, at last, I can show how the meta-theoretical presuppositions interact, and conspire, to make it impossible (on pain of inconsistency) to sustain an explanatory dimension characterised by complex causality and robust explanation. If the social world is reduced to observed, atomistic events (ontology), causality is reduced to event regularities (Humean), knowledge (epistemology) is reduced to (trying to) identify regularity in the flux of events and methodology is reduced to engineering closed systems so that event regularities can be presented in the form of functional relations, and regression equations, then deductivism cannot sustain anything other than Humean causality and emaciated explanation.

Because of its meta-theoretical presupposition, current research on the HRM–Performance link does not venture beyond sets of statements that facilitate deduction or prediction and the construction of hypotheses in terms of regularities of observable, atomistic events. These are expressed (qualitatively) as variables which, in turn, are expressed as functional relations or derivatives such as regression equations, allowing the hypotheses to be tested using quantitative data and statistical techniques. For deductivism, then, a *theory is merely a vehicle for delivering predictions and hypotheses in terms of regularities between events.* It is hardly surprising that a theory (explicitly or implicitly) designed for the sole purpose of delivering predictions and hypotheses fails to provide something quite different, namely explanation. This is a serious, if largely ignored, weakness

Implausible conception of the human

I said in the introduction that the concept of *the human* presupposed by the meta-theory underpinning empirical research on the HRM–Performance link is implausible. This is, however, difficult to show because empirical studies simply seek associations between sets of variables, and appear not even to mention *the human* in any way, shape or form. However, appearances can be misleading: even regression equations have presuppositions about *the human* buried within them. Allow me to try and tease out these presuppositions by recalling Lauren's regression equation.

$$A_i = a_s \text{SECT}_i + d_s \text{SIZE}_i + u_s \underline{\text{LINK}}_i + h_s \text{HRMS}_i + e_{ij}$$

Ignoring the control variables (SECT, SIZE and LINK) the equation suggests that: the firms' ability to innovate (A_i) is caused by HRM practices associated with performance-related pay, delegation of decision rights, interdisciplinary working groups; quality circles; planned job rotation; and integration of functions like sales, production/services and finance (HRMS_i).

Now, like the child questioning the 'Emperor's clothes', let us ask: What is the point of trying to demonstrate the existence of an association between HRM practices and some measure of organisational performance? The point, surely, is to inform various parties (e.g. HR practitioners, consultants and other stakeholders such as trade unions) that if their organisation adopts the kinds of HRM practices that are good 'predictors' of increased organisational performance, then performance in their organisation will increase. In a section entitled *Implications for Practitioners*, for example, Boselie *et al.* (2005, p. 81) sincerely hope that HR professionals learn lessons from these empirical studies. In short, these empirical studies presuppose temporal and spatial generalisablity.

What, then, does temporal and spatial generalisablity imply about *the human* buried in these studies? They presuppose that whatever it is the humans in these studies did, they will continue doing when placed in different temporal and spatial contexts. Even assuming the contexts do not change (a heroic assumption) they presuppose that humans will not change: humans will always respond in the same, predictable way to the same stimuli. To the extent that performance-related pay, for example, is a good 'predictor' of increased productivity, then the introduction of performance-related pay systems to other workplaces should cause an increase in productivity there too. To grasp the point, consider what would happen if this is *not* presupposed, and humans changed and responded differently. In this case, the models would probably cease to be good 'predictors'. What would be the point of having a good 'predictor' of increased productivity, if it could not predict what would happen to productivity in other workplaces? Paradoxically, the better the model is at identifying 'predictors' of increased organisational performance, the stronger is the commitment to the presupposition of unchanging humans.

The same point can be made with a little more meta-theoretical rigor. I demonstrated above that regression equations presuppose closed systems. Closing the system requires assumptions about the components internal to the system, and assumptions about causal factors external to the system. Critical realists refer to these assumptions as *intrinsic* and *extrinsic closure conditions* respectively. For our purposes, however, the former are the most interesting. To maintain event regularity, and hence closure, the *internal state* of the individuals that constitute the system must be engineered so that the individual *always* responds in the same, predictable way. The internal closure condition is maintained by a plethora of assumptions, most of which are unstated. One of the main assumptions relates to alleged calculative rationality. In Lauren's regression equation, workers increase their performance whenever performance-related pay systems are introduced. The concept of *the human* presupposed here is that of an atomistic entity: a bloodless non-human, empty of all internal social-psychological structure, except for the internal programme we endow it with to ensure that it *always* responds in the same, predictable way. This concept of *the human* is, arguably, implausible.[9]

Conclusion

The vast majority of empirical researchers are probably unaware that empirical research on the HRM–Performance link lacks theory – or if they are, they have not gone into print on the matter. Gould-Williams, for example, suggests he will discuss his results 'in light of HRM theory' (2004, p. 1) without feeling the need to explain what this theory is. Whilst a few empirical researchers (Wright and McMahan, 1992; Becker and Gerhart, 1996; Guest, 1997, 2001; Boudreau and Ramstad, 1999) are aware that empirical research on the HRM–Performance link lacks theory, to the best of my knowledge no-one has gone on to recognise the lack of explanatory power.[10]

There is however, a possible way out of this dilemma. Empirical researchers could point to theories lying outside their particular orbit, perhaps even to theories lying outside the field of HRM, and argue that the sought-after theory, explanation, and a plausible concept of *the human* in the workplace, might well reside therein. I would like to conclude by considering this possibility, because, rather than offering a real way out, it reveals just how deep the problems run.

Scattered throughout the literature is a bewildering array of approaches, perspectives, theories, models, maps, all at various levels of abstraction, generality, universality, particularity and concreteness (see Jackson and Schuler, 1995; Guest, 1997, 2001; McMahan *et al.*, 1999; and Ferris *et al.*, 2004 for overviews of at least some of these approaches). In what is probably a massive understatement, Jackson and Schuler (1995, p. 256) observe that: 'Although imperfect, potentially useful theories are relatively plentiful.' In no particular order, those theories that I am aware of are as follows: the normative model; the descriptive-functional model; the descriptive-behavioural model; the critical-evaluative model; the Michigan, Harvard, Guest's and Warwick models; HRM as a map; the universalistic, internal fit, best practice or one size fits all approach; the bundling or internal fit approach; the contingency or external fit approach; the configurational approach; individual – organisational performance linkages; General Systems Theory; the personnel systems & staff alignment perspective; the partnership or stakeholder perspective; the New Economics of Personnel; the strategic contingency approach; strategic, descriptive and normative theories of HRM; expectancy theory; action theory; the strategic contingency approach; strategic reference points theory; systematic agreement theory; AMO (ability, motivation and opportunity) theory; control theory; balanced scorecard approach; the job characteristics model; social exchange theory; labour process theory; the behavioural perspective; the role behaviour perspective; population ecology; cybernetic models; agency theory; transaction cost economics; resource-based theory/view; power/resource dependence theory; Institutional theory; critical theory; Marxist theory; and last, but probably not least, Foucauldian theory.

If buried underneath this bewildering array of approaches, perspectives, theories, models maps or whatever is something that might amount to a theory, or theories, of *the human* in the workplace, then a lot more *theoretical* work will be needed to identity it or them. If correct, this observation raises two problems.

First, with a few notable exceptions, theoretical work in this field is simply not being undertaken because the research is totally dominated by the deductivist method. Hoobler and Brown Johnston's extensive survey of the general HRM literature found that: 'statistical regression was by far the method of choice' (2005, p. 668). Boselie *et al.*'s (2005, p. 70) survey of the HRM–Performance literature observed that: Despite calls 'for more use of qualitative methods to examine this relationship, we found only a few wholly qualitative studies'. Without reflecting upon the nature of theory, and without taking explicit steps to develop it, we will not even begin the task of improving our understanding of *the human* in research on the HRM–Performance link.

Second, and perhaps even more worrying, some researchers suggest lack of theory will be corrected via meta-theory. That is, theory will develop if researchers continue doing more, and/or better, empirical work (Becker and Gerhart, 1996, p. 777; Guest, 1997, p. 267). Whilst Guest is aware of some of the problems, he does nothing to encourage researchers to explore other meta-theoretical perspectives; indeed, he counsels more of the same:

> After considering this catalogue of problems and challenges, some might be tempted to abandon this line of research. This would be unfortunate since exploration of the HRM–Performance link provides one of the major current research challenges in the field of HRM. It would also be unfortunate because, despite all the methodological shortcomings and possible sources of error, the research is making progress. (Guest, 2001, p. 1004)

More of the same, of course, means more of the deductive method. And as I have shown above, this will do nothing to improve our understanding of *the human* in research on the HRM–Performance link. It is time to re-think our theoretical and meta-theoretical presuppositions.

Notes

1. Rather than provide a long list of oft-cited papers, the interested reader should consult two recent surveys Wall and Wood (2005, p. 454) and Boselie *et al.* (2005, pp. 81–2).

2. On critical realism with a organisation and management studies flavour see: Ackroyd and Fleetwood (2000); Fleetwood and Ackroyd (2004); Fleetwood (2005); Fairclough (2005); Johnson and Duberley (2000); Lewis (2000); Reed (2005); Sayer (2000), and Fleetwood and Hesketh (2007) which specifically addresses meta-theory in HRM.

3. A deterministically closed system can be expressed probabilistically and can, thereby, be transposed to a stochastically closed system. It is important to note, however, that closed systems do not cease to be closed systems simply because we specify them stochastically. Under stochastic closure y and $x_1, x_2, \ldots x_n$ are still constantly conjoined, albeit under some well behaved probabilistic function. In effct, the claim 'whenever event x then event y' is transposed into the claim 'whenever events $x_1, x_2, \ldots x_n$ on average, then event y on average', or 'whenever the average value of events measured by variables $x_1, x_2 \ldots x_n$ are what they are, then the average value of event y measured by variable y is what it is'.

4. According to Hume: 'When I cast my eye on the *known qualities* of objects, I immediately discover that the relation of cause and effect depends not in the least on *them*. When I consider their *relations*, I can find none but those of contiguity and succession' (1888 and 1978, p. 77). And 'We have no other notion of cause and effect, but that of certain objects, which have been *always conjoin'd* together . . . We cannot penetrate into the reason for the conjunction (1888 and 1978, p. 93).

5. It is important to tackle the red herring here. It is true that the list of what *could, in principle*, be included in a robust explanation, could easily expand until it included, literally, everything, and go all the way back to the big bang. In practice, however, social scientists usually avoid a potential infinite regress by making use of *abstraction* (c.f. Sayer, 1998). That is, they make judgements about which factors need to be included and which can safely be excluded. This is of course fallible, and sometimes investigators get it wrong – but it is, in principle, no different than deciding upon which variables to include and which to exclude (c.f. Runde, 1998).

6. There are a few researchers who claim to do something similar, but their talk of 'examining the mechanisms' quickly evaporates into *measuring* the mechanisms (Meyer and Smith, 2000, p. 319). The same goes for Becker and Huselid (1999, p. 288) as their talk of providing us with 'rich detail in how leading firms use their HRM system' and 'an outline of theoretical rationale and empirical literature linking HRM systems with corporate financial performance' turns out to be yet more measurement.

7. Den Hartog and Verburg's (2004) attempt to deal with the hermeneutic issue of awareness of organisational culture soon collapses into attempts to *measure* culture.

8. See also Bacharach (1989, p. 498); Noon (1992, p. 18); Storey (1992, p. 40); Kane (1991, p. 247); Sutton and Straw (1995, p. 376); and Wright and MacMahan (1992).

9. This human is, of course, *homo economicus*. Most economists (and other social scientists who use this concept) do not assume this is a plausible conception of real human beings: they know real human beings do not act in this very rigid, calculatively rational way. Rather, they use this implausible concept of the human simply because it is expedient, it makes the formal logic work – I would say, it assists closing the system. In any case, it will be considered implausible by most contributors to this collection.

10. Many are prepared to recognise what might be called 'technical' problems with sample and response rates, adequacy of research design; reliability and validity of HRM measures, metrics, measurement, data and so on (Becker and Gerhart, 1996; Gerhart, 1999; Wright and Sherman, 1999; Gerhart *et al.*, 2000 and Wall and Wood, 2005). The problems I raise in this chapter, however, extend far beyond these 'technical' problems

References

Ackroyd, S. and Fleetwood, S. (2000) *Realist Perspectives on Organisation and Management*, London: Routledge.

Arthur, J. (1994) 'Effects of Human Resources on Manufacturing Performance and Turnover', *Academy of Management Journal*, Vol. 37, No. 3, 670–687.

Bacharach, S. (1989) 'Organisational Theories: Some Criteria for Evaluation', *Academy of Management Review*, Vol. 14, No. 4, 495–515.

Becker, B. and Gerhart, B. (1996) 'The Impact of Human Resource Management on Organisational Performance: Progress and Prospects', *Academy of Management Journal*, Vol. 30, No. 4, 779–801.

Becker, B. and Huselid, M. (1999) 'Overview: Strategic HRM in Five Leading Firms', *Human Resource Management*, Vol. 38, No. 4, 287–301.

Becker, B., Huselid, M. and Ulrich, D. (2001) *The HR Scorecard: Linking People, Strategy and Performance*, Harvard: Harvard Business School Press.

Boselie, P., Dietz, G. and Boon, C. (2005) 'Commonalities and Contradictions in HRM and Performance Research', *Human Resource Management Journal*, Vol. 15, No. 3, 67–94.

Boudreau, J. and Ramstad, P. (1999) 'Human Resource Metrics: Can Measures be Strategic', *Research in Personnel and Human Resources Management*, Supplement 4, 75–98.

Den Hartog, D. and Verburg, R. (2004) 'High Performance Work Systems, Organisational Performance and Firm Effectiveness', *Human Resource Management Journal*, Vol. 14, No. 1, 55–79.

Fairclough, N. (2005) 'Discourse Analysis in Organisation Studies: The Case for Critical Realism', *Organisation Studies*, Vol. 26, No. 6.

Ferris, G., Hall, A., Royle, M. and Martocchio, J. (2004) *Organizational Analysis*, Vol. 12, No. 3, 231–254.

Fleetwood, S. (2001) 'Causal Laws, Functional Relations and Tendencies', *Review of Political Economy*, Vol. 13, No. 2, 201–220.

Fleetwood, S. (2005) 'The Ontology of Organisation and Management Studies: A Critical Realist Approach', *Organisation*, Vol. 12, No. 2.

Fleetwood, S. (2006) 'Re-thinking Labour Markets: A Critical Realist – Socioeconomic Perspective', *Capital & Class* No. 89, 59–89.

Fleetwood, S. and Ackroyd, S. (2004) *Critical Realist Applications in Organisation and Management Studies*, London: Routledge.

Fleetwood, S. and Hesketh, A. (2006) 'High Performance Work Systems, Organisational Performance and (Lack of) Predictive Power', *Journal of Critical Realism*, Vol. 5, No. 2.

Fleetwood, S. and Hesketh, A. (2007) *The Performance of HR: Towards a New Meta Theory*, Cambridge: Cambridge University Press.

Gerhart, B. (1999) 'Human Resource Management and Firm Performance: Measurement Issues and their Effect on Causal and Policy Inferences', *Research in Personnel and Human Resources Management*, Supplement 4, 31–51.

Gerhart, B., Wright, P., McMahan, G. and Snell, S. (2000) 'Measurement Error in Research on Human Resources and Firm Performance: How Much Error is There and How Does it Influence Size Estimates', *Personnel Psychology*, Vol. 53, 803–834.

Gould-Williams, J. (2004) 'The Effects of "High Commitment" HRM Practices on Employee Attitude: The Views of Public Sector Workers', *Public Administration*, Vol. 82, No. 1, 63–81.

Guest, D. (1997) 'Human Resource Management and Performance: A Review and Research Agenda, Process', *International Journal of Human Resources Management*, Vol. 8, No. 3, 263–276.

Guest, D. (2001) 'Human Resource Management: When Research Confronts Theory', *International Journal of Human Resources Management*, Vol. 12, No. 7, 1092–1106.

Hiltrop, J.-M. (1996) 'The Impact of Human Resource Management on Organisational Performance: Theory and Research', *European Journal of Human Resource Management*, Vol. 14, No. 6, 628–637.

Hoobler, J. and Brown Johnston, N. (2005) 'An Analysis of Current HRM Publications', *Personnel Review*, Vol. 33, No. 6, 665–676.

Hume D. (1888 and 1978) *A Treatise of Human Nature*, Oxford: Clarendon Press.

Huselid, B. (1995) 'The Impact of Human Resource Management Practices on Turnover, Productivity, and Corporate Financial Performance', *Academy of Management Journal*, Vol. 38, No. 3, 635–672.

Jackson, S. and Schuler, R. (1995) 'Understanding Human Resource Management in the Context of Organizations and their Environments', *Annual Review of Psychology*, Vol. 46, 237–264.

Johnson, P. and Duberley, J. (2000) *Understanding Management Research*, London: Sage.

Kane, J. (1991) 'Towards a Modernized Model of Science', *Human Resource Management Review*, Vol. 1, No. 4, 245–251.

Laursen, K. (2002) 'The Importance of Sectoral Differences in the Application of Complementary HRM Practices for Innovation Performance', *International Journal of the Economics of Business*, Vol. 9, No. 1, 139–156.

Lawson, T. (1997) *Economics and Reality*, London: Routledge.

Lawson, T. (2004) *Reorienting Economics*, London: Routledge.

Lewis, P. (2000) 'Realism, Causality and the Problem of Social Structure', *Journal for the Theory of Social Behaviour*, Vol. 30, No. 3, 249–268.

MacDuffie, J. (1995) 'Human Resource Bundles and Manufacturing Performance: Organizational Logic and Flexible Production Systems in the World Auto Industry', *Industrial and Labor Relations Review*, Vol. 48, No. 2, 197–221.

McMahan, G., Virick, M. and Wright, P.M. (1999) 'Alternative Theoretical Perspectives for Strategic Human Resource Management Revisited: Progress, Problems, and prospects', *Research in Personnel and Human Resources Management*, Supplement 4, 99–122.

Meyer, J. and Smith, A. (2000) 'HRM Practices and Organisational Commitment: Test of a Mediation Model', *Canadian Journal of Administrative Sciences*, Vol. 17, No. 4, 319–331.

Noon, M. (1992) 'HRM: A Map, Model or Theory?' in Blyton, P. and Turnbull, P. (eds), *Reassessing Human Resource Management*, London: Sage.

Reed, M. (2005) 'Reflections on the Realist Turn in Organisation and Management Studies', *British Journal of Management Studies*, Vol. 42, No. 8.

Runde J. (1998) 'Assessing Causal Economic Explanations', *Oxford Economic Papers*, No. 50, 151–172.

Sayer, A. (1998) 'Abstraction: A Realist Interpretation' in Archer, M., Bhaskar, R., Collier, A., Lawson, T. and Norrie, A. (eds), *Critical Realism: Essential Readings*, London: Routledge.

Sayer, A. (2000) *Realism and Social Science*, London: Sage.

Storey, J. (1992) *Developments in the Management of Human Resources*, Oxford: Blackwell.

Sutton, R. and Straw, B. (1995) 'What Theory is Not', *Administrative Science Quarterly*, Vol. 40, No. 3, 371–385.

Wall, T. and Wood, S. (2005) 'The Romance of Human Resource Management and Business Performance, and the Case for Big Science', *Human Relations*, Vol. 58, No. 4, 429–462.

Whetten, D. (1989) 'What Constitutes a Theoretical Contribution?', *Academy of Management Review*, Vol. 14, No. 4, 490–495.

Wright, P. and McMahan, G. (1992) 'Theoretical Perspectives for Human Resource Management', *Journal of Management*, Vol. 18, No. 2, 295–320.

Wright, P. and Sherman, S. (1999) 'Failing to Find Fit in Strategic Human Resource Management: Theoretical & Empirical Problems', *Research in Personnel and Human Resources Management*, Supplement 4, 53–74.

4

The human side of skills and knowledge

Irena Grugulis

The goal of decent work is best expressed through the eyes of people. It is about your job and future prospects; about your working conditions; about balancing work and family life, putting your kids through school or getting them out of child labour. It is about gender equality, equal recognition, and enabling women to make choices and take control of their lives. It is about personal abilities to compete in the market place, keep up with new technological skills and remain healthy. It is about developing your entrepreneurial skills, about receiving a fair share of wealth that you have helped to create and not being discriminated against; it is about having a voice in your workplace and your community. . . . For everybody, decent work is about securing human dignity.

(ILO, 2001, pp. 7–8 cited in Green, 2006, pp. 19–20)

Attempting to capture the human side of work is a fascinating, if fraught process. Workers' relationships with their employers, their colleagues and their customers, the way that work is designed as well as how (and how generously) it is rewarded all play a part in (among others) whether workers are treated with dignity and respect, whether their wages and working conditions are decent and whether they have a voice in workplace issues. Skills and knowledge are central to these issues. They can provide individual workers access to interesting and more highly rewarded work as well as equipping collective groups with bargaining power, status and a basis on which they may influence workplace decisions. But it is not clear whether these elements, desirable as they may be, are what makes work human nor whether it is their absence that dehumanises.

61

This chapter explores skills, the growing emphasis on soft skills and emotions in work, and knowledge work from the perspective of what each contributes to, or detracts from, the humanity of workers. It is not a straightforward debate. Work is a social process and workers may take pleasure in forming friendships in unpromising environments or find themselves alienated by work that is high status, well rewarded, intrinsically interesting yet all consuming. But it is an important one and one that is generally neglected by most commentators on employment (though see Green (2006) for an exception to this).

Given this focus on humanity, a key issue underlying some of these discussions is the extent to which things are getting better. After all, in many developed countries people are living longer and their general health and standard of living is far better than that previous generations might have expected. It does not seem unreasonable to assume that work too should mirror these advantages. And to a certain extent it has. Work is less dangerous, less immediately threatening to health and well being (a result, perhaps, of the shift from manufacturing dominated economies to ones where most jobs are located in the service sector), while both wages and working conditions have improved in most countries (Green, 2006).

All of which are to be welcomed. However, acknowledging these changes for the better does not necessarily mean that we enjoy the best of all possible workplaces in the best of all possible worlds. Work is, after all, a negotiated order with negotiations that are permanently ongoing (Edwards and Wajcman, 2005). Employers' interests only partially coincide with those of their employees and power relations are unequal. This means that changes in the type of work undertaken or the location in which it is conducted or the product or service being produced may well alter many work processes but they do not necessarily do anything to change workplace relations. This tension between employer and employee, an ingrained peculiarity of the nature of work, is central to the way that organisations function. It is also a key mediating factor in the way that the general trends noted above are introduced into workplaces and experienced by individual workers and when we seek humanity, it is that experience that is key.

This chapter considers the nature of skilled and deskilled labour, the impact on work of 'new' soft skills and personal qualities, working with and through emotions, and knowledge work. These are all topics that are central to any discussion of employment but are rarely reviewed from the perspective of the human. Doing so gives rise to some interesting tensions and raises questions about the standard assumption that discretion is inevitably a 'good thing'. It also considers the issue of power, particularly the way that different interpretations of skill or ways of working may confer advantage on either the employee or the employer. This does not mean that power is necessarily synonymous with humanity but rather, in a relationship that is already asymmetrical, it is unlikely that *powerlessness* is compatible with human working conditions (at least in the long term). Throughout the chapter the social nature of work is acknowledged, both with respect to the way it complicates discussions on skills and as a very significant factor in the way that work is humanised or dehumanised. These discussions are not easy ones and not conducive to simple or universal answers but hopefully starting to set them out may help to focus attention on the human side of work and encourage judgements that go beyond economic rationale.

Skills and deskilling

Traditionally, skill has required some form of thoughtful or competent input from workers, it has incorporated knowledge and expertise, discretion over aspects of the way work is done or job design as well as some form of decision-making power (see, for example, Littler, 1982; Cockburn, 1983). Essentially, skilled work involves the worker in some way. Because workers can exercise discretion over how tasks should be arranged, or what exactly constitutes a job well done, work is more likely to be meaningful. And, since their input is necessary for satisfactory completion, workers gain negotiating power, status and money. In Ainley's (1993) words this is the 'workmanship of risk' as opposed to the 'workmanship of certainty'.

Such discretion, decision-making power and (occasionally) autonomy contrast markedly with the alienating and dehumanising effects of *deskilling*, when all task and job based decisions are taken away from the worker. Frederick Taylor's (1949) mythical labourer Schmitt, for example, was told how to hold his shovel, raise it once loaded and transfer its contents elsewhere; while Charlie Chaplin's unfortunate character in *Modern Times* was trapped working on a conveyor belt, tightening bolts as they travelled past him at speeds he could not control. Nor are such examples historical relics: the work undertaken by staff at McDonald's is regulated by buzzers and lights, buns arrived pre-sliced and burgers pre-prepared, while dispensers take away any need to exercise judgement over even such minutiae as the amount of ketchup which should go into each burger (Leidner, 1993; Ritzer, 1996; Royle, 2000). Elsewhere modern factories use sophisticated time management systems to time activities down to a tenth of a second (Garrahan and Stewart, 1992; Delbridge, 1998). These are workplaces where errors can often be traced back to the individual worker who made them but where that worker has little opportunity to adjust the pace of their work, amend the quality of products or redesign the job itself. In the words of one member of a typing pool, 'Janey gives us the work and I sit down and type all day' (Webster, 1990, p. 51).

In deskilled work, people are simply a routine part of the production process, cogs in the machinery who perform their instructions by rote. There is nothing individual or distinctive they can add to the process to make it better or to make it peculiarly their own. Indeed, one of the central ideas behind deskilled work is that labour and labourers are interchangeable; homogeneous products mass produced by homogeneous workers. This can provide firms with competitive advantage: a customer who buys a McDonald's burger in Madrid can feel reasonably confident that it will be the same as those on sale in Montreal, Milan or Milton Keynes. It also has implications for productivity. Adam Smith's (1776/1993) description of pin manufacturing estimates the capacity of individual craft workers at less than twenty pins a day. Ten workers, each endlessly repeating one part of the manufacturing process could produce between them some 48,000 pins a day. Work is completed more quickly and satisfactory outcomes are no longer dependent on workers making the right decisions. Workers are not expected to know about the product they are producing, or to make decisions on how they might best work or to judge the quality of their own labour. Their role is simply to follow orders.

Designing work in this way effectively dehumanises it. As Marx (1964) noted, being employed on tasks over which they have no control alienates workers from what they produce, the process of production, themselves and their fellow workers. Personality cannot be expressed through work and work is transformed into a process where workers' humanity is denied. Adam Smith (1776/1993) having put forward his model for productivity went on to comment on the devastating effect it would have on those engaged on such numbing and repetitive tasks. Interestingly, his solution was to offer them further education, not as a means of escape from routinised labour but to re-humanise them after alienating shifts at work.

So far, it seems, so simple. Craft work, which engages workers' expertise, where they may exercise their judgement and in which they may take a pride in a job well done is set against routinised and repetitive actions which require employees only to follow instructions and where they have no control over even the pace and intensity of work. And yet in focussing only on these aspects of work and, crucially, in neglecting research accounts which explore workers' perspectives, we risk missing other human and humanising aspects of employment. Work is, after all, a social process and the quality of a job cannot be judged simply and solely by the skills required of workers. Employees may also value pay, status, friendships, security or responsibilities. Admittedly, many of these elements move in tandem with skills (or skills may move in tandem with them). These variables are not independent ones. Certainly perceptions of skill are linked to status, both by external observers and workers themselves, so that those with high status will be deemed to be highly skilled and those with low status low skilled (Burchell *et al.*, 1994; Gallie, 1994). Moreover securing status and control over work can enable workers to increase skills (Turner, 1962) and, through these, pay.

Nonetheless, even the most apparently degraded and simplified tasks may require worker familiarity, dexterity or competence, often at speed. Delbridge's (1998) account of electrical assembly reveals how important it was for workers to work quickly; Rainbird *et al.*'s (2004) research into work in a cook-freeze centre reveals how women became 'experts at putting 80 grammes [*sic*] of meat into the containers'; while Sennett's (1998) description of working at McDonald's shows how, when equipment broke down, employees would prove unexpectedly adept at running repairs.

Then too, routines and routinisation are not universally condemned. Leidner's (1993) study of trainee insurance people whose sales patter, from descriptions of the product to pauses and jokes, was scripted by their employers, reveals how much they appreciated the reassurance of knowing they had robust information to work with which had proved to be successful. These scripts may have taken away their opportunity to shape the majority of the sales task but they also provided security. Finally the social elements of work, friendships and collegiality can occur in even the most unpropitious of settings including noisy factories (Burawoy, 1979; Pollert, 1981; Delbridge, 1998); slaughterhouses (Ackroyd and Crowdy, 1990) and call centres (Wray-Bliss, 2001; Korczynski, 2002).

It seems that worker input is still required even from 'unskilled' workers, that deskilling and routinisation may help as well as alienate, and that for those who value friendships rather than work, degraded work environments are no bar to satisfaction. This should be no surprise. After all, workplaces are not laboratories where potential sources of satisfaction or dissatisfaction can be reduced to a small number of variables. In complex social systems real humans may take pleasure from a range of factors. However, it is also dangerous to conclude on the basis of these studies that skill or discretion or autonomy do not matter. After all, simply because some workers have discovered pleasurable, human elements in certain types of workplaces does not mean that those workplaces are pleasurable places. The fact that friendships are formed should not excuse poor treatment, low pay or degrading work conditions (though for the individual worker it can make these far more bearable). And the security that trainees feel in routine might be contrasted with the frustration it engenders in workers who are already skilled (Felstead *et al.*, 2006). It is still useful to consider skill when assessing the human side of work. From the perspective of work design alone (and clearly work should not be judged solely against this criterion) deskilled work is, by definition, not intrinsically satisfying and would play no part in a humanised workplace.

The changing nature of skill

This, then, is what might be described as the traditional idea of skill: knowledge, expertise, experience, job design or social status that confers some sort of power in the labour market and that may make work more human. But as Payne (1999, 2000) notes, both work itself and employers' definitions of skill are changing and these changes have consequences for employees. Some 30 to 50 years ago, 'being skilled' involved technical capabilities or distinctive occupational knowledge, today the emphasis is on soft skills and personal qualities, although *which* soft skills and what exactly they involve actually varies widely. According to Hillage *et al.* (2002, pp. 33–36) the skills currently most sought by employers are communication, customer handling and teamworking. Keep (2001) drawing on a range of studies, found many suggestions including positive attitudes towards change, self-confidence, self-promotion, exploring and creating opportunities and political focus. Research in the 'style labour markets' of the hospitality industry reveals a demand for a persona that is 'passionate, stylish, confident, tasty, clever, successful and well-travelled' (Nickson *et al.*, 2001; Warhurst and Nickson, 2001, p. 14). Government documents recommend the development of positive attitudes to life and work, getting on with work mates, working as a team and getting information and advice (Payne, 1999). While in the USA employers seek work attitude, punctuality, loyalty (Lafer, 2004); friendliness, teamwork, ability to fit in (Moss and Tilly, 1996); and dedication to work and discipline in work habits (Cappelli, 1995). The lists are lengthy and bring together a confused morass of personal traits, attitudes, qualities and pre-dispositions (Brown and Hesketh, 2004).

Given that this book focuses on the human side of work, such a shift in emphasis might well be considered positive, as an indication that work is breaking down the old bureaucratic straitjacket to become a legitimate site for human feelings and emotions. As Bolton (2005a) notes, organisations are starting to prescribe emotions rather than proscribe them. It is certainly true that emotions can bring a great deal of pleasure to workers. According to Wharton (1996) workers who work with their emotions are more likely to be satisfied in the workplace than those who do not. Pierce (1995, 1996) emphasises how hard pressed paralegals coped by personalising the relationships they had with the lawyers they worked for. Even in the most regulated and alienating of jobs, nice customers, positive emotional exchanges and being able to actually help another person can boost employees' spirits enormously (Korczynski, 2001, 2002). Leidner's (1993) account of McDonald's employees shows how much pleasure they gained from interactions with customers. As 'Steve' and 'Theo' comment (p. 136):

> It's just fun, the people are fun! . . . They make my day, they really do. I mean, sometimes, I can come to work – like yesterday, I wasn't really happy. I was somewhat in the middle. This guy came in, he was talking real low, and his friend said, 'Why don't you talk up?' . . . I told him to turn his volume up [I laugh], and he said something . . . and I just started smiling. Ever since then, I've been happy. . . . The guests out here, . . . they're friendly and fun. I just love to meet them, you know? I mean, it's nice working for them, it's nice serving them. Some, you know – well, I'd say one out of ten guests will probably try to give you a bad time. But the rest of them, they'll just make my day.

> Well, I enjoy working with the public, 'cause they're fun to be with. Some of them are a trip. So I enjoy it, find it very amusing.

This is the positive side of emotion work. Interacting with pleasant people, helping customers and receiving thanks and appreciation in return and it is small wonder that workers enjoy this side of the process.

But this is not an untrammelled emotional arena in which employees are free to display the feelings that spontaneously occur and the emotions they are required to express are not necessarily those that are most enjoyable, psychologically valuable or therapeutic. Rather, they are the ones their employers consider most useful in the workplace, whether the requirement is for warmth, anger, calm or empathy (Hochschild, 1983; Putnam and Mumby, 1993; Mann, 1999; Callaghan and Thompson, 2002; Bolton, 2005a). Conformity to emotion rules is not novel, nor is it restricted to employment. As Goffman (1959) notes, many social responses are enacted with others in mind (as opposed to pure and 'authentic' emotional reactions). So people will look mournful at funerals and happy at weddings, quarrelling couples will postpone their argument rather than fight in front of strangers and young people on dates will attempt to create a good impression. However locating these emotions in the workplace imposes an additional dimension on them since the act entered into is one that the employer, rather than the employee has chosen.

This is a key point and should materially affect our assessment of workplace emotions. It is management who decide on the feelings employees should display and the ones they should attempt to generate in their customers. In the words of Colin Marshall, an ex-chairman of British Airways:

> We . . . have to 'design' our people and their service attitude just as we design an aircraft seat, an in-flight entertainment programme or an airport lounge *to meet the needs and preferences of our customers.* (cited in Barsoux and Manzon, 1997, p. 14, emphasis added)

The issue then, is not that of re-emotionalising the workplace but of introducing (occasionally compulsorily) feelings that the employer requires demonstrating in specific and specified ways. Work is not designed to fit workers, rather workers are redesigned to conform to the needs of work (Putnam and Mumby, 1993).

What this implies, just as work itself involves the sacrifice of time, or independent action, or activity, or freedom of movement is that (if only during working hours) employees relinquish control of their emotions. But noting that workers' emotional freedom is limited does not necessarily mean employers are able to exert total, hegemonic control over what employees feel (Bolton, 2000, 2005a). After all, workers do not leave their humanity or their capacity to feel emotions unprompted by managers at the factory gates. Colleagues and customers may inspire genuine emotional responses. The call centre workers described by Callaghan and Thompson (2002) gave freely of their time to late night callers because they felt empathy for them, not because they were told to do so by management (see also Bolton and Boyd, 2003). Then too, Bolton's studies of nurses reveal professional and protective feelings to patients and anger or irritation at the increasing bureaucratisation of the health service rather than emotional dupes mindlessly following 'feeling rules' (Bolton, 2005a,b).

Moreover, there are great variations in the way that different firms put their emotional demands into practice from the degrading suggestion to Harvard university clerical staff to 'think of yourself as a trash can. Take everyone's little bits of anger all day, put it inside you, and at the end of the day, just pour it into the dumpster on your way out the door' (Eaton, 1996, p. 296) to the professional socialisation required of lawyers (Mann, 1999). Hochschild (1983) usefully calls on Marx to distinguish between work, over which employees have some control, and labour which is almost entirely regulated. So to a certain extent the potential problems and pitfalls here repeat the issues of control considered with technical skills.

But these soft skills and emotional demands also raise issues that technical skills did not. Soft skills are not certified and, unlike technical skills which were often judged by occupational and professional peers (or their professional bodies), many soft skills exist largely in the eye of the beholder and are valuable only when authorised and legitimated by employers (Brown and Hesketh, 2004). Since different employers may have very divergent ideas over which particular traits are desirable and how they should be demonstrated (Rees and Garnsey, 2003) and even a shared vocabulary of soft skills may not translate into common meanings (Hirsch and Bevan, 1988); soft skills may not be particularly portable.

Ironically, while judgement about the possession or otherwise of desirable qualities is assumed by the employers, responsibility for demonstrating them is devolved to the individual workers. They are accountable for making sure that they are sufficiently loyal, punctual, teamworkers, effective communicators, self-confident, friendly or whatever else it is that employers claim to want. Ehrenreich's (2006) study of unemployed middle and senior managers in the USA reveals just how hard many of them tried, generally without success, to demonstrate whatever personal traits and dispositions were required. Yet as Lafer (2004) points out, many of these are not individual qualities and listing them as such neglects their reciprocal and relational aspects. Teamworking, communication and friendliness are not activities carried out in isolation. More fundamentally, a great deal of workplace behaviour, from strikes, absenteeism and turnover to active co-operation and commitment, reflect heavily on workers' relationships with their employers. Lafer (2004) draws on research by Moss and Tilly (1996) in two warehouses in the same district of Los Angeles both of which employed present and past gang members. While managers in one complained of high turnover, laziness and dishonesty, in the second, which paid several dollars per hour more, managers had few complaints and turnover was a modest two per cent. These are issues that, in the past, would have been considered industrial relations or personnel problems and for which management would have considered themselves at least partially responsible. Today they are labelled as skills and responsibility is located firmly on the individual worker (Keep, 2001).

This means that training which focuses on soft skills may be a problem rather than a solution. It can detract attention from dull and alienating tasks, in the words of a call centre supervisor interviewed by Kinnie *et al.* (2000) it could provide 'fun and surveillance'. But, it may not actually be able to change an employee's soft skills and, when all training focuses on behavioural qualities, may deprive them of opportunities to learn technical skills which might provide more career advantages. Soft skills based programmes in

Canada and the USA designed to get people into work generally mean that even the successful attendees gain jobs which pay only just over the minimum wage and which participants are likely to leave quite quickly (Butterwick, 2003; Lafer, 2004).

An emphasis on soft skills may also result in gendered and racialised stereotypes being used to make judgements. So, women are hired for call centre jobs because they are women rather than as a result of anything they did in their interviews (Taylor and Tyler, 2000) or confined to customer care, front-line roles and denied access to higher paying, high status career track work (Skuratowicz and Hunter, 2004; Hebson and Grugulis, 2005) while black men are rated as less loyal and ambitious than their white colleagues (Maume, 1999). This is not to argue that discrimination in the labour market is in some way a new phenomenon. On the contrary it is firmly established (Moss-Kanter, 1977) and power and status in the labour market has long been equated with skill (Gallie, 1994). Rather, it is to express concern that these 'new' skills are themselves so vulnerable to discriminatory judgements.

Soft skills, it seems, carry with them few of the material advantages that technical skills confer on workers, at least at the disadvantaged end of the labour market. Despite repeated claims by employers that these skills are in short supply, pay rates for the sort of jobs in which they dominate are seldom high (Bolton, 2004), perhaps because such work is predominantly undertaken by women, perhaps because even when social interactions are reasonably complex they are such a common feature of human interaction that these skills are considered 'natural' or at least widespread (Payne, 2006). Even the emotional pleasure workers get from engaging in emotion work can be questioned. After noting workers' exceptionally high levels of satisfaction with work Korczynski (2001, p. 92) goes on to observe that the turnover figures in the call centres he studied were high and to note wryly that '[w]orkers, it seems, were so satisfied with the job that they were leaving in considerable numbers'. Workers who already possess high levels of technical skill or educational qualifications have a different experience of soft skills. The traits demanded are likely to advantage them as much as their employers (or can be used against their employers), demand for technical skills is rarely diminished and soft skills may provide access to more interesting work (see, for example, Brown and Hesketh, 2004; Grugulis and Vincent, 2004).

It seems that even given the enduring aspects of emotional freedom at work it would be disingenuous to assess employer demands for emotions in the workplace against the same scales and criteria as 'personal' feelings. Going further, classifying personal traits and qualities as soft skills creates a whole range of problems. It is not that employers have not before demanded a particular personality or character from those they hire, these are long established practices (see, for example, Beynon, 1975; Grugulis *et al.*, 2004). Rather, labelling these personal qualities 'skills' inappropriately individualises responsibility for them, reshapes work based training in ways that may confine those at the bottom of the labour market to a narrow range of jobs on the same horizontal job grade (Grimshaw *et al.*, 2002) and may institutionalise discrimination.

Knowledge work and knowledge workers

If emotion work and soft skills contain few grounds for optimism, it may be that knowledge work provides more promising prospects. After all, if, as suggested above, skills and knowledge make work itself more intrinsically interesting and also mean that employers are likely to treat employees better, then increases in the skills and knowledge that workers can exercise at work may well be a positive development. And there are numerous commentaries and predictions suggesting that in the future nations will aim to be 'knowledge societies' gaining competitive advantage through the innovation, creativity and input of their specialised 'knowledge workers'. It is a model of the market which sets the individual worker centre stage and one which has been taken up with enthusiasm by policymakers (see, for example, Department for Education and Skills/DTI/H M Treasury/Department for Work and Pensions, 2003).

Since these workers are (both individually and collectively) important to their firm's performance and since the knowledge that they possess is often tacit (Nonaka and Takeuchi, 1995), knowledge work is peculiar to the individual, not readily codifiable and knowledge itself is often extended when it is shared. As a result, research into enclaves of knowledge workers shows that managerial effort is put into making work a pleasant place to be and eliciting commitment from the workers. Social support systems, good environments and excellent working conditions take the place of tight supervision and rigid control routines (Alvesson and Karreman, 2001; Alvesson and Sveningsson, 2003) to the extent that Hackley (2000) compares managing knowledge workers to wartime submarines on 'silent running' where everyone knows what to do and no-one gives orders. Colleagues who need help arrive bearing cookies or coffee (Starbuck, 1993), even virtual teams simulate social interaction through videoconferencing (McKinlay, 2000), and workers have extensive freedom and the flexibility to determine their own schedules or places of work (Grugulis *et al.*, 2000). Not only are conditions in these workplaces excellent, the perks are also generous – in one workplace including biscuits from Harrods or Fortnum and Mason, weekend shooting parties and a chauffeur driven Mercedes (Robertson *et al.*, 2003).

As with emotion work however, this is not a freedom from control but a shift to a different type of control. Rather than regulate or prescribe employers encourage normative control (Etzioni, 1961), a moral orientation to the organisation, so that employees do what will benefit the firm, not because they are coerced or bribed but because they are genuinely working to its benefit. Social activities encourage gift exchange, rather than economic exchange between colleagues so workers may be more generous with advice, or time or support (Grugulis *et al.*, 2000). And this form of control too comes at a price. The first is that work may be so interesting that it is all consuming. The type of professional workers observed here frequently work long hours and this can be carried to the extent that friendships, marriages, family ties and individual health suffers (Kidder, 1981; Kunda, 1992). Indeed, one of Kunda's (1992) interviewees joked that their freedom effectively meant, 'you can choose which twenty hours of the day you work'. Normative control also involves a great deal of conformity with freedom in work offset against the acceptance of social and cultural norms. In the organisation observed by Grugulis *et al.* (2000) workers were predominantly white, male and aged between 20 and 40 and the extensive calendar of social events, paid for and hosted by the firm, were only notionally voluntary (one woman, who preferred not to join in the company socials was sacked on the basis that she was not a 'people person'). For those who enjoyed this form of control (and many did and wanted more rather than less of it) it was clearly preferable to be managed through friendships, funded socials and generous salaries and benefits than extensive regulation or supervision but this was still a form of control and employees were required to conform to it.

More fundamentally though, there is little evidence that this type of knowledge work is likely to dominate any economy in the foreseeable future. Indeed, many of the numerous knowledge management initiatives are simply a modern variant of traditional deskilling and a separation of conception from execution since they carefully map out work activities and strip workers of their decision-making and discretionary powers so that services or production become more efficient (see, for example, Davenport and Klahr, 1998). As Brown and Hesketh (2004) point out, knowledge *work* does not invariably require knowledge *workers*. The scientists, consultants, researchers and lawyers, whose working practices are described above are, not the vanguard of the 'typical' organisation of the future (Thompson, 2004) but a self-conscious elite, a group of experts with impeccable academic credentials, recruited against almost impossibly demanding selection criteria from top institutions (Blackler *et al.*, 1993; Starbuck, 1993). Even organisations with more mixed workforces have very different recruitment processes for their knowledge elite and seem to operate on the assumption that only a small number of staff will ever be able to aspire to such roles (Brown and Hesketh, 2004). At his most optimistic Reich (1991) estimated that only a minority of workers would be symbolic analysts with most confined to more 'routine production services' or 'in-person services' (pp. 174–182). His figures are reflected in job growth. The booming service sector in Britain and the USA certainly includes knowledge workers, scientists, architects, consultants, lawyers, academics and the like. But it also covers, and in far greater numbers, cleaners, carers, security guards, waitresses and receptionists. Such person-to-person services, while often low status, poorly paid and unskilled, are difficult to automate and likely to remain a significant feature of the labour market for the foreseeable future.

It seems then, while knowledge workers themselves are likely to enjoy extremely good working conditions, we cannot rely on working conditions for all (or even many) becoming more human through the spread of knowledge work. These people are an important group but also an elite one (Thompson, 2004) and it is little surprise that the elite are treated well or that they are treated differently to other workers.

Discussion and conclusions

Where then does this take us in our journey to humanity through skills and knowledge and in search of humanity in skills and knowledge? Technical skills perhaps provide the clearest answer, not because they are necessarily inevitably good but because deskilling is necessarily bad. By its very nature deskilling extracts the human, personal, crafted elements from work and reduces workers' input to actions learned by rote. They may still take pleasure from friendships formed at work, Delbridge's (1998) account of factory life paints a vivid picture of the camaraderie and the shared enjoyment of 'Our Tune' on the radio; from the financial independence work grants; or from the few spaces for expertise or speed of performance that work allows but welcome as these are, they should not detract from the fact that the deskilled work itself dehumanises those who undertake it, encouraging them to 'go into robot' as Hochschild's (1983) flight attendants did, 'switching off' and just doing the job in hand.

Emotion work and soft skills present a slightly more complex picture. Many workers take pleasure in the emotional aspects of their employment, after all, providing comfort to those who are seriously ill may be taxing but it is a worthwhile occupation (James, 1993); and even serving burgers with a smile (Leidner, 1993) or assisting those who telephone call centres (Korczynski, 2002) can provide those who do the work with a 'buzz'. This is not to deny that the emotions deployed are those that management prescribe and workers in these situations often have very little official freedom over their responses. As Callaghan and Thompson (2002) note, even dropping your voice inappropriately during a sentence can result in additional (remedial) training. Yet in reality workers in front-line roles may carve out spaces of freedom, misbehaviour and resistance. Engaging genuinely with those they come into contact with, joining with colleagues and customers to mock official systems and scripts or simply going through the motions of whatever acts are required for the sake of the pay packet (Hochschild, 1983; Taylor and Bain, 2003; Weeks, 2004; Bolton, 2005a).

Perhaps it is most helpful here, since dehumanising work should not be excused on the grounds of ineffectiveness, to distinguish as Hochschild (1983) does between emotion *work*, over which the employee has some degree of control and which is itself intrinsically interesting, meaningful or pleasurable and emotional *labour* where control rests firmly in the hands of others and workers simply follow orders. This is also reflected in the extent to which workers are expected to accept hostility and abuse from customers as a natural part of their lot. As one trade unionist pointed out, if the customer is always right, those who serve them are always wrong (Eaton, 1996, p. 304). Emotion work can be an unequal exchange that strips employees of their dignity and their right to consideration or it can be a means of asserting the mutuality of courteous treatment. The route chosen materially affects how human a workplace is.

Soft skills, meanwhile, are remarkable for the relative powerlessness workers have when assessing them. They are personal qualities and traits that may well reflect how well employers treat employees but which are likely to be judged by the employer and assumed to be the responsibility of the employee. As a result, they are vulnerable to prejudice. For workers who already have high levels of skill or excellent educational qualifications, the issues are rather different. Many of the soft skills required may bring additional (and often interesting) dimensions to their work and many of these workers can use those skills to carve out areas of influence which benefit them and not their employer (see, for example, Brown and Hesketh, 2004; Grugulis and Vincent, 2004). For those at the other end of the labour market and even workers with intermediate skills, an emphasis on soft skills seems to ensure that they have less influence rather than more. Given how key an element of control is, in both the discussions on technical skills and emotion work, this is an important point.

Of all the three areas considered here, knowledge work seems to offer the best prospects. Knowledge workers are experts who are crucial to the successful functioning of their organisations and who, in consequence, are treated with every consideration. But that consideration is due to the fact that they are members of an elite and it is neither surprising, nor a harbinger of better treatment for the majority, when those at the top enjoy special privileges. Moreover, these experts are often more than capable of dehumanising their work themselves. Kunda's (1992) interviewees spoke of work as something that was fascinating, wonderful, all consuming, but also contaminated, 'shit' and 'crap'. Work invaded their home lives to the exclusion of all else, marriages, relationships and individual health failed on a regular basis and there was often little sign that those who had suffered one divorce or breakdown had changed their behaviour sufficiently to avoid another. To qualify as human, work must necessarily be limited so that it allows space for workers to take pleasure (and time) outside their workplaces, to enjoy good health and to form satisfying relationships.

This influence on the world outside work is an issue that has only briefly been touched on in this chapter but it is an important one and one that has been taken up by other authors. Brown (2001) and Lloyd and Payne (2004, 2005) in particular have argued that, in order to achieve genuine improvements in skill in the workplace there must, and should, be genuine changes in the way firms compete and the way society is organised. At firm level Brown (2001) argues for co-operative competition, positive high trust labour relations and a view of human capability which permits contributions to work decisions from more than a small minority of workers. Lloyd and Payne (2004, 2005) point out that such steps are likely to be ineffective unless accompanied by broader social change including a more equal distribution of income, labour and social rights, access to health, welfare and education and relatively high wages.

This link to the world beyond the workplace is an important one. Just as workplaces are social spaces and work should be judged on its social effects as well as the skills and knowledge needed in and for employment, so too are work and workplaces part of a broader society. The injustices, inequalities and discrimination found in that wider society are likely to be reflected in work. As a result, the analytical boundaries of any study of humanity in work need to be defined very broadly.

But such breadth should not be taken as an excuse for inaction. Granted, many workplace problems (racism, sexism, educational and health problems) are unlikely to have originated in employment but work can be a means of (at least partially) addressing them, of introducing or restoring dignity, of providing a route out of poverty or a source of pride. Just because we acknowledge that society as a whole may be racist or sexist it does not follow that we should accept with equanimity the racism and sexism that occur at work. It is, of course, rare to find those in charge of workplaces to be primarily motivated by issues of social justice, but it would be nice to see these and other aspects of the human regularly deployed in discussions of work and work design.

Humanity in work is a complex area and there is no single element that can be pointed to with certainty as the dividing line between human and degrading treatment. Even discretion, probably the closest pivotal element from this discussion on skills and knowledge, is no cure-all. But noting that an area is complex and that there are no easy answers should not be considered an admission of defeat. Because there is no one definition of humanity does not mean there are no ways to improve workplaces and asking ourselves that question, rather than how to make work absolutely human, might provide an easier route to improvement.

References

Ackroyd, S. and Crowdy, P.A. (1990) 'Can culture be managed? Working with "raw" material: the case of the English slaughterman'. *Personnel Review* 19:5, 3–13.

Ainley, P. (1993) *Class and Skill: Changing Divisions of Knowledge and Labour*. London and New York: Cassell.

Alvesson, M. and Karreman, D. (2001) 'Odd couple: making sense of the curious concept of knowledge management'. *Journal of Management Studies* 38:7, 995–1018.

Alvesson, M. and Sveningsson, S. (2003) 'Good visions, bad micro-management and ugly ambiguity: contradictions of (non-) leadership in a knowledge-intensive organization'. *Organization Studies (after Jan 1, 2003)* 24:6, 961–988.

Barsoux, J.-L. and Manzon, J. -F. (1997) 'Becoming the world's favourite airline: British Airways 1980–1993'. Bedford: European Case Clearing House.

Beynon, H. (1975) *Working for Ford*, Wakefield: EP Publishing Ltd.

Blackler, F., Reed, M. and Whitaker, A. (1993) 'Editorial introduction: knowledge workers and contemporary organisations'. *Journal of Management Studies* 30:6, 851–862.

Bolton, S.C. (2000) 'Emotion here, emotion there, emotional organisations everywhere'. *Critical Perspectives on Accounting* 11:155–171.

Bolton, S.C. (2004) 'Conceptual confusions: emotion work as skilled work'. In Warhurst, C., Grugulis, I. and Keep, E. (eds) *The Skills that Matter*, Basingstoke: Palgrave Macmillan.

Bolton, S.C. (2005a) *Emotion Management in the Workplace*, Basingstoke: Palgrave Macmillan.

Bolton, S.C. (2005b) ' "Making up" managers: the case of NHS nurses'. *Work, Employment and Society* 19:1, 5–23.

Bolton, S.C. and Boyd, C. (2003) 'Trolley dolly or skilled emotional manager? Moving on from Hochschild's *Managed Heart'. Work, Employment and Society* 17:2, 289–308.

Brown, P. (2001) 'Skill formation in the twenty-first century'. In Brown, P., Green, A. and Lauder, H. (eds) *High Skills: Globalization, Competitiveness and Skill Formation*, Oxford: Oxford University Press.

Brown, P. and Hesketh, A. (2004) *The Mismanagement of Talent: Employability and Jobs In the Knowledge Economy*, Oxford: Oxford University Press.

Burawoy, M. (1979) *Manufacturing Consent*, London: University of Chicago Press.

Burchell, B., Elliot, J., Rubery, J. and Wilkinson, F. (1994) 'Management and employee perceptions of skill'. In Penn, R., Rose, M. and Rubery, J. (eds) *Skill and Occupational Change*, Oxford: Oxford University Press.

Butterwick, S. (2003) 'Life skills training: "open for discussion" '. In Cohen, M.G. (ed.) *Training the Excluded for Work*, Vancouver and Toronto: UBC Press.

Callaghan, G. and Thompson, P. (2002) 'We recruit attitude: the selection and shaping of routine call centre labour'. *Journal of Management Studies* 39:2, 233–254.

Cappelli, P. (1995) 'Is the "skills gap" really about attitudes?' *California Management Review* 37:4, 108–124.

Cockburn, C. (1983) *Brothers: Male Dominance and Technological Change*. London: Pluto Press.

Davenport, T.H. and Klahr, P. (1998) 'Managing customer support knowledge'. *California Management Review* 40:3, 195–208.

Delbridge, R. (1998) *Life on the Line in Contemporary Manufacturing*. Oxford: Oxford University Press.

Department for Education and Skills/DTI/H M Treasury/Department for Work and Pensions. (2003) *21st Century Skills, Realising our Potential: Individuals, Employers, Nation*, Norwich: HMSO.

Eaton, S.C. (1996) ' "The customer is always interesting": unionised Harvard clericals renegotiate work relationships'. In Macdonald, C.L. and Sirianni, C. (eds) *Working in the Service Society*, Philadelphia: Temple University Press.

Edwards, P. and Wajcman, J. (2005) *The Politics of Working Life*. Oxford: Oxford University Press.

Ehrenreich, B. (2006) *Bait and Switch: The Futile Pursuit of the Corporate Dream*. London: Granta Publications.

Etzioni, A. (1961) *A Comparative Analysis of Complex Organisations*, New York: Free Press.

Felstead, A., Bishop, D., Fuller, A., Jewson, N., Lee, T. and Unwin. L. (2006) 'Moving to the music: learning processes, training and productive systems – the case of exercises to music instruction'. Presented at 24th International Labour Process Conference, 10–12 April, Birkbeck College, London.

Gallie, D. (1994) 'Patterns of skill change: upskilling, deskilling or polarisation?'. In Penn, R., Rose, M. and Rubery, J. (eds) *Skill and Occupational Change*, Oxford: Oxford University Press.

Garrahan, P. and Stewart, P. (1992) *The Nissan Enigma: Flexibility at Work in a Local Economy*, London: Mansett.

Goffman, E. (1959) *The Presentation of Self in Everyday Life*, Harmondsworth: Penguin.

Green, F. (2006) *Demanding Work: The Paradox of Job Quality in the Affluent Economy*, Princeton and Oxford: Princeton University Press.

Grimshaw, D., Beynon, H., Rubery, J. and Ward, K. (2002) 'The restructuring of career paths in large service sector organisations: "delayering", up-skilling and polarisation'. *Sociological Review* 50:1, 89–116.

Grugulis, I. and Vincent, S. (2004) 'Whose skill is it anyway? Soft skills and organisational politics'. Presented at 22nd International Labour Process Conference, 5–7 April, AIAS, Amsterdam.

Grugulis, I., Dundon, T. and Wilkinson. A. (2000) 'Cultural control and the "culture manager": employment practices in a consultancy'. *Work, Employment and Society* 14:1, 97–116.

Grugulis, I., Warhurst, C. and Keep, E. (2004) (eds) 'What's happening to skill'. *The Skills that Matter*, Basingstoke: Palgrave Macmillan.

Hackley, C. (2000) 'Silent running: tacit, discursive and psychological aspects of management in a top UK advertising agency'. *British Journal of Management* 11:3, 239–254.

Hebson, G. and Grugulis, I. (2005) 'Gender and new organisational forms'. In Marchington, M., Grimshaw, D., Rubery, J. and Willmott, H. (eds) *Fragmenting Work: Blurring Organisational Boundaries and Disordering Hierarchies*, Oxford: Oxford University Press.

Hillage, J., Regan, J., Dickson, J. and McLoughlin, K. (2002) 'Employers Skill Survey 2002'. In *Research Report*. Nottingham: DfES.

Hirsch, W. and Bevan, S. (1988) *What Makes a Manager?* Brighton: Institute of Manpower Studies, University of Sussex.

Hochschild, A.R. (1983) *The Managed Heart: Commercialization of Human Feeling*, Berkley: University of California Press.

ILO (2001) *Reducing the Decent Work Deficit: A Global Challenge*. Geneva: International Labour Office.

James, N. (1993) 'Divisions of emotional labour: disclosure and cancer'. In Fineman, S. (ed.) *Emotion in Organisations*, London: Sage.

Keep, E. (2001) 'If it moves, it's a skill'. Presented at ESRC seminar on The Changing Nature of Skills and Knowledge, 3–4 September, Manchester.

Kidder, T. (1981) *The Soul of a New Machine*, Boston/Toronto: Little, Brown and Co.

Kinnie, N., Hutchinson, S. and Purcell, J. (2000) 'Fun and surveillance: the paradox of high commitment management in call centres'. *International Journal of Human Resource Management* 11:5, 967–985.

Korczynski, M. (2001) 'The contradictions of service work: call centre as customer-oriented bureaucracy'. In Sturdy, A., Grugulis, I. and Willmott, H. (eds) *Customer Service: Empowerment and Entrapment*, Basingstoke: Palgrave.

Korczynski, M. (2002) *Human Resource Management in Service Work*, Basingstoke: Palgrave.

Kunda, G. (1992) *Engineering Culture: Control and Commitment in a High-Tech corporation*, Philadelphia: Temple University Press.

Lafer, G. (2004) 'What is skill?' In Warhurst, C., Grugulis, I. and Keep, E. (eds) *The Skills that Matter*, Basingstoke: Palgrave Macmillan.

Leidner, R. (1993) *Fast Food, Fast Talk: Service Work and the Routinizations of Everyday Life*, Berkeley and Los Angeles: University of California Press.

Littler, C. (1982) *The Development of the Labour Process in Capitalist Societies*. London: Heinemann.

Lloyd, C. and Payne, J. (2004) 'The political economy of skill'. In Warhurst, C., Grugulis, I. and Keep, E. (eds) *The Skills that Matter*, Basingstoke: Palgrave Macmillan.

Lloyd, C. and Payne, J. (2005) 'A vision too far? Mapping the space for a high skills project in the UK'. *Journal of Education and Work* 18:2, 165–185.

Mann, S. (1999) *Hiding What We Feel, Faking What We Don't: Understanding the Role of Your Emotions at Work*. Shaftesbury: Element.

Marx, K. (1964) *Karl Marx: Early Writings*, trans. and ed. by Bottomore, T. New York: McGraw-Hill.

Maume, D.J.J. (1999) 'Glass ceilings and glass escalators: occupational segregation and race and sex differences in managerial promotions'. *Work and Occupations*, 26:4, 483–509.

McKinlay, A. (2000) 'The bearable lightness of control: organisational reflexivity and the politics of knowledge management'. In Prichard, C., Hull, R., Chumer, M. and Willmott, H. (eds) *Managing Knowledge: Critical Investigations of Work and Learning*, Basingstoke: Macmillan.

Moss, P. and Tilly, C. (1996) 'Soft skills and race: an investigation into black men's employment problems'. *Work and Occupations* 23:3, 252–276.

Moss-Kanter, R. (1977) *Men and Women of the Corporation*. New York: Basic Books.

Nickson, D., Warhurst, C., Witz, A. and Cullen, A.-M. (2001) 'The importance of being aesthetic: work, employment and service organisation'. In Sturdy, A., Grugulis, I. and Willmott, H. (eds) *Customer Service: Empowerment and Entrapment*, Basingstoke: Palgrave.

Nonaka, I. and Takeuchi, H. (1995) *The Knowledge Creating Company: How Japanese Companies Create the Dynamics of Innovation*, New York and Oxford: Oxford University Press.

Payne, J. (1999) 'All things to all people: changing perceptions of "skill" among Britain's policy makers since 1950s and their implications'. In *SKOPE Research Paper No. 1*, Coventry: University of Warwick.

Payne, J. (2000) 'The unbearable lightness of skill: the changing meaning of skill In UK policy discourses and some implications for education and training'. *Journal of Education Policy* 15:3, 353–369.

Payne, J. (2006) 'What's wrong with emotional labour?' In *SKOPE Research Paper*. Oxford and Warwick: Universities of Oxford and Warwick.

Pierce, J.L. (1995) *Gender Trials: Emotional Lives in Contemporary Law Firms*. Berkley: University of California Press.

Pierce, J.L. (1996) 'Reproducing gender relations in large law firms: the role of emotional labour in paralegal work'. In Macdonald C.L. and Sirianni, C. (eds) *Working in the Service Society*, Philadelphia: Temple University Press.

Pollert, A. (1981) *Girls, Wives, Factory Lives*, Basingstoke: Macmillan.

Putnam, L. and Mumby, D.K. (1993) 'Organisations, emotions and the myth of rationality'. In Fineman, S. (ed.) *Emotion in Organisations*, London: Sage.

Rainbird, H., Munro, A. and Holly, L. (2004) 'Employer demand for skills and qualifications'. In Warhurst, C., Grugulis, I. and Keep, E. (eds) *The Skills that Matter*, Basingstoke: Palgrave Macmillan.

Rees, B. and Garnsey, E. (2003) 'Analysing competence: gender and identity at work'. *Gender, Work and Organization* 10:5, 551–578.

Reich, R. (1991) *The Work of Nations: Preparing Ourselves for 21st Century Capitalism*, New York: Vintage Books.

Ritzer, G. (1996) *The McDonalidization of Society*, Thousand Oaks, California and London: Pine Forge Press.

Robertson, M., Scarbrough, H. and Swan, J. (2003) 'Knowledge creation in professional service firms: institutional effects'. *Organization Studies (after Jan 1, 2003)* 24:6, 831–857.

Royle, T. (2000) *Working for McDonald's in Europe: The Unequal Struggle*, London: Routledge.

Sennett, R. (1998) *The Corrosion of Character*, New York and London: Norton.

Skuratowicz, E. and Hunter, L.W. (2004) 'Where do women's jobs come from? Job resegregation in an American bank'. *Work and Occupations* 31:1, 73–110.

Smith, A. (1776/1993) *Wealth of Nations*, Oxford and New York: Oxford University Press.

Starbuck, W. (1993) 'Keeping a butterfly and an elephant in a house of cards: the elements of exceptional success'. *Journal of Management Studies* 30:6, 885–921.

Taylor, F.W. (1949) *Scientific Management*, London: Harper and Row.

Taylor, P. and Bain, P. (2003) ' "Subterranean worksick blues": humour as subversion in two call centres'. *Organization Studies* 24:9, 1487–1509.

Taylor, S. and Tyler, M. (2000) 'Emotional labour and sexual difference in the airline industry'. *Work, Employment and Society* 14:1, 77–96.

Thompson, P. (2004) 'Skating on thin ice: the knowledge economy myth'. Glasgow: University of Strathclyde/ Big Thinking.

Turner, H.A. (1962) *Trade Union Growth, Structure and Policy*. London: Allen and Unwin.

Warhurst, C. and Nickson, D. (2001) *Looking Good, Sounding Right*, London: Industrial Society.

Webster, J. (1990) *Office Automation: The Labour Process and Women's Work in Britain*, New York and London: Harvester Wheatsheaf.

Weeks, J. (2004) *Unpopular Culture: The Ritual of Complaint in a British Bank*, Chicago and London: University of Chicago Press.

Wharton, A.S. (1996) 'Service with a smile: understanding the consequences of emotional labour'. In Macdonald, C.L. and Sirianni, C. (eds) *Working in the Service Society*, Philadelphia: Temple University Press.

Wray-Bliss, E. (2001) 'Representing customer service: telephones and texts'. In Sturdy, A., Grugulis, I. and Willmott H. (eds) *Customer Service: Empowerment and Entrapment*, Basingstoke: Palgrave.

5

Making capital: strategic dilemmas for HRM

Paul Thompson

> While HRM does need to support commercial outcomes (often called the 'business case'), it also exists to serve organizational needs for social legitimacy.
>
> (Boxall *et al.*, 2006, p. 4)

As the quote illustrates, Human Resource Management (HRM), in theory and practice, has strategic (or economic) and normative (or legitimacy) dimensions. In part this reflects its origins. From the beginning HRM was compelled to engage in product differentiation to distinguish itself from a set of functional practices. To project itself as something that was not 'simply a new sign tacked on the personnel manager's door' (Thomas, 1988, p. 3), HRM had to sell itself on both its promise of organisational and human growth.

These dimensions and then tensions between them have become embedded in HR contrasting approaches taken in the relevant literatures. Admittedly, HRM is not a homogeneous body of scholarship. One distinction is between those who see HRM itself as a distinctive approach to managing the employment relationship based on a high skill, high commitment workforce and a central role for human capital in firm strategy (Storey, 1985; Guest, 1987, 2002); and those who take a more contingent perspective and seek to identify the appropriate fit between particular HR practices and contexts (Boxall and Purcell, 2003). We will return to such distinctions later, but both groups seek to identify practices that generate efficiency and legitimacy and thus they grapple with the central tension about the management of work and employment relations.

The more far-sighted and less prescriptive scholars in the field recognise these tensions and call for organisations to find a 'strategic balance' between their economic and justice/legitimacy objectives (Paauwe and Boselie, 2006). But identifying a need for balance and finding the means to achieve it are different things. This chapter has two main contentions. First, both the strategic and normative dimensions of HRM are underpinned by conceptions of human capital and those conceptions are frequently disabling. Second, the tension is becoming more difficult to manage in the contemporary conditions of corporate governance and political economy and that this is diminishing the credibility of HRM to other organisational stakeholders.

The human capital narrative: origins, variations and consequences

Economists (e.g. Becker, 1964) originally claimed that, like business, individuals made decisions about 'investment' in the expectation of greater returns, in this case by increasing their human capital through undergoing education and training. Typically for neo-classical thinking, this view emphasises individual, calculable and rational behaviour. Implicitly there is an assumption that such actions pay off for employers because more human capital means more productive workers. Whatever the origins and limits of such arguments, they enabled the terms of debate about competitive advantage to be shifted by emphasising that the quality and skills of the workforce can have a significant effect on productivity.

There are widely acknowledged limits to such arguments. In particular, they take no account of the systematic variations in the amount of human capital available to individuals and the structural constraints that shape people's choices. In addition, employers make choices about how much and what kinds of human capital are available to the workers who undertake jobs. Radical economists (Doeringer and Piore, 1971) therefore developed alternative accounts that emphasise two different sets of labour market rules, focusing on institutions rather than individuals. Such theorists

> do not argue that labour supply differs according to the "human capital" that workers decide to invest in themselves. Instead, they are concerned with the skills which employers decide to give workers. (Fevre, 1992, p. 32)

In the first instance, internal labour markets enable employers to use extensive job hierarchies in order to recruit, reward and retain within the firm. In the second, dual labour markets, help to explain how employers create and benefit from secondary 'segments' where wages are lower, job structures are flatter and career prospects and job security minimal.

Both theories explain why the normal laws of supply and demand do not work in real labour markets. But such critiques can bolster HRM perspectives as they focus on the employment relationship, albeit within the confines of the labour market. In particular, internal labour markets have been an important sub-plot in the human capital narrative as they identify how employers and employees can achieve some degree of mutual gains through long-term commitment and joint regulation.

However, given the substantial changes in markets, work relations and employment systems arising out of the decay of the old Fordist arrangements, from the middle of the 1980s HRM theorists began to make a new, more contingent argument; that changes in the external environment have made the internal assets of the firm more significant and strategic. The drivers were generally seen as the dynamic duo of (more specialised and volatile) product markets and (programmable) technologies. Given the need for innovation and flexibility, human assets – the skills, knowledge and attitudes of employees – become the crucial competitive advantage. In parallel, there is a shift towards soft controls: practices intended to *generate* commitment through a combination of culture-led changes and delegation of authority. Given the primacy of human capital, command and control were seen to be displaced by what some call 'soft HRM' – culture, trust, empowerment and self-direction as a means of co-ordination (Walton, 1985). As O'Reilly and Pfeffer (2000) argued, HRM is values-led, puts culture first and has consistent people-centred practices that are supported by senior management. In most people's eyes, HRM became indivisible from a humanistic message about growth and development. From this viewpoint, the employment relationship is a 'thick' one, 'involving recognition, respect, trust and, perhaps most importantly, reciprocal obligation' (Bolton and Houlihan, this book, Chapter 1).

What was being promoted was a productive synergy between a new content (enhanced human capital) and a new context (flexible markets and technologies). In this context, the dominant HRM model is a human capital/high involvement one (Kaufman, 2004). A *strategic* approach to HRM is said to be marked, in part, by investment in the workforce and this would be associated with enhanced skills, training, career structures and skill and knowledge-based reward systems. In turn, this forms the basis for mutual gains and shared interests through the employment relationship. The management of people is thus given a seat at the top table. Typical of this approach was Pfeffer's (1994, 1998) 'profits through people' message. He examined seven practices that successful organisations needed to have in order to make a difference, including employment security, selective hiring, self-managed teams and decentralised decision-making, high compensation linked to organisational performance, training, minimal status differences and extensive openness in sharing information.

Royal and O'Donnell (2003) sum up the perspective by arguing that sustainable human resource practices are those which stress the importance of long-term employment, organisational membership and performance. They need to be internally consistent and consistent with the broader context in which the firm is operating. Such thinking forms the grounds on which the concept of high performance work systems (HPWS) was developed. Cohesiveness has been a key theme from an early stage, with the package of high-commitment practices sustained by a strategic orientation and a high level of integration between corporate, functional and operational levels of the business (Kochan *et al.*, 1986).

This approach was the underlying basis of the 'bargain' for employees to buy into HPWS or new transactional psychological contracts. As one of the most authoritative studies supporting HPWS argued, workers need incentives to acquire new skills and knowledge, and to engage in discretionary effort, whilst for employers, 'increasing training, employment security, and pay incentives for non-managerial employees has the greatest effect on plant performance' (Appelbaum *et al.*, 2000, p. 8).

That is the 'theory'. There has, inevitably, been huge pressure on HRM academics to demonstrate a pay-off, that such practices are prominent and make a difference. Central to this burden is identifying 'the mediating variables between strategic human resource management and performance' (Royal and O'Donnell, 2005, p. 132). Huselid's (1995) longitudinal study is amongst the best known and oft-quoted. Examining the relationship between human resource policies and organisational performance, his findings indicated that those which target their approach to the development of human capital outperformed those who did not. Many others followed in its wake. Whilst scope and settings differed, the broad themes remained the same: people-centred management practices which emphasise long-term relationships with their employees, recruitment, retention, skill acquisition and internal career mobility, tend to perform better with regard to innovation, product development, attracting and retaining good staff, and financial performance (Royal and O'Donnell, 2003).

Such arguments have been augmented by claims from two other sources. Resource-based views (RBV) of the firm (Barney, 1991) see human capital as a key invisible asset that is increasingly valuable, non-substitutable and hard to replicate. Whilst originating in a shift in the strategy literature from external factors to internal sources as means of sustainable competitive advantage, such views have 'brought legitimacy to HR's assertion that people are strategically important to firm success' (Wright *et al.*, 2005, p. 18). Wright *et al.* go on to refer to such resources as a 'human capital pool' and note that most research sees HR practices as the mechanism that manages or activates that latent competitive advantage. In this sense, there is a considerable overlap with the above-described HPWS perspectives – both study the relations between HR practices and performance and both assume that HR activities lead to the kind of workforce that can enhance that performance. RBV perspectives are a typically optimistic human capital narrative in that the 'pool' is seen as synonymous with a highly skilled, motivated workforce and that HR and other managers can capture that talent and align interests in a mutually beneficial way (Boxall, 1996).

What is less typical is the dominant emphasis on aligning the people management system with other internal systems. Alternate human capital narratives replace a notion of a static or latent stock of human capital with an assumption that some external driver – rather than, say, HR practices – triggers the enhanced pool. In recent years academic and policy discourse has been dominated by exactly such a narrative in the form of the knowledge economy thesis (Reich, 1993; Nonaka and Takeuchi, 1995; World Bank, 2002). Here, the (thinking) skills and knowledge of the employee are seen as displacing the traditional factors of production as the key asset for firms.

Studies are often vague or imprecise on the causes of such outcomes, but the underlying theme is that of a productive synergy between the knowledge and skill needs of innovative, high tech, service-based firms in dynamic product markets and the greater availability of highly educated, better trained labour. Whatever the drivers, the outcome is the same – creative work based on the intangible features of knowledge. Knowledge is transformed literally into human *capital*. This is reflected in the claim made by the OECD (2001, p. 148) that 'knowledge capital is beginning to challenge money and all other forms of capital'. In such circumstances the *labour* market becomes a much more important focal point of economic life in that 'power in the knowledge economy resides more with workers than owners or managers' (Bennis, 1999, p. 37).

This harks back to a central premise of human capital theory that individuals rather than firms own that resource. If this logic is followed there is less emphasis on management as such in that knowledge workers are essentially free agents who, in a 'war for talent' can dictate the terms of the employment relationship (Pink, 2001). Though this maximum autonomy/minimal management view is repeated in other literatures, such as those on the creative economy (Florida, 2002), a knowledge economy perspective is compatible with the kind of soft HRM views discussed earlier that focus on values, commitment and trust-based displacement of command and control methods.

Profits through people: a plot in search of practice

The human resource management profession faces a crisis of trust and a loss of legitimacy in the eyes of its major stakeholders. The two-decade effort to develop a new 'strategic human resource management' (HR) role in organizations has failed to realize its promised potential of greater status, influence, and achievement. (Kochan, 2006)

As we have seen, the human capital narrative, in its various guises has enabled HRM theorists to make two inter-related core claims about these approaches to managing work and people. The most significant is that organisations that employ such approaches to work organisation, particularly in a systematic and strategic fashion, can foster high levels of satisfaction, commitment and mutual gains among their employees. Largely as a result of their impact on employees, these approaches to work organisation contribute to superior organisational performance in terms of measures such as labour productivity and turnover. Despite the volume of evidence that seemingly makes it difficult to dispute the proposition that new forms of work organisation are associated with superior performance, such claims have faced two kinds of questioning. The first, from critical workplace scholars, often from a labour process perspective, focuses on the classic rhetoric–reality gap, questioning the extent and character of HC/HPWS practices.

As Jenkins and Delbridge note elsewhere in this book, 'there are major question marks over the extent to which current practice on the manufacturing shopfloors of North America and the European Union matches these imperatives'. Though referring more broadly to HRM, traditional critiques have focused on the 'continuities and constraints associated with lean production and other new management practices' (Thompson and Newsome, 2004, p. 147). As they point out, there is a wealth of qualitative research that illustrates the 'dark side' of new managerial regimes and HPWS in terms of enhanced controls and work intensification in the US (Graham, 1995; Parker and Slaughter, 1995; Rinehart *et al.*, 1997), UK (Danford, 1998; Delbridge, 1998); and Europe (Sandberg, 1995).

This is not merely an empirical critique. As Fleetwood (this book, Chapter 3) outlines, the preference for measurement and metrics in HPWS scholarship draws a deductive epistemology that places event regularities above explanation, and an ontology that ignores the active agency and interests of labour that is assumed to respond in unproblematic ways to HR initiatives. The failure to treat divergent interests is a significant factor in the unwillingness or inability to account for the impact of capitalist relations of production and changes in political economy on fragile and contested employment relations (Godard, 2004).

By focusing on the dynamic nature of workplace change in the context of broader political economy, and qualitative methodologies that can reach beneath the surface of managerial rhetoric and highlight the experience of employees, labour process and other critical research is able to offer an important corrective to the human capital narrative. But the rival approaches and methodologies mean that the two literatures exist in largely parallel universes.

The methodological gap, at least, need not be insurmountable. Some pro-HPWS research has been undertaken with more mixed methodologies, notably Appelbaum *et al.*'s (2000) *Manufacturing Advantage*. Moreover, though most Labour Process Theory (LPT) research has been based on case studies or ethnographies, it is not in principle hostile to quantitative approaches. As Thompson and Harley (2006) argue, survey and related methods can also be used to test dominant rhetorics against worker voice and management practice. That is not to discount criticisms of the robustness of HPWS studies. Even within its own ranks, the methodological limitations to finding clear relations between HR practices and performance have been well aired and as Wright *et al.* (2005, p. 26) note, 'as yet no study has demonstrated anything close to a full causal model through which HR practices are purported to impact on performance'. The absence of such a model is not seen by these and other authors as a barrier to more rigorous (in their case longitudinal) studies of HR from an RBV perspective.

Up to a point they may be right, though the faith in bigger and better science is somewhat naïve. In a more general sense, this is a bit like carrying on fiddling whilst Rome burns. The position taken in this chapter is to accept that the potential link between investment in human capital, superior performance and mutual gains is real, indeed, one of the few British studies which explicitly adopts a LPT perspective found such positive associations (Ramsay *et al.*, 2000). However, there is also a need to recognise that external conditions are making it ever more difficult for that investment to be either a corporate priority or sustainable, or both.

If Kochan is right in his above assessment, the crisis of legitimacy for HRM cannot arise primarily from weaknesses in scholarship. This is a profoundly practical crisis and to unravel its origins and effects there is a need to question more deeply the origins, nature and weaknesses of HRM's love affair with the notion of human capital on the one hand, and on the other its historic failure to get to grips with other kinds of capital, whether the political economy of capitalism in general or contemporary financial markets in particular.

Contexts and causes

The progressive appeal of human capital arguments is understandable. 'Profits through people' and investment in the workforce offers a practical workplace and societal politics in a context in which HRM has to demonstrate legitimacy and effectiveness in often hostile economic and political environments. But what if in contemporary capitalism people are not 'our most important asset'? A wide range of contemporary research is now available that refutes or at least questions such claims.

HRM takes capitalism for granted, both in general and in its particular forms. More specifically, it does not conceptualise capitalism as setting structural limits to the degree to which the interests of labour and capital can converge or be managed successfully. Nor does it conceptualise the dynamics of capitalist political economy as a significant influence on firm behaviour. In particular, HRM has been largely silent on the question of capital markets. Theories such as the knowledge economy, in fact, write capital out of the picture as a factor of production. What Stiles and Kulvisaechana (2003) refer to as a 'supportive environment' tends to foreground the immediate context and at best stretch to product markets, labour markets and technologies. As we saw earlier, HRM built much of its optimistic predictions around a scenario where those contingencies were combining in a manner that facilitated human capital strategies.

Some strands of HRM discourse do draw on wider contexts, including some research in international and comparative HRM that seek to show how models and practices vary across cultures and reflect laws, cultures and institutions (Boxall et al., 2006). The best of such analyses overlap with comparative employment relations literatures that locate firm-oriented analysis within the webs of inter-locking national institutions. Such frameworks can explain trends such as the persistence of a 'low skills equilibrium' in a particular economy such as the UK (Crouch et al., 1999). They can also offer an important corrective to the belief that American, or indeed any other, styles of management are universal or inevitable. A good example of the latter is Jacoby's (2004) study of how firms in Japan and the United States are responding to the pressures of globalisation. In contrast to the USA, HR departments in Japan are occupying a more central position in the corporation and corporate governance arrangements do not give a choice only to shareholders. Paradoxically, however, the strengths of such studies can also be their limitation. Emphasis on national difference can submerge common and convergent trends in institutional detail. There are a number of wider and more general trends that are inimical to the human capital narrative.

Such arguments rest, in part, on the assumption of an ever-expanding supply of high quality, high skill jobs. That is not what the facts of job growth and skill formation show. The largest growth is in routine jobs in hospitality and retail, or in personal services in the private and public sectors and few have any relation to high tech employment (Brown *et al.*, 2001; Thompson, 2004). Where does that leave high skill or knowledge work? Despite repeated optimistic claims that the majority of jobs fall into this category, more rigorous analysis of official occupational data indicates that those that could be classified as knowledge workers with substantial 'thinking skills' account for a relatively small minority in the US and UK (Brown and Hesketh, 2004), and Australia (Fleming *et al.*, 2004). Some of these are, admittedly, amongst the *fastest* growing, but only alongside a range of low-end service jobs that rely on social competencies rather than knowledge. An increasing number of commentators are referring to these trends as the development of an hourglass economy (Nolan, 2001). We can therefore say that the human capital pool may be, if not shrinking, at least segregating.

Second, there is limited evidence that employers, at least in Anglo-Saxon economies, are delivering on the commitment to invest in other aspects of human capital, whilst employees are asked to invest in themselves. Trends are uneven, for example job tenure rates in the UK are not falling overall; but there is evidence of long-term decline in traditional career structures and internal labour markets, and falling investment in training (Cappelli, 2001). Even mainstream management voices have raised serious concerns about the violation of the traditional psychological contract as the burden of risk is increasingly transferred to employees, who are exhorted to take over responsibility for skill and career development and/or abandon any hope of stable, long-term employment (Robinson and Rousseau, 1994; Deal and Kennedy, 1999).

The greatest cause of insecurity and instability is the perpetual restructuring that began in parts of the economy in the 1980s, but spread to many more sectors through rationalisation and downsizing in the 1990s. Even those that did not lose their jobs have to bear the costs of low morale, increased workloads and threats to their pensions (Biewener, 1997; Green, 2001; Beynon *et al.*, 2002). The role played by HR departments in this process is particularly instructive. Reflecting on her research into changes in the banking sector in the US, Smith notes that the old employment relations

> buffered employees from coercive regulation by the market and had generated "surplus commitment" to the bank. Yet, in the mid-1980s, that same infrastructure produced the architects of and technicians for corporate retrenchment, personnel now charged with chiselling away at both the job and the psychological security that led employees to regard the Bank as a progressive employer. (Smith, 1999, p. 1)

A third key factor undermining investment in HC is the growth of outsourcing and fragmented employment systems. The externalisation of labour and the growth of multi-employer networks produce significant tensions in the management of the employment relationship. For labour, employment often becomes more precarious, whilst for management the shift to market-based transactions across permeable inter-organisational boundaries can make it more difficult to generate and sustain commitment, or even to sustain a stable management style and strategy across a variety of structures and contracts (Rubery *et al.*, 2005). The new relationships are also likely to impact on the behaviour of employees – leading to more calculative attitudes towards learning and sharing knowledge. In turn this may make organisations even more cautious about investment in HC because they fear that it will be lost through exit or redundancy. As Rubery *et al.* (2005, p. 233) observe

> In these circumstances, it would be sensible not to place too much faith in the power and pervasiveness of notions of commitment, as evidenced in the doctrines of human resource management.

To some extent the above factors are more symptoms than causes. There is a growing realisation that we now have a form of financialised economies in which capital markets rather than product or labour markets are the dominant drivers of firm behaviour (Littler and Innes, 2003; Thompson, 2003). Shareholder Value, in the context of an enhanced and active market for corporate control, has become a growth regime in its own right. This regime is marked by a focus on asset management and generation, market share and anticipated revenue streams.

In circumstances where downsizing and perpetual restructuring are the norm in many sectors, progressive objectives in work and employment spheres, notably investment in firm-specific assets (skills, training, employment stability and careers), are difficult to sustain and increasingly disconnected from wider trends in corporate governance. Not surprisingly firm-level industrial relations settlements and partnerships, whilst desirable, are also harder to sustain as macro pressures work their way through to the local level (Jenkins and Delbridge, this book, Chapter 11). This is why I refer to contemporary political economy as 'disconnected capitalism' rather than vaguer labels such as vigorous or turbo capitalism (Thompson, 2003).

It is possible that pursuit of shareholder value may be compatible with stable, HPWS systems in particular circumstances. But if productivity and performance in product markets is of declining relative significance, it is also not surprising that even firms that have achieved gains in productivity and market share through the appropriate HPWS measures are not immune from destructive effects of enhanced demands for shareholder value (Konzelmann and Forrant, 2003). Whilst such developments may lead to 'both managers and non-managers find(ing) themselves aligned together in opposition to corporate-level restructuring' (Jenkins and Delbridge, this book, Chapter 11), senior management have been increasingly immunised from the destructive effects by tying their interests to the corporate and financial elite via stock options and executive remuneration packages. What has been created is a new mutual gain from above between senior executives and finance capital that is destructive of the traditional mutual gains from below between labour and firm-level management.

What of the role of HR in these processes? Kochan (2006) suggests that as traditional intra-firm alliances declined, HR professionals aligned themselves increasingly with line management and especially senior executives. After all, who else is facilitating these executive deals and packages? Of course, this may be a question of level in the hierarchy. But even if mid-level HR managers may want to pursue higher performance and high-commitment policies, at least in some sectors, the levers they are pulling are often outweighed or countermanded by corporate decision-makers in thrall to financial markets. As Kunda and Ailon-Souday (2005) demonstrate, the dominant form of market rationalism has little time for culture and is more interested in reducing than transforming the workforce. In this context, whilst many of the prescriptions of HRM are laudable, they are increasingly out of step with this 'new normative climate of impermanence, transience, and fluctuation' (Smith, 1999, p. 3).

Re-conceptualising 'people are our most important asset'

The flaws of a particular narrative do not mean that labour power has ceased to be an asset for firms or an object for managerial intervention. What is required is some substantial re-conceptualisation. First, we need to critically recast the insight that 'hard' HRM is concerned with the 'full utilisation of labour' (Storey, 1995). The partial break with Taylorism and Fordism from the mid-1980s onwards relied primarily on a *qualitative intensification of labour* (Thompson, 2003, pp. 362–364). But this intensification required the mobilisation of something new, whether described as 'knowledge*ability*' (Thompson *et al.*, 2000), knowledge worked (Brown and Hesketh, 2004), or the 'extra-functional skills' of the 'new model worker' (Flecker and Hofbauer, 1998). Under-specified notions of human capital make it difficult to develop a critique of the tide of work intensification, presenteeism and mobilisation of emotional labour associated with this 'full utilisation'.

Second, that there has been a decisive shift in the skill requirements of employers, but one that rests more on 'capitalizing on humanity' than investing in human capital (Thompson *et al.*, 2000). As the introduction to a recent volume on skills sets out, paralleling the shift from explicit to tacit knowledge has been one from *technical to social skills* (Warhurst *et al.*, 2004). Whilst employers may have in the past thought 'positive attitudes' were desirable, they were not regarded as *skills* integral to the job. Today, in much service and other work, 'person-to-person' social competencies are seen as the key asset. This has been confirmed in wider research in the UK, France and the US that has found that attitudes, dispositions and appearance are frequently more important than level of education and training (Mounier, 2001; Warhurst and Nickson, 2001; Lafer, 2004). Such trends are reflected in the language of social policy and vocational training such as 'transferable skills', 'generic skills' and 'employability'. The latter confirms the previously noted transfer of responsibility for investment in human capital from employers to employees. Because the 'new' soft skill currencies such as positive attitudes, ability to work as a team and communication are generic, they are hard to connect to any notion of high skills or knowledge (Brown *et al.*, 2001, p. 40). But they do constitute an asset for firms and can be understood better through the concept of social rather than human capital. Less individualistic than the human variant, social capital draws our attention to the relational components of work systems, notably the dependence on teamworking in many job contexts.

Third, we have to reconsider the locus of the 'investment' made through HRM practices. Increasingly managerial practice is to *identify the social and personal capital* held by the actual or potential employee. Employers may be choosing to invest more in recruitment and selection processes that can identify workers with the appropriate personal characteristics, than in skill development and learning (Callaghan and Thompson, 2002; Brown and Hesketh, 2004). This helps to understand the apparent paradox of strong investment in some HR practices in contexts such as call centres, despite the low discretion work (Houlihan, 2002).

The search for legitimacy: alternate narratives?

HR theorists and practitioners are not blind to the kind of changes discussed in the previous sections. But their respective locations in the academic and business divisions of labour require the re-fashioning of a narrative that can continue to link investment in human capital to organisational performance. There are a number of potential sources for this re-fashioning.

The most obvious pathway is through a revival of economic models of HRM. The increased centrality of the accounting function in Anglo-Saxon capitalism has meant for some time that what were then known as personnel specialists have tried to emphasise human resource accounting (Armstrong, 1995). In recent years, consultants and business academics have argued that companies do not have have systematic means for measuring intangible assets, notably knowledge and human capital. Elias and Scarbrough (2004) and Royal and O'Donnell (2003) catalogue a variety of such attempts to monitor and measure people as assets contribution to added value, retention and growth factors, and not least, returns to shareholders. Royal and O'Donnell's (2005) own model of human capital analysis seeks to combine traditional financial analysis with a number of qualitative approaches that can be adopted by securities analysts in industries such as investment banking. Such metrics and measurements are clearly of benefit to practitioners as they enable 'a link between the HR function and other managerial groups, not least senior management' (Elias and Scarbrough, 2004, p. 36).

Most human capital narratives assume a set of universal best practices that generate mutual benefit for employees and employers. A growing number of HR academics have articulated a more contingent position that seeks to identify 'what HR practices are profit-rational in which contexts' (Boxall and Purcell, 2003, p. 10). This can be reinforced by a notion of multiple bottom lines that recognise the salience of social legitimacy as well as cost effectiveness. Part of the reason for a retreat to contingency has been a recognition that large parts of the service sector do not require a human capital/high involvement approach in order to be competitive in product markets. For example, Batt and Moynihan (2002) argue that varied work organisation and HR practices in call centres reflect product market segmentation between high value (professional service model) and low value (mass production) customers.

The final alternative narrative is that of the knowledge economy. As noted earlier, the thesis depends on the idea that possession of human capital by a growing army of professionals and experts with the firm or 'free workers' such as contractors and consultants outside, is the central productive resource in the contemporary economy. This view is particularly important as it refreshes the human capital narrative and allows for a logical escape hatch from the well-publicised problem of job insecurity and blocked careers inside the hierarchies of large corporations.

There are a number of limitations to these alternative narratives. It may well be possible to develop effective metrics to measure the supposedly intangible assets of highly skilled expert labour in knowledge-intensive firms. Moreover, some in these ranks, such as the 'hired guns' and itinerant contractors identified in Barley and Kunda's (2004) Silicon Valley study, may develop ways of organising their working life through staffing agencies and horizontal networks. But such an orientation has little to offer in the mass of low-level service or manufacturing jobs, nor to the large number of clerical and semi-professional workers operating technology-driven expert *systems*. Nor are their sufficient numbers of free agents to make that particular form of individual human capital generalisable across the economy.

With respect to the 'best fit' argument, any attention paid to variations in institutional and product market context is beneficial. But it doesn't ultimately resolve the problem that external capital market conditions are making it harder for high performance and progressive HR practices to flourish even where they meet the dual conditions of internal consistency and external fit (Konzelmann and Forrant, 2003). There may be multiple bottom lines, but when shareholder value logic is dominant there is likely to be only one winner. And that still leaves the awkward question of what is the normative basis of an appeal of HRM to (the majority) low road sectors? This is linked to a wider problem and point. A pre-disposition to argue for progressive practices solely on the basis of the business case means that human capital arguments instrumentalise labour. What if equal opportunity or work–life balance is not good for the bottom line? Do we stop arguing for them?

Conclusion: resolving the practical and intellectual dilemmas?

The human capital narrative was given force within the context of the employment relationship by a projected double alignment between the interests of labour and capital over mutual investment in labour power and between the strategic, functional and operational levels of the firm. This chapter has demonstrated that in the conditions of financialised capitalism both these alignments have fractured, if not broken down. The problem in the modern capitalist employment relationship is not the existence of divergent interests, but the diminished capacity of management to produce sustainable mutual gains from them.

None of the attempts to fashion an alternative narrative of human capital is satisfactory, but defects will not make it defunct. For academics there will always be enough potential evidence of links between people and profits to explore and related methodological and conceptual problems to solve. And if that is not deemed desirable, academics can take always refuge in analysis *of* HRM. As Boxall *et al.* (2006, p. 3) argue, 'Analytical HRM privileges explanation over prescription. The primary task of analytical HRM is to build theory and gather empirical data in order to account for the way management actually behaves in organising work and managing people across different jobs, workplaces, companies, industries and societies.'

But the reason why the human capital narrative will not disappear is more practical. Unlike academics, practitioners cannot remove themselves to become commentators on their own actions. But they can use the narrative as a commentary to explain and legitimise those actions. As Harley and Hardy (2004) argue, managers can use the progressive language of HRM to establish the legitimacy of their practices, even if the latter bear little resemblance to the former. This is a recurrent feature of modern business. Vicki Smith astutely notes that at the same time that big banks were rationalising and downsizing their operations, 'The very same infrastructure was responsible for introducing managerial measures and methods that were comparatively punishing – all the while couching it in a way consistent with a broader rhetoric about community, individual empowerment, and opportunity' (1999, pp. 1–2).

However, spinning a rhetorical narrative that is increasingly out of touch with real events is a risk. In his exploration of the importance and changing basis of social legitimacy to the work of HR specialists in the USA, Tom Kochan (2006) argues that the quest for senior management approval has gone too far, has ignored the fraying American 'social contract', and calls for a major re-evaluation of the values and professional identities that inform specialist HR roles. But the question remains: can HR managers put some distance between them and their employers?

One of the themes of this book is that changes in the content and context of employment relations has rendered such relations thin and increasingly removed the human. Institutions mediate the relationships between economic imperatives and the human. However desirable Kochan's call, a reason for scepticism is that in environments that produce thin employment relations, there is little to compel the corporate elite to balance their claims against other interests or to provide HR specialists with means and motive to re-align their practices and alliances. In comparison, a parallel plea from Looise and Paauwe (1998, p. 158) that 'Within a Western European socio-economic setting, it is important to do justice to the various stakeholders that represent their claims vis-à-vis the management of human resources' has greater institutional leverage and countervailing power resources to make feasible. Ultimately it may be easier to find the human outside rather than inside the employment relationship.

Note

1. Parts of this chapter draw on Thompson and Harley (2006).

References

Appelbaum, E., Bailey, T., Berg, P. and Kalleberg, A.I. (2000) *Manufacturing Advantage: Why High-Performance Work Systems Pay Off*, Ithaca: Cornell University Press.

Armstrong, P. (1995) 'Accountancy and HRM', in Storey, J. (ed.), *Human Resource Management: A Critical Text*, London: Routledge, pp. 142–166.

Barley, S. and Kunda, G. (2004) *Gurus, Hired Guns, and Warm Bodies: Itinerant Experts in a Knowledge Economy*, Princeton: Princeton University Press.

Barney, G. (1991) 'Firm Resources and Sustained Competitive Advantage', *Journal of Management*, 17:11, 99–120.

Batt, R. and Moynihan, L. (2002) 'The Viability of Alternative Call Centre Production Models', *Human Resource Management Journal*, 12:4, 14–34.

Becker, G. (1964). *Human Capital*, New York, Columbia University Press.

Bennis, W. (1999) 'The Leadership Advantage', in Hesselbain, F. and Johnston, R. (eds), *On Mission and Leadership*, New York: The Drucker Foundation.

Beynon, H., Grimshaw, D., Rubery, J. and Ward, K. (2002) *Managing Employment Change*, Oxford: Oxford University Press.

Biewener, J. (1997) 'Downsizing and the New American Workplace: Rethinking the High Performance Paradigm', *Review of Radical Political Economics*, 29:4, 1–22.

Boxall, P. (1996) 'The Strategic HRM Debate and the Resource-based View of the Firm', *Human Resource Management Journal*, 6:3, 59–75.

Boxall, P. and Purcell, J. (2003) *Strategy and Human Resource Management*, London: Palgrave.

Boxall, P., Purcell, J. and Wright, P. (eds) (2006) 'Human Resource Management: Scope, Analysis, and Significance', *Oxford Handbook of Human Resource Management*, Oxford: Oxford University Press.

Brown, P. and Hesketh, A. (2004) *Playing to Win: Managing Employability in the Knowledge-Based Economy*, Oxford: Oxford University Press.

Brown, P., Green, A., and Lauder, H. (2001) *High Skills: Globalization, Competitiveness, and Skill Formation*, Oxford: Oxford University Press.

Callaghan, G. and Thompson, P. (2002) ' "We Recruit Attitude": The Selection and Shaping of Call Centre Labour', *Journal of Management Studies*, 39:2, 233–254.

Cappelli, P. (2001) 'Assessing the Decline of Internal Labor Markets', in Berg, I. and Kalleberg, A. (eds), *Sourcebook of Labor Markets: Evolving Structures and Processes*, New York: Plenum.

Crouch, C., Finegold, D. and Sako, M. (1999) *Are Skills the Answer? The Political Economy of Skill Creation in Advanced Industrial*, Oxford: Oxford University Press.

Danford, A. (1998) *Japanese Management Techniques and British Workers*, London: Mansell.

Deal, T. and Kennedy, A. (1999) *The New Corporate Cultures: Revitalizing the Workplace after Downsizing, Mergers and Renengineering*, New York: Texere.

Delbridge, R. (1998) *Life on the Line in Contemporary Manufacturing*, Oxford: Oxford University Press.

Doeringer, P.B. and Piore, M.J. (1971) *Internal Labor Markets and Manpower Analysis*, Lexington, MA: D.C. Heath.

Elias, J. and Scarbrough, H. (2004) 'Evaluating Human Capital: An Exporatory Study of Management Practice', *Human Resource Management Journal*, 14:4, 21–40.

Fevre, R. (1992) *The Sociology of Labour Markets*, Hemel Hempstead: Harvester Wheatsheaf.

Flecker, J. and Hofbauer, J. (1998) 'Capitalising on Subjectivity: The "New Model Worker" and the Importance of Being Useful', in Thompson, P. and Warhurst, C. (eds), *Workplaces of the Future*, London: Macmillan.

Fleming, P., Harley, B. and Sewell, G. (2004) 'A Little Knowledge is a Dangerous Thing: Getting Below the Surface of the Growth of "Knowledge Work" in Australia', *Work, Employment and Society*, 18:4, 725–747.

Florida, R. (2002) *The Rise of the Creative Class*, New York: Basic Books.

Godard, J. (2004) 'A Critical Assessment of the High Performance Paradigm', *British Journal of Industrial Relations*, 42:2, 349–378.

Graham, L. (1995) *On the Line at Subaru-Isuzu: The Japanese Model and the American Worker*, Cornell University: ILR Press.

Green, F. (2001) 'It's Been a Hard Day's Night: The Concentration and Intensification of Work in Late Twentieth Century Britain', *British Journal of Industrial Relations*, 39:1, 53–80.

Guest, D. (1987) 'Human Resource Management and Industrial Relations', *Journal of Management Studies*, 8:3, 503–521.

Guest, D. (2002) 'Human Resource Management, Corporate Performance and Employee Well-Being: Building the Worker into HRM', *Journal of Industrial Relations*, 44:3, 335–358.

Harley, B. and Hardy, C. (2004) 'Firing Blanks? An Analysis of Discursive Struggle in HRM', *Journal of Management Studies*, 41:3, 377–400.

Houlihan, M. (2002) 'Tensions and Variations in Call Centre Management Strategies', *Human Resource Management Journal*, 12:4, 67–85.

Huselid, M. (1995) 'The Impact of Human Resource Management Practices on Turnover, Production and Corporate Financial Performance', *Academy of Management Journal*, 38, 635–672.

Kaufman, B.E. (ed.) (2004) 'Toward an Integrative Theory of Human Resource Management', *Theoretical Perspectives on Work and the Employment Relationship*, Cornell: Cornell University Press.

Kochan, T. (2006) 'Social Legitimacy of the Human Resource Management Profession: A U.S. Perspective', in Boxall, P., Purcell, J. and Wright, P. (eds), *Oxford Handbook of Human Resource Management*, Oxford: Oxford University Press.

Kochan, T.A., Katz, H. and McKersie, R. (1986) *The Transformation of American Industrial Relations*, New York: Basic Books.

Konzelmann, S. and Forrant, R. (2003) 'Creative Work in Destructive Markets', in Burchell, B., Deakin, S., Michie, J. and Rubery, J. (eds), *Systems of Production: Markets, Organization and Performance*, London: Routledge, pp. 128–158.

Jacoby, S. (2004) *The Embedded Corporation: Corporate Governance and Employment Relations in Japan and the United States*, Princeton, NJ: Princeton University Press.

Kunda, G. and Ailon-Souday, G. (2005) 'New Designs: Design and Devotion Revisited', in Ackroyd, S., Batt, R., Thompson, P. and Tolbert, P. (eds), *The Oxford Handbook of Work and Organization*, Oxford: Oxford University Press.

Lafer, G. (2004) 'What is Skill? Training for Discipline in the Low-Wage Labour Market', in Warhurst, C., Grugulis, I. and Keep, E. (eds), *The Skills that Matter*, London: Palgrave.

Littler, C.R. and Innes, P. (2003) 'Downsizing and Deknowledging the Firm', *Work, Employment and Society*, 17:1, 73–100.

Looise, J.C. and Paauwe, P. (1998) 'Human Resources Management: Evolving Paradigms and Research Issues from an Integrated Stakeholder Perspective', in Evers, G.H.M., van Hees, G.B. and Schippers, J.J. (eds), *Work and Organisation Research in the Netherlands*, Dordrecht: Kluwer Academic Publishers, pp. 139–169.

Mounier, A. (2001) *The Three Logics of Skill in French Literature*, Sydney: NSW Board of Vocational Education and Training.

Nolan, P. (2001) 'Shaping Things to Come', *People Management*, 27 December, 30–31.

Nonaka, I. and Takeuchi, H. (1995) *The Knowledge-Creating Company*, Oxford: Oxford University Press.

O'Reilly, C.A. and Pfeffer, J. (2000) *Hidden Value: How Great Companies Achieve Extraordinary Results with Ordinary People*, Harvard: Harvard Business School Press.

OECD (2001) *Devolution and Globalisation*, Paris: OECD.

Paauwe, J. and Boselie, P. (2006) 'Human Resource Management and Societal Embeddedness', in Boxall P., Purcell, J. and Wright, P. (eds), *Oxford Handbook of Human Resource Management*, Oxford: Oxford University Press.

Parker, M. and Slaughter, J. (1995) 'Unions and Management by Stress', in Babson, S. (ed.), *Lean Work: Empowerment and Exploitation in the Global Auto Industry*, Detroit: Wayne Sate University Press, pp. 41–54.

Pfeffer, J. (1994) *Competitive Advantage Through People*, Boston: Harvard Business School Press.

Pfeffer, J. (1998) *The Human Equation: Building Profits by Putting People First*, Boston: Harvard Business School Press.

Pink, D. (2001) *Free Agent Nation*, New York: Warner Business.

Ramsay, H., Harley, B. and Scholarios, D. (2000) 'Employees and High Performance Work Systems: Testing Inside the Black Box', *British Journal of Industrial Relations*, 38:4, 501–532.

Reich, R. (1993) *The Work of Nations*, London: Simon & Schuster.

Rinehart, J., Huxley, C. and Robertson, D. (1997) *Just Another Car Factory? Lean Production and its Discontents*, New York: ILR-Cornell University Press.

Robinson, S. and Rousseau, D. (1994). Violating the Psychological Contract: Not the Exception but the Norm, *Journal of Organizational Behaviour*, 16, 289–298.

Royal, C. and O'Donnell, L. (2003) 'The Human Capital Classification Process Evaluating Companies Using a Qualitative Lens', Working Paper, School of Organisation and Management, University of New South Wales.

Royal, C. and O'Donnell, L. (2005) 'Embedding Human Capital Analysis in the Investment Process: A Human Resources Challenge', *Asia Pacific Journal of Human Resources*, 43:1, 117–136.

Rubery, J., Earnshaw, J., Marchington, M., Cooke, F.L. and Vincent, S. (2005) 'Changing Organisational Forms and the Employment Relationship', in Salaman, G., Storey, J. and Billsberry, J. (eds), *Strategic Human Resource Management: Theory and Practice*, London: Sage.

Sandberg, A. (ed.) (1995) *Enriching Production*, Aldershot: Avebury.

Smith, V. (1999) Essay on Russell Jacoby's *Postmodern Manors: Welfare Capitalism at the End of the Century*, Accessed online at http://aom.pace.edu.lcms/Smith.httn 1–4.

Stiles, P. and Kulvisaechana, S. (2003) 'Human Capital and Performance: A Literature Review', Background Paper for UK Government Task Force on High Commitment Management, University of Cambridge. Accessed online at http://accountingforpeople.govuk/task.htm.

Storey, J. (1985) 'The Means of Management Control', *Sociology*, 19:2, 193–211.

Storey, J. (1995) *Developments in the Management of Human Resources*, Oxford: Blackwell.

Thomas, R.J. (1988) 'What is Human Resource Management?' *Work, Employment and Society*, 2:3, 392–402.

Thompson, P. (2003) 'Disconnected Capitalism: Or Why Employers Can't Keep Their Side of the Bargain', *Work, Employment and Society*, 17:2, 359–378.

Thompson, P. (2004) *The Knowledge Economy Myth*, Glasgow: Big Thinking.

Thompson, P. and Harley, B. (2006) 'HRM and the Worker: Labour Process Perspectives', in Boxall, P., Purcell, J. and Wright, P. (eds), *Oxford Handbook of Human Resource Management*, Oxford: Oxford University Press.

Thompson, P. and Newsome, K. (2004) 'Labour Process Theory, Work and the Employment Relation' in Kaufman, B.E. (ed.), *Theoretical Perspectives on Work and the Employment Relationship*, Cornell: Cornell University Press.

Thompson, P., Warhurst, C. and Callaghan, G. (2000). 'Human Capital or Capitalising on Humanity? Knowledge, Skills and Competencies in Interactive Service Work', in Prichard, C., Hull, R., Chumer, M. and Willmott, H. (eds), *Managing Knowledge*, London: Palgrave.

Walton, R.E. (1985) 'Towards a Strategy of Eliciting Employee Commitment Based on Policies of Mutuality', in Walton, R.E. and Lawrence, P.R. (eds), *Human Resource Management, Trends and Challenges*, Boston: Harvard University School Press.

Warhurst, C. and Nickson, D. (2001) *Looking Good and Sounding Right*, London: Industrial Society.

Warhurst, C., Grugulis, I. and Keep, E. (eds) (2004) *The Skills that Matter*, London: Palgrave.

World Bank (2002) *Building Knowledge Economies: Opportunities and Challenges for EU Accession Countries*, Paris: World Bank.

Wright, P.M., Dunford, B.B. and Snell, S.A. (2005) 'Human Resources and the Resource-Based View of the firm', in Salaman, G., Storey, J. and Billsberry, J. (eds), *Strategic Human Resource Management: Theory and Practice* (2nd edition), London: Sage.

part II

Searching for the human in HR practice

6

HRM and the menu society: the fetishisation of individual choice at work

Marek Korczynski

This chapter analyses the way in which many Human Resource Management (HRM) practices present a menu of choices to individual employees in such a way as to enchant employees through the very process of individual choice. This fetishisation of individual choice is seen as pernicious for it serves to obscure the operation of power within the workplace. The chapter argues that we must ask key critical questions about HRM menus in the workplace. The menu is an artefact that draws attention to itself as offering choice, but critical analysis needs also to consider what is not on the menu. We also need to consider who constructs the menu, and to consider how far, in fact, the menu constructs employees as *individuals*.

This introductory section outlines the key theoretical argument concerning the operation of the menu in society more widely. The following section outlines a number of areas where we can see the menu in operation within mainstream HRM practice. The conclusion examines in more detail the key critical questions thrown up by the concept of the operation of the menu within HRM.

It is has been widely observed that at the heart of the HRM project is a move towards individualisation within employment (Guest, 1990; Legge, 1995). While there has been a tendency to see this move to individualisation as linked to the marketisation (Cappelli, 1999) of the employment relationship, what I focus on in this chapter is the way in which individualisation occurs in the context of an enchanting presentation of a menu of choices to individuals. Important here are the concepts of the *enchanting myth of individual sovereignty* and the concept of *the operation of the menu in society*. Each is explicated in turn.

It is useful to characterise people's sense of their individual autonomy as enchanting myths of individual sovereignty. Such visions of the autonomous individual enchant in the sense that George Ritzer uses in *Enchanting a Disenchanted World* (1999). The process of enchantment involves the creation of pleasurable dreams and fantasies around an array of time, space, self-image, social relations, and material products. Ritzer argues, contra Weber, that the development of rationalisation within capitalism has not meant the death of enchantment – seen by Weber mainly in terms of the decline of religion. Ritzer points out that enchantment lives on as a key social process in the way in which firms systematically seek to enchant consumers. Processes of enchantment are central to contemporary 'entertainment' (Wolf, 1999), or 'Disneyized' societies (Bryman, 2003). The concept of enchantment is a useful one for it implies active agency on the part of the enchanted. A story teller cannot enchant a passive audience. People may be active agents in the creation of enchanting myths of individual sovereignty. The word 'myth' is used not only in the sense that the rhetoric of sovereignty clashes often with reality but also in a way that calls on Levi-Strauss's thesis that 'the purpose of myth is to provide a . . . model capable of overcoming a contradiction' (1963, p. 229).

Korczynski and Ott (2006) have argued that a key way in which enchanting myths of individual sovereignty are propagated is through the operation of the menu in society. The restaurant menu serves as the basis for the metaphor. The restaurant menu is created to enchant and appeal to the customer, and it does this not only substantively through the descriptions of the available food, but also formally through the placing of the customer as the autonomous figure who chooses between available alternatives. This ritualised emphasis on autonomous choice can make the act of choosing as delicious as the actual food consumed. The customer here consumes the enchanting myth of sovereignty. For management, the genius of the menu is that it offers to the customer the image of sovereignty through autonomous choice, whilst at the same time constraining that choice. A menu not only offers choices but it necessarily constrains options. In this way it allows rationalised production of food to go on unconsidered in the kitchen (see Gabriel, 1988). In other words it allows often-rationalised structures of power to operate alongside the myths of sovereignty within the 'free' sphere of consumption. It plays a key role in the creation of what Wood (1995, p. 99) has called the 'illusion of variety and choice' in restaurants that exists alongside the largely standardised meals that are served. What the menu leaves unsaid is that what is not on this menu is not available. But this message is present only by its absence, and the menu thus offers the customer the comfortable opportunity to experience the pleasure of choice.

The menu may also be attractive to a person not only because it places them as the autonomous chooser between alternatives but also because it operates as a form of filter which promises the opportunity to exercise real and meaningful choice. The menu enables and constrains, and it can enable by constraining. It lends shape and pattern to the plethora of alternatives that are available in many social spheres in contemporary societies. In many social spheres people are confronted with increasingly fantastic amounts of information, more information than it is possible for an individual to process. In this situation meaningful choice is impossible. As Warde (1994, p. 892) argues, 'if people were making choices every time they confronted a situation of consumption, social life would become insupportable'. A filtering mechanism is needed to process the information to give the opportunity of meaningful choice. In many social spheres the menu operates exactly as this filtering mechanism.

Crucially, Korczynski and Ott (2006) argue, the operation of the menu both as mode of enchantment and as apparently neutral information filter can facilitate the operation of power, particularly through the structuring of choice, at the same time as propagating myths of sovereignty to individuals. A form of menu is presented, and with the same implications, not only in restaurants and cafes but also in a wide range of social settings. Korczynski and Ott (2006) explicate how the menu operates within consumption, production and citizenship. Here I focus on the way in which the menu often operates at the heart of a number of key HRM practices.

The menu and HRM practices

This section draws out how many HRM practices operate with the menu at their centre:

- the 'cafeteria system' of training provision and benefit options;
- the list of choices available to individuals within the process of performance appraisals and in coaching dialogues;
- the range of options given to people in stress management and counselling situations;
- the range of personality types available to people within Belbin teamwork training courses;
- the range of options regarding the aims of quality circles and other micro-level forms of participation.

The 'cafeteria system' of training provision and benefit options

In the presentation of what is called a 'cafeteria system' of training and benefits options the central role of the menu in HRM practices rises to the surface. In the cafeteria system the individual worker is presented with a menu of choices to put together an individual benefits/training package. The term 'cafeteria system' recalls the restaurant root of the menu metaphor. There is no accident in the use of the term for it recalls the enchantment offered by a menu of choices to customers at a café or restaurant. The term emphasises the process of choice that is available to individuals. By prioritising the enchanting process of choice it serves to marginalise key issues regarding the actual substantive value and meaning of the choices offered.

Examining the pensions mis-selling scandals that occurred in the UK in the 1990s we can see something of this at work. In millions of cases, individuals were sold private, individual, pension schemes having been persuaded of their value in relation to collectively oriented employer, or occupation-based pension schemes. The deregulation of the financial services industry in the 1980s allowed, for the first time, the opportunity to offer a menu of choices to individuals regarding pension schemes. Financial service firms' sales staff, fuelled by commission payment systems, were quick to enchant individuals with the new menu of choice. Mis-selling here involved both the enchantment of individualised choice through the menu and the false presentation of the menu as a neutral information filter (when in fact it was often a heavily biased menu, created to maximise commission earnings, rather than to maximise the individual's welfare). The outcome for millions was that although they experienced the enchantment of choice, their financial interests were often seriously compromised.

Although there are no commission-driven sales staff at work in organisations offering a cafeteria system of training and benefits options, the dangers of the processes of enchantment through choice, and the presentation of the choices as a mode of neutral information-filtering, although less accentuated, are still present. The individual in a UK firm offering a menu of training options may feel the enchantment of choice but it is very unlikely that they will experience the same quality of training that is offered in more collectively oriented training systems such as exist in Norway and Austria. The cafeteria system, indeed its very name, promotes the fetishisation of individual choice.

The list of choices available to individuals within the process of performance appraisals and in coaching dialogues

The performance appraisal is at the sharp end of the contradictory HRM project. It is where the management must exert control over a worker in such a way as to not only promote a better work ethic, but also a better work ethic which is self-authored by the worker. This is the essence of the 'commitment' to which business writers such as Peters and Waterman (1982) refer. Note already that it is 'worker' in the singular that is being used. HRM has tended to replace previous more collective-based reward systems with individual-centred systems. The key way in which management attempts to get the individual worker to author their own work ethic is through the menu and its ritualised presentation. The performance appraisal is structured as a (pseudo) dialogue in which the manager guides the worker through a series of stages in each of which the worker is presented with a menu of options: 'How do you rate your performance over the last six months against the targets that were agreed at your last appraisal meeting . . . Exceeded targets; Met targets; Fell below targets?' 'If you fell below targets, was this because: (a) your focus was not as it should have been; (b) your skills and knowledge need to be developed; (c) the support systems were not in place?' There is a constant emphasis on the range of choices that face the individual worker. In Zeus and Skeffington's (2002, p. 150) 'how to' book on coaching they devote a whole section to the importance of developing an *awareness of choices* in staff who are to be coached (or appraised). Even when performance of the individual is below management standards, the authors still stress that a menu of choices must be presented to individuals. Coaches are advised to 'emphasise that it is the coachee's [*sic*] choice to change his or her performance' (emphasis added) (p. 229).

Within an overall exertion of hierarchical power, the worker is placed in a position of choice by the mediation of the menu of options. In this way, management hopes that the worker can emerge from the performance appraisal with the commitment to do 10 per cent better in the next period. If it is to be true commitment it must be self-authored and the process of its generation must involve the development of the enchanting myth of individual sovereignty. Of course, the menu of choices offered by management are rarely neutral. In a moment of rare candour, Zeus and Skeffington's (2002, p. 168) prescriptive text on coaching notes that

> According to Socrates, when we ask a question we already have half the answer. Asking the right questions at the appropriate time is a core dialoguing skill of a

successful coach. Our questions guide the coachee in a particular direction – in that sense our questions are never neutral. Questioning is a tool whereby we direct the coaching dialogue.

The point is clear: the appearance of choice within dialogue must be there but, at the same time, managers should aim to structure that choice to meet their interests.

The range of options given to people in stress management and counselling situations

Another of the contradictions of the HRM project is that while its rhetoric suggests the existence of a contented workforce it is also the case that HRM implicitly acknowledges this as a fabrication through the proliferation of stress management courses and counselling sessions in organisations. Within these stress management courses the primary focus is upon the individual worker (Newton *et al.*, 1995). The aim is to make the individual worker 'stress fit', able to cope with the pressures of their working lives. Central to the operation of these stress management approaches is the presentation to the individual worker of a menu of options which they can adopt in their own stress management. Diamond and Diamond (2006, p. 30), in their 'how to' book on motivating staff, stress that management should seek to create situations of choice for staff even in stressful situations. For instance they recommend that management use the following phrases when staff are experiencing stress and abuse:

- You cannot control everything that happens. You can control how things affect you.
- You cannot control how customers speak to you, but you can keep your stress level down by controlling your reaction.

For an example of the sort of menu of options that are presented to individuals we can turn to Mann (1999). This managerialist text prescribes that those who are suffering from stress through the delivery of emotional labour (Hochschild, 1983) in their jobs should choose from a menu of stress management techniques. Individuals are encouraged to choose from a menu of strategies to cope with the stressful aspects of emotional labour:

- Calming strategies – such as deep relaxation techniques and taking a few deep breaths 'when faced with the prospect of having to hide boredom or anger from a customer' (Mann, 1999, p. 136).

- Displacement techniques – here anger is expressed but deflected away from the person or situation that provoked the negative reaction.
- Visualisation techniques – here the worker is encouraged to visualise going through a stressful event, with the change that in the visualisation scenario, 'you say exactly what you feel . . . Be as forceful, rude, abusive as you like' (p. 143).
- Cognitive restructuring techniques – here the worker is asked to rethink their approach to emotional labour, to approach their own work as an act and to take pleasure in skilful acting, and re-imagine stressful incidents through self-talk.

Here, as in many other stress management approaches, the individual worker is placed as the sovereign individual, owner of their own emotions, through the process of choice among the menu of alternatives. At the same time as the worker is encouraged to experience a sense of their own sovereignty, power structures are enacted. The whole approach depoliticises the issue of stress. By focusing on the individual and making the individual stress fit, it deflects from an examination of the organisational causes of stress – in the case of emotional labour delivery, for instance, management's insistence that workers put up with a high level of customer abuse. Further, it depoliticises by focusing on the individual and marginalises the collective workforce, and its institutions such as trade unions, who would be more likely to challenge the organisational, rather than the individual, causes. Consider, for instance, call centres in which, research shows, many staff experience high levels of stress (Korczynski, 2002; Taylor *et al.*, 2003). Trade unions in call centres can act to lower stress levels by lowering the target levels of calls taken and sales made that management may seek to unilaterally impose; whereas the presentation of a menu of choices to individuals seeks to deal with stress by offering different modes of individual accommodation to the (given) stressful situation.

The range of personality types available to people within Belbin teamwork training courses

One of the most common forms of training courses run in organisations involves the development of teamwork through the Belbin (1981) principles. The process involves individuals filling in a self-reporting questionnaire in which the questions are designed to assess the key personality characteristics of individuals. The questionnaires are then analysed and individuals are placed into one of a number of character types. Each character type is set up to match on to a particular role within what is seen as an ideal division of labour within a team. So the character types range from 'chairman [sic]' who is 'calm, self-confident and controlled', to a 'company worker' who is 'conservative, dutiful and predictable', to a 'resource investigator' who is 'extrovert, enthusiastic, communicative and explores opportunities and develops contacts' (p. 74). Overall, the process can be seen to effectively legitimise power structures by implicitly legitimising the idea that a strict division of labour should exist within teams. The process involves the reproduction of power structures and it also involves the promotion of enchanting myths of individual sovereignty. In the Belbin process people make themselves up as particular types of individuals and in this process the menu is central. People are not simply labelled as character types by an outside observer; rather they make themselves up as that character type freely through the process of choice from the menu of options in the questionnaire. They assign themselves points with regard to how a menu of statements applies to themselves. For instance, in being questioned about their involvement with other people in a project an individual can agree to the statement 'I have an aptitude for influencing people without pressurising them' or 'my general vigilance prevents careless mistakes and omissions being made' (p. 148). Further, in the Belbin training process, the menu does not just operate within the questionnaire but also, implicitly, within the range of possible character types that one can be. Those who make themselves up to be a 'company worker' can look across the menu of character types and think to themselves that in fact they would like to be a 'chairman' sort of character. They will easily find further training courses or self-help books to guide them in their journey of becoming. Individuals come to discipline themselves, and allow power structures to be reproduced, through the mediating role of the menu.

The range of options within micro-level forms of participation

The following interchange between managers at a call centre was noted in research I and my colleagues conducted in the USA (see Frenkel *et al.*, 1999). It concerns the identification of a problem and the aim to address it in a way that involves the call centre workers' participation:

> 1st Manager: We need to address it [the problem] as a group, with staff representation. We need to create a quick focus group on this.
> 2nd Manager: We as managers need to define a correct policy first before the focus group otherwise the staff preference may not meet our needs. I want to be the driver. I don't want staff to be the driver. I want their feedback.

1st Manager: This is where our morale hurts. If we dictate again, there's a problem.

2nd Manager: There are ways to win them over without dictating. Sometimes management need to define standards, set goals.

1st Manager: Yes, then go to them and ask them about options on how to reach that goal.

What we see here is tension within management regarding the need to involve workers in decision-making – to avoid the resentment that comes from coercion – and the danger that workers may make decisions that are not in keeping with management wishes. The ultimate proposed solution to this problem involves the use of the menu. The managers decide that the outcomes need to be pre-decided by management but that it can be dressed up as involving participation by management asking worker feedback regarding a menu of options regarding different processes of achieving that goal.

This is a revealing example for it shows how the menu can potentially be used as a way of offering participation and choice while at the same time systematically and significantly constraining that choice. At another site in the research project a manager spoke of the importance of 'guided democracy' in team meetings, whereby he would ensure that the 'team gets what's good for them' by effectively pre-deciding an objective and involving the team in choosing from a menu of options on how to achieve that goal. The menu is used by management within micro-forms of participation in an attempt to solve the fundamental contradictions in managing the labour process, whereby management must seek both worker compliance and worker cooperation (Hyman, 1987).

Menus and questions

This concluding section argues that the menu in the society/HRM metaphor throws up questions that promote a critical sociological investigation into the nature of the workplace. The three key questions that its use highlights are expounded in turn.

What is not on the menu?

The menu itself, aided by the ritualised presentation that often accompanies it, calls attention to itself, to the substantive choices that it offers to the person, whether as a consumer, a worker, or a citizen. The idea of the menu in society, however, also calls our attention to what is not on the menu. It calls attention to absences in choices offered and to what these absences signify. It poses the questions whether there are patterns in what is absent in menus, and whether these patterns directly or indirectly match the interests of powerful segments of the social sphere. So, for instance, in the example of menu in Belbin teamwork training, it can be noted that what is not on the menu is the person who would like to be fully involved at all stages of the production process, from conception to design to implementation. An argument then can be constructed that this patterned absence fits the sort of specialism in the division of labour advocated by Frederick Taylor. The question of what is not on the menu speaks directly to what Lukes (1974) terms the 'third dimension' in the operation of power, involving a 'consideration of the many ways in which potential issues are kept out of politics' (p. 24). It also speaks directly to the critical media studies analysis of 'agenda-setting'. It may be that on investigation the absences in menus are not patterned in ways that meet the interests of powerful segments in organisations. The point is not to assume a certain answer to the question. The point is the importance of asking the question in the first place.

Who writes the menu?

The menu draws attention to the substance of the choices that it offers and perhaps to itself as an elegant artefact. The idea of the menu in society forces us to look beyond this to also ask who has written the menu. As sociologists it is not enough for us to point out how patterned absences on menus may suit the interests of powerful groups in organisations, it is also beholden on us to examine the social processes by which these absences are written into the menu. To do otherwise is to lapse into the laziness of functionalist analysis. In examining the authorship of menu, it may be that we immediately see the operation of a technocratic elite of experts who seek to maintain a monopoly on the right to author menus in particular social spheres. For instance, Bauman (1988, p. 67) intimates the importance of technical experts and the perpetuation of their power systems in the provision of choice to consumers:

> individuals depend on the market and the experts for being individuals – that is being able to make free choices . . . Individual freedom becomes an important link in the process of reproduction of the power structure.

It may also be that we see the clash of competing authors, perhaps the technical expert, the chef, fighting with the instrument of capitalist rationality, the restaurant manager, over what should be on and not be on the menu. Again the point is not to assume an answer to the question, but rather to stress that the menu metaphor directs us towards this crucial question. If menus are increasingly necessary as a form of information filter in making proper informed decisions, the key issue becomes the governance of the menu-writing process. A key challenge for the development of a more humane workplace becomes the creation of a democratic form of governance here. There may be much to be learned from revisiting the debates in the 1970s regarding technocracy.

How does the menu create us as individuals?

The menu through its form, and its often-ritualised presentation, promotes an enchanting myth of individual sovereignty. Critical investigation guided by the idea of the menu in society can take this as a starting point and probe how far and in what ways this form of enchantment is actually enacted by people. The promotion of enchantment should not be read as equivalent to its enactment. Myths of individual sovereignty promoted by a menu are likely to be thin and fragile. To return to a point made in the introduction, one of the key qualities of enchantment is that it must involve an active role on the part of the enchanted. Critical investigation can focus upon understanding both the active embracing of this enchantment, and the active or passive resistance to it. Critical investigation can look at the cracks of disillusionment where enchantment fades. For instance, disillusionment is likely to occur where the absences of the menu rise into clear view. Think of the restaurant customer who orders a meal from a menu only to be told that the dishes are no longer available. Disappointment at the unavailability of a specific dish may elide into disillusionment as the artifice of the menu, its functioning as that which offers and constrains choice, comes into view.

Critical social theory needs to articulate the gaps between the current workplace and a humane workplace. The concept of the menu within HRM practices contributes here by bringing out how the fetishisation of individual choice can often serve to obscure the operation of power. A humane workplace would be one where the operation of power is not obscured but is left open for critical and democratic scrutiny. Questions such as what is not on the menu and who writes the menu should not be left to lie dormant in the corner while the menu of choice dazzles us all. Rather they should be first-order questions to consider in the creation of a more humane workplace.

References

Bauman, Z. (1988) 'Is there a postmodern sociology?' *Theory, Culture and Society*, 5: 217–37.

Belbin, R. (1981) *Management Teams*, Oxford: Butterworth-Heinemann.

Bryman, A. (2003) *The Disneyization of Society*, London: Routledge.

Cappelli, P. (1999) *The New Deal at Work*, Cambridge, MA: Harvard University Press.

Diamond, H. and Diamond, L. (2006) *Perfect Phrases for Motivating and Rewarding Employees*, New York: McGraw-Hill.

Frenkel, S., Korczynski, M., Shire, K. and Tam, M. (1999) *On the Front Line*, New York: Cornell University Press.

Gabriel, Y. (1988) *Working Lives in Catering*, London: Routledge.

Guest, D. (1990) 'Human resource management and the American dream', *Journal of Management Studies*, 27:4, 378–97.

Hochschild, A. (1983) *The Managed Heart*, Berkeley: University of California Press.

Hyman, R. (1987) 'Strategy or structure? Capital, labour and control', *Work, Employment and Society*, 1:1, 25–55.

Korczynski, M. (2002) *Human Resource Management in Service Work*, Basingstoke: Palgrave.

Korczynski, M. and Ott, U. (2007) 'The menu in society: Mediating structures of power and enchanting myths of individual sovereignty', *Sociology* 40: 911–928.

Legge, K. (1995) *Human Resource Management*, Basingstoke: Macmillan.

Levi-Strauss, C. (1963) 'The structural study of myth' in *Structural Anthropology*, New York: Basic Books.

Lukes, S. (1974) *Power*, Basingstoke: Macmillan.

Mann, S. (1999) *Hiding What We Feel, Faking What We Don't*, Boston: Element.

Newton, T., Handy, J. and Fineman, S. (1995) *'Managing' Stress: Emotion and Power at Work*, London: Sage.

Peters, T. and Waterman, R. (1982) *In Search of Excellence*, New York: Harper and Row.

Ritzer, G. (1999) *Enchanting a Disenchanted World*, California: Pine Forge Press.

Taylor, S., Baldry, C., Bain, P. and Ellis, V. (2003) 'A unique working environment: Health, sickness and absence management in UK call centres', *Work, Employment and Society*, 17:3, 435–58.

Warde, A. (1994) 'Consumption, identity-formation and uncertainty', *Sociology*, 28:4, 877–98.

Wolf, M. (1999) *The Entertainment Economy*, New York: Times Books.

Wood, R. (1995) *The Sociology of the Meal*, Edinburgh: Edinburgh University Press.

Zeus, P. and Skeffington, S. (2002) *The Coaching at Work Toolkit*, Sydney: McGraw-Hill.

7

Putting the missing H into HRM: the case of the flexible organisation

Karen Legge

Introduction

Andrew Sayer (2000) has argued that we need to consider the 'moral economy', that is what moral norms concerning the good and the just should be embodied in and guide choices and action in organisations. Instead of being preoccupied with the instrumental rationality of performativity and efficiency (Cooper and Burrell, 1988), we should focus on the substantive rationality of what an organisation should be seeking as its ultimate aim or purpose in its relationships with its stakeholders and society as a whole. If organisational life is the dominant, indeed 'carceral' way of living in radical modernity (Burrell, 1988; Giddens, 1990), what should constitute a 'good' organisational life? What values and beliefs about the nature of our humanity should inform the organising process?

In this chapter I wish to address this issue in relation to the growth of flexible organisation or, more properly, the flexible organising that is seen to be a characteristic of post-Fordism (see, e.g., Procter, 2005). I will first address the question of what constitutes the human, particularly with reference to human resource management (HRM). I will then consider the nature of flexible organisation and the reasons for its emergence. The discussion will then focus on the paradoxes and contradictions embodied in various issues associated with flexible organisation, such as commitment and insecurity, empowerment and control, producer and consumer relationships and identities and work–life balance. Finally, I will consider the extent to which it is possible to 'put the human back into human resource management' in a capitalist society.

What do we mean by human?

This is a difficult question to address in a postmodern age when notions of essentialism are under attack, where identity (paradoxically) is seen as produced through acts of consumption and where relativism prevails. Nevertheless, pre-modern and modern ethical theory is helpful in initiating a discussion.

Most ethical theorists, whether deontologists (who emphasise the rules and principles governing action) or teleologists (who evaluate all actions in terms of whether they achieve a desired end state or purpose) prioritise reason as the defining characteristic of humanity and therefore as the basis on which we should address questions about the 'good' and the 'right' (fair distribution of the good). Thus Aristotle, in identifying the ultimate end of human action as happiness or 'flourishing', argues that it is best achieved through acting in accordance with reason and following the 'Golden Mean' of fitting behaviour based on traditional virtues – the 'rationality of emotions' as Normann (1998, p. 27) puts it. For Kant a person's moral consciousness and, hence, moral law is based on pure reason. For ethicists as different as contractarians (e.g., Rawls) and utilitarians (Bentham, Mill) the human ability to make rational calculations is central to the ethical systems they propose.

What at first sight appears a contrasting approach is that of Hume (1985/1740) who identifies 'sympathy' or 'fellow-feeling' as characteristic of humanity (indeed he uses sympathy and humanity interchangeably) (Normann, 1998, p. 54). By this he means the capacity to be moved or affected by the happiness or suffering of others. However, this is rather different from the notion of morality as individual, non-universalisable, non-reversible, unconditional 'being for the Other' as advocated by Levinas (1987) and as developed by Bauman (1993). Rather, it rests on the assumption that the reason one person might give for a judgement or action can be understood by another person, that they may see the reason as permissible, that a common point of view may be developed. Someone's suffering cannot be directly experienced, but by empathising and internalising the pain, we can be motivated to act to alleviate it. 'What we can do is to take up the reasons of others and make them our own' (Blackburn, 2001, p. 132). Both Bauman and Hume, however, would be at one in agreeing that sympathy tends to decline with physical and psychological distance.

What do we mean by human in HRM?

HRM itself is riven by the contradiction that it has to secure both the control and consent of employees or, to put it in Marxist terms, to assist in the realisation of surplus value through simultaneously enacting and obscuring the commodity status of labour (Braverman, 1974; Burawoy, 1979; Hyman, 1987). 'Consent' is required for three reasons. First, because labour is notionally free, people can sell their labour capacity to another employer. Secondly, because an employment contract is indeterminate and cannot remove employee discretion (Baldamus, 1961), it is necessary to harness that discretion in the interests of the employer (nowadays termed 'generating commitment'). Thirdly, because people may engage in resistance if they object to the implications of instrumental rationality/extracting their surplus value at the point of production for their terms and conditions of employment (Ackroyd and Thompson, 1999). It seems self-evident that in the process of securing consent it is likely to be more effective to recognise people's humanity rather than treat them as the commodities that early control processes, such as scientific management, implied.

A 'reasonable' person might suggest that in deciding what might constitute the human face of HRM two issues need addressing:

1. What is the nature of a worthwhile and fulfilling life?
2. How should people relate to each other? (Normann, 1998, pp. 215–16).

The answers I might give are as follows. A worthwhile and fulfilling life at work should entail opportunities for need satisfaction and personal development (Maslow, 1943) that might be expressed in terms of Hackman and Oldham's (1976) classic requisite task attributes (optimising skill variety, task identity, task significance, autonomy and feedback). It should also build on the Aristotelian idea (very much taken up by MacIntyre [1981] and Sennett [1998]) that a person should be able to develop an integrated narrative of their life, rendering their life meaningful to themselves and to their community, including the work community, as a whole. How well this can be achieved will partly depend on how people relate to each other. All the ethical theories have something useful to say on this issue.

First, Kant (1949/1788) identified the characteristics of reason as consistency, universality and a priori derivation. From this we have his fundamental moral law, the 'Categorical Imperative' ('categorical' because it is absolutely binding and 'imperative' because it gives you instructions of how to act). For an action to be moral it must (a) be amenable to be made consistently universal (b) respect rational beings as ends in themselves and never *solely* as means to the ends of others (c) stem from and respect the autonomy of rational beings. To treat someone as an end is to offer them a rational argument for acting in a particular way and, assuming their rationality, leave it to them to evaluate the argument and freely decide on a course of action. To treat someone as a means is to seek to make a person do something to further one's own purpose (which may be against their best interests) by exerting manipulative influence or coercion. The emphasis here is that in dealing with other people we respect their autonomy, treat them equally and generally obey the maxim of 'do as you would be done by'.

Second, the utilitarianism's belief in 'the greatest happiness to the greatest number' (however difficult to operationalise, the problem of lack of knowledge of consequences, the issue of unjust consequences) at least alerts us to the desirability of the objective that organisations should seek to optimise the social welfare of the many (including employees and customers), not just that of the few (top management and shareholders).

Third, as anticipated in the utilitarians' position, we have the issue of the fair distribution of the good. This has been addressed at all levels of analysis. Thus, at the individual level, we might use the ideas contained in Adam's equity theory of satisfaction (1963) and at group and organisational level those of distributive and procedural justice (Folger and Cropanzano, 1998) – essential in designing a just industrial relations system. At organisational and societal level two ethical approaches can inform HRM: Rawls' (1971) 'egalitarian theory of justice' and stakeholder analysis (Freeman, 1984).

Briefly, Rawls' approach is very much Kantian in that he attempts to derive principles of distributive justice that should be acceptable to all rational people and, hence, universal. Suppose we assume a 'veil of ignorance' where we know only that we are human but not our social, gender, ethnic or other characteristics. What, rationally, could we agree as a basis of fair treatment? Rawls' answer is the formulation of two principles of justice: (a) each person should have an equal right to the most extensive basic liberty compatible with like liberty for others; (b) social and economic inequalities should only exist where they are reasonably expected to be to everyone's advantage and attached to positions open to all. Imagine the implications of

Rawls' proposals for work and organisational design, for training and career development and diversity policies!

Similarly, popular versions of stakeholder theory assert that organisations should not just be answerable to shareholders, as Friedman (1970) would maintain, but to all groups that have a 'stake', who may potentially benefit from or be harmed by the organisations' actions – employees, customers, suppliers, local communities. The stakes of each group are reciprocal, since each can affect the others in terms of costs and benefits as well as rights and duties. From this principle of reciprocity two rules have been derived (a) that the organisation should be managed for the benefit of all its stakeholders, that their reciprocal rights should be protected and that they must participate in decisions that affect their interests; and (b) that management must act in the interests of stakeholders as their agent and in the long-term interests of the organisation to ensure its survival and hence those of each stakeholder group. While useful as heuristics, both Rawls' and stakeholder models may be criticised as utopian – containing unresolved potential contradictions (e.g., between the short and long term) and ignoring issues of power.

So, on the basis of this short review, what might be a humanistic approach to managing human resources in flexible organisations? First, there should be 'good' jobs based on Hackman and Oldham's (1976) requisite task attributes, combined with developmental opportunities for self-actualisation and a collegial organisational climate. This would roughly satisfy Kantian, Humean and Aristotelian principles. Second, 'good' employment conditions might be defined as a 'fair' relationship between employee inputs (skill, effort, time) and material outcomes in relation to others (including other employees in the same or comparable organisations and other stakeholders). This should be reached by negotiation and agreement, with the organisation additionally committed to a duty of care towards the employee. This would comply with Adam's equity theory of satisfaction, and stakeholder theory and would not be incompatible with Rawl's theory of justice. Randy Hodson's (2001, p. 264) judgement about what constitutes 'dignity at work' outlines a humanistic approach to HRM. For him, *human* resource management involves the creation and enforcement of norms which provide both protection from mismanagement and abuse and the creation of bilateral structures of participation that provide opportunities for employees to realise their human potential through creative, meaningful and productive work. Respect for individual autonomy and social reciprocity is the bedrock of such an approach and the antithesis of treating people ('labour'!) as a commodity.

The nature and causes of flexible organisation

In order to assess whether flexible organisation might be a fertile ground for developing humanistic work and employment policies, it is necessary to identify both the nature of flexible organisation and the reasons for its emergence.

Flexible organisation is usually characterised in oppositional terms to Fordism. Fordism is characterised as involving manufacturing, machine bureaucracy (later, the M form), vertical integration, hierarchical job structures with high levels of specialisation and fragmentation, male blue-collar workers/female carer division of labour, standard full-time employment contracts and often high levels of union density. In contrast, flexible organisation (and post-Fordist regimes generally) is characterised by the service sector, networked organisational relationships, flatter hierarchies, teamworking and empowerment, dual earner/dual carer work model, non-standard contracts and low levels of unionisation (Rubery, 2005). Furthermore, flexible organisation may be seen at two levels: intra-organisational/organisational flexibility (e.g., flexible firm model, business process re-engineering, 'lean' organisation) and inter-organisational flexibility (e.g., networked forms, virtual organisation). A brief word about both these forms of flexibility may be useful as background to subsequent arguments. (A more detailed overview may be found in Procter, 2005.)

Considering intra-organisational/organisational flexibility first, an early model (more prescriptive than empirically descriptive at the time of its inception) was Atkinson's (1984) famous 'flexible firm' model, notable for its differentiation of an organisation's employees into the 'core' and 'periphery'. Whereas 'core' labour was supposed to be 'functionally' flexible (i.e., able to be deployed between activities and tasks to match changing workloads, production methods or technology), employees in the periphery (i.e., those on non-standard contracts and insourced and outsourced labour) were supposed to be numerically flexible (i.e., disposable when not required due to fluctuations in demand). A further proposition was that the periphery should protect the stability of employment of the core. A more recent model is the Japanese inspired 'lean' organisation, which marries together both intra- and inter-organisational flexibility. In theory, lean organisation brings together the 'hardware' of total quality management (TQM) quality procedures and associated 'Japanese' production processes (e.g., just-in-time (JIT), statistical process control, supply chain management, total productive maintenance, material resources planning, zero defects/right first time, benchmarking) with the 'software' of 'high commitment' HRM and work practices (e.g., careful recruitment and selection, with emphasis on traits and competency, extensive use of systems of communication, teamworking with flexible job design, emphasis on training and learning, involvement in decision-making with responsibility (so-called 'empowerment'), performance appraisal with tight links to contingent pay) (Rees *et al.*, 1996; Legge, 2000). Also involved is business process engineering, in which the organisational logic is to cut out anything within the organisation or along its supply chain (people, structures, technologies, materials) that does not add value.

Clearly, from the above, inter-organisational flexibility is implicated with intra-organisational/organisational flexibility, through, for example, insourcing and outsourcing. However, inter-organisational flexibility goes further than that. Organisations have tended to become smaller, more specialist and more interdependent with other organisations (Colling, 2000, 2005; Marchington *et al.*, 2005). Large organisations now tend to be a network of disaggregated and quasi-independent cost centres, affiliated businesses and co-operative alliances. Spin-offs and franchises are commonplace. Furthermore, whole industries may be organised as elaborate, often global, supply chains (Ackroyd, 2005, pp. 249–51; Procter, 2005). At a macro level, such developments have been theorised in terms of flexible specialisation/the 'second industrial divide' (Piore and Sabel, 1984) and by regulation theory/post-Fordism (Aglietta, 1979).

To some extent we can be sceptical about the extent to which the intra-organisational/organisational models of flexibility have been enacted other than in a piecemeal and pragmatic fashion and whether they have lived up to their promise of increasing organisational effectiveness. (For an extended critique of the flexible firm model, see Legge, 2005; and of 'lean' organisation, Ackroyd and Procter, 1998; Legge, 2000). Indeed, Proctor (2005, p. 479) maintains that 'none [of such models] appears to have established itself much beyond the settings in which it was originally established'. Furthermore, he suggests that it is the 'extent to which they take their place in particular organized systems' that makes the greater contribution to an organisation's effectiveness than its 'intrinsic properties' (Procter, 2005, p. 464). Nevertheless, there can be no doubt that 'flexibility' has become a mantra in liberal market economies and that *parts* of the package (e.g., teamworking, outsourcing, downsizing) *have* been widely implemented (Marchington *et al.*, 2005).

It is important to establish why the notion of flexible organisation first came into prominence in the 1980s and has gained pace ever since, because it gives clues as to its theoretical and empirical compatibility with achieving a humanistic HRM. First, the initiator was undoubtedly the crisis of Fordism (in its broadest sense) (Jessop, 1994) and the rise of political leaders in the US/UK committed to neo-liberal economic policies. (Indeed, Atkinson's 'flexible firm' model emerged from the Rightwardly leaning Institute of Manpower Studies.) 'Flexibility' resonates with a cluster of ideas from freeing up markets to eroding the 'rigidities' of seniority rules and demarcation lines 'imposed' by 'over-powerful' trades unions. The crisis in Fordism was signalled by the falling levels of profitability and innovation in US mass production in the 1970s and, importantly, by the perceived causes for this fall: overly diversified, overly centralised and overly functionally differentiated corporations that were too large, too bureaucratic and too unresponsive to the marketplace. This was seen as being compounded by non-engaged workforces alienated by deskilling and job fragmentation. This was not good news for a capitalist regime committed to the logic of accumulation associated with growth.

The perception of crisis was fuelled in the 1980s and 1990s by the rise of innovative foreign competitors, notably Japan and, subsequently, the 'Asian Tigers'. Japan's achievement, particularly in consumer electronics and automobiles, was to secure cost reduction, rapid product innovation and modification *and* quality (defined as conformity to specification) in contrast to Fordism, where cost reduction had gone hand in hand with standardisation and variable quality. Initially, Japan's success was attributed first to organisational cultures that generated a shared vision, a collective commitment to organisational goals and high levels of employee involvement (expressed, for example, through TQM). Secondly, it was attributed to a commitment to organisational (cross-functional) learning/innovation/ responsiveness (expressed through ideas about 'continuous improvement' (*kaizen*) and the 'internal customer'). The message of the iconic *In Search of Excellence* (Peters and Waterman, 1982), that America's home-grown excellent companies had achieved their excellence through the adoption of management practices reminiscent of Japan, was highly influential, although based on methodologically suspect research and amenable to a very different (and ideological) interpretation (Guest, 1992). Only belatedly in the late 1980s and 1990s was there recognition that Japan's success could also be attributed to its business system, in particular to its dualistic industrial structure of the *keiretsu* of interlocking businesses resting on the graduated pyramid of subcontractors (Whitley, 1992; Dore *et al.*, 1999). By the 1990s and beyond, competition from Asia was also seen as expressive of the perceived intensification of competition resulting from ICTs-facilitated globalisation. Despite the debate between hyperglobalists (e.g., Ohmae,

1989), sceptics (e.g., Hirst and Thompson, 1999; Rugman, 2000) and transformationalists (e.g., Held *et al.*, 1999) about the nature and extent of globalisation, in the decade of the 1990s, 'globalisation' joined with 'flexibility' as the mantra of neo-liberal economies.

At the same time, under the stimulus of the shift from Keynesianism to neo-liberalism, and encouraged by highly liquid, *laissez faire* financial markets, in the US and UK in particular, the idea that the maximisation of 'shareholder value' should be the lodestone of corporate strategy emerged. (There are echoes here of Friedman's (1970) dictum that 'the social responsibility of business is to increase profit'!) The upshot was that many large conglomerates in the 'old' economy of commodity manufacture and processing abandoned their traditional 'retain and re-invest' in favour of a 'downsize and redistribute' allocative regime (Lazonick and O'Sullivan, 2000; Lazonick, 2005). This involved focusing (and sometimes redefining) on the core business/competencies, massive divestiture and downsizing, with accompanying spin-offs and outsourcing, and the distribution to shareholders (and top management via stock options) of the realised value. The idea was to produce 'leaner', 'fitter', more 'agile' (anorexic?) (Legge, 2000) organisations that could get closer and be more responsive to the customer and develop a renewed capacity for innovation. Customer focus and innovation, as in the Japanese model, were seen to be the road to profitability in the old economy.

At the same time, notably in the UK, Thatcherism and New Labour's embracing neo-liberal values massively stimulated intra and inter-organisational flexibility, not just through privatisation and (under Thatcher) anti-union legislation, but through the insistence that public sector services be subject to the discipline of the marketplace in the interests of efficiency and customer responsiveness. As a result, over the last twenty years, via a tranche of initiatives such as purchasers/provider contracting, 'Best Value', market-testing, Private Finance Initiatives (PFI), Public Private Partnerships (PPP), much work in the public sector services is now subcontracted to specialist private firms, motivated by profit rather than public service values. The notion of an entitled citizen is now replaced by the rhetoric of customer choice.

This brings us to the final justification for flexibility – the discovery in the 1990s of 'consumer sovereignty'. From the Fordist position of 'Any colour, so long as it is black' and a 'caveat emptor' attitude to quality failures, the notion that 'the customer is always right' was glamorously restated in terms of seeking 'to meet or exceed our customers' expectations'. The 1990s saw a recognition that just as the production regime of Fordism was failing to generate desired profit, so its standardised products and services were failing to meet expectations of a generation who had higher expectations than their parents who knew of the poverty of the inter-war years and wartime scarcity. Such customers demanded customised, differentiated, high-quality goods and services. Indeed, postmodernists, such as Baudrillard (1983), argued that Marx's analysis of capitalism as concerned with commodity production was outdated, and that capitalism was now concerned predominately with the production of signs, images and symbols rather than the commodities themselves. People were looking to define their shifting identities by their patterns of consumption, rather than their roles as producers, so the argument went, but via the images and symbolic value of the products consumed, rather than purely through products' use value. The fashion and style of 'cool', high mark-up products and services could be realised only if organisations kept their finger on the pulse of the fickle, ever-changing demands of the credit card–loving, debt-accepting, ready-to-complain postmodern consumer. Flexible, responsive organisation was the route to achieving the speedy delivery of the right product/service, of the right quality, at the right time and at the right price.

The theme that links all these reasons for the emergence of flexible organisation is the dynamic of capitalist accumulation, of surplus value being generated at the point of production *and* realised as profit in the marketplace. In order to judge whether flexible organisation, *when embedded in this dynamic*, is likely to be supportive of a moral economy and humanistic HRM, it is useful to explore some of its paradoxes and contradictions.

The contradictions and tensions of flexible organisation

Job insecurity vs. organisational commitment

The *logic* of flexible organisation is to promote job insecurity. Further, the organisation of flexible production in the UK does not appear to adhere to the 'Japanese' model of multiskilling/core functional flexibility. Rather it opts for semi-skilled, product-focused work teams, controlled through the indirect allocation of costs and threat of redundancy/outsourcing if productivity is not deemed satisfactory. The core members on permanent contracts appear as vulnerable to cost-based downsizing and outsourcing as those on non-standard contracts (Ackroyd and Procter, 1998; Burchell *et al.*, 2001; see also Capelli, 1995 for similar US experience). There is much evidence too of a growth in labour intensification in all grades of employees, whether welcomed by *some* aspirant professional/managerial workaholics or tolerated as protection against job loss (Green, 2003). Stress also results from the so-called 'survivor syndrome' and pressures to achieve work/family balance in cultures of long hours and presenteeism (Noer, 1993; Capelli, 1997b) (see below).

What is clearly evident is that from the 1980s, in the UK and US, the growth of jobs has been polarised (Lazonick and O'Sullivan, 2000; Edwards and Wajcman, 2005, Ch. 2). On the one hand there are the 'Macjobs' – well-paid, managerial and professional knowledge work whether in the old or in the new IT- and media-based economies. On the other, there are the 'Mcjobs' – poorly paid work in the rapidly expanding service sector, in fast food, retail and personal services (Goos and Manning, 2003, cited in Edwards and Wajcman, 2005, p. 29). The jobs that are being squeezed are the middle range of erstwhile 'good' jobs available to those with little formal educational qualifications – the craft and semi-skilled (but permanent) jobs in manufacturing and clerical grades, both archetypal of Fordist bureaucracies (Sennett, 1998). It is the educated that are the winners (with increasing numbers of women in their ranks) and those lacking formal qualifications that are the losers (mainly from ethnic and disadvantaged backgrounds, the young, the old, immigrant labour and men without qualifications).

Yet, there are few clear winners in this polarisation. The mantra of 'global competitiveness' encourages governments in the developed West (but particularly in liberal market economies) to cut back on employees' rights and welfare. These may be perceived as costs, as eroding a country's ability to compete in tradeables and encouraging portfolio and foreign direct investment to shift to where costs are lower. Even when firms do not outsource jobs to developing countries/export processing zones, the threat of relocation may be used to put a downward pressure on wages of the average worker (Standing, 1999). Further, among the managerial elite, some are more equal than others. If the 1980s in the UK were marked by high levels of job loss among blue-collar, manufacturing workers, in the 1990s it was the turn of the delayered and downsized middle managers, forced to trade security of employment for questionable employability (Gratton *et al.*, 1999). There is US evidence too of a decline in the practice of internally promoting managers and UK evidence that middle managers perceive a loss of career opportunities and job security with the rise of flexible organisation (summarised by Edwards and Wajcman, 2005, p. 66). Nevertheless, such trends appeared more apparent in the lower managerial/supervisory grades than among more senior managers (Edwards and Wajcman, 2005, p. 69). With corporate restructuring in liberal market economies and the exceptional compensation packages offered to very senior executives, it has been argued that there is a new division of labour 'between the small number of top executives who are protected from market forces and everyone else' (Kunda and Ailon-Souday, 2005, p. 211).

At the same time as flexible organisation appears to be promoting job insecurity, senior managers are calling for more *committed* employees. These are seen as employees who have internalised the corporate vision of customer sovereignty, quality and innovation and who are 'prepared to go the extra mile' in the interests of the organisation and customer (and their own job security?). The late 1980s and 1990s saw a fashion for 'cultural change' programmes. These were aimed at encouraging employees to exercise the discretion in their jobs in the organisation's interests by internalising espoused corporate values, rather than going through the motions of 'resigned behavioural compliance' (Ogbonna and Wilkinson, 1990; see also Legge, 2005, Ch. 6). A Marxist might say of this that not only is labour intensification the order of the day, but employees are encouraged to collude in their own exploitation. Whereas Fordism might have been content to govern the body, some see cultural change programmes, particularly when backed-up by Foucauldian disciplinary practices, as an attempt at 'governing the soul' (Rose, 1990; Willmott, 1993). There is evidence that some employees are prepared to embrace many of the values embodied in flexible organisation (quality, customer care), not as 'cultural dupes' but as seeing advantages such as enhanced security of employment, greater job interest being an outcome (Collinson et al., 1998). Many, however, are 'bothered and bewildered' and highly cynical of management initiatives (Knights and McCabe, 2000; Collinson and Ackroyd, 2005, pp. 318–20). The contradiction of demanding organisational commitment, which has been defined in terms of long-term involvement in an organisation (Porter et al., 1974), at the same time as adopting policies that entail job insecurity, is self-evident. Capelli's (1997a, p. 10) comment that 'more is expected of employees while less is offered to them' is apposite.

The 'reality' of 'empowerment'?

In relation to flexible organisation, empowerment is often seen in terms of granting some measure of autonomy to 'self-managed' teams and 'responsible autonomy' (Friedman, 1977) to individuals. As such, it may be welcomed and enjoyed by the individuals involved. But the empowerment granted is first and foremost in the interests of management rather than for the job satisfaction of employees. Both TQM and JIT imply highly fragile production systems that rely for smooth running on employees exercising their initiative. Employees may have increased discretion at operational level, but subject to accountability to managerial standards derived from an agenda firmly set by management.

Two well-known studies illuminate the limited nature of empowerment in flexible organisations. In discussing empowerment in relation to BPR, Willmott (1995) suggests that 'empowered work' is assumed simply to be the opposite of fragmented and degraded work, a reversal of Taylorist/Fordist work ('functionalist humanism') rather than the expansion of processes of self-determination ('democratic[anti] humanism'). Hence, he suggests that in BPR 'empowerment' is better typified as

'false charity' – 'charity' because [at least] it seeks to bestow the gift of greater discretion and involvement on employees; and 'false' because it is motivated less by any concern to ameliorate structural inequalities that make such gestures possible than it is by a calculation that such a change will engender enhanced performance and profitability. (Willmott, 1995, p. 93)

Sewell (1998) and Barker (1993) analysing what they describe as empowerment involving 'concertive' control point to the introduction of TQM and a cultural change programme involving teamworking where ostensibly the team members set the rules and norms of work behaviour. However, as a result, they monitor and sanction colleagues' performance in the interests of and to parameters set by management more tightly than the previous forms of technical and bureaucratic control (cf., Edwards, 1979). Sewell and Barker (2005, p. 81) suggest that the team members are equivocal about such empowerment, experiencing it as 'simultaneously constraining *and* liberating, coercive *and* protective' (authors' italics), providing tangible rewards such as perceived autonomy, greater job security, protection from free-riders but at the cost of labour intensification.

Turning to specialist project teams, Sennett (1998), in a nostalgic lament for the securities of a lost Fordist era, takes an even more sceptical view of such teamworking and its effectiveness. Teamworking, he argues, in the interests of group cohesion, backgrounds dissent, the reality of intra-team competition and issues of power relationships. Pseudo-autonomy is matched by teams' denial of responsibility and scapegoating of 'change' as the responsible agent in which all are victims. The existence of power without authority in teams, Sennett argues, encourages the deep acting of a mask of co-operation and respect for team members, while looking for opportunities for freeloading, escaping responsibility for failed projects and claiming ownership of successes. The short-term projects and fluid team membership do not allow for the establishment of loyalties and trust, particularly in an environment of delayering and downsizing.

Finally, it could be argued that, pressured by appeals to shareholder value and customer sovereignty, the traditionally most 'empowered' employees, managers and professionals are increasingly constrained by short-term targets in the private sector, and monitoring and auditing in the public sector (Power, 1997).

Producer–consumer tensions

This manifests itself in two ways. First, the desire of many consumers for high-quality products at low cost encourages the modes of flexible organisation outlined, with accompanying job insecurity and labour intensification. If we as consumers object to the employment relationships and work patterns of flexible organisation, it could be argued that we collude with the consumerist culture that has brought this about (Legge, 2005, pp. 35–39).

Secondly, as consumers, we expect a pleasant service encounter when purchasing a manufactured product, but we may have enhanced expectations of the encounter when it constitutes the service we are purchasing – what Korczynski (2002) terms 'customer enchantment'. The customer needs to be kept happy and certainly not experience the backlash of antagonisms that might be intrinsic to the employment relationship (Edwards and Wajcman, 2005, p. 33). The skills required are likely to involve the ability to display customer-expected feelings and aesthetics; in any encounter the employee is expected to look and sound 'appropriate'. In certain circumstances – when employees have some autonomy in their expression of feelings, and the interactions occur in socially embedded relationships with customers and clients, as in many of the traditional 'caring' jobs in the public sector – real satisfactions may result for both parties and 'spaces' and 'fine lines' may be drawn that facilitate the management of inherent tensions (Bolton, 2005; Korczynski, 2002). However, in many routine service encounters, the opposite may prevail. That is, employees may be required not only to 'act out' displays of feeling scripted by management, but to internalise such feelings, in a context of an unequal relationship with a powerful customer. The employee may also be required to 'look the part' and follow various grooming and dress conventions. In such circumstances, Hochschild (1983) argues that the emotional *work* that we all engage in becomes transformed into emotional *labour*, in which not just our physical bodies but our very appearance and personality becomes commodified in the interests of capitalism.[1] While flexible organisation is not responsible for emotional labour, it is implicated in many service sector sites where this occurs. At the same time, 'customer enchantment' may appear little more than management rhetoric as increasingly the customer is transformed into the unpaid producer of a service that may frustrate and irritate rather than enchant – witness the lengthy option choosing, telephone queuing and (sometimes) difficulty in understanding the non-English accent of the customer service (!) rep in any interaction with a distant call-centre (Bolton and Houlihan, 2005).

Work–life balance

The change in the world of work, of which flexible organisation is a manifestation, has several characteristics that put pressure on work–life balance. First, there is the intensification of work and the long hours culture of liberal market economies emphasising shareholder value and customer sovereignty. Secondly, there is a culture of consumerism in which people want more, better and more often. Thirdly, there is the growth in the service sector that provides jobs for women aspirant for increasing material living standards and for their own independence and development. The latter two factors encourage the growth of dual-earner households.

If we put this potent mix together, several issues emerge (for a detailed discussion, see Edwards and Wajcman, 2005, Ch. 3). First, many people experience time pressure, of too much to do, in too little time. This is partly a function of the fact that while individual working hours are polarising (some working very long hours and others very short hours), household hours are rising due to most women continuing or returning to paid employment. With the 24/7 flexibility of large parts of the service sector, many of these hours, particularly those worked by the low paid, are at non-standard, unsocial times that eat into family life. Similarly, a long hours culture (often worked semi-voluntarily to demonstrate 'commitment' in the pursuit of job security/promotion) has the same effect. In coping with time pressures, mechanisation may play a part (e.g., pre-prepared meals, microwaves, cars), ironically promoting consumerism and fuelling the need for two incomes. While time devoted to childcare by both men and women is increasing, this is an activity that is less amenable to mechanisation, but which again can promote consumerism as parents, guilty of the lack of family time, indulge their children with the latest peer-prescribed 'must have' items.

Second, while there appears to be some convergence in the hours of housework undertaken by men and women, this appears to be less the result of men doing more than time-constrained working women doing less (Edwards and Wajcman, 2005, p. 53). This is particularly the case where dual earners are both working at full-time, career-oriented jobs that demand long hours. Among more affluent families this has resulted and is reflected in the generation of another form of casual, flexible work organisation, namely the employment of domestic, often migrant, workers – what has been termed 'the global care chain' (Ehrenreich and Hochschild, 2003 cited in Edwards and Wajcman, 2005, p. 59). Casually employed migrant workers are also heavily involved in the fast-food and restaurant industry that similarly supports time-pressured families (Schlosser, 2002). Thus we have an ironic situation. What might be seen as exploitation of time-pressured families can be translated into their creation of their own form of flexible organisation with its potential for the exploitation of casual labour through lack of normal employment rights. In the case of live-in domestics, this may extend to an intrusion into their private personal lives (Edwards and Wajcman, 2005, p. 59).

Finally, while IT, particularly PCs, laptops and mobile phones, may facilitate beneficial flexibilities in managing work–life balance (e.g., through teleworking), it allows the boundary between work and home to be permeated and all too frequently for work to colonise the home rather than vice versa (e.g., Bell and Tuckman, 2002).

Does capitalism deliver humanistic HRM?

On the basis of this analysis, can it be said that flexible organisation, *in the context of a capitalist liberal market economy*, supports a humanistic approach to HRM?

The overwhelming evidence is that flexible organisation is associated with a polarisation in the nature of jobs and material rewards between the 'haves' and 'have nots'. A revealing statistic is that in 1965 the pay of the average CEO in America was 44 times that of the average worker; by 1998, this had risen to 419 times (O'Sullivan, 2000, p. 200, cited in Edwards and Wajcman, 2005, pp. 206–207). It is both managerial and professional jobs *and* semi-skilled/unskilled, poorly paid jobs in the service sector that are the fastest growing in the UK and US (Edwards and Wajcman, 2005, p. 67). The decline is in semi-skilled/skilled permanent jobs in manufacturing. Whereas the service sector jobs are largely non-unionised, the latter, in Fordist regimes, were unionised. This meant that jobs were embedded in structures that provided the basis for unions' control over work: delimited and well-defined job classifications, contractually specified rules about seniority, overtime arrangements, job postings; and formal grievance and negotiating procedures to regulate the effort–reward bargain. Although one might argue that union power restricted individual worker autonomy, gave rise to restrictive practices and so on, it bought with it a large measure of individual job security and protection (Legge, 2006). With the passing of Fordism and the rise of flexible organisation, this is now eroded.

On the other hand, we have the growth in professional and managerial jobs in both the old and new sectors of the economy. Ironically, a major source of such growth has been in business services consultancies advising on outsourcing and business process reengineering, in specialist IT companies to whom many large organisations now outsource their IT and (particularly in the UK public sector) in jobs concerned with managing contracts with subcontractors (Colling, 2005). When the skills of such employees are seen as key to organisational effectiveness (or to use the jargon, 'the source of high value-added and competitive advantage'), their individual bargaining power is likely to be high. As a result, such employees may enjoy work that is high on Hackman and Oldham's (1976) requisite task attributes, offering genuine empowerment and high material rewards. Even if job security is no longer guaranteed, training and development opportunities may secure a high level of employability and the prospect of a 'portfolio career', for some individuals, may enhance their feelings of autonomy and independence. Such work may be argued to deliver well on the ethical criteria defining *human* resource management outlined earlier. If employees' skills and knowledge are respected in their own right, the criteria of Kantian ethics are fulfilled. If recognition and career development leads to self-actualisation and the achievement of a coherent narrative that renders life meaningful, then such work and employment conditions score highly in Aristotelian terms.[2] If high material rewards are received, this might be justified in Rawlsian terms, if one believes in the 'trickle down' effect. (High pay is necessary to retain scarce and valuable skills, which are necessary for organisational success, which is necessary for economic growth, which in turn is to everyone's advantage.) Even if it is recognised that such employees may not be respected as ends in themselves but, instrumentally, as means to organisational success, this may still be justified in terms of utilitarianism.

Nevertheless, even among this privileged group, flexible organisation also delivers job insecurity, labour intensification/workaholic life-styles and the erosion of autonomy through the proliferation of short-term targets and auditing activities. MacIntyre (1981) would argue that the exigencies of management roles, which are exacerbated by flexible organisation, prevent the achievement of the Aristotelian ideal. Role fragmentation, inauthenticity and an unbalanced development of potentiality deprive managers of developing an integrated narrative of their lives and, hence, rendering their lives meaningful to themselves and their communities. Sennett (1998, p. 28) similarly sees the 'corrosion of character' as a consequence of flexibalisation and as a threat to all workers: 'How can human beings develop a narrative of identity and life history in a society composed of episodes and fragments?'

The answer of course is that we develop identity through consumption. The surplus value generated at the point of production needs to be realised in the marketplace. It is not surprising then that in *aggregate*, real wages have risen steadily over the last twenty years promoting a consumer boom in developed countries. Capitalism, in comparison to other economic systems, delivers, as the reinvigorated economies of east Europe and China attest. As Smith (1776/1961) would advocate, capitalism promotes the very really virtues of productive efficiency through individual freedom of choice and action.

Nevertheless, I would argue that the non-humanistic employment policies and practices of flexible organisation are also an inevitable consequence of neo-liberal capitalism with its prioritising shareholder value/short-term profit. The logic of accumulation, untempered by the corporatist underpinnings of the Fordist regime, gives rise to a form of human resource management where *resource management* is the priority. If people are viewed as commodities, this is the logical outcome. If employees as stakeholders lack the power of the markets, market values will take precedence. If the people working for an organisation are not technically its employees (as may be the case with agency and outsourced labour), it is not surprising if they are physically or psychologically distanced and treated with little sympathy, in Hume's (1985) and Bauman's (1993) terms. High-commitment HRM will be on offer to those employees who are regarded as valuable and non-substitutable in the task of achieving organisational competitive advantage and profit. All other employees are likely to be regarded as a cost to be minimised, constrained only by the need to maintain employee consent and social legitimacy. Humanistic HRM is more likely to flourish in economies that adopt the co-ordinated market economy model of capitalism, which promotes the values of employment regulation, skill development, participation and corporatism. If we want to develop a moral economy in the UK, we might be better served by adopting the continental European model of capitalism, rather than that of the USA.

Notes

1. There has been an extended critique of Hochschild's work, centring on her conflation of the subjective experience of emotional labour and the objective conditions of workers under capitalism. (For an extended discussion, see Korczynski, 2002; for an excellent summary, see Edwards and Wajcman, 2005, pp. 33–41.)
2. Hochschild (1997) has argued that when work is intellectually absorbing and exciting, and collegiality is high, 'work' can become home and, given the problems of time constraints in managing the domestic scene, 'home' can appear like hard work. This is a useful counterbalance to the popular maxim that 'no one on his deathbed has said "I wish I'd spent more time at the office"; many have said "I wish I'd spent more time with my family" '.

References

Ackroyd, S. (2005) 'Introduction: Part IV', in Ackroyd, S., Batt, R., Thompson, P. and Tolbert, P.S. (eds), *Oxford Handbook of Work and Organization*, Oxford: Oxford University Press, pp. 449–61.

Ackroyd, S. and Procter, S. (1998) 'British manufacturing organization and workplace relations: some attributes of the new flexible firm', *British Journal of Industrial Relations*, 36:2, 163–83.

Ackroyd, S. and Thompson, P. (1999) *Organizational Misbehaviour*, London: Sage.

Adam, J.S. (1963) 'Towards an understanding of inequity', *Journal of Abnormal and Social Psychology*, 67: 422–36.

Aglietta, M. (1979) *A Theory of Capitalist Regulation*, London: New Left Books.

Atkinson, J. (1984) 'Manpower strategies for flexible organisations', *Personnel Management*, 16:8, 28–31.

Baldamus, W. (1961) *Efficiency and Effort*, London: Tavistock.

Barker, J.R. (1993) 'Tightening the iron cage: concertive control in self-managing teams', *Administrative Science Quarterly*, 38:3, 408–37.

Baudrillard, J. (1983) *Simulations*, New York: Semiotext(e).

Bauman, Z. (1993) *Postmodern Ethics*, Oxford: Blackwell.

Bell, E. and Tuckman, A. (2002) 'Hanging on the telephone: temporal flexibility and the accessible worker', in Whipp, R., Adam, B. and Sabelis, I. (eds), *Making Time: Time and Management in Modern Organizations*, London: Sage, pp. 115–25.

Blackburn, S. (2001) *Being Good*, Oxford: Oxford University Press.

Bolton, S.C. (2005) *Emotion Management in the Workplace*, London: Palgrave.

Bolton, S. and Houlihan, M. (2005) 'The (mis)representation of customer service', *Work, Employment and Society*, 19:4, 685–703.

Braverman, H. (1974) *Labor and Monopoly Capitalism*, New York: Monthly Review Press.

Burawoy, M. (1979) *Manufacturing Consent*, Chicago: University of Chicago Press.

Burchell, B., Ladipo, D. and Wilkinson, F. (eds) (2001) *Job Insecurity and Work Intensification*, London: Routledge.

Burrell, G. (1988) 'Modernism, postmodernism and organizational analysis 2: the contribution of Michel Foucault', *Organization Studies*, 9:2, 221–35.

Capelli, P. (1995) 'Rethinking employment', *British Journal of Industrial Relations*, 33:4, 563–602.

Capelli, P. (1997a) 'Introduction', in Capelli, P., Bassi, L., Katz, H., Knoke, D., Osterman, P. and Useem, M. (eds), *Change at Work*, New York: Oxford University Press, pp. 3–14.

Capelli, P. (1997b) 'The effects of restructuring on employees', in Capelli, P., Bassi, L., Katz, H., Knoke, D., Osterman, P. and Useem, M. (eds), *Change at Work*, New York: Oxford University Press, pp. 173–207.

Colling, T. (2000) 'Personnel management in the extended organization', in Bach, S. and Sisson, K. (eds), *Personnel Management* (third edition), Oxford: Blackwell, pp. 70–90.

Colling, T. (2005). 'Managing human resources in the networked organization', in Bach, S. (ed.), *Managing Human resources* (fourth edition), Oxford: Blackwell, pp. 90–112.

Collinson, D. and Ackroyd, S. (2005) 'Resistance, misbehaviour and dissent', in Ackroyd, S., Batt, R., Thompson, P. and Tolbert, P.S. (eds), *The Oxford Handbook of Work and Organization*, Oxford: Oxford University Press, pp. 305–26.

Collinson, M., Rees, C. and Edwards, P.K. (with Innes, L.) (1998) *Involving Employees in Total Quality Management: Employee Attitudes and Organizational Context in Unionized Environments*, London: DTI.

Cooper, R. and Burrell, G. (1988) 'Modernism, postmodernism and organizational analysis: an introduction', *Organization Studies*, 9:1, 91–112.

Dore, R., Lazonick, W. and O'Sullivan, M. (1999) 'Varieties of capitalism in the twentieth century', *Oxford Review of Economic Policy*, 15: 102–20.

Edwards, R. (1979) *Contested Terrain: The Transformation of the Workplace in the Twentieth Century*, London: Heinemann.

Edwards, P. and Wajcman, J. (2005) *The Politics of Working Life*, Oxford: Oxford University Press.

Ehrenreich, B. and Hochschild, A. (2003) *Global Women: Nannies, Maids and Sex Workers in the New Economy*, New York: Metropolitan.

Folger, R. and Cropanzano, R. (1998) *Organizational Justice and Human Resource Management*, Thousand Oaks, CA: Sage.

Freeman, E. (1984) *Strategic Management: A Stakeholder Approach*, Boston, MA: Pitman.

Friedman, A.L. (1977) *Industry and Labour*, London: Macmillan.

Friedman, M. (1970) 'The social responsibility of business is to increase profit', *New York Times Magazine*, 13 September.

Giddens, A. (1990) *The Consequences of Modernity*, Cambridge and Oxford: Polity and Blackwell.

Goos, M. and Manning, A. (2003) 'Mcjobs and Macjobs: the growing polarisation of jobs in the UK', in Dickens, R., Gregg, P. and Wadsworth, J. (eds), *The Labour Market under New Labour: The State of Working Britain.* Basingstoke: Palgrave Macmillan.

Gratton, L., Hope Hailey, V., Stiles, P. and Truss, C. (1999) *Strategic Human Resource Management: Rhetoric and Human Reality*, Oxford: Oxford University Press.

Green, F. (2003) 'The demands of work', in Dickens, R., Gregg, P. and Wadsworth, J. (eds), *The Labour Market Under New Labour: The State of Working Britain*, Basingstoke: Palgrave Macmillan.

Guest, D.E. (1992) 'Right enough to be dangerously wrong: an analysis of the *In Search of Excellence* phenomenon', in Salaman G. *et al.* (eds), *Human Resource Strategies*, London and Milton Keynes: Sage/Open University Press, pp. 5–19.

Hackman, J.R. and Oldham, G.R. (1976) 'Motivation through the design of work: test of a theory', *Organizational Behavior and Human Performance*, 15: 250–79.

Held, D., McGraw, A., Goldblatt, D. and Perraton, J. (1999) *Global Transformations*, Cambridge: Polity.

Hirst, P. and Thompson, G. (1999) *Globalization in Question* (second edition), Cambridge: Polity.

Hochschild, A. (1983) *The Managed Heart: Commercialization of Human Feeling*, Berkeley: University of California Press.

Hochschild, A. (1997) *The Time Bind*, New York: Metropolitan Books.

Hodson, R. (2001) *Dignity at Work*, Cambridge: Cambridge University Press.

Hume, D. (1985/1740) *A Treatise of Human Nature*, Harmondsworth: Penguin.

Hyman, R. (1987) 'Strategy or structure? Capital, labour and control', *Work, Employment and Society*, 1:1, 25–55.

Jessop, R. (1994) 'Post-Fordism and the state', in Amin, A. (ed.), *Post-Fordism: A Reader*, Oxford: Blackwell.

Kant, I. (1949/1788) *Critique of Practical Reason, The Philosophy of Immanuel Kant*, iv, trans. L.W. Beck, Chicago: University of Chicago Press.

Knights, D. and McCabe, D. (2000) 'Bewitched, bothered and bewildered: the meaning and experience of teamworking for employees in an automobile company', *Human Relations*, 53:11, 1481–517.

Korczynski, M. (2002) *Human Resource Management in the Service Sector*, Basingstoke: Palgrave Macmillan.

Kunda, G. and Ailon-Souday, G. (2005) 'Managers, markets and ideologies: design and devotion revisited', in Ackroyd, S., Batt, R., Thompson, P. and Tolbert, P.S. (eds), *The Oxford Handbook of Work and Organization*, Oxford: Oxford University Press, pp. 200–19.

Lazonick, W. (2005) 'Corporate restructuring', in Ackroyd, S., Batt, R., Thompson, P. and Tolbert, P.S. (eds), *The Oxford Handbook of Work and Organization*, Oxford: Oxford University Press, pp. 577–601.

Lazonick, W. And O'Sullivan, M. (2000) 'Maximizing shareholder value: a new ideology for corporate governance', *Economy and Society*, 29:1, 13–35.

Legge, K. (2000) Personnel management in the lean organization', in Bach, S. and Sisson, K. (eds), *Personnel Management* (third edition), Oxford: Blackwell, pp. 43–69.

Legge, K. (2005) *Human Resource Management, Rhetorics and Realities* (Anniversary Edition), Basingstoke: Palgrave Macmillan.

Legge, K. (2006) 'The ethics of HRM in dealing with individual employees without collective representation', in Pinnington, A., Macklin, R. and Campbell, T. (eds), *Ethical Issues in HRM and Employment*, Oxford: Oxford University Press.

Levinas, E. (1987) *Collected Philosophical Papers*, trans. A. Lingis, The Hague: Martinus Nijhoff.

MacIntyre, A. (1981) *After Virtue*, London: Duckworth.

Marchington, M., Grimshaw, D., Rubery, J. and Willmott, H. (2005) *Fragmenting Work*, Oxford: Oxford University Press.

Maslow, A.H. (1943) 'A theory of human motivation', *Psychological Review*, 50: 370–96.

Noer, D. (1993) *Healing the Wounds: Overcoming the Trauma of Layoffs and Revitalizing Downsized Organizations*, San Francisco: Jossey-Bass.

Normann, R. (1998) *The Moral Philosophers: An Introduction to Ethics* (second edition), Oxford: Oxford University Press.

Ogbonna, E. and Wilkinson, B. (1990) 'Corporate strategy and corporate culture: the view from the checkout', *Personnel Review*, 19:4, 9–15.

Ohmae, K. (1989) 'Managing in a borderless world', *Harvard Business Review*, 67:3, 52–61.

O'Sullivan, M. (2000) *Contests for Corporate Control*, Oxford: Oxford University Press.

Peters, T.J. and Waterman, R.H. Jr (1982) *In Search of Excellence, Lessons from America's Best Run Companies*, New York: Harper and Row.

Piore, M. and Sabel, C. (1984) *The Second Industrial Divide*, New York: Basic Books.

Porter, L., Steers, R., Mowday, R. and Boulian, P. (1974) 'Organizational commitment, job satisfaction and turnover among psychiatric technicians', *Journal of Applied Psychology*, 59: 603–609.

Power, M. (1997) *The Audit Society: Rituals of Verification*, Oxford: Oxford University Press.

Procter, S. (2005) 'Organizations and organized systems: from direct control to flexibility', in Ackroyd, S., Batt, R., Thompson, P. and Tolbert, P.S. (eds), *The Oxford Handbook of Work and Organization*, Oxford: Oxford University Press, pp. 462–84.

Rawls, J. (1971) *A Theory of Justice*, Oxford: Oxford University Press.

Rees, C., Scarbrough, H. and Terry, M. (1996) 'The people management implications of leaner ways of working', Report by IRRU, Warwick Business School, University of Warwick, *Issues in People Management*, No. 15, London: Institute of Personnel and Development, pp. 64–115.

Rose, N. (1990) *Governing the Soul: The Shaping of the Private Self*, London: Routledge.

Rubery, J. (2005) 'Labor markets and flexibility', in Ackroyd, S., Batt, R., Thompson, P. and Tolbert, P.S. (eds), *The Oxford Handbook of Work and Organization*, Oxford: Oxford University Press, pp. 31–51.

Rugman, A. (2000) *The End of Globalization*, London: Random House.

Sayer, A. (2000) 'Moral economy and political economy', *Studies in Political Economy*, 61: 79–103.

Schlosser, E. (2002) *Fast Food Nation*, New York: Perennial.

Sennett, R. (1998) *The Corrosion of Character*, New York: Norton.

Sewell, G. (1998) 'The discipline of teams: the control of team-based industrial work through electronic and peer surveillance', *Administrative Science Quarterly*, 43:2, 397–429.

Sewell, G. and Barker, J.R. (2005) 'Max Weber and the irony of bureaucracy', in Korczynski, M., Hodson, R. and Edwards, P. (eds), *Social Theory at Work*, Oxford: Oxford University Press, pp. 56–87.

Smith, A. (1776/1961) *The Wealth of Nations*, London: Methuen.

Standing, G. (1999) *Global Labour Flexibility, Seeking Distributive Justice*, Basingstoke: Macmillan.

Whitley, R. (1992) *Divergent Capitalisms*, Oxford: Oxford University Press.

Willmott, H. (1993). ' "Strength is ignorance; slavery is freedom": managing culture in modern organizations', *Journal of Management Studies*, 30:4, 515–52.

Willmott, H. (1995) 'The odd couple?: re-engineering business processes; managing human relations', *New Technology, Work and Employment*, 10:2, 89–98.

8

'HAVE IT YOUR WAY®': resources, citizens and the culture of deceit

Martin Parker

HAVE IT YOUR WAY®
This cup makes a statement about you. It says 'Hey, look at me, I'm an ambitious and decisive person.' You could have gone larger, but you didn't. You could have gone smaller, but you decided against it. No, you know exactly what you want in life, and that you should always have it your way®.

(Text from a medium-sized Burger King paper cup, 2006)

Introduction

The language of Human Resource Management is very similar to the language spoken by this Burger King cup.[1] In the most obvious sense, it is a lie, an intentional form of deceit. Cups do not talk, and buying a medium-sized soft drink merely suggests that I wanted a medium-sized soft drink. But were I to return to the counter, and demand that this lie was rescinded I would immediately have to deal with the problem that this cup makes its sense within a particular social context. Marketing and advertising make sense in the context of the ubiquity of the language of marketing and advertising – from people selling soft drinks, political parties, corporations and even selling marketing itself. The Kings of Burger King rule a world of lies, half truths, and selective claims. It would be a mistake to judge them as if they were really making true statements.[2]

Now this is true, but it is also defeatist. It means that in a world of soft soap we can only smile ruefully and sip our soft drink. There is no point in

137

berating the migrant with poor English who served us, or the duty manager who has been on shift for 14 hours and is wondering what to get her children to eat when she finally gets home. The area manager is somewhere on the motorway, and the UK Head-Office is 150 miles away. The 'creative' from the advertising agency who wrote the text in response to Burger King's brief probably really wants to be a novelist, and would tell me that she was just doing her job.[3] So, when Burger King claim that their managers must 'share our passion to deliver our customer promise to every customer, everyday' the people who wrote that sentence, and the people who read it, know that it is a lie. When they say 'Our managers enjoy working for BURGER KING® and often refer their friends for career opportunities with us,' I bet they could not provide me with evidence. And when they say 'Career opportunities are unlimited,' you might wonder whether the words 'career' 'opportunity' and 'unlimited' are being used in the same ways that they are in ordinary language. I suppose they might as well say 'this language makes a statement about you. It says that you are a modern and caring company. You could have been more honest, but you weren't. You could have employed fewer adjectives, but you decided against it. No, you know exactly what you want from your employees, and that you should always have it your way.®'[4]

However, as Habermas (1979) argued, the odd thing about language is that someone can turn round and hold you to what you said. Or, in more prosaic ways, when a big company makes certain claims about its activities, it needs to hold to them or risk being exposed (Klein, 2000). Language is, in some sense, performative, in that it does something in making claims. A promise (like Burger King's promises) once made, cannot be unmade without some other sort of act of language. Unless it is exposed as a false promise, in which case all future promises will be treated with the scepticism they deserve. So when an organisation claims that its people are its first priority, there is a sense in which this statement is one that should be taken at face value. (Whatever we might think about its placement within a culture of deceit.) This might be a very dangerous thing to do to such statements, because then the half-truth needs to become true, or become nothing more than a lie that has been exposed as a lie.[5] In order to do this I will connect Burger King's claims with a perennial concern in social and political theory – that of citizenship (Marshall, 1950; Giddens, 1982; Barbalet, 1988; Plant and Barry, 1990; Turner, 1990, 1991; Ahrne, 1996). I will suggest that HRM language might be seen as a latent model of organisational citizenship, and, moreover, that it might be used against management in order that employees can have it their way for a change.

Belonging to organisations

Since Peters and Waterman's *In Search of Excellence* (1982) there has been increasing visibility given to attempts at reconstructing organisational membership. Consultants and gurus have been prolific in developing formulations of belonging – culture, family, mission and so on. In the most general terms what unifies these approaches is that they are aimed at the hearts of organisational members. Demonising the autocratic manager, the accountant, the bureaucracy and the stopwatch, modern HRM likes to claim that the best organisations are built through the development of the people within them. Not only are these new commitment-led organisations supposed to be more humanitarian, but are also more efficient and profitable. The key ideas of this new age management have been that cultures can be excellent, management can disseminate visions, teams share missions and communities be true to themselves.

Unsurprisingly, the response from critical management academics has often not been positive. Marxist, Weberian and Foucauldian responses have all focused on control strategies, ideology, self-surveillance and discipline in suggesting that this form of organisation is actually an internalised coercion (for example Silver, 1987; Miller and Rose, 1990; du Gay, 1991; Kunda, 1992; Willmott, 1993; Grint, 1994). Neither are contemporary attempts to construct the committed worker a new phenomenon. What Thompson and McHugh call 'moral machinery' (1990, p. 50) was a vital component of the early factory system, and Sharon Beder (2000) has documented a century of US attempts to sell the work ethic to workers. Early versions of control were not limited to Taylorism, particularly with regard to habits of individual self-discipline, temperance and fidelity or Fayol's recognition that *esprit de corps* mattered. Ford's 'Sociological Department' is perhaps the best-known example but Smith *et al.* (1990) remind us that many organisations, Cadbury in their example, employed a powerful paternalism. The development of Human Relations, organisational psychology and so on clearly echoed similar concerns and provoked similar critique, for example W.H. Whyte's formulation of the 'organisation man' (1961).

That being said, it seems to me that contemporary formulations of 'moral machinery' are much more pervasive. I argue below that their current popularity provokes some central questions about the nature of individuals' affiliation to work organisations and the varied ways in which these affiliations might be manipulated. Putting the point rather crudely, it is as if we are being asked to weaken or relinquish wider (and increasingly contested) affiliations to nation, gender, occupation, ethnicity, profession, region and so on in favour of (supposedly) uncontested organisational membership. Whilst scepticism concerning such developments is very convincing, subversive engagement is a tactic that might produce some interesting outcomes.

I am not the first person to attempt linking 'citizenship' to organisations and working life. Marshall himself (1950) referred to 'industrial citizenship' as an emergent subcategory of political citizenship. More recently, various related usages seem to have become more common. Miller and O'Leary (1993) have used the term 'economic citizenship' to refer to a new governmental practice based on a customer orientation and related to the political language of enterprise (Miller and Rose, 1990). There is also a strand of work in psychology that uses the term 'organisational citizenship' to refer to something like 'organisational commitment' (for example, Organ, 1990; Vinten, 1994), and a body of work on 'corporate citizenship' that means something like corporate social responsibility (for example, Andriof and McIntosh, 2001; Matten and Crane, 2005). My adoption of the term 'organisational citizenship' differs from these uses in referring primarily to what might be called the political constitution of an organisation. It is similar to some of the ideas contained in Handy (1997) and Manville and Ober (2003), though both of those works appear to be remarkably smug about the radical possibilities of such an idea. Mine is not an argument about how workplace democracy can make organisations more efficient and profitable,[6] but an argument about the radical possibilities for subverting hypocrisy.

Employees and citizens

Consider this, fairly representative, quote from a pop management text.

> One might think of corporations as big families. Management acts to develop its people by caring for and training them, setting goals and standards for excellent performance. Every member of the organisation, from the CEO to the lowliest clerk, shares some responsibility for the organisation's products and services, and the unique patterns with which they carry out their responsibilities distinguish their 'family' from those of their competitors. To perpetuate the culture, each employee passes valued traits along to succeeding generations. (Hickman and Silva, 1985, pp. 57–58)

Behind the homely language are a set of assumptions about the nature of the organisation and its members. First, 'we are all in this together'. An organisation is a group of people oriented towards a common goal because it is a community that shares a particular set of ideas. However, different members of the organisation have different rights and responsibilities.

Everyone is important but some people and groups set targets, shape values and make strategies, whilst others perform work with machines or deal with administration. Finally, and most importantly, the argument developed in the rest of Hickman and Silva's book is that even if this 'family' metaphor is not accurate for a particular organisation, management must act as if it were in order to maximise profit and happiness. In other words, if you treat your organisation as a 'big family' then it will come to be one. 'Family' is here used as a metaphor. It implies a set of strongly shared values, a blood that is thicker than water, a joyful reproduction of human things with caring parents at the head of the table and grateful children getting treats for doing their homework. Whether this is an accurate description of families is irrelevant, because this is a metaphor with a prescriptive intent. If it is not true of your organisation then it should be.

But there is more to humanised resource management than cosy ideas of family as unity. There is also an assumption that management must convince their workforce of the value of shared goals, they must *sell* the vision and not impose it. This family is a liberal one where the parent explains to the child why they must eat their greens, and only smacks them as a last resort if they do not listen to reason. Hence there is much in these texts about management as coaching, about tolerating creative mistakes, about stimulating innovation, about replacing bureaucracy with adhocracy. As Janssens and Brett (1994, p. 32) rather neatly put it, centralisation and formalisation should be replaced by socialisation. Links are often also made with ideas of capitalist democracy and its superiority over autocratic command states, economies and organisations. Ouchi (1981), for example, suggested that mission and vision statements are something like a constitution, a bill of rights for employees. In order to want to achieve high productivity the employee must be trusted, and must trust those who guide them – the 'clan' form of organisation. More recently, Handy (1997) suggested that the 'Citizen Corporation' must satisfy many different stakeholders, and Manville and Ober (2003) suggested that Athenian democracy provides a model for best organising human capital. It seems to me that these formulations of management, worker and organisation contain an implicit notion of reciprocity that is potentially very interesting. If the managerial bias and the political smugness can be ignored, then it may be that these ideas might help to construct an idea of representative democracy in organisations.

Let's begin with some clarification of the concept of the citizen.

citizen, *n.* any member of a political community or STATE who enjoys clear rights and duties associated with this membership, i.e. who is not merely a 'subject'. (Jary and Jary, 2000, p. 68)

The use of dictionary quotation implies definitional precision, a juridical and rational specification. These legislative ideals are implied in much of the literature on citizenship. One version of the idea can be found as 'progress' – social 'evolution' tends to move social organisations away from the arbitrary use of physical coercion by despots to the use of legalistic codes operated in a universalistic fashion by institutions formally independent of the state. Both autocracy and democracy are methods for ensuring social order but the latter is assumed to be better at finding resolutions that meet the good of the greatest number in the most equitable fashion. The modern idea of a 'social contract' assumes that the human becomes a citizen when they accept the force of these resolutions, when they accept responsibilities in return for rights. The state guarantees and the citizens accede. Following Marshall's seminal contribution (1950) these rights may analytically (and historically) be divided into civil, political and social but in all three spheres the underlying story is still clear. The citizen is listened to when the subject was not and the further we travel towards democracy, the better the consultation will get.

In organisational theory a similar story of modernisation can be told. Before bureaucracy and scientific management, organisations were in the dark ages – rife with inefficiency, despotism and patronage. Writers like Taylor and Weber are suggested to have recognised or brought into being a new way of thinking about organisations that conceptualised them as logically structured machines. Bureaucracies operated without hatred or passion, according to the legislative rulebook, and every member (but particularly those at the bottom) was subject to the disciplines of time and motion. Attendance was ensured by the pay-packet, obedience with the threat of dismissal and efficiency by the man in the white coat with the stopwatch and clipboard. Organisational science then developed away from these origins. Mayo invented human relations, Maslow humanistic psychology. Organisational development and HRM replaced hiring, firing and time sheets. Now, the proponents of this story suggest, organisational and societal change has meant that the external coercions of bureaucracy and work-study are being (or should be) replaced by a new kind of post-bureaucratic commitment-based organisation. In order that private sector, or marketising public sector, organisations become more 'efficient' writers suggest that we must grow to love our jobs, make suggestions as to how they might be improved, and engage in 360° appraisal.

The convergence between these two narratives – the rise of the citizen and the rise of the new organisation – suggests some powerful analogies. After all, if organisations wish to operate within the framework of a shared mission statement then management are logically forced to acknowledge the reciprocity implied. To put it another way, for an organisational rulebook to be transformed into a 'bill of rights' requires the recognition of a universalism that positions managers and subordinates in similar ways. It seems to me that the rhetoric, if not the practice, of HRM is very much related to this recognition. The reciprocity of rights and responsibilities becomes a language upon which the commitment-based organisation (or the nation-state) is built. Now to be clear here, I am certainly not suggesting that either of these narratives are empirically accurate descriptions of managerial or state histories and practices. What I think is interesting is the similarity of the stories and their conceptions of the democratic process. Most importantly, I want to explore the possibility that when certain forms of language are used they imply that other voices must be allowed into the parliament. In order to do this I will now develop the implications of this suggested convergence, beginning with the organisation and then moving back to some ideas about citizenship.

Power, resistance and globalisation

In 1992, I worked at Staffordshire University and received a copy of its mission statement. Though I was aware it was being developed, I (and all the colleagues I talked to) had no input into the words that I read. Oddly however, it spoke for me – on my behalf. I had commitment and ability, I was open and enthusiastic. The statement told me what I believed higher education was for, what my students wanted, what I as an academic wanted and so on. It was full of inclusive terms – 'we', 'us', 'our' and 'The University recognises . . . ', 'The University will . . . ', 'The University believes . . . ' and so on. This mission statement was intended to articulate, and also perhaps create, a community of interest and a common culture. Of course it failed. I did not recognise the organisation that I worked for in that description. It was, at best, a waste of paper and at worst a document that actually strengthened my distrust of management. I do not believe that my response was unusual. There is a great deal of evidence to suggest that most employees at most organisations are similarly cynical about the company song, tie, scarf, pen, magazine and so on (Ackroyd and Thompson, 1999).

This is often a language of fake community, what Gouldner once called 'pseudo-gemeinschaft' (1952, p. 347). But employees are not dupes who simply absorb whatever is produced by their HRM departments. If they do echo them it is likely to be with a degree of irony that almost entirely undermines their intent. As other critics of new wave management have argued, language of this kind can be seen as an attempt to engineer consent whilst favouring an already privileged group (Silver, 1987; du Gay, 1991; Willmott, 1993; Parker, 2000). Its use does not mean that consent exists, or indeed that it is expected by the managers who write and approve such documents. I assume here that many HR managers and management consultants are not dupes either, and that they understand how much their language conceals and what other symbolic or ritual functions it is intended to perform within the culture of deceit.

However, an acknowledgement of the role of resistance and ironic reflexivity does not mean that mission statements are inconsequential, particularly if they are tied to appraisal, promotion and payment systems. Indeed, a broadly Foucaudian line of argument would suggest that these attempts to define the meaning of 'membership', what it means to be 'one of us', are central to understanding the formulation of subjectivities within any workplace (Knights and Willmott, 1989). As various authors have suggested, this is a new attempt to 'make up' managers, a practice that combines various elements in order to constitute a new form of subjectivity (Miller and Rose, 1990; Miller and O'Leary; 1993; du Gay *et al.*, 1996; Pritchard, 1996). The idea of a committed organisational member is a powerful moral machinery that replaces the external stick with the internal carrot. Grey's (1994) classic paper on the training of accountants illustrates the point well – to succeed means defining career as a project of the self. Thus the member who, even partially, accepts a version of their organisation's common mission can achieve a very happy coincidence – an increase in their possibility of status and reward as well as the warm feeling that what they are doing is valued. This 'organisation wo/man' is dedicated to enterprise in the pursuit of supposedly collective goals, and exercises self-surveillance in order to erase signs of disloyalty. Whilst there are problems with Foucaudian arguments (not least that they underplay the possibility that people are very often doing one thing and thinking another) they are powerful ways of rephrasing HRM as Orwellian 'unfreedom' (Willmott, 1993). New wave employees may only be able to echo the manager's voice, not to challenge it.

The implications of this argument could be suggested to have particular resonances in global network societies (Castells, 1996). As understandings of national identity become increasingly permeable to economic and cultural flows their importance as sites for a rooted identity may begin to decline. Simultaneously (and perhaps consequentially), established understandings of class, ethnicity, locality, even gender and sexuality are suggested to be increasingly liquid. Perhaps one of the only solidities that is emerging is that capitalist organisations operate on a global basis and have economies greater than many medium-sized countries. Even if this sketch is only partially accurate this may be one reason why organisational membership becomes increasingly possible. Management strategies attempt to disentangle employees from previous (possibly weakening) cultural, political or spatial affiliations and tie them strongly to their organisation as a bulwark in an increasingly fragmented world.

Now I willingly acknowledge the empirical problems with this argument. There is no agreement that a coherent global corporate citizenry exists – though Sklair makes a persuasive argument about a 'trans-national capitalist class' (2000). In any case, the globalisation thesis has many critics, some who suggest nationalism is still a key foci of identity (Calhoun, 1993), and others that there is nothing really new here anyway (Bamyeh, 1993). Once again I would suggest that what is important is not so much whether the story is true, but whether enough people believe in it. The idea of the warm communities of a previous era being increasingly fragmented by the turbulence of late capitalism does suggest that the remaining stable institutions could become resources for identity construction. This means that the idea of self-actualisation or identity construction through work is increasingly seen as credible by many people and that is in itself a matter of interest. As Miller and Rose put it – 'there is no longer any barrier between the economic, the psychological and the social' (1990, p. 27). We are always at work.

Citizens and organisations

Attempts to create commitment-based organisations can also be seen as attempts to delineate the rights and responsibilities of the corporate citizen. Both the language of HRM and the language of citizenship involve making assertions of normative commonality, suggesting that the state is a society or nation, or the organisation a community or culture. They also both involve articulating the rights of the member (citizen, employee) and their obligations to the institution (state, organisation). Yet, as has been suggested many times in the literature on citizenship (for example, Turner, 1990, 1991), the concept is extremely contested. The key logical problem hinges on whether it is deemed an inclusive or exclusive classification. If the former, then citizenship becomes a unifying category that takes priority over other divisions – gender, class, ethnicity and so on. However, the latter view forces us to recognise that there is no single position that will not in some way reflect values that construct certain kinds of people as lesser citizens, or even non-citizens. Either the Other's difference is denied, subsumed within false incorporating claims, or the Other's difference is emphasised and they become no longer fully human, uncivilised. Finding a middle ground is difficult because it requires an explication of shared values, of the boundaries of behaviour that must be crossed before citizenship is restricted or revoked. In any case, as Marshall was aware, in any complex society 'citizenship is the architect of legitimate inequality' and hence our explication of shared values must include decisions on how much inequality we will tolerate and in which spheres (Minson, 1993). If such difficulties were not enough, it is also fair to say that the language of citizenship provides little help in the practical resolution of everyday conflicts. Reframing practical problems in what Minson calls a 'romantic republican' language makes them no more amenable to solution. For example, simply telling someone that they have 'rights' does little to adjudicate on the corresponding 'rights' claims of all other citizens. There is (apart from metaphysics) no place outside local values that can legitimate the constitutional tablets coming down from the mountain.

All that being said, I would still argue that the idea of citizenship is still a useful one. A state, or organisation, can be viewed metaphorically as a social contract and, if the metaphor is shared widely enough, that will shape conduct. In any case, it seems inescapably true that we participate in forms of social organisation which allow us to do some things that we could not achieve on our own, but this participation in itself means that we cannot do other things. Of course we do not usually participate as equals and so our rights and responsibilities are not equally distributed either. White, able-bodied, heterosexual, middle class and middle-aged males construct citizenship in most modern states. This means that institutional practices are hence often exclusive; they stress revoking membership if responsibilities are not met. Yet, using the symmetry of the same starting point it is possible to suggest that the concept can be *tactically* used to stress rights. Putting it simply, if managers talk about responsibilities then there is an opening for their subordinates to represent themselves and their superiors within the same logic. This is pretty much what Marshall (1950) wanted to argue in suggesting that citizenship rights may have begun as specifications of a formally free labour force – civil rights supporting bourgeois capitalism – but that their extension into the political and social spheres increasingly problematised the class inequalities that were characteristic of capitalism in the first place. In other words, the very dualism of rights and responsibilities is often uncomfortably double edged for those who claim them to be important.

The tactics of organisational citizenship

> Behind the citizenship debate is the quest for an adequate account of the public within which the good life could be realised on the basis of universalistic social participation, irrespective of colour, creed, class, age or gender. (Turner, 1991, p. 217)

In this chapter I am suggesting that perhaps the manager's smug voice can be used against him, that the rest of the metaphorical 'family' can ask the father to eat his greens too.[7] Staffordshire University's mission statement said 'people matter above all else'. It said that management was a matter of motivating the commitment of employees. This may be bland rhetoric but it did not say that profits or certain members matter above all else (which may be true), or that they did not care what employees think (which may also be true). The point is that within the language is the possibility that employees might take them at their word. 'If you really do care what we think, then listen to this.' If management is prepared to present a version of the organisational citizen as one that accepts responsibilities then they are, discursively at least, also forced to accept the reciprocity implied – that all citizens have rights. Most importantly, this might mean that management will be forced to listen to some other accounts of the organisation, to establish and institutionalise ways of articulating and mediating different claims to rights as *their* responsibility.

Of course organisational democracy does not need to wait for the formulation of mission statements, but a certain kind of engagement could begin with them. That being said, I do not think that an organisation will change simply because an employee starts quoting the mission statement back at them. The managers who wrote them may not believe in them either and, as I indicated earlier, the culture of deceit provides legitimacy for such half-truths anyway. Mission statements are documents that will be read by insiders and outsiders, superiors and subordinates in many different ways and their meaning is inseparable from a local context (Swales and Rogers, 1995; Pritchard, 1996). To treat them as legislative statutes would be politically naive, but a practice of organisational democracy might begin with a text that appears to mimic an organisational bill of rights. This could be an arena within which challenges might be made using the same language of civil and political citizenship that management wish to claim as belonging to everyone. In a sense, much HRM language provides an opening because it relies for its persuasiveness on an alliance with a language of modernising emancipation. This is both its strength and its central tactical weakness.

If such a hypothetical contest were joined within an organisation then there would seem to be three broad options. First management could simply ignore the rights claims of workers, in which case HR language would be exposed as mere deceit. Secondly, management could abandon their commitment-led language and re-institute or further strengthen the coercions of time and motion. Thirdly, the optimistic scenario, a dialogue might be joined and further specification of the rights and responsibilities of the organisational citizen might result. In favour of the optimistic scenario I suggest three points. The first is that managers, like most other people, would probably rather think of themselves as democrats than autocrats and it is embarrassing to be revealed (to oneself and others) as a liar where such matters are concerned.[8] Secondly, to move towards more explicitly coercive controls is (according to the influential narrative of organisational evolution) to travel backwards in history. The narrative may be flawed, but if managers give it legitimacy then it may have important consequences. Thirdly, and probably most importantly, in all workplaces, managers need workers co-operation in some form or another. This is most obviously true in organisations that rely on strategies of 'responsible autonomy' (rather than 'direct control') for certain groups of subordinates (Friedman, 1977). Options one and two would result in expensive and time-consuming direct control strategies being required for all workers. Not only would this be technically difficult, it would also increase expense very substantially indeed. Even Burger King does not rely on direct control for assistant managers and above.

However, even if I am correct and some kind of dialogue about rights and responsibilities was joined, there would be no way of avoiding the problems with inclusive and exclusive definitions of citizenship identified above. Like states, organisations are not normatively homogeneous and neither are their 'goals' ('missions') uncontested. Specifying the mission of Burger King would have to (at least) make reference to customers, public health specialists, vegetarians, environmentalists, trade unions, residents of the local area, suppliers and the whole range of different employees. Most importantly, it would also require that the organisation's management acknowledged the limitations that all of these varied claims to rights placed on their responsibilities. Opening up the language of organisational citizenship is not the solution to these problems, but it does allow the questions to be legitimately asked.

Before concluding I want to bring the argument back to the state. Considering the position of the principled organisational traitor will illustrate my point. A member or group might disagree fundamentally with an organisational policy on ethical-political grounds, and agitate inside and outside the organisation to get that policy changed. This includes various forms of industrial action, 'whistleblowing' or even sabotage but does not include any activity that was stimulated by the expectation of personal financial gain – espionage or insider dealing for example. Clearly, the member will be involved in activities that may result in their citizenship rights being revoked for reasons that many other organisational members, not just management, will find perfectly valid. As far as I can see this is a matter that cannot be resolved within the organisation itself for obvious reasons. If I had been sacked by Burger King for publicly accusing management of lying on their paper cups I would not want my jury to consist only of Burger King employees. The example does not invalidate the arguments I have been putting forward above, but it does point to the importance of augmenting them with an acknowledgement that the possibilities of organisational citizenship must be defined by a judicial context. In other words, we are back to the inclusion/exclusion problem – the question of what behaviours invalidate the social contract in a given organisation.

As far as I can see the only current contenders to deal with such problems are various arms of the state. Matters of organisational treachery could only be resolved, however partially, by recourse to wider notions of justice and public interest. As Marshall hinted, a collectivist conception of 'industrial citizenship' may well be a development of individualistic conceptions of rights in the civil, political and social arenas (1950, see Giddens, 1982; Minson, 1993). This must mean that the institutional frameworks within which such resolutions might take place would have be arranged as a system of laws or codes which were binding on all organisations operating within a given arena. Locally agreed mission statements/constitutions would have to be subordinated to, and hence be framed within, broader assumptions about the rights and obligations of workers as well as how much legitimate inequality between workers and management will be tolerated. Laws – about consultation, representation, employment rights, discrimination, trade union organisation and so on – could be the only bulwark that ensures that the fragile organisational citizenship I have been outlining could be protected in practice. It may seem a little odd to be relying on the state to guarantee so much, but any formulation of citizenship, and certainly organisational citizenship, is going to be parasitic on state, or multi-state, institutions for the time being (Barbalet, 1988, p. 109). After all, corporations do not yet issue passports.

Conclusion

I have a strong feeling that more cynical or pragmatic readers will suggest that this is a hopelessly utopian argument.[9] I can only respond, rather glibly, that if we give up on imagining alternatives then we give up on the possibility of change. To put the same thing in a more theoretical manner, what I am doing is something like imagining Habermas's 'ideal speech situation' – the assumption that all members involved in communication are oriented towards mutual understanding (1984). Habermas wishes to persuade us that this is a rational and progressive way to think about language because he believes that any communication contains a 'gentle but obstinate, a never silent although seldom redeemed claim to reason' (1979, p. 3). This provides us with the possibility that the language of the Burger King cup could be clearly understood as deceitful, and not just a normal part of our culture. Treating such language 'as if' it were true then exposes hypocrisy, or solicits change. In other words, if the mission statement is partially constituted and popularised through an alliance with the language of liberal democracy then perhaps it might also be undone or exceeded by liberal democracy too.

I would like to conclude by acknowledging the paradox at the heart of this chapter. I am uneasy about attempts to manipulate the identity of organisational members – to make them into corporate acolytes. As Willmott (1993) suggests, strong forms of culturalism can be seen as an Orwellian 'newspeak', an attempt to impose a form of self-consciousness that serves the powerful and suppresses debate and discontent. Yet at the same time I am aware that the idea of working for an organisation that I can believe in is a very attractive one. I do not want to feel that 'my job is my job and my soul is my own' as if the two worlds never met (Rippen, 1993) and I would be very happy if (in my organisation) phrases about care, value and community actually meant something. In other words, I want to find meaning at work and to feel that my organisation is doing worthwhile things. The paradox is that some senses of belonging that might be real and fulfilling to some people strike others as vacuous propaganda.

> With $11 billion in annual sales and more than 11000 restaurants worldwide, BURGER KING® is sizzling with growth plans as hot and juicy as our flame-broiled burgers. [. . .] Just as we have provided customers with unlimited ways to treat their taste buds, we are also a company with a full menu of employment options. Whether you're looking for an exciting opportunity to shape a career with a global leader, or for a terrific part-time job close to home, Burger King Corporation offers some very juicy possibilities! Any wonder why we're focused on attracting and retaining top-notch people? Any wonder why we're

glad that you're here exploring how our opportunities might suit your needs? (www.bk.com/CompanyInfo/careers/index.aspx, 29/3/06)

Burger King's definition of the juicy benefits of organisational citizenship is, at first sight, my definition of false consciousness. On the other hand I suppose I do want to carry on eating burgers. I would also very much like the people who make my burgers to be content, to be well paid, to feel they are doing a good job for an organisation that appreciates their efforts and so on.[10] I am, of course, not certain they will want to be organisational citizens in the way I have outlined above – partly because of the responsibilities that will follow from their rights. But then surely that is the whole point. The promise of liberal formulations of citizenship are that they are not fixed categories but socially constructed ones that ideally follow from negotiations about the acceptable boundaries of behaviour. Since such ideals are now widely applied as governmental practices in the civil, political and social contexts I see no reason why they might not also be applied to organisations. Unless there really is no escape from the culture of deceit, from the smell of bullshit? As George Bernard Shaw put it, echoing Habermas, 'The liar's punishment is, not in the least that he cannot be believed, but that he cannot believe anyone else.'

Notes

1. This chapter is a revised version of Parker's (1997) 'Organisations and Citizenship', *Organisation*, 4:1, 75–92 (1997). A different version again appears as chapter three in Parker (2002). Thanks to the editors for their comments on this version.
2. Arthur (2003) provides a nice discussion of utility and its relation to truth in the context of business, and Frankfurt (2005) is a nice discussion of the difference between lies and 'bullshit'.
3. As Nietzche put it 'the most common lie is that which one lies to himself, lying to others is relatively an exception'. Frankfurt (2005, p. 56) also notes that at least the liar has some relation to truth, whilst the bullshitter is 'neither on the side of the true nor on the side of the false'.
4. 'BURGER KING, HAVE IT YOUR WAY and the Crescent Logo are registered trademarks of Burger King Corporation. © 2005 Burger King Corporation. All rights reserved.'
5. My apologies for simplifying Habermas's universal pragmatics down to this sort of example. For the full details, see Habermas (1979; 1984). Frankfurt School and later critical theory seems to be partly defined by the idea of soliciting emancipatory possibilities from the trivialisations of market managerialism (see Parker, 2003).
6. See Johnson (2006) for an extended critique of such claims.
7. Something that might happen in some families already.
8. This is important, because it is not an implication of this chapter that all the people who participate in the culture of deceit are liars intentionally. They probably do it because they feel that they have no choice, or forget that they too hate bullshit in many areas of their lives. See Frankfurt (2005).

9. For a robust criticism of the original paper, see Hancock (1997).
10. This is the point in the argument where real utopians and mere liberal democrats would part company. For more on industrial democracy, worker self-management and utopian alternatives to BURGER KING® see Parker *et al.* (2006).

References

Ackroyd, S. and Thompson, P. (1999) *Organisational Misbehaviour*. London: Sage.
Ahrne, G. (1996) 'Civil Society and Civil Organisations', *Organisation*, 3:1, 109–120.
Andriof, J. and McIntosh, M. (eds) (2001) *Corporate Citizenship: Awakening the Possibilities*. London: Greenleaf.
Arthur, A. (2003) 'A Utility Theory of Truth', *Organization*, 10:2, 205–221.
Bamyeh, M. (1993) 'Transnationalism', *Current Sociology*, 41:3.
Barbalet, J. (1988) *Citizenship*. Milton Keynes: Open University Press.
Beder, S. (2000) *Selling the Work Ethic: From Puritan Pulpit to Corporate PR*. London: Zed Books.
Calhoun, C. (1993) 'Nationalism and Civil Society', *International Sociology*, 8, 387–411.
Castells, M. (1996) *The Network Society*. Oxford: Blackwell.
du Gay, P. (1991) 'Enterprise Culture and the Ideology of Excellence', *New Formations*, 13.
du Gay, P., Salaman, G. and Rees, B. (1996) 'The Conduct of Management and the Management of Conduct', *Journal of Management Studies*, 33:3, 263–282.
Frankfurt, H. (2005) *On Bullshit*. Princeton University Press.
Friedman, A. (1977) *Industry and Labour*. London: Macmillan.
Giddens, A. (1982) 'Class Division, Class Conflict and Citizenship Rights', in A. Giddens (ed.) *Profiles and Critiques in Social Theory*. London: Macmillan.
Gouldner, A. (1952) 'The Problem of Succession in Bureaucracy', in Merton, R. *et al.* (eds) *Reader in Bureaucracy*. New York: Free Press.
Grey, C. (1994) 'Career as a Project of the Self and Labour Process Discipline', *Sociology*, 28, 479–497.
Grint, K. (1994) 'Reengineering History', *Organisation*, 1, 179–201.
Habermas, J. (1979) *Communication and the Evolution of Society*. Boston: Beacon Press.
Habermas, J. (1984) *The Theory of Communicative Action: Volume 1*. Oxford: Polity.
Hancock, P. (1997) 'Citizenship or Vassalage? Organisational Membership in the Age of Unreason', *Organisation*, 4:1, 93–111.
Handy, C. (1997) 'The Citizen Corporation', *Harvard Business Review*, 75:5, 26–27.
Hickman, C. and Silva, M. (1985) *Creating Excellence*. London: Unwin.
Janssens, M. and Brett, J. (1994) 'Coordinating Global Companies', in Cooper, C. and Rousseau, D. (eds) *Trends in Organisational Behaviour*. Chichester: Wiley.
Jary, D. and Jary, J. (eds) (2000) *Dictionary of Sociology*. London: Collins.
Johnson, P. (2006) 'Whence Democracy?' *Organization*, 13:2, 245–274.
Klein, N. (2000) *No Logo: Taking Aim at the Brand Bullies*. London: Flamingo.
Knights, D. and Willmott, H. (1989) 'Power and Subjectivity at Work', *Sociology*, 23, 535–558.
Kunda, G. (1992) *Engineering Culture*. Philadelphia: Temple University Press.
Manville, B. and Ober, J. (2003) *A Company of Citizens: What the World's First Democracy Teaches Leaders about Creating Great Organizations*. Boston, MA: Harvard University Business School.
Marshall, T. (1950) *Citizenship and Social Class and Other Essays*. Cambridge: Cambridge University Press.
Matten, D. and Crane, A. (2005) 'Corporate Citizenship', *Academy of Management Review*, 30:1, 166–179.

Miller, P. and O'Leary, T. (1993) 'Accounting Expertise and the Politics of the Product', *Accounting, Organisations and Society*, 18:2/3, 187–206.

Miller, P. and Rose, N. (1990) 'Governing Economic Life', *Economy and Society*, 19:1, 1–31.

Minson, J. (1993) *Questions of Conduct*. Basingstoke: Macmillan.

Organ, D. (1990) 'The Motivational Bases of Organisational Citizenship Behavior', in Staw, B. and Cummings, L. (eds) *Research in Organisational Behavior*, Vol. 12. Greenwich, CT: JAI Press.

Ouchi, W. (1981) *Theory Z*. Reading, MA: Addison-Wesley.

Parker, M. (1997) 'Organisations and Citizenship', *Organisation*, 4:1, 75–92.

Parker, M. (2000) *Organizational Culture and Identity*. London: Sage.

Parker, M. (2002) *Against Management*. Oxford: Polity.

Parker, M. (2003) 'Business, Ethics and Business Ethics: Critical Theory and Negative Dialectics', in Alvesson, M. and Willmott, H. (eds) *Studying Management Critically*. London: Sage.

Parker, M., Fournier, V. and Reedy, P. (2006) *The Dictionary of Utopias and Alternative Organization*. London: Zed Books.

Peters, T. and Waterman, R. (1982) *In Search of Excellence*. New York: Harper Collins.

Plant, R. and Barry, N. (1990) *Citizenship and Rights in Thatcher's Britain*. London: IEA Health and Welfare Unit.

Pritchard, C. (1996) 'Making Managers Accountable or Making Managers?' *Educational Management and Administration*, 24:1, 79–91.

Silver, J. (1987) 'The Ideology of Excellence: Management and Neo-Conservatism', *Studies in Political Economy*, 24, 105–129.

Sklair, L. (2000) *The Transnational Capitalist Class*. Oxford: Blackwell.

Smith, C., Child, J. and Rowlinson, M. (1990) *Reshaping Work: The Cadbury Experience*. Cambridge: Cambridge University Press.

Swales, J. and Rogers, P. (1995) 'Discourse and the Projection of Corporate Culture', *Discourse and Society*, 6:2, 223–242.

Thompson, P. and McHugh, D. (1990) *Work Organisations*. London: Macmillan.

Turner, B. (1990) 'Outline of a Theory of Citizenship', *Sociology*, 24, 189–217.

Turner, B. (1991) 'Further Specification of the Citizenship Concept', *Sociology*, 25, 215–218.

Vinten, G. (ed.) (1994) *Whistleblowing: Subversion or Corporate Citizenship*. London: Paul Chapman.

Whyte, W.H. (1961) *The Organisation Man*. Harmondsworth: Penguin.

Willmott, H. (1993) 'Strength is Ignorance; Slavery is Freedom; Managing Culture in Modern Organisations', *Journal of Management Studies*, 30, 515–552.

9

Searching for the human in the HR practice of diversity

Fiona Wilson

Introduction

Just how human, or indeed effective, is the HRM practice of diversity management? The goal of this chapter is to use the research literature to date to trace the story of the development of the practice of equality and diversity management and the research that has evaluated the extent of its success. Evidence that concern for equality and diversity in organisations has had a positive impact on numbers from diverse groups and the terms of their employment should show in statistics on employment trends; is it there? While equal opportunity approaches, underpinned by law, aim for workplaces where individual characteristics like sex and race are of no significance in the treatment humans receive, the core idea behind managing diversity appears to be to encourage organisations to recognise and celebrate differences. Human Resource (HR) practice is concerned to capture diversity as both a reflection of difference but also as a means of dissolving difference in order to encourage equality of opportunity. If the HR function is simultaneously attempting to utilise difference whilst ensuring there is no difference in treatment, this could be difficult to manage (Maxwell, 2004; Foster and Harris, 2005). This can appear as a contradiction, creating tension in HR practice, process and outcome. The chapter is written to stimulate discussion and debate about just how human the HR practice of diversity can be considered to be.

155

HRM and its concern with diversity

Human Resource Management (HRM) is characterised as having a concern with organisational performance as its long-term strategic primary goal, adopting a unitarist perspective and a corresponding belief that employers and employees can be beneficiaries of 'good' HRM if employees are nurtured and developed as valuable members of an organisation (Storey, 1987). An essential part of that nurturing and developing could be expressed in valuing diversity within the organisation, diversity of, for example, gender, religion, race, physical ability/disability, educational background, sexual orientation, ethnicity and age. Broadly, managing diversity means a systematic and planned commitment to recruit and retain employees from diverse demographic backgrounds (Thomas, 1992).

Human Resource Management is a central business function, carried out by line managers and senior executives rather than professional personnel or HR managers (Harley and Hardy, 2004). My view is that HR faces a fundamental dilemma. It is a function that on the one hand is required to operate like an efficient bureaucracy making sure, for example, that employment law is implemented and followed, a suitably diverse range of people are recruited to and selected for vacant jobs, employees are appraised and are paid fairly. It should operate as an ideal bureaucracy, without bias, without 'regard for persons' (Weber, 1948, p. 215), taking the human out of human resources. On the other hand it is required to represent the interests of those who are treated unfairly or unequally, so with regard to persons. It could also be argued that while the rhetoric of HRM is about facilitating the development of human skill, knowledge and experience, providing organisations with competitive advantage, it is at the same time at odds with the promotion of equal opportunities (Dickens, 1994, 1998). If diversity management is viewed in isolation from other strategic HR decisions as Leopold *et al.* (2005) contend, then the H could well be missing from HRM. Before looking further at this very human problem that HRM faces, let us look at diversity management and its critics.

Diversity management and its critics

Diversity emerged as a research topic in the 1990s following practitioners' growing interest in how to 'manage' an increasingly diverse demographic workforce (Nkomo and Cox, 1996). Managing diversity has been frequently presented as a viable long-term strategy likely to yield the firm some crucial economic benefits (Prasad *et al.*, 1997) as an 'alternative approach' (Kandola and Fullerton, 1994) and 'new way forward' (IPD, 1996) for beleaguered equality policies. Research aimed to provide evidence of discrimination in the workplace and for a 'business case' for diversity. Managing diversity is seen as an important and powerful management tool to harness the energies of all organisational members of service in the global battle for organisational success (Litvin, 1997). Managing diversity appears to encourage organisations to recognise difference, respond to it and value it (Liff, 1997). Difference is seen as a resource to be managed; differences among employees leads to broader competences and experiences. Employers should promote an image of the organisation as an 'inclusive' place to work by encouraging applications from 'diverse' individuals so that these employers become 'employers of choice' which enhances their ability to recruit the most talented and skilled individuals (Cox and Blake, 1991). A diverse workforce can raise organisational efficiency and effectiveness (McLeod *et al.*, 1996).

Thomas (in Gordon, 1992) defined managing diversity as learning to cope

> with unassimilated differences. It's about managing people who aren't like you and who don't necessarily aspire to be like you... It's taking differences into account while developing a cohesive whole... The goal is an organization that is able to function as productively with heterogeneous workers as it once did with homogeneous ones.

Heterogeneity is then being presented as something new and different from the past. It is a problem or a challenge if people who are being managed are different and deviant from a norm. While managing diversity might present a challenge, I would disagree that it is something new. While it might have been presented as a new replacement for beleaguered equality policies, organisations have always been faced with heterogeneity, for example old and young employees, men and women, single and married, heterosexual and homosexual. Diversity has been viewed as a 'problem' since at least the Second World War (Prasad and Elmes, 1997).

Not surprisingly, since the early 1990s, the diversity approach has received some criticism. It has been accused of 'upbeat naivety' (Prasad *et al.*, 1997, p. 5) due to the way it de-emphasises the conflicts, problems and dilemmas involved in implementing meaningful diversity policy (Kirton and Greene, 2005). Consultants who have been engaged in organisational diversity programmes at companies such as Digital (Walker and Hanson, 1992) and Xerox (Sessa, 1992) have offered their own personal accounts of successes, presenting the 'happy face' of diversity without paying much attention to race tensions, gender frustrations or ongoing resistance (Prasad *et al.*, 1997).

The underlying assumptions about the nature of diversity and its management have been questioned in the Organisation Studies and HRM research literature. One assumption being questioned is that socio-demographic characteristics are considered as 'immutable differences' (Northcraft and Neale, 1994, p. 637) and 'factors that make up the essence of who we are as human beings' (Moorhead and Griffin, 1995, p. 526). A problem with this assumption is that diversity is seen as primarily a group phenomenon (Litvin, 1997) so that individuals are reduced to being a member of a socio-demographic category such as 'women' or 'migrant workers' with almost no attention to individual differences or within-group variation. Secondly, such groups are seen as objective, 'natural', clear and obvious. But Litvin (1997, p. 201) asks, how would you classify 'a bisexual female with a speech impediment whose father is a "white" person from Spain and whose mother is a member of the Zulu nation of southern Africa'? The categories constructed through the discourse of workforce diversity are hard-pressed to accommodate the complexity of real people and the power differences that exist between both groups and individuals. A third problem is the view of identity as a given fixed essence (Litvin, 1997; Zanoni and Janssens, 2003); for example by looking at gender or race essential differences in attitude, personality and behaviour are highlighted and seen as given or fixed or unchangeable. Yet we know that the meanings attached to these categories are socially constructed. For example, we know that gender is about the social creation of ideas about appropriate roles for women and men and these change with time and place. There is nothing immutable about them. Disabilities can change. For example a person with cancer can go into remission. The underlying assumptions are then not difficult to question and undermine.

Practitioners' texts often argue that organisations should recruit and manage diverse personnel to face the increased diversity among customers (Cox, 1991; Cox and Blake, 1991; Thomas, 1991); the diversity of the employees should 'mirror' the diversity to be found amongst the customers. They discuss the 'business case' of diversity, the potential economic benefits of a diverse workforce and present best practices to help organisations realise them. Thomas and Ely (1996) labelled this as 'the access-and-legitimacy' perspective on diversity. The assumption is that employees with a certain socio-demographic profile, for instance from a particular cultural background or native language, bring skills and insights into the organisation to better reach and serve customers with similar cultural and linguistic characteristics. Yet, as Janssens and Zanoni (2005) note, this perspective has yet to be empirically investigated. It remains unclear which customers' socio-demographic differences, under what conditions, become salient enough to legitimise the provision of a diversity-customised service.

While some like Litvin (1997) have been critical of how diversity is constructed as group phenomenon of employees belonging to the same category, another criticism of the business case for diversity, and how in particular diversity is treated in textbooks on organisational behaviour, is that if it defines diversity broadly so that every employee can be seen as 'different' in terms of age, background, gender, race and so on, and portrayed as working within a classical meritocracy. It is each person's responsibility to grasp opportunities (Liff and Wajcman, 1996). Zanoni and Janssens (2003) argue that this conceptualisation hides power in diversity. It represents organisations as arenas where differences and competences are valued and individuals receive the same opportunities. Diversity is assumed to be a universal and objective fact that can be described, measured and used. Diversity is seen as a reality in current organisations rather than being conceived as a social construction reflecting existing power relations. Their research found that HR managers generally define diversity on the basis of a few selected diversity axes and as a group phenomenon. These definitions fix diverse employees' representations by constructing them solely as members of reference groups sharing given essences such as disability or gender. Diverse employees are discursively denied full subjectivity and agency. Managers are most interested in how difference can be used to attain organisational goals. If it can be, difference is constructed positively; if it cannot then difference is constructed negatively as lack. Diversity discourses clearly reflect existing power relations between managers and employees in the organisation.

It would also appear that there is an underlying, unspoken, unexplored assumption inherent in the concept of managing diversity, in my view. If you manage diversity, have a more diverse workforce, then you will have achieved greater equality. Simply put, diversity equals equality. But does it? Increasing the numbers of disabled or ethnic mix could actually increase the level of discrimination rather than lower it. Are equality approaches and policies more successful than the diversity approach?

Equal opportunity approaches and policies and their critics

Another strand of the research and literature has looked at equal opportunities policies. Equal opportunities approaches or policies are underpinned by a legal framework that stresses the importance of treating people equally (Liff, 1997). There has been a growth in the number of companies adopting formal policies, developing equality initiatives and practices, and signing up to initiatives like Opportunity Now, Race for Opportunity and Positive about Disabled People (Dickens, 2000). However it has been argued that these are not worth the paper they are written on, and companies like Ford (United Kingdom), Coca Cola and Microsoft have been described as having company practice which falls far short of espoused values of equal opportunity enshrined in company policies (Hoque and Noon, 2004). Equal opportunity policies can be a façade behind which unfair practices, prejudice and inequality thrive (Young, 1987; Liff and Dale, 1994; Hoque and Noon, 1999). Case study analysis has shown that members of organisations pay only lip service to policy, few clear procedures are adopted from the policy, and managers are able to subvert the procedures that are developed (Liff and Dale, 1994). Hoque and Noon (2004) found that while there was evidence of a reasonably widespread uptake of formal written Equal Opportunities policies, there is also considerable evidence that many of those policies lack substance, as they are not supported by practices.

Wetherell *et al.* (1987) found that people will see the provision of equality of opportunity for women as highly desirable, but they can also argue that in practice equal opportunities cannot be available and can justify inequality of opportunity. This Wetherell *et al.* called 'unequal egalitarianism'. Similarly Gill (1993) identified a number of different ways in which broadcasters were able to account for a lack of female DJs on local radio stations. The explanation lay in the lack of employment in the women themselves or in factors external to the radio station. McVittie *et al.* (2003) also found that those responsible for employment do not state that they are opposed to employing older workers but attribute the lack of older workers to factors out of the control or influence of their organisations. People can then account for the marginalisation of disadvantaged groups and at the same time sustain that marginalisation.

It may be that companies are adopting equal opportunity policies as 'insurance policies' against potential problems, or as a direct response to a particular problem, to demonstrate that they are responsible employers, or as a result of pressure or for competitive advantage, for example to expand a customer base (see Jewson *et al.*, 1990, 1995; and Dickens, 1999, 2000). Where the aim is to enhance the external or internal image of the organisation there is a greater likelihood that the EO policy will be little more than an 'empty shell' (Hoque and Noon, 2004). Where the aim is to address a particular concern, for example a skills shortage, the policy is more likely to be backed by substance. It may be thought that even in instances where policies are more than just a paper exercise they have only a limited effect. For example, Opportunity Now has been criticised for failing to have any positive impact on women in non-managerial jobs (Richards, 2001). Some managers may be more willing than others to allow employees to job share or take parental leave, so employees' access to these practices might depend on the individual line manager. Low levels of awareness among employees concerning family-friendly practices to which they are entitled will limit their impact (Bond *et al.*, 2002). Hoque and Noon 2004 found that provision of job sharing, parental leave and nursery places was available to only a minority.

One organisation, the British Army, started discussing the management of diversity in the late 1990s, having been stung by criticism about levels of discrimination in its ranks (Woodward and Winter, 2006). Following concerns about the level of racism in the Army, an Equal Opportunities Action Plan was launched in October 1997 which set out objectives and mechanisms for monitoring compliance on a range of measures to combat harassment and discrimination on the basis of ethnicity and sex, and to ensure equality of opportunity for all. Around the same time a 'gender free' model for the assessment of physical capabilities of recruits was introduced, as well as an announcement that the proportion of posts open to women in the Army would be increased from 47 to 70 per cent. These policy frameworks for expanding opportunities for women's participation were accompanied by public policy statements on equal opportunities including the 1999 Defence White Paper (MoD, 1999). Diversity management for the Army is a managerial tool for maximising the performance of every individual. However, Woodward and Winter (2006) argue that the problem is that the structural sources of social disadvantage are left unattended. Attention is diverted from the construction of difference through social practice and towards the management of difference. The existence of social difference, thus unconsidered and unattended, is then assumed as a given, rather than understood as the outcome of social practice. This has important ramifications for women soldiers, and the failure to analyse the sources of difference have allowed an essentialist interpretation of gender difference to hold sway. Essentialist interpretations include interpreting female difference as disruptive to cohesion by their very presence; by being non-men, women are intrinsically disruptive to unit cohesion. Similar arguments are to be found about the incompatibility of non-heterosexuals. All types of difference that deviate from a white, male, heterosexual norm are in some way problematic for the Army (Dandeker and Mason, 2003).

While researchers have looked at organisations like the army, the newspapers have been discussing lack of equality in government. Government too have been concerned to bring about greater equality and introduced a Civil Service Diversity Plan. Back in 1998, they said that women should fill 35 per cent of the top 4000 jobs in Whitehall. (One wonders why it is not 50 per cent.) It is currently about 29 per cent (*The Times*, 2005). The upper echelons of the Civil Service also appear out of reach for most ethnic minority Whitehall workers. Trevor Phillips, the Chair of the Commission for Racial Equality, has called the higher levels of the Civil Service the 'snowy peaks' as virtually all of the ethnic minority civil servants are in the lower grades; above grade five they are almost all white (*The Independent*, 2006). The Commission for Racial Equality said it was so dismayed by the inaction, it was now considering legal action (*Evening Standard*, 2006).

Due to the closeness of personal relationships, it might be thought that small- and medium-sized businesses would be better than large organisations, like the Civil Service, in managing equality of opportunity. However, although they employ over 55.6 per cent of the labour force, they are not associated with good equality practice (Woodhams and Lupton, 2006). In a survey, only 18 per cent of respondents reported that they took active steps to redress gender imbalances in their workforce. Many organisations were actively perpetuating direct and indirect discrimination (Woodhams *et al.*, 2004). Both Collinson (1991) and Lupton (2000) have found that HR specialists were prepared to collude with line managers to circumvent formal equality policies.

The evidence of greater diversity and equality of opportunity

Is there any evidence that concern for equality and diversity in organisations has had a positive impact on numbers from diverse groups and the terms of their employment? What do the statistics show? Looking first at ageism, as this is the form of discrimination most frequently cited by employees, necessitating new regulations to prevent it in October 2006 (Johnson, 2006), the statistics show that the numbers of older workers are rising. The percentage of those over 50 increased from 30.8 to 31.7 per cent of the population between 1971 and 1998. By 2050, it is predicted that 47 per cent of individuals will be 65 and older compared to 27 per cent in 2003 (OECD, 2004). However the participation of the over-50s in employment in the United Kingdom has been declining. The labour force participation rate for those aged 50 and above fell from 44.1 per cent in 1971 to 34.1 per cent in 1997 (McVittie *et al.*, 2003). These figures combined with findings from other studies (e.g., Phillipson, 1998; Campbell, 1999) suggest that older workers are increasingly absent from the workforce. Of course, you could argue that older workers are choosing to retire early. But research shows that the under-representation of older workers is an outcome, at least in part, of employment practices adopted by employers who favour the recruitment and retention of younger workers rather than older ones (Laczko and Phillipson, 1991; Taylor and Walker, 1997). The BBC, for example, while having a very public commitment to equal opportunities, were found to be increasingly excluding those aged over 50 over a 15-year period (Platman and Tinker, 1998).

Human Resource Management has largely remained silent with regard to issues faced by ethnic minorities at work (Kamenou and Fearfull, 2006), yet people from ethnic minorities groups have lower levels of economic activity than white people and higher levels of unemployment. The wide gap between the percentage of those employed from ethnic minority groups and white people has been consistent over the past 20 years (CRE, 2006). The ethnic minority employment rate for Great Britain was 59 per cent compared to an overall employment rate of 75 per cent in 2002. Discrimination testing (where two or more testers equally matched in every respect except their ethnicity apply for the same job vacancy at the same time) has consistently uncovered substantial levels of racial discrimination (Brown and Gay, 1985; CRE, 1996). An important consequence of low employment rates, a high inactivity and unemployment rate for ethnic minority groups is that income is much lower than for white people (CRE, 2006). Ethnic minority women face both racial and gender stereotypes that are often exacerbated by stereotypical perceptions concerning their culture and religion. Ethnic minority women generally have problems identifying mentors and are often excluded from influential networks (Bell *et al.*, 1993; Kemenou, 2002; Kemenou and Fearfull, 2006). Asian women find that their cultural and religious backgrounds are often used to stereotype them as submissive and lacking in career ambition (Rana *et al.*, 1998). This in turn has negative repercussions on their career opportunities and earnings.

Income inequities exist between men and women from all backgrounds; the gap between them remains 'stubbornly large' (Cotton and Worman, 2006). Clara Freeman, the Chair of Opportunity Now, the organisation that promotes the business benefits of an inclusive workforce, notes the 'pay chasm' that exists between men and women despite equal opportunities legislation as women's annual salaries are 25 per cent lower than men's when overtime and bonuses are taken into account (Freeman, 2004). Why do we still have this discrepancy? She says it is because addressing pay disparity takes time, effort and dedication. Most employers are vacillating between ignoring the issue or being scared of the can of worms they suspect will come with a pay audit. Both attitudes are expensive and short-sighted. (See also the Women and Work Commission Report found at www.womenandequalityunit.gov.uk.) Recent research by Olsen and Walby (2004) shows that there has been little change in the full-time gender pay gap since the mid-1990s and in the female part-time/male full-time pay gap since the mid-1970s. The majority of employers have no plans to carry out equal pay audits and nearly a fifth do not allow staff to discuss pay with their colleagues (IDS, 2003). There are many examples of organisations that have been accused of not closing the pay gap. For example, government departments and agencies were given a year to submit equal pay action plans, but only 19 of 93 government departments offered any proposals to close the pay gap (*BBC News*, 2003).

What about appraisal? For example do women and ethnic minorities appear to be equal when appraised? Appraisal is a process in which individuals are differentiated, in which effort and value is judged. It is defined as a 'formal organizational mechanism for controlling the performance of work tasks on a rational, subjective and continuous basis' (Coates, 2004, p. 567). Women are more likely to be at a disadvantage where the appraiser is male with masculine values and frames of reference (Thomas, 1987; Alimo-Metcalfe, 1992; Thomas, 1996). The process of appraisal can help reproduce unequal treatment of women (Wilson, 2004). The process has also been found to be discriminatory for ethnic minority managers (Rana, 2003). Bosses rated ethnic minority male managers as less competent than their peers.

The statistics on the size of the disabled population in relation to employment suggests that they too are still a significantly marginalised employment group (Woodhams and Danieli, 2000). The Labour Force Survey of 1997–98 (Office for National Statistics, 1998) showed that the percentage of disabled people in employment is 40.5 per cent. The process of actively managing diversity for this group is more elusive, less prescriptive and less accessible than for others, Woodhams and Danieli (2000) argue. The disabled are a heterogeneous group so there are no collective group-based characteristics or particular skills and attributes that can be seen to be the property of this group to be valued and to make the business case. Also the removal of organisational barriers, which impede organisational goals and individual fulfilment, is problematic. Not only would the costs be prohibitive but also what may enable one disabled person may disenable another.

One of the many problems faced by those in HR who want to promote equality and diversity is that not everyone supports the notion of a level-playing field in the workplace; moving towards the reality may be seen as threatening to some men and women. There is thought to be a backlash (Faludi, 1991; *Business Week*, 1994; Burke and Black, 1997; Burke, 2005) particularly in North America. This is resistance men exhibit towards policies, programmes and initiatives that promote the hiring and advancement of marginalised groups and has been described as a growing 'white rage' by Prasad and Mills (1997). While diversity programmes have a 'platitudinous façade' there can be 'passionate disagreement' raging beneath (Ellis and Sonnenfeld, 1994). However, a backlash does not need to be an active campaign to stop equality. The issues of inequality can be treated with apathy (Dick and Cassell, 2002), simply be ignored and left to one side.

So how human is the HR practice of equality and diversity?

The widespread adoption of equality policies appears to coexist with the continuing evidence of differential labour market experience by members of different social groups (Liff, 1999). Equal opportunities legislation has not brought about equality of opportunity for all (Wilson, 2003). The legislation does little to rectify the more indirect forms of discrimination as by their very nature they do not appear discriminatory, but rather are part of normal everyday working patterns (Townley, 1994). Diversity discourse remains silent on the enduring 'demographic characteristics of those in positions of power' (Ramsey, 1994, p. 424). It has also remained relatively silent on the very little progress that has been made towards equality of opportunity for all. Managing or celebrating diversity, it could be argued, is no more than a 'pre-emptive ideological project that aims to neutralise race and gender' (Cavanaugh, 1997, p. 44). While the inequalities and discrimination are left uncovered or ignored, the status quo will be maintained. Faced with inequities, staff are unlikely to believe they are in receipt of 'good HRM' or feel valued as the H in HRM.

How then should HR face the dilemma of whether it should operate without 'regard for persons' (Weber, 1948, p. 215), thus taking the human out of human resources; or should it represent the interests of those who are treated unfairly or unequally, so with regard to persons? The dilemma of whether it operates without or with regard for persons should not be glossed over, but often is in the rhetoric of diversity management. I would suggest that it would be helpful to firmly situate the H in HR so that diversity and equal opportunities are more actively managed. Human Resource Management needs to ask if their equal opportunities and diversity policies are supported by practice and what evidence is there to suggest success. This may then mean operating with regard to persons who are clearly unequal, disadvantaged and being discriminated against. The statistics discussed in this chapter on lack of progress in terms of equality demonstrate there is no meritocracy. The business case for diversity is currently couched in mainly economic terms rather than human ones. The rationale for legal compliance and equality is pushed into the background offering HR little incentive to ask what are the human (rather than the purely economic) benefits of a diversity-customised service?

For there to be change, difference and diversity need to be recognised as socially constructed, reflecting power relations, and not immutable. Individuals bring different attributes and differing levels of power into organisations; it would, therefore, be helpful to treat them as individuals facing discrimination, rather than as members of homogeneous groups. In doing so, the HR function will need to think long and hard about whose interests it represents – those senior managers who may wish to keep the economic costs low and in whose interests inequality could serve, or those who are currently unequal and whose interests would be better met by investment so they are truly nurtured, developed and valued. The management of diversity has to be more than just rhetoric.

References

Alimo-Metcalfe, B. (1992) 'Different gender – different rules: assessment of women in management', in Barrar, P. and. Cooper, C.L. (eds) *Managing Organizations in 1992, Strategic Responses*, Routledge, London.

BBC News (2003) 'Equal pay warning to government' (http://newsvote.bbc.co.uk).

Bell, E.L., Denton, T.C. and Nkomo, S.M. (1993) 'Women of color in management: towards an inclusive analysis', in Larwood, L. and Gutek, B. (eds) *Women in Management: Trends, Issues, and Challenges in Managerial Diversity*, Sage, California.

Bond, S., Hyman, J., Summers, J. and Wise, S. (2002) *Family-Friendly Working?: Putting Policy into Practice*, Joseph Rowntree Foundation/The Policy Press, York.

Brown, C. and Gay, P. (1985) *Racial Discrimination: 17 years After the Act*, Policy Studies Institute, London.

Burke, R.J. (2005) 'Backlash in the workplace', *Women in Management Review*, 20:3, 165–176.

Burke, R.J. and Black, S. (1997) 'Save the males: backlash in organizations', in Burke, R. (ed.) *Women in Corporate Management*, Kluwer, Dordrecht.

Business Week (1994) 'White, male and worried', 31 January.

Campbell, N. (1999) *The Decline in Employment among Older People in Britain, CASE Paper 19*, Centre for Analysis of Social Exclusion, London.

Cavanaugh, J.M. (1997) '(In)corporating the other?', in Prasad, P., Mills, A.J., Elmes, M. and Prasad, A. (eds) *Managing the Organizational Melting Pot: Dilemmas of Workplace Diversity*, Sage, London, Chapter 2.

Coates, G. (2004) 'Entrusting appraisal to the trust', *Gender, Work and Organization*, 11:5, 566–588.

Collinson, D. (1991) 'Poachers turned gamekeepers: are personnel managers one of the barriers to equal opportunities?' *Human Resource Management Journal*, 1:3, 58–76.

Cotton, C. and Worman, D. (2006) 'Payback time', *People Management*, 9 February, 42.

Cox, T. (1991) 'The multicultural organization', *Academy of Management Executive*, 5:2, 34–47.

Cox, T. and Blake, S. (1991) 'Managing cultural diversity: implications for organizational effectiveness', *Academy of Management Executive*, 5:3, 45–56.

CRE (Commission for Racial Equality) (1996) *We Regret to Inform You . . .* CRE, London.

CRE (Commission for Racial Equality) (2006) *Statistics: Labour Market* (www.cre. gov.uk/research/statistics-labour).

Dandeker, C. and Mason, D. (2003) 'Diversifying the uniform: the participation of minority ethnic personnel in the British Armed Services', *Armed Forces and Society*, 29:4, 481–507.

Dick, P. and Cassell, C. (2002) 'Barriers to managing diversity in a UK constabulary: the role of discourse', *Journal of Management Studies*, 39:7, 953–976.

Dickens, L. (1994) 'Wasted resources? Equal opportunities in employment', in Sisson, K. (ed.) *Personnel Management: A Comprehensive Guide to Theory and Practice in Britain*, Blackwell, Oxford.

Dickens, L. (1998) 'What HRM means for gender equality', *Human Resource Management Journal*, 8:1, 23–40.

Dickens, L. (1999) 'Beyond the business case: a three pronged approach to equality action', *Human Resource Management Journal*, 9, 9–19.

Dickens, L. (2000) 'Still wasting resources? equality in employment', in Bach, S. and Sisson, K. (eds) *Personnel Management* 3rd edition, Blackwell, Oxford, pp. 137–169.

Ellis, C. and Sonnenfeld, J.A. (1994) 'Diverse approaches to managing diversity', *Human Resource Management*, 33:1, 79–109.

Evening Standard (2006) 'Whitehall accused of ignoring law on race equality checks', 21 February, Author Martin Bentham.

Faludi, S. (1991) *Backlash: The Undeclared War Against American Women*, Crown Publishers Inc., New York.

Foster, C. and Harris, L. (2005) 'Easy to say, difficult to do: diversity management in retail', *Human Resource Management Journal*, 15:3, 4–17.

Freeman, C. (2004) 'Women play salary catch-up', *People Management*, 25 March, 27.

Gill, R. (1993) 'Justifying injustice: broadcasters' accounts of inequality', in Burman, E. and Parker, I. (eds) *Discourse Analytic Research: Repertories and Readings of Texts in Action*, Routledge, London, pp. 75–93.

Gordon, J. (1992) 'Rethinking Diversity', *Training*, January, 23–30.

Harley, B. and Hardy, C. (2004) 'Firing blanks? An analysis of discursive struggle in HRM', *Journal of Management Studies*, 41:3, 377–400.

Hoque, K. and Noon, M. (1999) 'Racial discrimination in speculative applications: new optimism six years on?' *Human Resource Management Journal*, 9:3, 71–82.

Hoque, K. and Noon, M. (2004) 'Equal opportunities policy and practice in Britain: evaluating the "empty shell" hypothesis', *Work, Employment and Society*, 18:3, 481–506.

IDS (Incomes Data Services) (2003) *Equal Pay: Lack of Progress May Make Gender Pay Audits Mandatory*, Editorial from IDS report 879, April.

The Independent (2006) 'Civil Service's "racial bias" attached', 14 March, Colin Brown.

IPD (1996) 'Managing diversity', *An IPD Position Paper*, IPD, London.

Janssens, M. and Zanoni, P. (2005) 'Many diversities for many services: theorizing diversity (management) in service companies', *Human Relations*, 58:3, 311–340.

Jewson, N., Waters, S. and Harvey, J. (1990) *Ethnic Minorities and Employment Practice: A Study of Six Employers*, Research paper no. 76, Employment Department, Sheffield.

Jewson, N., Mason, D., Drewett, A. and Rossiter, W. (1995) *Formal Equal Opportunities Policies and Employment Best Practice*, Employment Department Research Series, no. 69, Employment Department, Sheffield.

Johnson, A. (2006) 'Be ready for the age discrimination laws', *Personnel Today*, 4 April, 21–24.

Kandola, R. and Fullerton, J. (1994) 'Managing the mosaic: diversity in action', *Institute of Personnel and Development*, London.

Kemenou, N. (2002) *Ethnic Minority Women in English Organizations: Career Experiences and Opportunities*, Unpublished PhD thesis, Leeds University Business School, Leeds.

Kemenou, N. and Fearfull, A. (2006) 'Ethnic minority women: a lost voice in HRM', *Human Resource Management Journal*, 16:2, 154–172.

Kirton, G. and Greene, A.M. (2005) *The Dynamics of Managing Diversity: A Critical Approach*, 2nd edition, Elsevier Butterworth Heinemann, Oxford.

Laczko, F. and Phillipson, C. (1991) *Changing Work and Retirement*, Open University Press, Milton Keynes.

Leopold, J., Harris, L. and Watson, T. (2005) *The Strategic Managing of Human Resources*, Prentice Hall, Harlow.

Liff, S. (1997) 'Two routes to managing diversity: individual differences or social group characteristics', *Employee Relations*, 19:1, 11–26.

Liff, S. (1999) 'Diversity and equal opportunities: room for a constructive compromise?' *Human Resource Management Journal*, 9:1, 65–75.

Liff, S. and Dale, K. (1994) 'Formal opportunity, informal barriers: black women managers within a local authority', *Work, Employment and Society*, 8:2, 177–198.

Liff, S. and Wajcman, J. (1996) 'Sameness and difference revisited: which way forward for equal opportunity initiatives?' *Journal of Management Studies*, 33:1, 79–94.

Litvin, D.R. (1997) 'The discourse of diversity: from biology to management', *Organization*, 4:2, 187–209.

Lupton, B. (2000) 'Pouring the coffee at interview? Personnel's role in the selection of doctors', *Personnel Review*, 29:1, 48–64.

Maxwell, G. (2004) 'Minority report: taking the initiative in managing diversity at BBC Scotland', *Employee Relations*, 26:2, 285–295.

McLeod, P.L., Lobel, S.A. and Cox, T.H. (1996) 'Ethnic diversity and creativity in small groups', *Small Group Research*, 27, 248–264.

McVittie, C., McKinlay, A. and Widdicombe, S. (2003) 'Committed to (un) equal opportunities? "New ageism" and the older worker', *British Journal of Social Psychology*, 42, 595–612.

MoD (Ministry of Defence) (1999) *Defence White Paper 1999 Cm 4446*. The Stationery Office, London, available on line at http://www.mod.uk/publictions/whitepaper 1999/index.htm.

Moorhead, G. and Griffin, R.W. (1995) *Organizational Behaviour: Managing People and Organizations*, Houghton Mifflin, Boston, MA.

Nkomo, S. and Cox, T. (1996) 'Diverse identities in organizations', in Clegg, S.R., Hardy, C. and Nord, W.R. (eds) *Handbook of Organization Studies*, Sage, London, pp. 338–356.

Northcraft, G.B. and Neale, M.A. (1994) *Organizational Behaviour: A Management Challenge*, 2nd edition, The Dryden Press, Fort Worth, TX.

OECD (2004) *Aging and Employment Policies – UK*, OECD Publications, Paris.

Office for National Statistics (1998) *Labour Force Survey*, Office for National Statistics, London.

Olsen, W. and Walby, S. (2004) *Modelling Gender Pay Gaps*, EOC working paper, EOC, November, Manchester.

Phillipson, C. (1998) 'Changing work and retirement: older workers, discrimination and the labour market', in Bernard, M. and Phillips, J. (eds) *The Social Policy of Old Age*, Centre for Policy on Ageing, London, pp. 76–92.

Platman, K. and Tinker, A. (1998) 'Getting on in the BBC: a case study of older workers', *Ageing and Society*, 18:5, 513–535.

Prasad, A. and Elmes, M. (1997) 'Issues in the management of workplace diversity', in Prasad, P., Mills, A.J., Elmes, M. and Prasad, A. (eds) *Managing the Organizational Melting Pot: Dilemmas of Workplace Diversity*, Sage, London, Chapter 15.

Prasad, P. and Mills, A. (1997) 'From showcase to shadow: understanding the dilemmas of managing workplace diversity', in Prasad, P., Mills, A.J., Elmes, M. and Prasad, A. (eds) *Managing the Organizational Melting Pot: Dilemmas of Workplace Diversity*, Sage, London.

Prasad, P., Mills, A., Elmes, A. and Prasad, A. (1997) *Managing the Organizational Melting Pot*, Sage, London.

Ramsey, V.J. (1994) 'Even handedness in work force diversity courses', *Journal of Management Education*, 18, 424–427.

Rana, E. (2003) 'Council appraisals discriminate, public sector', *People Management*, 9:2, 11.

Rana, B.K., Kagan, C., Lewis, S. and Rout, U. (1998) 'British South Asian women managers and professional: experiences of work and family', *Women in Management Review*, 13:6, 221–232.

Richards, W. (2001) 'Evaluating equal opportunity initiatives: the case for a "transformative" agenda', in Noon, M. and Ogbonna, E. (eds) *Equality, Diversity and Disadvantage in Employment*, Palgrave, Basingstoke, pp. 15–31.

Sessa, V.I. (1992) 'Managing diversity at the Xerox Corporation: balanced workforce goals and caucus groups', in Jackson, S.E. (ed.) *Diversity in the Workplace: human resource initiatives*, Guilford, New York, pp. 37–64.

Storey, J. (1987) 'Developments in the management of human resources: an interim report', *Warwick Papers in Industrial Relations*, Industrial Relations Research Unit, The University of Warwick, UK, p. 17.

Taylor, P. and Walker, A. (1997) Age discrimination and public policy, *Personnel Review*, 26:4, 307–318.

Thomas, P.J. (1987) 'Appraising the performance of women: gender and the naval officer', in Gutek, B.A. and Larwood, L. (eds) *Women's Career Development*, Sage Publications, London.

Thomas, R.R. (1991) *Beyond Race and Gender: Unleashing the Power of Your Total Workforce my Managing Diversity*, AMACOM, New York.

Thomas, R.R. (1992) 'Managing diversity: a conceptual framework', in Jackson, S.E. (ed.) *Diversity in the Workplace: Human Resource Initiatives*, Guilford, New York, pp. 306–318.

Thomas, R. (1996) 'Gendered cultures and performance appraisal: the experience of women academics', *Gender, Work and Organization*, 3:3, 143–155.

Thomas, D.A. and Ely, R.J. (1996) 'Making differences matter: a new paradigm for managing diversity', *Harvard Business Review*, September–October, pp. 79–90.

The Times (2005) 'Civil Service Diversity Plan – the issue explained', 8 November.

Townley, B. (1994) *Reframing Human Resource Management, Power, Ethics and Subject*, Sage, London.

Walker, R.A. and Hanson, W. (1992) 'Valuing differences at digital corporation', in Jackson, S.E. (ed.) *Diversity in the Workplace: Human Resource Initiatives*, Guilford, New York, pp. 119–137.

Weber, M. (1948) 'Bureaucracy', in Gerth H.H. and Wright Mills, C. (eds and trans.) *From Max Weber: Essays in Sociology*, published as 1991 edition, Routledge, London, pp. 196–244.

Wetherell, M., Stiven, H. and Potter, J. (1987) 'Unequal egalitarianism: a preliminary study of discourse concerning gender and employment opportunities', *British Journal of Social Psychology*, 26, 59–71.

Wilson, F.M. (2003) *Organizational Behaviour and Gender*, 2nd edition, Ashgate, Aldershot.

Wilson, F.M. (2004) 'Caught between difference and similarity: the case of women in academia', *Women in Management Review*, 20:4, 234–248.

Woodhams, C. and Danieli, A. (2000) 'Disability and diversity – a difference too far?' *Personnel Review*, 29:3, 402–417.

Woodhams, C. and Lupton, B. (2006) 'Gender-based equal opportunities policies and practice in small firms: the impact of HR professionals', *Human Resource Management Journal*, 16:1, 74–97.

Woodhams, C., Lupton, B. and Raydon-Rennie, S. (2004) *Gender-Based Equal Opportunities in SMEs: Establishing Policy and Practice*, Report published by Manchester Metropolitan University Business School, Manchester.

Woodward, R. and Winter, P. (2006) 'Gender and the limits to diversity in the contemporary British Army', *Gender, Work and Organization*, 13:1, 45–67.

Young, K. (1987) 'The space between words', in Jenkins, R. and Solomos, J. (eds) *Racism and Equal Opportunity Policies in the 1980s*, Cambridge University Press, Cambridge, pp. 93–109.

Zanoni, P. and Janssens, M. (2003) 'Deconstructing difference: the rhetoric of human resource managers' diversity discourses', *Organization Studies*, 25:1, 55–74.

10

Human resource development or developing human capability?

Jane Bryson

This chapter discusses the area of HRM practice that comes within the general description of human resource development (HRD). Two important, but seldom discussed, questions underpin the chapter: is it reasonable to expect employers to contribute to HRD? And what is it reasonable to expect of HRD practitioners?

First, in a search for definition, the chapter explores what seems to constitute the general territory of HRD activity. Then an analysis of the broader literature of work and learning, and a small but emerging stream of critical HRD, illustrates the insular and organisationally focused nature of most HRD commentary. It suggests that despite a changing HRD vocabulary, for example from training and development to learning and development and an emphasis on lifelong learning in the rhetoric of HRD, the practice of human resource development is almost exclusively concerned with the achievement of organisational ends and not about contributing to society, or the workforce or the individual. This concern is underpinned by the pervasive assumptions of resource-based views of the firm and human capital theory which assert (despite heavy criticism) that it is not reasonable to expect employers to act in the development interests of employees who may then leave the organisation, or may not use all their skills for the benefit of the organisation. It is argued that these particular theoretical perspectives have become unquestioned normative drivers of HRD, and that it is time to reorient HRD to human capability. Thus the core tensions between the economic and the social and between organisational ends and individual needs, with which HRM must grapple, are epitomised in HRD.

This chapter proposes that two requirements must be met if the human is to be put back into HRD practice. The first, is that HRD practitioners need to clarify their ethical underpinning by determining the answer to such questions as – what are the action – guiding principles that they adhere to?; in whose interests do they practice?; and what is the purpose and scope of their practice? In order to do this the second requirement is that HRD practitioners need to explore a broader range of conceptions of HRD practice and theoretical frameworks than the organisationally bound and largely short-term focused paradigms which have dominated thinking to date. This chapter suggests that Sen's capability approach to human development provides one framework within which to reorient HRD to the notion of developing human capability and permits the canvassing of a broader range of concerns in searching for the identity and ethical principles of HRD practice. These arguments are supported by empirical evidence in the form of recent case study research (by this author and others; see Bryson *et al.*, 2006; Bryson and Merritt, 2005) which applied a human capability lens to the development practices of organisations. The chapter concludes with challenges to employers and HRD in order to create organisations as capability enhancing institutions.

Defining HRD

The definition of HRD is not as straightforward as one would imagine or hope, being described as 'frustrating, elusive and confusing' (McGoldrick *et al.*, 2001, p. 344). Indeed, the picture becomes murkier depending on whether one consults general HRM textbooks, professional/practitioner associations or the academic literature. Some would also argue that variation can also be traced to whether we heed American or European perspectives, and whether they are adult education, industrial training or HRM-inspired (McGoldrick *et al.*, 2001; Swanson, 2001). This chapter attempts to rely on United Kingdom/European perspectives but has incorporated some American literature recognising that it forms part of the mosaic of influences on HRD thought and practice.

Any general HRM textbook will contain a chapter on HRD usually focused on training and development although more recent publications will now refer to learning and development (e.g., Beardwell *et al.*, 2003; Torrington *et al.*, 2004). Other topics sometimes contained under the rubric of HRD in such texts may range across career development, management development and competence, through noting the strategic connections of HRD to recruitment and selection decisions and to performance management. Some texts, particularly from the United States, will also include individual, team and organisational learning (e.g., Russ-Eft *et al.*, 1997).

However, if we refer to professional associations and the standard setting bodies for HRM practitioners a subtly different picture of HRD emerges. For instance, in the United Kingdom and Ireland, the Chartered Institute of Personnel and Development (CIPD) list of HR practices does not refer to human resource development. It has a category called 'training' which deals mainly with the design, delivery and evaluation of training. It has another category called 'learning and development' which includes career development, coaching and mentoring, management development, e-learning and self-development. Issues of organisation development are contained under the title of 'corporate and HR strategy'. Interestingly, the CIPD host an annual 'HRD' conference which they note is 'the largest event for learning and development professionals in Europe' (www.cipd.co.uk/hrd) and conduct an annual learning and development survey which 'provides data on current and emerging trends and issues in learning, training and development' (CIPD, 2006). Given that CIPD is the national body accrediting professional development for HRM (from university programmes to consultant-led short courses) one could reasonably assume that the absence of a specific HRD practice category both influences and is reflective of current practice.

If one delves into the academic literature the picture varies again. Debates over the definition of HRD range from advocating it should not be defined (Lee, 2001) through a reluctance to impose a single meaning (Stewart and Beaver, 2004), to a loose consensus on HRD as some combination of training and development, career development and organisation development to improve individual and organisational effectiveness (Hezlett and Gibson, 2005; McLagan, 1989). Large bodies of literature exist on all these topic areas, sometimes discussed within the rubric of HRD but often debated as their own fields of enquiry and practice. A rise in the volume and presence of the work and learning literature also fits with the previously noted practitioner move from training to a learning and development orientation.

The key debates that have dominated the HRD literature in recent years have centred on the controversy over whether HRD should focus on learning or whether it should focus on organisational performance (Bierema, 2002; McGoldrick *et al.*, 2001; Russ-Eft, 2005; Taylor *et al.*, 2004). Meanwhile the more fundamental question of who should benefit from HRD has remained unanswered and largely unexamined (Bierema and Cseh, 2003; Cervero and Wilson, 2001; McGoldrick *et al.*, 2001). This is disturbing for a number of reasons. If it is not clear what or whom HRD practitioners stand for or the purpose and scope of their activities, then they are doomed to act solely as agents of those who do know what they want, that is managers/employers. Consequently, HRD as an area of practice will continue to suffer from an uncertain identity.

A number of commentators, most notably Legge (2005), have demonstrated the gap between the rhetoric and the reality of HRM practices. Similar observations emerge in HRD. For example, changing production processes and organisational arrangements are cited as stimulating interest in HRD in recent decades (Van der Veen, 2006). Initially this occurred through organisation development and an emphasis on facilitation and learning in teams and organisations, and more recently through coaching and mentoring and an emphasis on individual autonomy and creative thinking. However, Van der Veen points out that this portrayal of HRD is at odds with recent evidence which reports a decrease in the autonomy of United Kingdom workers (Ashton *et al.*, 2000). Others have observed that much of the writing on HRD matters focuses on management development and large organisations only, neglecting non-managerial development and smaller organisations (Stewart and Beaver, 2004; Wexley, 1991).

Recently, a critical HRD stream has emerged taking its lead from the more established fields of critical management studies and critical adult education and learning. Critical HRD highlights the contested and political nature of knowledge (Fenwick, 2005; Schied *et al.*, 2001), pursues issues of equity, justice and organisational democracy (Fenwick, 2005), and exposes and challenges human capital and other theories taken up by HRD that perpetuate commodification of human learning and unfair inequities (Baptiste, 2001; Bierema and Cseh, 2003). It also challenges the performance and learning outcome focus of HRD, and the illusion of commonality of worker/manager/organisation interests. However, Fenwick (2005) notes many theoretical and practical dilemmas in trying to construct critical HRD, and in particular the need to move beyond naïve or idealistic prescriptions to find possibilities to 'reconceptualise critical approaches to foster human well-being and meaningful work in ways that also support organisational well-being and sustainability' (p. 231).

HRD in practice

Indeed, the broader research literature confirms that HRD practice largely confines its concerns to achieving organisational ends. Even within the more humanistic organisation development and organisational learning-related HR practices human development is merely instrumental to organisational performance. For instance, the assumed mutuality of purpose and outcome for individual and organisation of learning activity has been widely questioned (Antonacopoulou, 2001; Fenwick, 1998; Gherardi, 2000; Thomson et al., 2001; Van der Veen, 2006). Others have noted the shift of organisations' risks to individuals (Beck, 1992). This is evidenced in a number of ways. These include employer reluctance to invest in or support development that is not firm-specific or that has no immediate organisational pay-off (Keep, 2000) and a desire to recruit ready-made skills and capability.

Associated with this are an expectation that government will help provide that supply of labour and a shift towards expecting workers to invest their own time and money in development even though employers persist in acting as if they own worker capabilities (Antonacopoulou, 2000; CIPD, 2006). There is also a persistent tendency for skilled employees to receive more development opportunities than those less skilled; and a marked tendency to focus on skills and thus on training or coaching-related development, rather than on organisational opportunities to use skills and capabilities. In this regard the large, and expanding, literature on work and learning is becoming very informative to the HRD field. It offers an increased understanding of the importance of situated learning (Lave and Wenger, 1991), the impact of organisational affordances and invitational qualities on individual engagement with learning (Billett, 2002; Bryson et al., 2006), expansive and restrictive learning environments in workplaces (Fuller and Unwin, 2004) and social networks (Coffield, 2000). Despite this growing range of insights, however, the practice of HRD still favours certain occupational groups or types of employees and seemingly remains relentlessly focused in favour of organisational outcomes (Rainbird et al., 2004). This may be because HRD practitioners perceive their role as purely to serve organisational ends with the employee merely a (human) input to that equation.

Worldwide the more qualified you are the more development opportunities you get. This was the conclusion of the OECD international adult literacy survey which showed a noticeable relationship between social background, educational attainment and adult education participation across 12 countries (Rubenson, 2001). This picture is repeated when we examine access and uptake of HRD opportunities by employees in organisations. The recent Workplace Employment Relations Survey in the United Kingdom (Kersley et al., 2005) reports some increase in off-the-job training for core experienced employees since 1998, but provision is still not universal or consistent. The CIPD survey of learning and development (2006) reports that only 28 per cent of organisations in the survey include all employees in their talent management development strategy with most focusing effort on management or those they identify as 'high potential'. Sixty per cent of organisations surveyed had no formal talent management strategy at all. Commenting on the survey's findings Clutterbuck and Megginson (2006) note that 'there is an increasing emphasis on short-term task performance at the expense of the long-term development of organisational capability through people' (p. 17). Keep (2000) observes that certain groups of workers in the United Kingdom (part-time, older, low-status jobs, those in small businesses and the less qualified) are at risk of receiving very little non-task-specific training. Indeed

> large swathes of the adult workforce are not being provided with broader learning opportunities of any sort by their employers (with) the expectation that the state and individuals will have to step in to fill the gap. (p. 1)

He argues that the wider social benefits of learning are ignored by employers as they are not seen as relevant to their HRD investment decisions.

Recent research confirms that current HRD practices are often driven by notions of human capital, that is investing in worker skills and knowledge solely in order to increase productivity, performance and other organisationally valued outcomes (Bates and Chen, 2005). As a result, HRD largely ignores any role that employers may have in developing human capability for the good of society and the individual, in addition to the organisation. Bates and Chen investigated the value priorities of HRD professionals who they classified into three occupational groups: managers, practitioners, and academics. They designed survey questions around three broad value streams derived from a review of the HRD literature. These streams were identified as performance, learning and meaning-in-work. The 'performance' paradigm focused on individual job performance and organisational performance. It did not acknowledge any role or goal for HRD beyond the boundaries of the organisational work system. The 'learning' paradigm focused on providing individual learning experiences and building learning systems in order to increase short- and long-term work related learning capacity. Thus, although it is largely organisation or work bound, unlike the performance paradigm it did acknowledge value in outcomes that may not immediately impact organisational performance. The 'meaning-in-work' paradigm focused on enabling meaningful work and building socially responsible organisations. It recognised a role for HRD and organisations' contribution to long-term societal and human development. The survey found some revealing differences in value priorities based on nationality and on occupational role. Overall they found that the highest percentage of respondents believed the practice of HRD should be guided by performance-focused values and to a lesser degree by learning and meaning-in-work values. Interestingly, respondents who spent more time involved in organisational practice rated improving organisational performance higher, and rated building socially responsible organisations, enabling meaningful work and providing individual learning experiences much lower than those less actively involved in organisational practice, that is academics. Similarly, American respondents viewed the meaning-in-work values as significantly less important as a guide to HRD practice than did other nationalities.

Certainly, it is clear from the debates in the literature and from practice that HRD is contested ground – on the one hand a key strategic tool for the employer to construct, shape, control and constrain worker identity and performance, and on the other hand the potential key to economic growth, innovation, good citizens, human fulfilment and well-being. HRD appears to favour serving organisational ends. In order to discern what drives such widespread HRD norms we need to examine the current theoretical underpinnings of HRD and the role that theory plays.

HRD in theory

We use theories to explain behaviour and, sometimes, to excuse it. We also use theories to predict behaviour, and sometimes to drive it, that is to create a moral imperative. Thus a theoretical explanation that 'this is how organisations or employers are likely to behave' becomes a normative injunction that 'this is how they *should* behave'. This is the process by which good explanatory theory sometimes gets turned into poor practice-guiding doctrine. The positivistic disciplines, such as economics, are particularly adept at transforming explanatory models into moral imperatives, arguably never a reliable thing to do where human behaviour and choice is involved. Human Resource Development provides some classic examples of this phenomenon, most notably the adoption of human capital theory from economics, and the resource-based view of the firm from strategic management (and economics).

There is a widespread belief in the HRD literature that human capital theory, first expounded by Becker (1964), offers the greatest explanatory power of employer and worker behaviour in relation to training and development (Wang and Holton, 2005). According to this theory HRD focuses on training which is regarded as an investment with productivity and performance as the pay-off. As a result, it is argued, firms should only be interested in firm-specific training from which they will then derive all the pay-off as employees can only use the skills in that firm. Conversely, firms should not be interested in general training because they may not receive the benefit if another firm can offer higher wages or better conditions and thus attract generically trained workers away. Indeed this does, at one level, explain employer behaviour in relation to training investment and recruitment practices. But, at another level, particularly because few counter explanations are considered (or have gained currency), this theoretical view has excused and even driven this type of employer behaviour. So that, in relation to HRD, self-interested organisational behaviour for short-term gain is never weighed up against the medium- to longer-term impact on the industry, the organisation or individuals.

Human capital theory gained prominence alongside other similar influences from the economic and strategic management literature, such as Barney's (1991) resource based view of the firm. In this view resources are defined as tangible and intangible assets which can be used to organisational advantage. Resources which contribute to competitive advantage are those which create value for the organisation, are rare and difficult to imitate and which are effectively integrated within the organisation so that the benefits they create are appropriated by the organisation. In this model an organisation's employees and their patterns of interaction are regarded as resources which can be an important source of competitive advantage. Thus skills and knowledge of certain employees, as deemed worthy by the organisation, are characterised as the organisation's asset, to be retained through better pay, rewards and opportunities. This type of view, and the increasing emphasis on business strategy and strategic human resource management, has one could argue led to a view of HRD and other HRM practices as the organisation's strategic tool.

In recent years human capital theory has been widely criticised for its domination of thinking in HRD. Critics claims include that it commodifies learning (Baptiste, 2001), that it ignores power relations, that it is fixated on individualistic market relations and is unable to deal with the general problem of under utilisation of investment in learning (Livingstone, 1999). Others claim it only generates an efficient amount of HRD and training activity under very restrictive assumptions (Kaufman, 1994; Wang and Holton, 2005) that it ignores that HRD is embedded in work processes, and that it distracts attention from other processes by which HRD resources are allocated in organisations. In short, although human capital theory has some explanatory power, it also has shortcomings and is certainly not a universally appropriate practice-guiding principle.

Both human capital and resource-based views of the firm are explanatory theories which over time have been transmuted into practice guides or moral imperatives. The problem is that when this happens it means that no one has stopped to ask what should be the moral imperative or practice-guiding principles. In the case of HRD that might simply be stated as who should benefit from HRD and how should HRD be practised. Swanson (2001) argues that reducing HRD's concerns to questions of ethics is superficial, and that to truly resolve HRD issues requires the development of a solid theoretical base. He has suggested that HRD should draw in a more balanced way on its three core foundations: economic, systems and psychological theories. This chapter argues that ethical and theoretical concerns are complementary and thus need to be considered together. They perform two different functions, with theory facilitating the explanation and understanding of practice and ethical principles guiding practice. In HRD there is a need to re-evaluate theoretical explanations and the ethical drivers of practice. The normative thrust of current popular HRD theory and practice towards performance and narrow organisation interests could be profitably reoriented to a broader and longer-term perspective using theories that provide for a more rounded and practical approach. In particular, it is necessary to find ways for HRD to take proper account of the social embeddedness of work activity and human development. For this purpose, we now turn to the capability approach introduced by the work of Sen (1993, 1997).

Humanising HRD

The core thesis of this book argues for a more human-centred focus in HRM, through consideration of perspectives other than the purely economic, managerialist, or individualist. In particular, it seeks to balance these dominant economic perspectives with consideration of social relations and ethical choices. This chapter proposes that development economist Amartya Sen's work on capability provides a valuable framework for re-structuring HRD. Sen has long been concerned with issues of inequality and deprivation. In the 1960s he contributed to the development of social choice theory in economics. Later he demonstrated that widespread starvation can occur even though a country has sufficient food production. Instead he showed that it is social and economic factors which lead to starvation – poor food distribution, unemployment and high food costs. He argued that this occurred because the common political and economic focus is on non-interference (which he labelled negative freedom). His capability approach focused on positive freedom, a person's ability to be or do something. Famously, he was awarded the 'Nobel Prize for Economics' in 1998 for his economic work which emphasised human values and challenged the self-interest focus of other dominant economic theories.

Sen's capability approach turned understandings of economic development on their head. Sen suggested economic development be evaluated not by increases in GDP, or average income, but by levels of human development and well-being. The problem Sen was addressing was that if policies aim to increase only economic measures, such as GDP, that they may unintentionally create distortions around things of even greater value to individual or societal well-being. Thus the capability approach focuses on freedom as a more accurate way to build what people really value:

> the basic objective of development is to create an enabling environment for people to enjoy long, healthy and creative lives. This may appear to be a simple truth but it is often forgotten in the immediate concern with the accumulation of commodities and financial wealth. (United Nations Development Programme, 1990, p. 9)

The appeal of the capability approach for our purposes is that it is interdisciplinary, and focuses on multidimensional aspects of well-being including individual, organisational, and societal. Capability is described as the freedom to pursue various functionings, that is, to lead a type of life one has reason to value. Functionings are the valuable states and activities that make up people's well-being, such as good health, friendship, an educated mind, a good job – the things one values being or doing. The key idea of the capability approach is that social arrangements should aim to expand people's capabilities, their freedom to promote or achieve valuable beings and doings. Sen (1993) argues that together capability and agency are the real freedoms that development and other social processes should aim to expand. Employment arrangements are a significant form of social arrangement in which many people spend much of their time and thus employment should be concerned with capability.

Applied to employment, Sen's capability approach forces a closer examination of issues such as the quality of employment rather than just its quantity (Sehnbruch, 2004). It suggests that crude numeric measures of unemployment and employment would be strengthened by a measure of employment capability, that is a persons opportunity, freedom and appropriate functionings to be employed (Burchardt, 2002). Capability has also been used by Salais and Villeneuve (2004) as a way to bring together both the social and economic objectives of employment at an institutional level. They argue that 'capability develops (or declines) depending on the daily circumstances of life and work' (p. 12).

Indeed, we know that employment can utilise our functionings and capabilities. It does this by allowing us to contribute our effort to the organisation, to feel enabled and competent in our work, to increase our confidence in our abilities, to engage us in meaningful activity, to be an acknowledged member of society and of groups in our place of work, to remunerate us with resources through which we can support others and live the lives we want to live. That is, essentially employment can facilitate us to be capable. But, we also know that workplaces can be disempowering, that employers are more likely to be interested in achieving business outcomes than in promoting the well-being of workers. Indeed, because of this government policy and employment legislation attempt to provide institutionalised protections for employees and employers. They set ground rules for the employment framework and the experience of work.

As previously discussed human capital theory underpins many of the assumptions of human resource management. Thus the distinction between human capital and human capability, and the ways in which they fit together, is illuminating. According to Sen (1997, p. 1959) human capital refers to 'the agency of human beings, through skill and knowledge as well as effort, in augmenting production possibilities'. On the other hand human capability is about the 'ability of human beings to live lives they have reason to value'. Sen discusses the nature of the two concepts and some important points of comparison. First, both concepts focus on human beings and their abilities. In this respect they have a common reference point. Where they differ, however, is that human capital is often viewed in terms of its contribution to productivity within an organisation whereas human capability looks at its contribution in a much broader way in terms of the extent to which these abilities enhance people's lives in general. It could be argued that it is the same distinction that separates employers and employees. Employers want to grow people's abilities for use in production whereas employees are developing their abilities not only for work but also to contribute to their wider well-being. To some extent the definition of capability depends on whether you perceive individual capability as the end goal or whether you view the individual as an input to the overall goals of organisational capability. In short, a focus on human capability can provide a more integrated way of considering organisational ends, individual needs and societal outcomes. It forces a more strategic view of human development, one which accepts the connection between individual, society and organisation. Part of the role of HRD is to ensure that work contributes to and drives individual well-being. That means that HRD needs to pay attention to different things, not just training or learning, and to balance organisational and individual needs, while accepting some broader social responsibility.

Applying a human capability lens to HRD

A large strand of HRD literature and practice focuses on training and development, now learning and development, and what can be measured – training course attendance, cost and learning transfer. However, if we focus on human capability, the factors that workers and employers report as most influential on their development are not things that are necessarily a cost to, nor always measured by, the organisation.

Recent research by the author of this chapter and others (Bryson and Merritt, 2005) applied a human capability lens to development practices in a number of organisations across two production industries (wine-making and furniture manufacturing) in New Zealand. Initially, the work of Billett (2002), Fuller and Unwin (2004) and others examining the workplace as a learning environment provided us with useful frameworks, concepts and tools for our research (such as organisational affordances, invitational qualities of the workplace, individual learning histories, expansive versus restrictive environments). However, we struggled with the fact that organisational processes often seemed to be at the centre of focus in evaluating HRD or work-based learning. We wanted to put people and their capabilities at the centre of our analysis and then examine how processes or other factors served their development. We felt a gap in terms of ways to examine individuals and their capability development, that is, individuals in the context of their lives (as people, workers, citizens). In essence we wanted a meta-framework in which workplace learning is one, albeit important, piece. Sen's capability approach provided the theoretical and practical orientation for developing that framework through our research.

This approach enabled us to develop an understanding of a range of influences that organisations/employers can have in both facilitating and obstructing the development of human capability. It also allowed us to understand how capability is influenced by the individual themselves, their experiences and networks. Other influences the capability approach prompts one to consider include wider institutional arrangements such as the education system, labour market conditions and broader societal beliefs. This approach gives a richer and more accurate picture of the divergent factors contributing to HRD than a more narrow organisation-focused approach. The following summary of some of the relevant findings illustrates the richer picture obtained through the use of a human capability framework.

Exploring human capability development requires attention to the individual in the context of the social arrangements of teams, workplaces, occupations, industries, education systems and local communities. Because of this different questions are asked of a broader range of stakeholders, and thus different answers emerge than those generated by a standard HRD investigation. The common factors reviewed by an HRD approach might include training needs, range of available training interventions (from courses to mentoring programmes), training participation rates, costs of training, alignment with organisational plans, and possibly an assessment of learning environment. In addition to these factors, taking a human capability approach involves seeking input from what we called the 'capability community' surrounding an industry, that is owners, supervisors, workers, HR people, trade unions, industry bodies, education providers to that industry, equipment or other suppliers.

In the research, we investigated the wine-making industry in one region of New Zealand, and the furniture manufacturing industry in three regions. Wine-making is a high profile industry which operates to a seasonal rhythm and is generally located in the more scenically beautiful and climatically temperate regions. These regions also tend to attract significant tourism and outdoor recreational activity. As a result some people are attracted to live and work in the region for lifestyle reasons. Hence we were not surprised to find that for some workers capability goals included minimal or no employment-related capabilities because they genuinely 'lived their lives of value', had their main priorities, outside of work. This, in fact, suited vineyard employers with many jobs having no career path or prospect for change. The furniture manufacturing industry is mainly located in urban areas, and works hard to compete in a domestic market crowded with attractive international products. In an industry reliant on today's businesses training apprentices for the next generation of business, we found some employers unwilling to provide apprenticeships because: 'not productive enough, quick enough (involving) too much paper work and take(ing) too long'. Such employers were only interested in firm-specific training. On the other hand, in some businesses apprentices were supported by trade-qualified staff who believed that 'employers have a responsibility to train young guys'.

In the research we sought views on what helped human capability development and what hindered it in each industry, and in specific organisations. With employees, managers and workers, we also sought a brief capability development history of what had influenced their development choices over time (from education to job changes). Most people found it novel to be asked to reflect on these issues and once they relaxed were very open in response. As a result, this yielded a greater breadth and depth of information on both formal and informal influences on development. In particular, while identifying the development influences (positive and negative) within the organisation, a capability approach also helped us to focus on the influences from outside the organisation, and a far wider range of the informal but highly significant capability development activities within the organisation. For example, workers in the research reported key capability development experiences due to the regular encouragement and support of certain managers, supervisors and colleagues, and also from any key person, such as 'Mum' or a respected friend. These were important in increasing confidence and thus willingness to develop.

> Well I came here knowing nothing and I learn best from watching people. A couple of the guys here are pretty on to it and I just picked up from them . . . Everything from driving a tractor to pruning. (Vineyard worker)

> Fencing for example, I always put a strong fencer with one of the weaker ones and rather than me getting out there and teaching them, they learn from one of their own fellow workers . . . I find the best way is to marry up the stronger guys on a particular job with one of the weaker guys and say 'ok, off you go, I'll come and see you on Wednesday and see how you're getting on' sort of thing, and it works a treat. (Vineyard manager)

This was further emphasised in reflections by employees on what had hindered their capability development:

> Guys in the past who've been narrow minded about sharing knowledge or skill development. (Furniture worker)

> Certain people around say 'we'll help you and encourage you to learn things' . . . but nothing comes of it. It's all PC (politically correct) crap. (Vineyard Worker)

Focusing on capability also enabled researchers to discern the fine line between the employee classified with a 'good' attitude and those labelled with a 'bad' attitude. Beneath the 'bad' attitude often lay literacy issues, poor education and/or family experiences, poor employment experiences. In the workplace people who have had these experiences sometimes appear to lack confidence, or not be motivated:

> Self confidence – a lot of people are very unconfident about their ability to undertake training and achieving. (Furniture worker)

It is hard to find young guys with [a] work ethic and sense of responsibility and good social skills. (Employer)

In many of the furniture manufacturers we visited there was no HRD practitioner. Capability development was dependent on employers, supervisors, proactive employees and their wider social networks, and on industry and institutional initiatives. At an organisational level skill related pay systems, job design, and commitment of the business owner to development opportunities, were also reported as highly influential.

You really have to do it yourself . . . [the company] expects people to ask, to be proactive. (Vineyard worker)

If you don't have a good employer it makes it harder. (Furniture worker)

At an institutional level vocational education infrastructures and industry responses were influential, both positively and negatively. The reputation of apprenticeship training or other qualifications, the perception of availability of work in the industry, the experience of secondary school, were all important.

Our research shows (secondary school) students are diffident about making decisions particularly in the trades areas and that they tend to take the softer options in the easy to get jobs. They might be jobs that rolled over from school or they're the ones they can slip into very easily . . . crews in McDonalds, the car yard – washing cars, the supermarket; the easy things . . . [They are] fearful of entering education, having to make a positive commitment into a career . . . And that's something we're trying to break through but it's extremely difficult for us. (Vocational education provider)

Applying a human capability lens enabled us to examine the challenge of human development in organisational settings in far more depth, examining informal and formal learning, and other influences on the development and actual use of functionings and capabilities. It also meant that we investigated more broadly, beyond the organisation chart to the industry, the region, and the relevant vocational education arena. The research highlighted a number of organisational challenges that the HRD practitioner faces. First, there is a well-entrenched assumption that capability development is costly. However, not developing one's workforce may well be more costly in the medium term as industries enter a vicious circle of skill shortages. In addition, capability development need not be costly. For instance, we found particular employers willing to share their capabilities and develop others in a variety of ways. The challenge for the HRD practitioner or line manager is to differentiate between those employees genuinely not interested and those not confident about development. Also to design a workplace that utilises capabilities. At base, human capability reminds us that all people need encouragement to develop, to feel confident and capable, and that the boundary between the organisation and the rest of the world is highly permeable. Thus, any HRD investigation needs to consider relevant stakeholders beyond the confines of the organisational entity.

Broadly speaking, current human resource development practice aims to enhance learning to improve organisational performance. It does this through training, coaching and other processes. It is operational in outlook; success is measured by productivity, and return on investment to the organisation. It puts the organisational entity at the centre of the picture. Human capability development aims to enhance people's lives in general. It does this by focusing not only on organisational processes but also inviting us to examine the impact of social arrangements (labour markets, education systems, industries, organisations, teams and local communities) as they influence human development. It also attends to positive freedom and agency. Thus it pays attention to formal courses, on the job development, work design, rewards, coaching, encouragement and all the ways in which people develop their skills, knowledge, confidence, aspirations, functionings and capability. It is strategic in outlook, mindful of the interconnectedness of individual, organisation, industry, workforce but also personal life and the role of the individual in society. It puts the human at the centre of the picture. In many ways thinking about human capability enables one to combine the psychological, economic and systems perspectives which are regarded as important for a foundational theory of HRD (Swanson, 2001).

Challenging HRD

This chapter has reflected on a mixed picture of HRD, one in which practice is predominantly organisationally focused with the human solely as an input, a strategic asset, rather than a capable outcome. The normative thrust of human capital theory and resource-based views of the firm has pushed much HRD practice into serving task-specific, short-term organisational agendas. It also privileges those with power, the anointed high-flyers, management, and the qualified. The recent academic literature on critical HRD and work and learning challenges organisations to take a wider view of their impact on human development. This chapter has shown that different, wider perspectives can be developed. Sen's capability approach presents an alternative understanding of the drivers and barriers to human development within developing economies. The translation of the capability approach to work settings in capitalist economies does several important things: (1) it forces a questioning of the taken-for-granted norms driving government policy and employer/organisational behaviour with respect to human resource development; (2) it focuses on positive freedom, a person's ability to be or do something; (3) it is contextual, forcing an appreciation of social networks, communities and institutions within and beyond organisations and industries; (4) it challenges inequities; and (5) it provides a meta-framework within which the many insights of organisational learning, work and learning, and critical HRD, may sit.

These approaches are, of course, not without limitations. For instance, some would argue that Sen's capability approach works for a developing economy but struggles in the context of competitive capitalism. However, the two are not necessarily mutually exclusive. One could argue that taking a broader based capability perspective of HRD provides the balance that vigorous capitalism needs in the organisations and industries of a civilised society.

From this analysis we arrive at two questions, or challenges for HRD:

1. Is it reasonable to expect employers to contribute to human development?
2. What is it reasonable to expect of HRD practitioners/professionals?

Reasonable expectations

Amidst increasing emphasis on quality of work issues in European policy agendas, and debate over government investment in skills, the employer has been largely peripheral (Keep, 2000). Some regarding HRD critically argue 'that emancipatory educative practice within capitalist institutions is completely untenable' (Fenwick, 2005, p. 231). Others assert that 'corporations and the state continue to control the learning agendas of adults to fit their own economic and political interests' (Wilson and Cervero, 2001, p. 273). But few have pondered what might be reasonable expectations to hold of employers in relation to human development.

Sen's work reminds us that reorienting our perspective (as he did in economic development) can provide valuable insights and a path to progress. In economic development he shifted attention away from financial measures towards human development and well being measures. In HRD we have proposed shifting attention away from short-term cost and performance of the company and towards human capability and the sustained ability to perform as a member of different communities in society. It is well accepted in our capitalist economies that organisations are wealth-creating institutions. For most that wealth is equated to profit and return to shareholders. However, we also know that the nature of that wealth is not just monetary, and the greater wealth is human capability. This capability wealth contributes to the organisation, industry, and society over the short- and long-term. To accept this makes it reasonable to reorient employers to the purpose of the organisation as being two-fold: to produce or serve in order to survive/make money, and in order to contribute to societal well-being by enhancing human capability. HRD (and HRM) thus become central to the success of the organisation as a capability enhancing institution.

The task of HRD is to enhance human capability for the good of the individual, organisation and society. At a practice level this means attending to issues of opportunity, access and support for development at all levels of the organisation. It also means attending to longer-term issues for industry-wide workforce development and the place of the organisation within that development. It means assessing influences on capability development at the level of the individual, the organisation and institutionally. While this broad view of capability development may be in opposition to organisation focused perspectives it is fully compatible with, and arguably mandated by, first the significant public investment in capability development (through funding of skills and qualification infrastructures) and second by the increased expectations of individual investment in both time and cost. Thus, it is reasonable to expect employers to also contribute to developing human capability as they too benefit from it in both the short- and long-term.

The practice of HRD

So, where does this leave the HRD practitioner? The practice of HRM is in a difficult space, often lacking real power within organisational management, but also mistrusted by employees. This continued lack of HRM credibility within many organisations extends from evidence of limited involvement in essential organisational planning or change (CIPD, 2006; Sloman, 2006) through to assertions of a global crisis of trust in HRM (Kochan, 2003). Fenwick (2005) observes that HRM does not have much power within organisational hierarchy and that HRD practitioners may end up completely marginalised if they challenge core ideologies and practices. HRD has long been caught between a desire to serve individuals and serving organisational dominance (Schied et al., 2001; Townley, 1994). At base, HRD has not identified what it stands for, who it serves, and what it can (or should) do for those it serves (McGoldrick, et al., 2001; Ruona, 2000). Underpinning

HRD practice in organisations, which has been shown to be variable at best (and unfairly discriminatory at worst), is a failure to question the practice and guiding principles of HRD. That is, the ethical basis of HRD practices.

This failure explains, in part, the ongoing struggle with definition and credibility. One has to know what one stands for and why or the parameters will move with the whim of the 'client'. If there is no real consensus over the scope of HRD, or if it is fragmented into training and learning and development and across a range of other HR practices, then it makes it very difficult for its practitioners to know how to act. What should they be concerned with, the quality of training delivery or the depth of human capability in the wider community, or both? Are they strategic, serving a wider purpose, or purely operational concerned only with delivery? Answering these questions presents a major challenge to HRD practitioners seeking to discern the future direction of the discipline. Does the practitioner name change to learning and development indicate a first step toward embracing a view broader than human as organisational resource, or a step toward an independent profession advocating a clear identity and purpose or is it just another name change, another fad, in a practice looking for an identity?

Ultimately if HRD, or learning and development, practitioners remain focused on process and practice, and do not lift their eyes to purpose and principles then they remain pawns in a short-term organisational performance game. HRD, and HRM practitioners generally, need to decide whether they are merely doing a job as agents of management and the organisation, or whether they are exercising a broader perspective and social conscience in free and frank advice to the organisation. Do HRD practitioners think long term and strategically about human development, and balance this with short-term drivers. If HRD and HRM practitioners do not do this as part of their role for organisations then who will?

Acknowledgement

This research was made possible by funding from the New Zealand Foundation of Research, Science and Technology for the 'Developing human capability: employment institutions, organisations and individuals' project at Victoria University of Wellington. Thanks are also due to the two institutions who kindly hosted the author during her research and study leave: the ESRC Centre on Skills, Knowledge and Organisational Performance (SKOPE) at the University of Oxford, and the Centre for Industrial Relations and Human Resources at the University of Toronto.

References

Antonacopoulou, E. (2000) 'Employee development through self-development in three retail banks', *Personnel Review*, 29:4, 491–508.

Antonacopoulou, E. (2001), 'The paradoxical nature of the relationship between training and learning', *Journal of Management Studies*, 38:3, 327–350.

Ashton, D., Felstead, A. and Green, F. (2000) 'Skills in the British workplace', in Coffield, F. (ed.), *Differing Visions of a Learning Society*, Research findings UK, The Policy Press, Vol. 2, pp. 193–228.

Baptiste, I. (2001) 'Educating lone wolves: pedagogical implications of human capital theory', *Adult Education Quarterly*, 51, 184–201.

Barney, J. (1991), *Firm Resources and Sustaining Competitive Advantage*, Reading MA, Addison-Wesley.

Bates, R. and Chen, H.C. (2005) 'Value priorities of Human Resource Development professionals', *Human Resource Development Quarterly*, 16:3, 345–368.

Beardwell, I., Holden, L. and Claydon, T. (2003) *Human Resource Management: A Contemporary Approach*, 4th edition, UK, FT Prentice Hall.

Beck, U. (1992) *Risk Society: Towards a New Modernity*, London, Sage.

Becker, G.S. (1964) *Human Capital: A Theoretical and Empirical Analysis, with Special Reference to Education*, New York, Columbia University Press.

Bierema, L.L. (2002) 'The sociocultural contexts of learning in the workplace', *New Directions for Adult and Continuing Education*, 96, Winter, 69–78.

Bierema, L.L. and Cseh, M. (2003) 'Evaluating AHRD research using a feminist research framework', *Human Resource Development Quarterly*, 14:1, 5–26.

Billett, S. (2002) 'Toward a workplace pedagogy: Guidance, participation, and engagement', *Adult Education Quarterly*, 53:1, 27–43.

Bryson, J.E. and Merritt, K. (2005) The Role of Work in Developing Human Capability, paper presented at the 5th International Conference on the Capability Approach, September 2005, UNESCO, Paris, France.

Bryson, J., Pajo, K., Ward, R. and Mallon, M. (2006) 'Learning at work: Organisational affordances and individual engagement', *Journal of Workplace Learning*, 18:5, 279–297.

Burchardt, T. (2002). *Constraint and Opportunity: Women's Employment in Britain*. Paper presented at the Von Hugel Institute Conference–Promoting Women's Capabilities: examining Nussbaum's capabilities approach, September 2002, Cambridge.

Cervero, R.M. and Wilson, A.L. and Associates (2001) *Power in Practice: Adult Education and the Struggle for Knowledge and Power in Society*, San Francisco, Jossey-Bass.

CIPD (2006) *Annual Survey Report 2006: Learning and Development*, London.

Clutterbuck, D. and Megginson, D. (2006) 'In search of coaching cultures', *Reflections on the 2006 Learning and Development Survey: Latest Trends in Learning, Training and Development*, London, CIPD, pp. 17–19.

Coffield, F. (ed.) (2000) *Differing Visions of a Learning Society*, Research findings, UK, The Policy Press. Volumes 1 and 2.

Fenwick, T. (1998) 'Questioning the concept of the learning organisation', in Scott, S., Spencer, B. and Thomas, A. (eds), *Learning for Life*, Toronto, Thompson Educational Publishing, pp. 140–152.

Fenwick, T. (2005) 'Conceptions of critical HRD: Dilemmas for theory and practice', *Human Resource Development International*, 8:2, 225–238.

Fuller, A. and Unwin, L. (2004) 'Expansive learning environments: Integrating organizational and personal development', in Rainbird, H., Fuller, A. and Munro, A. (eds), *Workplace Learning in Context*, London, Routledge, pp. 126–144.

Gherardi, S. (2000) 'Practice-based theorizing on learning and knowing in organizations', *Organization*, 7:2, 211–223.

Hezlett, S.A. and Gibson, S.K. (2005) 'Mentoring and human resource development: Where we are and where we need to go', *Advances in Developing Human Resources*, 7:4, 446–469.

Kaufman, B.E. (1994) *The Economics of Labour Markets*, 4th edition, Texas, Dryden.

Keep, E. (2000) 'Learning organisations, lifelong learning and the mystery of the vanishing employers', *SKOPE research paper 8*, Oxford and Warwick Universities.

Kersley, B., Alpin, C., Forth, J., Bryson, A., Bewley, H., Dix, G. and Oxenbridge, S. (2005) *Inside the Workplace: First Findings from the 2004 Workplace Employment Relations Survey*, UK, Department of Trade & Industry.

Kochan, T. (2003) *Contemporary IR/HR Challenges: Global Perspectives*, special seminar November 2003 to the Industrial Relations Society of Queensland, Department of Industrial Relations of the Queensland government, and Griffith University, Australia.

Lave, J. and Wenger, E. (1991) *Situated Learning: Legitimate Peripheral Participation*, Cambridge, Cambridge University Press.

Lee, M. (2001) 'A refusal to define HRD', *Human Resource Development International*, 4:3, 327–341.

Legge, K. (2005) *Human Resource Management: Rhetorics and Realities*, Anniversary edition, New York, Palgrave Macmillan.

Livingstone, D.W. (1999) *The Education – Jobs Gap: Underemployment or Economic Democracy*, Toronto, Garamond Press.

McGoldrick, J., Stewart, J. and Watson, S. (2001) 'Theorizing human resource development', *Human Resource Development International*, 4:3, 343–356.

McLagan, P. (1989) *Models for HRD Practice*, Alexandria, VA, American Society for Training and Development.

Rainbird, H., Munro, A. and Holly, L. (2004) 'The employment relationship and workplace learning', in Rainbird, H., Fuller, A. and Munro, A. (eds), *Workplace Learning in Context*, London, Routledge, pp. 38–53.

Rubenson, K. (2001) 'The power of the state: Connecting lifelong learning policy and educational practice', in Cervero, R.M. and Wilson, A.L. and Associates (eds), *Power in Practice: Adult Education and the Struggle for Knowledge and Power in Society*, San Francisco, Jossey-Bass, pp. 83–104.

Ruona, W.E. (2000) 'Core beliefs in human resource development: A journal for the profession and its professionals', in Ruona, W.E. and Roth, G. (eds), *Philosophical Foundation of Human Resource Development Practice*, San Francisco, Berrett-Koehler, pp. 1–27.

Russ-Eft, D. (2005) 'Editorial: Reflections over the long haul', *Human Resource Development Quarterly*, 16:4, 429–433.

Russ-Eft, D., Preskill, H. and Sleezer, C. (1997) *Human Resource Development Review: Research and Implications*, Thousand Oaks, CA, Sage.

Salais, R. and Villeneuve, R. (eds) (2004) *Europe and the Politics of Capabilities*, Cambridge, Cambridge University Press.

Schied, F.M., Carter, V.K. and Howell, S.L. (2001) 'Silent power: HRD and the management of learning in the workplace', in Cervero, R.M. and Wilson, A.L. and Associates, *Power in Practice: Adult Education and the Struggle for Knowledge and Power in Society*, San Francisco, Jossey-Bass, pp. 42–59.

Sehnbruch, K. (2004) *From the Quantity of Employment to the Quality of Employment: An Application of the Capability Approach to the Chilean Labour Market*, California, USA, University of California.

Sen, A. (1993) 'Capability and Wellbeing', in Nussbaum, M. and Sen, A. (eds), *The Quality of Life*, Oxford, Oxford University Press, pp. 30–53.

Sen, A. (1997) 'Editorial: Human capital and human capability', *World Development*, 34:3, 1959–1961.

Sloman, M. (2006) ' "If only you'd asked us sooner": Involvement of learning and development professionals in organisational change', *Reflections on the 2006 Learning and Development survey: Latest Trends in Learning, Training and Development*, London, CIPD, pp. 13–15.

Stewart, J. and Beaver, G. (eds) (2004) *HRD in Small Organisation, Research and Practice*, London, Routledge.

Swanson, R. (2001) 'Human resource development and its underlying theory', *Human Resource Development International*, 4, 299–312.

Taylor, S., Shaw, S. and Thorpe, R. (2004) 'Neither market failure nor customer ignorance: The organisational limitations of employee training and development', in Stewart, J. and Beaver, G. (eds), *HRD in Small Organisation, Research and Practice*, London, Routledge, pp. 26–47.

Thomson, A., Mabey, C., Storey, J., Gray, C. and Iles, P. (2001) *Changing Patterns of Management Development*, Oxford, Blackwell.

Torrington, D., Hall, L. and Taylor, S. (2004) *Human Resource Management*, 6th edition, UK, FT Prentice Hall.

Townley, B. (1994) *Reframing Human Resource Management: Power, Ethics and the Subject at Work*, London, Sage.

United Nations Development Programme (1990) *Human Development Report*, Oxford, Oxford University Press.

Van der Veen, R. (2006) 'Editorial: Human resource development: Irreversible trend or temporary fad?', *Human Resource Development Review*, 5:1, 3–7.

Wang, G.G. and Holton III, E.F. (2005) 'Neoclassical and institutional economics as foundations for human resource development theory', *Human Resource Development Review*, 4:1, 86–108.

Wexley, K.N. (ed.) (1991) *Developing Human Resources*, Washington DC, BNA Books.

Wilson, A.L. and Cervero, R.M. (2001) 'Power in practice: A new foundation for adult education', in Cervero, R.M and Wilson, A.L. and associates (eds), *Power in Practice: Adult Education and the Struggle for Knowledge and Power in society*, San Francisco, Jossey-Bass, pp. 267–288.

part III

Searching for the human in workplace contexts

11

Disconnected workplaces: interests and identities in the 'high performance' factory

Sarah Jenkins and Rick Delbridge

Factories have been the birthplace of much management thinking. While only a minority of workers are now employed in manufacturing jobs, many HRM concepts and ideas have been first identified or articulated in industrial settings. In this chapter, we search for the human in contemporary factory organisation, and in particular reflect upon the widely reported (and debated) practices associated with 'High Performance Work Systems' (HPWS) (MacDuffie, 1995; Appelbaum *et al.*, 2000). We will offer a picture of the shopfloor experience emerging from a series of key studies, pointing to outcomes, successes and missed opportunities for human relations under prevailing factory regimes.

Recently, it has been argued that competition, especially in mature markets, has led to moves away from Taylorist conceptions of fragmented, low skilled work and simple rigid processes with the need for greater cooperation, flexibility, creativeness and innovation leading to shopfloor transformations founded on the engagement and incorporation of shopfloor employees into teams of skilled problem solvers (Womack *et al.*, 1990; Kenney and Florida, 1993; Cooke and Morgan, 1998). Consequently, there has been much talk of plants as 'learning factories' (Leonard-Barton, 1992; Fruin, 1997; Delbridge *et al.*, 1998), where knowledge is created and applied by highly trained workers (Fruin, 1992; Snell and Dean, 1992; Adler, 1993). In this vein, the future prospects of manufacturing industries in mature economies rely heavily on the ability of firms to meet challenging targets for higher creativity and value added, and these activities are likely to be founded on skilled and knowledgeable employees who are willing and able to commit discretionary effort in order to work creatively and collaboratively in creating knowledge.

Despite the fact that human resources are central to meet these ends, there are major question marks over the extent to which current practice on the manufacturing shopfloors matches these imperatives and hence the degree to which high performance is delivered (Delbridge, 2006). The problematic nature of the evidence on HRM and performance has been the subject of much debate and discussion (see Godard, 2004; Wall and Wood, 2005; Hesketh and Fleetwood, 2006 for recent examples). For some, this has been a question of research design, for example Wall and Wood's extensive review of the research attempting to link HR practices to organisational performance argues that the difficulties within this research agenda rest on a fundamental methodological flaw; as such they urge researchers to adopt a much more systematic, rigorous and longitudinal approach in order to identify the exact nature of causal relationships. For Godard (2004) and Hesketh and Fleetwood (2006), however, the problem with this research agenda is much more systemic.

Hesketh and Fleetwood (2006) argue that the fundamental problem lies at the level of ontology and the researchers' meta-theoretical conceptualisations (see also Fleetwood, this book, Chapter 3). Godard argues that the expectation of high performance work systems which offer a win–win scenario for employment relations, worker satisfaction and organisational performance is problematic because of the paradigm assumptions upon which the HPWS literature is based. Specifically, he points to the fact that these approaches fail to incorporate the political economy perspective which addresses the 'essentially political problems of distrust and conflict that arise out of the nature of the employment relationship and the associated economic costs of HPP [high-performance practice] adoption in liberal market economies' (Godard, 2004, p. 369). He argues that this HPP approach fails to address the deep-seated conflictual relations embedded in the employment relationship and it is this which renders it 'highly fragile and explains its variable adoption, depending on workplace context variables' (p. 371). Further, Thompson (2003) has suggested that disconnections between spheres of economic activity and business organisation under contemporary capitalism result in tensions at each level of activity, including the workplace. He argues that the necessary stability and coherence of employment relations required to encourage employee participation and the contribution of discretionary effort is undermined by the unstable and unpredictable nature of contemporary corporate governance and product markets. His notion of 'disconnected capitalism' draws attention to the interface between corporate governance, employment relations and workplace organisation.

In this chapter, we seek to complement and expand upon Godard's and Thompson's arguments through a review of the qualitative studies within contemporary factory shopfloors which aim to engage with, and give voice to, worker experiences and wider outcomes of HPWS in manufacturing contexts. The focus on in-depth studies of human relations in the factory allows a greater access to the so-called 'black box' of HPWS, where causal relations have been assumed rather than examined. For instance, within this framework there are implicit assumptions of what constitutes 'human nature' such that workers are viewed as embracing more responsibility and welcoming the opportunity to become 'empowered' and where human needs are seen to be served by engagement in teamworking to reduce alienation. It is presumed that workers are economically self-interested and will accept changes to the social organisation of work because it will ultimately lead to enhanced job security, better company profits and improved wages. We argue that in this approach the social nature of human relations is treated in an overly simplified manner.

Our review of the qualitative research demonstrates that human behavior is much more complex and socially embedded. We highlight three related sources of disconnect around employee *interests, identities* and *relations* that stem from the instrumental, economistic and performative approach characteristic of the implementation of HR and HPWS in western manufacturing.[1] These are discussed in terms of conflicting interests between employees and organisations, the fractured identities of both individual and collective employees with that of the organisation and fragmented relations between employees themselves. These have led to a paradox where 'high performance' systems are contributing to a fragmented, individualised and increasingly problematic set of shopfloor relations that result in lower levels of discretionary effort, creativity and innovation (see, for example, Delbridge, 1998), thus undermining the prospects of sustainable competitive performance. In the main body of the chapter we articulate more clearly these workplace disconnections by focusing on a range of studies from relatively orthodox or 'realist' approaches to constructionist or post-structuralist accounts (see O'Doherty and Willmott, 2001) in seeking to build on the strength of the ontological differences that have characterised critical research of the workplace (see Delbridge and Ezzamel, 2005).

Workplace disconnections

Conflicting interests

What do we mean by disconnected interests? Edwards *et al.* (2006, p. 129) establish a framework to evaluate workplace co-operation and identify that the focus of capital's interests is in the operation and expansion of the firm, responding to competition and establishing work processes which ensure workers employ reasonable levels of effort to complete tasks. Labor's interests generally revolve around the effort–wage bargain, working conditions, their ability to participate at work and the survival of the firm. In this respect it is important to note that these interests are the source of both co-operation and conflict within the workplace. However, critics of the HPWS literature identify that the conflictual nature of the employment relationship is often over-looked and ignored. Instead, terms such as 'empowerment' are used to portray these types of working arrangements as being of benefit to workers as they loosen management control and result in a positive sum relationship. As such the Labor Process tradition which focuses on the 'structured antagonism' between labor and capital at the heart of the employment relationship is ignored in favor of unitarist assumptions about the synchronicity of interests between management and workers. It is apparent that this theorisation of workers' nature, in part, stems from the Human Relations roots of the HPWS literature which pathologises conflict as irrational and where divergences of interest resulting in resistance are seen to emanate from psychological deviants. This draws upon Elton Mayo's conception of society which was inherently functionalist and adopted a systems view of society as stable. This approach leads on to a narrow conception of human interests and fails to capture the disconnected nature of labor and capital interests.

Research highlights that both managers and workers perceive different opportunities and constraints within HPWS regimes; even sympathetic reviewers of HPWS acknowledge that lean production techniques are not ultimately realised as the win–win scenario often offered-up by advocates. For example, Anderson-Connolly *et al.*'s (2002) quantitative study of the impact of lean manufacturing on employee well-being identifies that managers and workers shared some of the ill effects of lean in that both groups found work intensity unequivocally harmful. Anderson-Connolly *et al.* (2002, p. 408) recognise that workplace restructuring had elements which were both more stressful and humane – but the key feature is the way in which restructuring is implemented and this depends on many factors including 'the extent to which workers have articulated and can support their interest *vis a vis* management'. In relation to intensity, both managers and non-managers find themselves aligned together in opposition to corporate-led restructuring. This work reveals that there are complex sets of interests at stake within lean production techniques. Furthermore, qualitative research findings illustrate such deep-seated conflicts of interest within lean manufacturing factory contexts.

The intensive ethnographic study into North Plant by Ezzamel *et al.* (2003, 2001) illustrates how lean manufacturing was routinely and effectively resisted by workers. Ezzamel *et al.* (2003, p. 274) note that resistance to contemporary manufacturing practices was organised both formally and informally, was sometimes overt and systematic but was often also disparate, covert and spontaneous. It was organised by agents on an individual and collective basis sometimes with clear objectives and sometimes by expedient considerations depending on the specific set of circumstances. These acts emanated from the impact of lean production which limited the degree of un-planned responsible autonomy enjoyed by the workforce which had previously allowed them to develop 'a sense of themselves as independent subjects, seemingly and deservedly "free" from direct management control' (p. 275). Under these conditions, workers saw themselves as self-managing human agents who were capable of working more effectively and productively without direct management control. The introduction of lean undermined their self-organisation within the workplace.

Workers' resistance to lean production was born out of these sedimented practices based on years of tradition during which management and workers had negotiated levels of autonomy and discretion. The nature of resistance was inspired by the politics of the workplace in terms of the power relations between these two groups. For instance, as Ezzamel *et al.* (2003, p. 294) note, this resistance was not just articulated around the 'meanness' of lean but also the supposed benefits for workers especially in relation to the promise of polyvalence which was treated with scepticism. This approach recognises the diverse interests and power relations in the workplace, so that

> only by appreciating the presence and significance of labour in the politics of production, can a less partial way of interpreting the practical application of 'new' or 'higher performance' techniques be advanced. (Ezzamel *et al.*, 2003, p. 301)

Another illustration of how workers' interests are challenged by HPWS systems is apparent within Strangleman and Roberts' (1999) research into Coberg, a light engineering firm based in the North East of England. Coberg was seen as having a sophisticated HR strategy based on recording individual workers' competencies, including monthly meetings between individual workers and their team leader who marked their performance against a set of seven categories collectively described as the 'philosophy of work'. Changes implemented in the factory included developing a single status to dismantle previous skilled demarcations and replacing the traditional skilled apprenticeship training system with narrowly focused, firm specific on the job training. Additionally, the firm attempted to instil a new corporate culture which sought to denigrate old ways of doing things – leading to management labeling of the older skilled workers as 'jurassics'. This led to the social production of inter-generational subcultures. However, management attempted to reduce any outward resistance by opening up a 'window of opportunity' by allowing those who were unable to accept the changes in the company to retire. Strangleman and Roberts (1999, p. 54) note how, 'management had attempted to colonize the space which hitherto had been an autonomous setting in which the workers carved out their own set of practices and understandings. In the process of changing the culture of the organization, management had invaded such a space and was now defining its content'. In Coberg, management saw it as legitimate to not just re-design the labor process but also the attitudes and beliefs of workers.

Despite attempts to engineer social relations in the workplace, some older workers remained and contested the effect of these changes. These workers questioned the claims of management practices such as TQM, JIT and teamworking by identifying how 'the reorganization and fragmentation of work tasks, broke down established patterns of social relations; and finally there was the intellectual assault on the workforce to simultaneously build up the new culture and denigrate that of the past' (Strangleman and Roberts, 1999, p. 65). As one of the older workers put it,

> They've decorated the factory with ... Coberg confetti, it's posters, labels, booklets, pamphlets, leaflets, flags and banners ... they've pasted all over the place ... they paid a lot of money to put expensive clocks in the middle of the factory and they've covered it with a banner saying, 'your old ways won't do' ... It's like they're having a Japanese factory, you know, it's ... indoctrination and brainwashing.

A failure to match local level developments with corporate imperatives can be seen at Coberg where redundancies were deemed necessary. Further, the way in which a new round of redundancies was implemented questioned the whole basis of the new inclusive and empowered open culture – there was no prior consultation and instead a tannoy announcement in the factory was made and individual's names were called out, workers were then escorted off the premises; as one of the workers remarked, 'calling people, to go to Human Resources was like going to the firing line' (Strangleman and Roberts, 1999, p. 61). A worker tried to understand the approach taken by management,

> I know at the end of the day they are bosses and it's their factory, but I think the workforce deserves more than a moment's notice. I think no matter who you are you deserve a bit more than that . . . I'll trust them no more. It gets everybody's backs up and so, what they have been working towards the past few years, they've destroyed it all straight away.

The contradictions apparent in the adoption of the new working practices at Coberg meant that workers were expected to undergo a re-engineering of the self and to accept that they had to change and make considerable shifts in previous behavior.

Differences in interests are clear from both cases. Interestingly, in both Coberg and North Plant, conflicts emerged over issues of skill transition; especially attempts to instil single status and diminish the craft apprenticeship system. Management attempted to 'sell' lean as a more skilled and empowered type of working arrangements but workers contested these claims about the content of work because they had invested in the previous systems of skill and were sceptical about management claims. Additionally, workers were also aware that changes in the organisation of work would have a deleterious impact on their previous ways of working, especially when they had benefited from a degree of autonomy and discretion which had been negotiated with management and had been sedimented over years of custom and practice. Another point of conflict emerged over the revisionism of history evident as management attempted to change the culture of the workplace. In Coberg this was most pronounced in terms of how the past was denigrated and older workers were labeled and stigmatised. These case studies emphasise how the unitarist assumptions of lean and the human relations school legacy regarding the nature of stability and co-operation within the labor process were not realised in the operation of lean restructuring.

These in-depth qualitative case studies shine a light on the complexities of interests within the factory and warn against simplistic understandings and definitions of worker interests. In each of these cases, the context of the organisation provides a crucial backdrop for understanding the human facets of HRM and HPWS. In both North Plant and Coberg, lean production was introduced into existing factory settings which were the sites of power struggles, of periods of conflict and co-operation and replete with decades of workplace practices which were the outcome of negotiated settlements with local management over the effort–wage bargain. In these contexts, it is extremely naive to assume that workers 'wake up and see the light' of lean production as a wonderful new empowering way of working. Instead, it is apparent that workers will attempt to secure the outcomes of negotiations over the effort–wage bargain and will critically examine whether indeed these new practices will lead to enhanced autonomy and discretion. Instead, a more rounded understanding of human agency is required which conceives of workers as knowledgeable and capable of making judgments about whether these changes do in fact provide them with a better way of working compared with the previous production regime. To represent the human simply in terms of economic self-interest is to bypass 50 years of research on the social relations of work, from the seminal work of Donald Roy to present day qualitative studies into the realities of work.

It would seem that workers are aware and accept that there are disconnected and competing interests at the heart of the employment relationship, which cannot easily be resolved by HPWS. Given this, it may prove more fruitful for management to accept the existence of these disconnected interests rather than using smoke and mirrors to present an optimistic portrayal of laboring under lean. Recognition of these differences may lead to greater prospects for the resolution of conflict which goes beyond treating workers as irrational and appreciate the diversity of interests in the workplace which goes beyond narrow issues of economic self-interest. Additionally, these cases also bring to the fore the importance of understanding issues of worker identities in the workplace. We shall now turn to these issues in the next sections.

Fracturing identities

Investigating identities is complex and multi-faceted. Workers' identifications overlap with other social identities; for example, a worker may be a single-mother, a Muslim, a community activist. These are external identities which we bring to work, but identities are also formed and reinforced in work through different status positions, such as a team leader, a skilled operative or a union representative. As Jenkins (1996, p. 142) notes, there are ascriptive identities which are socially constructed and based on the contingencies of birth, such that gender is an ascriptive identity, and there are achieved or acquired identities which are assumed over time and are generally the outcome of self-direction. For Knights and Willmott (1989) and Willmott (1994) the conception of self-identity is based on individual's attempts to construct a narrative of themselves which allows individuals a sense of security and a source of meaning which can help guide actions. For example, identifying oneself as a conscientious and loyal team member will provide a framework for engagement and participation in the organisation and the team. Workers are likely to pursue a course of action which reinforces this notion of themselves rather than an approach which contravenes their sense of self. Drawing on Giddens' (1984) understanding of the knowledgeability and capability of human agency, this approach illustrates how a sense of self leads to certain courses of action so as to maintain and secure self-identity. In workplace contexts therefore, notions of self-identity can be reinforced by working experiences, such that a black Muslim father's status may be reinforced in the community by being, for example, a diligent and effective union representative. In other cases, these identities may conflict. For example, a team leader who is a single-mother may be expected to work unplanned over-time which causes a tension with child-care. Therefore, self-identity may be threatened and challenged by work experiences, or may be the source of conflict as management may attempt to manipulate identities to benefit the organisation.

Alongside self-identities, the concept of social identities refers to the interaction between personal identities and the social context. Thompson and McHugh (2002, p. 334) note that social identities represent 'the negotiated position between our personal identity and the meanings and images demanded of us in our current social context' such that, 'identity is a tool that we use to present ourselves as, and possibly transform ourselves into, images appropriate to our social, cultural and work context'. Further, there are collective identities which, as Ackroyd and Thompson (1999, p. 56) note, involve groups either defining themselves in distinction to groups outside themselves by actively cultivating their own internal standards, or by a combination of these. Issues of identity are clearly closely linked to those of interests and also power. Power relations are crucial to understanding how groups may collectively resist organisational practices which seek to either manipulate their identities or threaten their shared sense of meanings and values. Additionally, groups may use their power resources to protect their interests and collective identities against those not in the group, by seeking to demarcate themselves – as can occur around gender, age and race relations. Hence, conflicts and tensions can emerge between and within different groups depending on the specific context under which identity concerns become realised.

Our understanding of conflicting identities acknowledges the complexity and fluidity of workers' identities and appreciates the multiple external and internal identificatory frames of references involved in identity formations. This approach emphasises that workers' identities cannot easily be shaped, moulded and manipulated by organisations. There may be points of connection between the identities of workers and the goals of the organisation but there are also likely to be disconnections, conflicts and tensions relating to identity concerns. Under HPWS we contend that conflicts emerge as workers' collective and self-identities are threatened and challenged, we refer to this as fractured identities which appear when there are disconnections between workers' identifications and organisational goals and objectives. Drawing on the rich tradition of qualitative research, these themes shall be illustrated through the literature on teamworking.

Ezzamel and Willmott's (1998, p. 359) study of StitchCo focuses on the psychosocial and cultural-ideological dimensions of teamworking, but also demonstrates how it was embedded in a political economy of work organisation. Ezzamel and Willmott (1998, p. 360) critique the portrayal of teamwork as a win–win situation whereby workers' employment futures are secured and working conditions improved. In this sense human needs are portrayed in terms of being satisfied by working in more fulfilling jobs and organisation needs are secured because production is more efficient and effective. As such, teamworking is perceived as meeting essential human requirements with respect to making work interesting and fulfilling and providing workers with the opportunity to increase their responsibilities. For Ezzamel and Willmott (1998, pp. 360–361) 'a particular, humanistic and essentialist, conception of identity is assigned to employees' in which it is assumed that any normal human being will embrace the opportunity to assume increased individual responsibility, as refusing this 'empowerment is irrational because it violates their essential human needs'.

Ezzamel and Willmott draw on Giddens' (1991) conceptualisation of self-identity in terms of the capacity to maintain a narrative that is accompanied by a feeling of comparative well-being and security, that is, employees' positive and negative reactions to working arrangements in terms of the perceived implications of their historically and culturally conditioned sense of self-identity' (Ezzamel and Willmott, 1998, p. 365). At StitchCo, prior to the implementation of a team-based bonus system rewards were based on individual performance and moving to teams created a number of tensions. Workers felt that they were putting in greater effort but were not being rewarded because the overall team effort was calculated. The most skilled and hard working felt aggrieved because they felt their efforts were benefiting others (i.e., the younger workers with no family responsibilities). This led to interpersonal conflict within and between teams which revolved around 'competing expectations of, and demands, from work' (Ezzamel and

Willmott, 1998, p. 381). Teams were often comprised of high skilled and hard-working machinists who had family commitments and were motivated to increase the bonus systems alongside low skilled, younger machinists without family responsibilities who did not want the extra pressure of work. As such Ezzamel and Willmott (1998, p. 387) assert that

> members of each group tended to regard the interdependence of teamwork as a burden, not as a benefit (such that) only when unimpeded by the constraints or pressures of the managerial device of teamwork were machinists able to express their established and preferred sense of self-identity, unencumbered by the requirements to become self-managing.

The pressures on machinists to become self-managing disrupted and intruded on their capacity to maintain an established narrative of the self, such as that of 'mate' or of 'family provider' both inside and outside of work. Instead of employees' embracing teamwork as an opportunity to become more self-determining, Ezzamel and Willmott (1998, p. 388) found that 'they experienced teamwork as an intrusive and decisive form of control that set machinist against machinist as each was required to become the other's supervisor and controller'. The focus on teamworking and the pressures for machinists to become 'self-governing' violated their sense of self-identity because it eroded a sense of cooperative involvement and so workers 'restricted their boundaries of responsibility to the distribution of work according to available skills and personal preferences within the teams' (p. 390). Workers only minimally became involved in what was viewed to be management's realm of responsibility. For Ezzamel and Willmott (1998, p. 391) these non-unionised female workers in StitchCo factories were not so much antimanagement in a class-conscious way, but 'they regarded the move to teamwork as a more oppressive and divisive system of managerial control that threatened to disrupt a sense of self-identity vested in social relations with fellow machinists'.

In terms of the concept of self-identity, Ezzamel and Willmott (1998, p. 392) argue that resistance to teamwork was driven more by 'its inadvertent impugning of the machinists' sense of self-identity than their alienation from some supposed essence of humanity or the simulation of class-conscious associated with the intensification of their work'. Instead, they argue that 'their hostility and resistance to the new disciplines of teamwork is better explained by reference to the easier accommodation of machinists' self-identity as mates within the fragmented hierarchical line-work system' (p. 392). To conclude, Ezzamel and Willmott (1998, p. 393) note that 'when the organization or re-organization of work impugns the self-identity of employees – conflicts emerge which disrupt employers' narratives of self-identity'. For Ezzamel and Willmott (1998, p. 393) the organisation of work is as much about workers sustaining a narrative of self-identity as it is about receiving payments for expending effort, so that, 'in addition to understanding organizational innovation and resistance in terms of political-economic logics of domination and exploitation, it is necessary to appreciate how these logics are constructed, negotiated, and mediated through processes of self-identity formation that are themselves conditioned by extant and emergent practices of organizational control'. Additionally, Ezzamel *et al.*'s (2003, p. 297) research at North Plant noted that it was not just opposition in terms of the material conditions of work which was apparent in North Plant, but also 'identity concerns' which coalesced around preserving the social spaces at work which had been formed previously when management had sanctioned worker discretion and afforded them a degree of free time in exchange for their co-operation in managing production. As such Ezzamel *et al.* (2003, p. 300) conclude that 'the politics of the product at Northern Plant were shaped and re-shaped by employees' determination to resist and subvert initiatives that threatened to reduce the sphere of action in which they were able to confirm and embellish a sense of self-identity as highly knowledgeable agents of the production process'. In this sense, it is apparent that the prospects for successfully introducing HPWS is often subject to workers having to significantly change their patterns of behavior and their views of how new production arrangements may affect their self-identity.

Identity matters were also significant in McKinlay and Taylor's (1996) research on teamworking in Pyramid, a green-field microelectronics plant in a booming global market. The company was owned by Phoneco, an American multi-national which has experimented to a high degree into work organisation and labor regulation. The organisation undertook a widespread 'Japanisation' programme to achieve 'total customer satisfaction' and Pyramid was to lead the way in achieving the implementation of teamworking and to adopt a management approach based on commitment rather than control. The importance of this plant for the overall global strategy ensured that Pyramid was closely monitored by corporate headquarters. A central objective behind the introduction of JIT, TQM and problem-solving workgroups was to increase plant responsiveness and efficiency. In this organisation the autonomy and creativity of the worker was no longer to be an obstacle to the enterprise's success, as F.W. Taylor believed, but a central economic resource to be mobilised (McKinlay and Taylor 1996, p. 285)

However, as in StitchCo, workers felt uneasy and uncomfortable with the system of peer control and survey data revealed the level of dissatisfaction as fewer than 20 percent favoured assessing or being assessed by co-workers. It was felt that the system of peer review drained teams and workers of their confidence, was an intimidating experience which created and sharpened tension in the teams and most of all workers intensely disliked reviewing their team-mates. To demonstrate their displeasure with the peer review project there emerged a form of score trading and this negated the discriminatory intent in the system. Equalised scoring also became the norm. Ironically, the subversion of peer review was justified through identification with Pyramid's team-based culture. This related to the fact that if teams were meeting their output and quality targets, then it was widely considered unfair for any individual team-member to receive a negative score. This also led to deterioration in the formal disciplinary process of teams. Both trading and equalising of scores undermined the dual purpose of team development and discipline. Tit-for-tat scoring was corrosive for team morale while trading nullified the disciplinary content. For all categories the distrust of peer review hardened over time and the most profound opposition came from the longest serving employees. Peer review became increasingly problematic as the increased pressures on production intensified. Team meetings grew chaotic as more and more workers were involved and the formalities of peer review slowly collapsed under the strain. Where it continued it became more divisive and resulted in retaliatory scoring. In this way, McKinlay and Taylor (1996, p. 290) describe how 'the disciplinary purpose of team-based organization was deflected, moderated or completely thwarted by a tacit campaign of non co-operation'. Even this mildest form of protest posed serious questions for a work regime whose whole rationale was not just to manufacture consent but to sustain the positive commitment of the workforce. This commitment was significantly undermined by workers' identities as fellow workers who would not consent to disciplining one another and also because it contravened workers' sense of fairness. This refers to the divisions which were promoted between permanent and temporary workers, such that, many permanent workers considered the attempts to control temporary workers as a form of 'draconian discipline' which constituted a breach of the teamworking ethos (McKinlay and Taylor, 1996, p. 289). Thus resistance was realised as a consequence of the disconnected identities evident in the imposition of teamworking.

Workers' identities cannot be read in terms of narrow economic self-interest and the above studies highlight that workers had multiple identifications inter-relating with class, gender and age. Worker identities based on friendship ties and notions of fairness were key to understanding how resistance to teamworking was articulated. Within these contexts workers also had a strong sense of what was morally acceptable and disciplining their fellow workers transgressed their social norms. Hence, their identities were disconnected with that of the team ethos and the organisation value system. In both cases, workers were uncomfortable with the concept of the team as defined by management. These findings run counter to Barker's (1999) study of teamworking at ISE which displayed 'concertive control'. For Barker (1999, pp. 40–41)

> concertive control, as an ideal type, presents a general conceptualization of the complex ways through which we become willing participants in and creators of a system that controls our own behaviour. It is a powerful and persuasive system that demands our obedience, and we obey because the system reflects our own work values. (Under this system of control), Workers achieve concertive control by reading a negotiated consensus on how to shape their behaviour according to a set of core values, such as the values found in a corporate vision statement. (p. 39)

The above cases at StitchCo and Pyramid both illustrate a much less successful (for management) adaptation of teamworking and concertive control without the totalising tendencies inherent within the ISE case. Barker's (1999, p. 132) study argues that 'team members had to invest their own identities into the concertive discipline of their team and put a big part of their sense of human dignity on the line to be a team member'. In ISE, even though workers found teamwork to be more demanding and stressful, Barker argues that they remain committed to the disciplines of this organisation of work because it is of their own making and because within it is imbued their own dignity and sense of self. Barker (1999, p. 171) notes that 'their ethical community became a meaningful intensive anchor point that kept them feeling safe and comfortable in turbulent and changing conditions. It was a foundation that forged the bonds of identification. It won their hearts and minds'. The research from ISE illustrates how workers' identities were moulded by their team community because it was this aspect of their life which gave them meaning and, as such, the team members exerted strong pressure to maintain their way of working by inculcating new recruits and extending intense peer pressure.

The context of ISE is important in interpreting Barker's findings. The plant faced closure and there was a constant fear of job losses which drove the teams to perform. This resulted in high degrees of peer pressure to conform. New recruits expressed their sense of pressure and constant feeling of surveillance. This questions the vision of teamwork which expects workers to eagerly embrace high commitment practices because they prove to be for the good of all by satisfying workers' innate sense of fulfilment and increasing organisational productivity. Instead, the reality suggests a great deal of social coercion mixed with a strong economic threat that without the pressure and intensity of this type of work organisation, all jobs would be lost. Indeed, as Barker's research demonstrated, even some of the most dedicated disciples of ISE's team vision felt burnt out and expressed their weariness with the all encompassing approach that left little space for any aspect of their identities other than work. As he puts it, many workers felt that 'paying the price' of this type of team identification was too high. Sophie, one of the founding architects of teamworking at ISE, had left the organisation and noted,

> I guess I was just naïve, you know. And it took me a long time to open my eyes. I had kind of put ISE and Jack up on a pedestal. I thought teamwork was this great big wonderful thing. But they're really just another company out to make money. There are people there like Jack who had vision and wanted to make a difference, but it was, bottom line, out to make money. (quoted in Barker 1999, p. 133)

The findings suggest that not all workers are prepared to carry on paying the price of HPWS even if they were initially inclined to do so. In the studies of StitchCo and Pyramid, the sense of identification with the team found at ISE was not apparent because workers were not prepared to relegate all other aspects of their identities to the hegemony of the team ideology. Therefore, there was a fracturing of worker identifications around the notion and realities of teamworking. The following section considers the nature of relations between workers under HPWS in more detail by focusing on fragmented identities in the workplace.

Fragmenting relations

The second element of disconnected identities relates to the ways in which HPWS production techniques often reinforce, stimulate and exacerbate social divisions between workers, so that cleavages and fragmentations occur between different groups. Fragmented relations occur when there are conflicts between the identities of different workers, as the workplace is often marked by enhanced competition and pressure. Durand and Hatzfeld's (2003) rich ethnographic account of life on the line on Peugeot's Sochaux portrays a complex, in-depth account of how lean impacts upon social relations at work by examining workers relationships to the assembly line and to one another. They reveal how the production process impacts upon different groups of workers because of the individualising tendencies evident within the career paths and performance systems for workers, from which there emerges a complex mix of winners and losers. Their research reveals disparate groups within the factory – which they term as 'multiple identificatory points of reference' – such that there are distinctions on the shopfloor between temporary and permanent workers, younger and older workers and French and foreign workers. As such they note that

> the affinities expressed at work are generated, then, by a number of different *identificatory references* whose effects may interact in combination or contradiction, these references being assembled and rearranged into identity position as a function of the demands of the situation. (p. 120)

Durand and Hatzfeld's observations reveal the complexities of how identificatory references are played out in the factory. These references were most apparent in the relations between younger and older workers. This is expressed in the labels attached to the variety of age groups. Lively youngsters are the recent recruits who are committed to the organisation while disillusioned old-timers tend to be distanced and withdrawn. Within this group distinctions are made between those who are faithful to the organisation, the embittered few and the militants who identify with the union. Then there are the thirty-somethings who remain in a vulnerable position and are demarcated as anxious and disappointed. The experience of factory life creates tensions and a cleavage between these groups – getting older is a vulnerable position as life on the line gets more physically demanding. As such Durand and Hatzfeld (2003, p. 204) note that the situation at the plant produces inequalities between individuals through 'systems which reveal, reinforce and recompose social inequalities'. They stress that this is grounded in 'detailed observation of the social processes which – through industrial production, the organization of work and the rules of non-management – tend to reduce, or contrariwise to consolidate or reinforce, the differences that exist among employees as they enter the plant'.

These tensions over interests, self and social identities are interwoven and manifested in fragmented relations between younger and older workers identified at Peugeot were also apparent in the Coberg study of Strangleman and Roberts. As we saw, conflicts emerged when management attempted a revisionist history of the workplace which denigrated the past and labelled and stigmatised older workers at the expense of younger workers. In particular, tensions over skill transitions especially in relation to the instillation of a single status and the eradication of the craft apprenticeship scheme were apparent as these transgressed working class men's social identities and associations with craft and pride. Hence, there was a disconnection in the identification of older workers' sense of values, meaning and stability which went beyond narrow notions of economic self-interest and instead threatened to destabilise their social identities and served to fuel the distrust and opposition to the introduction of new practices by management and gave expression to resistance.

As well as age relations, the following case studies focus on how gender identities are also a feature of understanding the 'thick' nature of social relations and the complex interplay with internal and external identifications. Stephenson (1996) and Jenkins' (1999) research on women workers in factories in the North of England and Gottfried and Graham's (1993) research at Subaru-Isuzu in the United States emphasise the ways in which workers displayed concern for the welfare of their co-workers within the harsh realities of Japanese management practices. Jenkins' research was based on the production centre of Beverages Ltd a drinks manufacturers. The factory was located at the edge of a large council housing development and workers were drawn from the local close-knit community. The company had appointed a new management team to 'modernise' the work process, moved to a green-field site, invested in new technology and implemented a TQM and JIT production system. These changes resulted in the intensification of work, as the women were required to operate more machines, monitor their own production outputs and to undertake quality checks every 20 minutes. Bureaucratic and technological controls co-existed with traditional direct control by supervisors. Additionally, the organisation was marked by segregation between men and women. The women were employed on part-time contracts despite the fact that the transition to the new work process required them to work over-time on a regular basis. The rigid system of sex segregation was becoming increasingly difficult to sustain as the economic context became increasingly harsh and unemployed males applied for 'women's' shopfloor work. If recruited to production work, the men were quickly integrated into full-time hours in the male dominated areas. These disproportionate conditions created a heightened sense of injustice amongst the female workers, who were unable to achieve progression and increase their earnings.

However, the experience of segregation allowed women to draw upon collective resources to gain meaning and value from the social relations within the workplace. They drew upon their gender and class identity as factory women as a source of strength.

> To me management and factory are separate: they are the bosses and we are the factory. It's like that with men and women. (Kay – Machine Operator)

In this sense women felt a strong collective bond because of the injustices of the content of work which was intensified and the organisation of work around rigid sex segregation. In Beverages resistance coalesced around women's sense of moral outrage to the harsh sickness policy introduced by the HRM manager to re-engineer the workforce towards a much younger and accommodating 'greener' employees who would be physically capable of coping with the intensification of the JIT production system. As the Training Manager explained,

> There are more young ones now . . . for those over 45 years the job is actually quite hard. It's different to years ago, now it is a much more pro-active workforce. They are running multi-machines which is quite hectic and the staff have to be dexterous.

Additionally, it was feared that older women would not consent to the intensification of the new production regime as easily as younger workers and so the sickness policy attempted to socially engineer the workforce,

> We have had a total culture change, a lot of the older women wouldn't change and so it's easier to get young ones to go along with new things than it is to change older ones. (Training Manager)

The organisation and control of the labor process was imbued with class, gender and age relations. Hence, management identified the ideal worker as a younger woman who was malleable to the increased intensification of work. Consequently, the sickness regime transmitted the identification of this ideal which many women resented as being unjust. The women acknowledged that the application of the new sickness regime forced many women to attend work when they were genuinely ill, hence the women recounted tales of how their colleagues had been sacked after their first period of sickness absence in 20 years of service, some following close family bereavements, one when a new-born baby was sick and others when they had incurred injuries in the workplace. The interviews with the women demonstrated that they were knowledgeable actors aware of the inequities resulting from management policies which they forcibly articulated. Their opposition and resentment of these practices culminated in collective and symbolic acts of defiance as the women sabotaged the rest room.

In a similar vein, Gottfried and Graham's (1993, p. 616) case study of Subaru-Isuzu in the United States highlighted that despite the rhetoric of equality within HPWS a sexual division of labor emerged as gendered stereotypes informed the allocation of work which also impacted upon the distribution of promotion opportunities and pay. Similar to Beverages Ltd, women were viewed as unsuitable for higher skilled and higher paying production work and tasks. Sex segregation was therefore reinforced by formal mechanisms of task allocation but also through informal practices of male and female workers in the formation of gendered sub-cultures on the shopfloor. As the workplace resembled a more office-like environment rather than a factory environment and the rhetoric of equality pervaded the organisation, Gottfried and Graham noted how the male workers attempted to actively reassert their masculinity by preserving certain tasks and technologies as male. The female workers used social networks to bypass team boundaries and thus define them apart from male production workers.

The female networks facilitated women's resistance in the workplace and helped them to challenge many taken-for-granted practices which negatively impacted upon women workers. For example, women illustrated the dual burdens of home and work and challenged the separation between public and private spheres by illustrating the tensions in balancing work and home. The imposition of mandatory over-time was viewed as unjust in terms of worker rights and also contested on the basis of their responsibilities as wives and mothers and as such the women acted collectively and refused to work after normal hours. Additionally, the women workers supported a woman who complained of sex discrimination when she applied to be a team leader – the woman eventually won her case but it re-enforced amongst the workers a shared sense of unfairness. Gottfried and Graham (1993, p. 623) note that 'gendered subcultures allowed the women to come together for a common cause and to oppose work conditions perceived to be unfair'. As Gottfried and Graham remind us (1993, p. 624) 'agents do not merely follow inscribed organizational roles; they are creative social beings who negotiate realities on historically contextualized terrains'. As such, workers used the company's ideology of egalitarianism to their own ends by resisting company policies and rules which were perceived as unfair.

> Their acts of resistance become righteous acts of indignation as they expose how the company fails to play by its own rules. The workers' success in preventing mandatory shift rotation and refusing unscheduled over-time exemplifies how they can use resistance to negotiate and cooperate on their own terms. (p. 625)

The cases of Beverages Ltd and Subaru-Isuzu both identify the disconnections between men and women within lean working contexts. The impact of these social divisions developed and informed women's collective social identities based on their shared experiences of inequalities and injustice as wage laborers but also as mothers and carers in the domestic sphere. They were able to successfully use their gender and class identities as a power resource to provide them with a sense of meaning and value which served to demarcate them as a group against male workers and management and inform their resistance to working practices. However, for the all-female workforce in Delbridge's (1998) ethnographic study of Nippon CTV, a Japanese-owned color television plant based in South West England, the low-trust, high surveillance shopfloor was found to be a stressful and intimidating workplace for many. The tight quality control in the plant resulted in a culture of blame as workers attempted to avoid being held responsible for defects. This resulted in a fragmented and individualised shopfloor culture which undermined a collective and supportive team environment and so contradicts the notion of the team as a source of social and emotional support. In this context again the team did not provide the main source of identification for workers. However, in contrast to Beverages Ltd and Subaru-Isuzu, the relationships between the women workers also fractured, in this case along the lines of experience and competence noted by Ezzamel and Willmott (1998) in StitchCo.

Taken together, the cases shed some light on the nature of peer relations and the reasons for the fragmented relations evident within HPWS contexts. These fragmentations can result in strengthening relations among groups or sub cultures on the shopfloor. For example, with some of the female workers the disconnections from male workers and managers provided a sense of strength and support by reinforcing a collective social identity. However, Delbridge's research identifies the potentially isolating and individualising effects of these working practices.

Concluding remarks

The evidence on the effects of the adoption of HPWS in western manufacturers is at best variable both for workers and in terms of organisational performance. In this chapter we have considered in-depth qualitative research to examine why this is the case. The research provides support for the idea that there are deep-seated disconnections between the interests of workers and their organisations which undermine the prospects for successfully implementing HPWS without careful attention to the nature and context of employment relationships. Assumptions of shared interests and the aligning of individual and organisational objectives are not well founded. To date the evidence is that organisations' HRM practices are failing to meet employee expectations and provide a context where discretionary effort is willingly expended. Our review demonstrates that workers are knowledgeable and capable actors, who understand the importance of skills settlements, recognise sham empowerment rhetorics and the potentially negative impact of HPWS on their autonomy and discretion. Thus attempts to introduce HPWS that seek to change established skills demarcations and occupational distinctions may falter as employees feel their sense of self is under attack. Thus the issue of employee interests is inter-woven with conceptions of identity.

This chapter has drawn together research that has considered worker identities (both self and social) and how these are impacted by the shopfloor changes heralded under HPWS. It has shown that workers' identificatory frames of reference are far more complex and multi-faceted than is assumed in much of the HRM and HPWS literature. The disconnections pointed to by Godard and Thompson at the level of corporate activity and the political economy in their evaluations of HPWS are matched at the micro-levels regarding aspects of worker identity and social relations. The cases show that HPWS are often undermined because they involve heightening disconnections across the multiple aspects of workers' self- and social identity which result in fractured identities and fragmented relations. The research demonstrates that workers' identities are not easy to mould or displace as they are underpinned by social identities based on friendship and kinship ties. Workers' senses of identity are socially embedded within local traditions and norms of acceptability which revolve around moral concerns for the welfare and well-being of their fellow workers. Teamworking initiatives may invoke widespread disaffection and resistance as they promote or accentuate disconnections between workers in terms of both interests and identities; HPWS often exacerbate cleavages between younger and older workers, males and females, permanent and temporary workers and those with and without caring responsibilities. Under these conditions, HPWS are highly unlikely to yield the beneficial effects anticipated for either the workers or the organisation.

This examination of workplace disconnections provides a more complex and multi-faceted conception of the notion of human which moves beyond 'thin' relations based on narrow economic self-interest and instead sees the importance of 'thicker' socially embedded relations as evident in our portrayal of conflicted interests and fracturing identities. Moreover, these findings show the importance of conceiving workers as knowledgeable and evaluative as they reveal that workers made informed judgments and had a strong sense of self, context and fairness. The intertwining of interests and identities shows the complexity of workplace change and the need to evaluate and explain the outcomes of HPWS. Sometimes workers acted to protect their interests in ways that culminated in workplace divisions, most notably around differing concerns based on identity differences, in particular, age, gender, and temporary versus permanent employees. This can result in inter-worker conflicts and tensions. At other times, workers' identificatory frameworks were drawn upon to offset the harsh impact of HPWS and were often articulated in terms of moral concerns about fellow workers. As Sayer (2005, p. 951) suggests, this is 'primarily about relations to others, about how people should treat one another in ways conducive to well-being'. We would stress that human agency is rich, multi-faceted and complex and workers should be conceived as knowledgeable, capable, inventive and creative. The challenge for managers is to develop organisational contexts and employment relationships that encourage workers to display these qualities to the benefit of the organisation. Neither assumptions of self-interest nor unitarism provide a promising position from which to build such relations.

Note

1. Of necessity, we must restrict our discussion of manufacturing, in this instance to the case of large manufacturers operating in mature economies.

References

Ackroyd, S. and Thompson, P. (1999) *Organizational Misbehaviour*. London: Sage.
Adler, P. (1993) 'The "Learning Bureaucracy": New United Motor Manufacturing, Inc', *Research in Organizational Behavior*, 15, 111–194.
Anderson-Connolly, Grunberg, L., Greenberg, E. and Moore, S. (2002) 'Is Lean Mean? Workplace Transformation and Employee Well-being', *Work, Employment and Society*, 16:3, 389–413.
Appelbaum, E., Bailey, T., Berg, P. and Kalleberg, A.L. (2000) *Manufacturing Advantage: Why High-Performance Work Systems Pay Off*. Ithaca: Cornell University Press.
Barker, J. (1999) *The Discipline of Teamwork: Participation and Concertive Control*. Sage: Thousand Oaks.
Cooke, P. and Morgan, K. (1998) *The Associational Economy: Firms, Regions and Innovation*. Oxford: Oxford University Press.
Delbridge, R. (1998) *Life on the Line*. Oxford: Oxford University Press.
Delbridge, R. (2006) 'HRM in Contemporary Manufacturing', in Boxall, P., Purcell, J. and Wright, P. (eds) *Oxford University Press Handbook of Human Resource Management*, Oxford: Oxford University Press.
Delbridge, R. and Ezzamel, M. (2005) 'The Strength of Difference: Contemporary Conceptions of Control', *Organization*, 12:5, 603–618.
Delbridge, R., Kenney, M. and Lowe, J. (1998) 'UK Manufacturing in the 21st Century', in R. Delbridge and J. Lowe (eds) *Manufacturing in Transition*, London: Routledge.
Durand, J. and Hatzfeld, N. (2003) *Living Labour: Life on the line at Peugeot France*. Palgrave: Basingstoke.

Edwards, P., Belanger, J. and Wright, M. (2006) 'The Bases of Compromise in the Workplace: A Theoretical Framework', *British Journal of Industrial Relations*, 44:1, 125–145.

Ezzamel, M. and Willmott, H. (1998) 'Accounting for Teamwork: A Critical Study of Group-based Systems of Organizational Control', *Administrative Science Quarterly*, 43, 358–396.

Ezzamel, M., Willmott, H. and Worthington, F. (2001) 'Power, Control and Resistance in the Factory that Time Forgot', *Journal of Management Studies*, 38:8, 1053–1079.

Ezzamel, M., Willmott, H. and Worthington, F. (2003) 'Accounting and Management – Labour Relations: The Politics of Production in the "Factory with the Problem" ', *Accounting Organizations and Society*, 29, 269–302.

Fruin, M. (1992) *The Japanese Enterprise System*. Oxford: Oxford University Press.

Fruin, M. (1997) *Knowledge Works: Managing Intellectual Capital at Toshiba*. Oxford: Oxford University Press.

Giddens, A. (1984) *The Constitution of Society*. Cambridge: Polity Press.

Giddens, A. (1991) *Modernity and Self-Identity: Self and Society in the Late Modern Age*. Cambridge: Polity Press.

Godard, J. (2004) 'A Critical Assessment of the High-Performance Paradigm', *British Journal of Industrial Relations*, 42:2, 349–378.

Gottfried, H. and Graham, L. (1993) 'Constructing Difference: The Making of Gendered Subcultures in a Japanese Automobile Assembly Plant', *Sociology*, 27:4, 611–628.

Hesketh, A. and Fleetwood, S. (2006) 'Beyond Measuring the HRM-Organizational Performance Link: Applying Critical Realist Meta–theory', *Organization*, 13:5, 677–699.

Jenkins, R. (1996) *Social Identity*. London: Routledge.

Jenkins, S. (1999). Gendering Workplace Change: An Analysis of Women in Six Organisations, unpublished PhD thesis Northumbria University: Newcastle upon Tyne.

Kenney, M. and Florida, R. (1993) *Beyond Mass Production: The Japanese System and its Transfer to the United States*. Oxford: Oxford University Press.

Knights, D. and Willmott, H. (1989) 'Power and Subjectivity at Work: From Degradation to Subjugation in Social Relations', *Sociology*, 23:4, 1–24.

Leonard-Barton, D. (1992) 'The Factory as a Learning Laboratory', *Sloan Management Review*, Fall, 23–38.

MacDuffie, J. (1995) 'Human Resource Bundles and Manufacturing Performance: Organizational Logic and Flexible Production Systems in the World Auto Industry', *Industrial and Labor Relations Review*, 48:2, 197–221.

McKinlay, A. and Taylor, P. (1996) 'Power, Surveillance and Resistance: Inside the "Factory of the Future" ', in Ackers, P., Smith, C. and Smith, P. (eds) *The New Workplace and Trade Unionism*, London: Routledge.

O'Doherty, D. and Willmott, H. (2001) 'Debating Labour Process Theory: The Issue of Subjectivity and the Relevance of Poststructuralism', *Sociology*, 35, 457–476.

Sayer, A. (2005) 'Class, Moral Worth and Recognition', *Sociology*, 39:5, 947–963.

Snell, S. and Dean, J. (1992) 'Integrated Manufacturing and Human Resource Management: A Human Capital Perspective', *Academy of Management Journal*, 35:3, 467–504.

Stephenson, C. (1996) 'The Different Experience of Trade Unionism in Two Japanese Transplants', in Ackers, P., Smith, C. and Smith, P. (eds) *The New Workplace and Trade Unionism*, London: Routledge.

Strangleman, T. and Roberts, I. (1999) 'Looking Through the Window of Opportunity: The Cultural Cleansing of Workplace Identity', *Sociology*, 33:1, 47–67.

Thompson, P. (2003) 'Disconnected Capitalism: Or why Employers can't Keep their Side of the Bargain', *Work, Employment and Society*, 17:2, 359–378.

Thompson, P. and McHugh, D. (2002) *Work Organisations: A Critical Introduction*. Basingstoke: Palgrave.

Wall, T. and Wood, S. (2005) 'The Romance of Human Resource Management and Business Performance, and the Case for Big Science', *Human Relations*, 58:4, 429–462.

Willmott, H. (1994) 'Theorizing Agency, Power and Subjectivity in Organization Studies', in Parker, M. and Hassard, J. (eds) *Towards a New Theory of Organizations*, London: Routledge.

Womack, J., Jones, D. and Roos, D. (1990) *The Machine that Changed the World*. New York: Rawson Macmillan.

12

Rethinking humanity in care work – extract from *Hardwork: Life in Low-pay Britain*

Polly Toynbee

The following chapter is taken from Polly Toynbee's book *Hard Work: Life in Low-pay Britain* (2003), a moving account of what it is to work in various service-sector work settings classified as low-skilled and low-paid. From Polly's experiences taking up the role of dinner lady, hospital porter, care home assistant and cleaner it is difficult to single out any one occupation for special attention. However, in our search for the human, the experiences of working as a care assistant in a home for the elderly richly conveys the socially embedded nature of work. Polly's account oozes humanity: Sister Prunella the efficient but kind matron determined to maintain dignity for the elderly in her care; Dorcas, the much loved senior care assistant who contributes not only to the care of the elderly residents at Hazeldene but also to the staff whom she nurtures and buffers from the emotional traumas the work involves; and Polly herself, who engages fully in the care of residents such as Minnie who states she 'just wants to die tonight'. These are encounters that, as Polly confesses, 'strike through your heart'.

Perhaps what strikes through our heart is that this humanity is in full view despite the imperatives of the market that ensure care assistants barely earn the minimum wage, that they do not have enough supplies to carry out their caring labour, that their work is intensified by unrealistic patient: carer ratios and finally, that they receive no support in terms of sickness benefit, health insurance or pension provision. At the end of the care-work chapter we have included the first three pages from the following chapter 'it doesn't have to be this way'. The chapter on care work truly conveys the extent to which organisations entirely rely on the mutuality of human

219

ties and the miracle that is care-work, while the 'conversation with Mr Jones' represents an organisation's best efforts to squeeze the human out, through a focus on social relationships as mere economic exchanges.

(Sharon and Maeve)

Care home

I was always drawn towards the more welcoming, less forbidding job ads because it was never my intention to seek out the worst jobs with the worst employers, but just the average, everyday at around the minimum wage.

> Care Assistant. Required to work within a private residential centre to assist qualified nursing staff. Experience desirable, qualifications an advantage, but caring and understanding more important than either. Must have good English to understand instructions and be co-operative to work in a friendly team environment.

The only drawback was the usual one: just £4.85 an hour for shifts that included evenings and weekends.

Hazeldene turned out to be a genteel nursing home with an air of a respectable, if somewhat depressing, modern provincial hotel set down on the border between Lambeth and Wandsworth. Its receptionists were good at the 'Have a Nice Day' smile and the care assistants all wore smart hospital uniforms subtly suggesting hosts of fully qualified nurses. However, even if this was a posh home, like all the others it didn't pay posh wages or a London weighting allowance.

As with everywhere else, applying for a job could not be done by post or phone. Cheap labour's time is priceless, meaning unpaid. Never mind the time of day or breaking into working hours, you have to leg it here and there to get a job. I had to take two buses down there and two back again to collect the application forms, another double bus ride down there again the next day to return the forms with all the required documents, and then come back a week later for an interview. The interviews were only on Tuesdays in the early afternoons, breaking into the working day, hard for anyone already in a job: the boot is always on the employer's foot.

There was something overawing about the atmosphere at Hazeldene. Their genteel air made them even better than other employers at making applicants for jobs feel nervous, apologetic, uncertain, in fear of rejection and grateful for their time in considering you. The lower paid the job, the more employers make you feel it is you who is being done the favour. They keep you on tenterhooks, conveying a general expectation that they are more likely to reject than accept you – until suddenly, before you know it, you are working for them. Then you realise that, never mind the airs and graces of employers, virtually anyone not visibly mad or bad who will take these wages can get any of these jobs. Brooms, mops and wheelchairs will be thrust into your hands with a lofty *de haut en bas* that cleverly disguises employer's eagerness.

My interview was with Sister Prunella, the Head of Nursing, who was a stately black middle-aged woman wearing the company office uniform of patterned shirt and matching pleated skirt, like an air-hostess. She had the stern air of an old-fashioned matron, a way of looking you up and down with a slight hint of disfavour. Scuffed shoes? Broken fingernails? She explained that the company now has forty-six nursing homes, with more opening all the time, including a brand-new one that was being built next door to this for care-assisted independent living.

I knew that many small independent nursing homes were going to the wall because the state pays too little for each patient, especially in the south-east, but I knew also that the big companies in this sector are booming. This was founded in the early 1980s at the start of the great Thatcher boost to private nursing homes. The Conservative government caused local authorities to close most of their homes by offering DSS payments for patients who went into private homes, but no funds to councils for those in local authority homes. Here at Hazeldene, said Sister Prunella, there were 140 patients on four floors, mainly in their late eighties and nineties. Some were privately paid-for, some were NHS-funded, 'But we make no distinction whatsoever in how people are treated.'

She was far more diligent in checking my application form than anyone else. I was impressed (and alarmed). Her interviewing technique involved going back over the same questions, looking for any slight discrepancy, a clever manoeuvre because it is easy to lie once but harder to remember you lie afterwards. For example, I could not know remember exactly how long I had claimed to work for my mother – two years or three? Sister Prunella tripped me up, I stumbled and she eyed me severely. Nor could I remember exactly what job I had claimed that I did for my partner. Cleaning? Housekeeping? I got by, just, I thought. Like all the other job interviewers, she was scrupulous about taking my passport. She also took my police check and said she would write to both my references. She was the only employer who actually bothered to write to my referees and wait until she had received back good references before I was offered the job. (No employer is proof against mendacious references from private referees.)

'We aim to be not good, not better, but the best!' was a mantra she kept repeating with greater emphasis each time. I was genuinely impressed. She talked about treating the patients with kindness and above all with respect.

'I don't want any of that "John, darling, just pop into bed!" talk. Some of these people were professionals or doctors and they deserve our best respect. You must find out how they like to be addressed first.' She spoke warmly of the residents, some physically weak, some mentally weak, some, she claimed, just living there for the company because they were lonely. I would, she said, be part of a team caring for a group of patients whom I would get to know, so I would learn what each wanted and how they liked to be treated. She returned often to an ethos of kindness, politeness and respect: 'Not good, not better, but the best!'

'This was the most effective instruction I encountered, emphasising the things that matter. Carillion's staff at the Chelsea and Westminster Hospital certainly got none of this, it was just 'Here's your wheelchair and off you go', without a word about kindness to patients. The difference sprang mainly from the fact that Sister Prunella was hiring me directly rather than through an agency. Her own standard of work would be judged by the quality and behaviour of her own staff. Carillion, on the other hand, were using distant agencies and anyway were not themselves directly responsible for the hospital's reputation, which remained, precariously, in the hands of the NHS managers who no longer hired or managed their own people. The closer to the actual employer, the stronger the sense of belonging, for both sides. Sister Prunella was a force to be reckoned with: she made it seem a great honour to be summoned back for a second interview the next week.

So I made a fourth visit to Hazeldene, sixteen buses in all and now a whole morning in the middle of the week without any warning that this second interview would in fact take several hours. As I arrived the crisp young receptionist at the desk, decked out in the universal company air-stewardess kit, looked briskly at me as I asked where to go for my interview. Tossing her golden pony-tail, she pointed rather imperiously down the corridor to a residents' lounge.

There I found myself with seven other women and one man, when to my surprise the receptionist herself followed me through the door and joined us. I had got her quite wrong. She turned out not to be imperious, but rather nervous as this was her first day in her new job and she too had been sent in for induction and a viewing of the company videos. This was a good example of the powerful effect of uniforms: they gave the passing public a spurious trust in the competence, qualification and experience of even the most transient of workforces.

Now we came under instruction from Jody, the Nursing Manager. What we expected to be more interviews turned out to be an induction session, without anyone formally offering the job, laying down the terms and conditions or giving us a written contract to take home. Jody was about my age, a jolly-hockey-sticks kind of nurse who had trained in 1965 at Bart's Hospital, full of bounce. She took us through the fire drill and showed us a company fire-safety video. Our instructions were startling: if the fire bell goes, forget heroism, abandon the patients and get the hell out was the basic message. 'Suppose you are all residents', she said looking at us grouped in the residents' chairs around the television in the lounge. 'Suppose that television set blew up and caught fire. You should just leave the room, shut the door, set off the fire alarm, shout Fire! out in the corridor and leave them. Yes, I know it sounds terrible, but they are behind a fire door and if you open it the flames and the fumes will spread and kill a lot more people than them. Just get out.' I am sure this is all standard fire-brigade doctrine. The tenor of much of our induction seemed to be about protecting the company from being sued either by patients or by staff. 'If you do not obey these instructions, you could be legally liable, as well as the company.' The video taught of dangerous toasters too full of crumbs, irons, Carmen rollers, televisions and above all cigarettes. 'Ok team?' Jody would ask, after each point. We were already a company team.

We were taught how to lift patients – never by the arms but by grasping them round the waists and shoulder, always with bent knees. Mainly we were being warned not to lift them at all. EU law says men cannot lift more than twenty-five kilos – a sack of potatoes – and women no more than sixteen kilos (eight bags of sugar). If we lifted any weight more than that, the company would not be to blame for any damage we did to our backs. If a patient was dropped, the company was not to blame but we would be for lifting too heavy a weight. So we were introduced to the electric Sarita hoist and the Trixi Lift hoist by which patients were to be heaved out of chairs or off the floor and on to beds or commodes. The Trixie took a long time to settle a patient into. It was a complicated sling device that left the patient swinging helplessly in the air, undignified but safe and painless for both carer and patient. This was all serious and essential information, for Jody described how she had destroyed her back during her nurse training, lifting patients without help in the days before hoists or instruction.

Listening to this good advice and looking back, it seemed all the more perverse that Carillion's Chelsea and Westminster porters were given no such instruction. It only took a couple of hours to learn and after that porters could have been far more useful around the hospital, lifting patients the right way instead of leaving it all to the nurses because they were 'trained' for it, wasting time waiting for the nurses to come and do it instead of doing it ourselves. But saving nursing time would be of no interest to Carillion as they only employ the porters, not the nurses, the workforces inefficiently divided between different employers. As for electric hoists, I never saw one at the Chelsea and Westminster and suspect the nurses were still left to lift far more than the EU rules permit.

The Hazeldene training on respecting patients' rights was good, too. Never restrain a patient: the company can be sued for false imprisonment. So those who keep falling out of bed at night can never be tied in, but must sleep on mattresses on the floor. People can never be left alone even for a moment belted into a wheelchair. 'We asked a social worker if we could just belt in one difficult patient briefly to give her meals, to stop her pacing up and down all day and night, but her social worker said no, it would be against the law. These are free people, as free as you or I. You can no more force someone here to do something against their will than you can some stranger in the street.' (Which is all very well in theory until confronted in real life by a patient insisting on climbing inside a broom cupboard, convinced it is her bedroom: a certain amount of force turned out to be necessary to stop another one choosing to sit in among the buckets and bags of soiled pads, whatever her rights.)

Jody gave examples of the dangers of institutionalisation. 'If a patient decides she doesn't want to go to the dining-room one day, no problem, you bring her lunch to her room. Then if she does it again the next and the next day, you do not, repeat NOT, assume that from now on Mrs So-and-so always has her lunch alone. That is institutionalising her. You take the time to find out why. You ask her and you get her to tell you. Maybe she'll say she hates the way someone eats who she sits next to on her table. No problem, move her table in the dining-room. Maybe she'll say she's had a bowel movement and she's afraid she smells. Well, sort out her problem. Meal times here are very, very important to the residents, the most social times of the day, really looked forward to.' All this sounded like good care. Sister Jody was as thorough and as enthusiastic as Sister Prunella, both of them keenly proprietorial about their residents – 'Not good, not better, but the best.'

When I arrived to start work the next week, the staff changing-room was packed with care assistants hurriedly putting on their uniforms for the shift. There were not enough lockers to go round and there was a waiting list for them, so the rest of us piled our bags under Sister's desk for safety. Sister Prunella issued me with a second-hand light-blue nurse's jacket with epaulettes and the company logo on the pocket, together with a pair of navy blue trousers. I liked it very much. Like a magic spell, it made me feel like a nurse as soon as I put it on, crisp and capable. A whole new uniform would be ordered for me, for which £10 would be deducted from my wages. She said she was giving me an easier start on the partly private second floor, where she handed me over to the floor sister on duty that day, Sister Davina, who sat me down and explained, 'On this floor many people are paying a lot of money, so we have to go the extra mile. When they call on the bell, we answer however often they call. Whatever they want, they can have.'

It was shift change-over time and Sister Davina read out the case notes of each resident to the gathering of all the care assistants on this new shift. I was the only white face on the floor, all the others being West Indian or African, with a few Indian nurses who had been recruited from India by the company a few months ago to serve out their time at Hazeldene as 'adaptation nurses'. After these indentures they would eventually become fully qualified nurses in Britain, free to work anywhere. (There has recently been a scandal about the many nurses employed in this way by some care homes, and often paid less than ordinary nurses, one in three having paid large sums to the employers or agencies who brought them over. But I had no reason to suppose it was happening here.)

For my first day I was assigned to Dorcas, the senior care assistant, who had worked there for six years. Dorcas was one of those dynamos on whom employers so often rely without ever acknowledging the value of what they have. 'Don't you worry!' she said, sensing my anxiety. 'It's a lot to learn but you will pick it up, the same way we all did!' and she threw a welcoming arm round me. 'We are all nice people here, that's what keeps us going, isn't it?' The others laughed, breathing in her infectious camaraderie. Majestic, warm, wise, meticulous about details, fussy about every kind of cleanliness and gentle with the residents, Dorcas was approaching her fiftieth birthday within the week, with a husband, seven children and eleven grandchildren to help her celebrate. She was given to breaking into hymns from time to time. She hugged everyone and everyone hugged her, she was the star of the second floor, invaluable and beloved of the residents whom she took me round to meet, going from room to room to introduce me to each one of them.

Even after six years at Hazeldene and many more years' experience in other nursing homes before that, Dorcas was still paid only a little more than me, something over £5 an hour. Like most of the others, Dorcas did at least a 48-hour week, because, she said, it was the only way she could pay her bills. Her thirty-year-old daughter used to work as a care assistant here on the floor above, but she had given it up for higher pay as a bus conductor, a job with a fraction of the responsibility, worry and sheer hard work.

As Dorcas took me to say hello to each of the thirty-five residents on our floor, the full dreadfulness of what lay ahead hit me. They were very frail indeed, most of them demented to varying and often deceptive degrees. Virtually, all were incontinent, which is usually the last straw preventing people surviving in their own homes. The routine, Dorcas explained, was bathing and dressing them to get them up, which took most of the morning. Then there was lunch and feeding and, before you knew it, it was time to do it all over again to get them back to bed. That was our day's work and the residents' whole lives.

You get used to changing wet and soiled pads reasonably easily. The first time you think you might not, but surrounded by all these care assistants who do it scores of times a day without a thought, you just get on with it because it must be done. Someone has to do it and that someone is us. The real fear is the danger of knocking people over, letting them fall, hurting them or doing the wrong thing. But after changing people a few times, wiping and washing bottoms and elderly genitals, the shock of it wears off. That is not the true horror of this job. What never wears off is the shock of the old. Dealing all the time with the most pathetic old people – most of them in pain from various sores on their legs, in misery and despair, many wishing to die – strikes you through the heart. I left the place after each shift hardly able to speak with the wretchedness of it all. In their little dying rooms, no amount of ruched valances, potted plants on their window sills, photos of smiling fit great-grandchildren could ever overcome the awfulness of their condition: they had come here never to return to the outside world. This was it, all there was left of life, nowhere to go. Their varied lives had shrunk down to the narrow confines of the dull and sometimes painful routines of eating, being washed, dressed and undressed. Yes, there were cookery, flower-arranging, exercise classes and other activities on offer but most were too far gone for that. It was not the fault of the nursing home – this was superior to most – but watching over these people's fragile remnants of life made the job hard to bear. No prison is so lacking in hope. This is death row.

My first evening I took a tray in to Minnie who was sitting hunched in her chair, plucking at her knitted waistcoat. I was bringing her a small plate of elegantly cut sandwiches without crusts, a dish of tapioca with a dollop of jam and a cup of tea.

'Take it away!' she said. 'Take it away!' I urged her to try a little. 'You see', she said very clearly, 'I am hoping not to be here tomorrow.'

Was she leaving, going somewhere? From the furniture in her room – they were allowed to bring in anything of their own that would fit into their rooms. Her chest of drawers and a smaller dresser looked as if she was here for good. 'I feel', she said looking up at me, 'I feel that one ought not to go on a full stomach. It doesn't seem right, does it?'

I tried a smile and said, 'You'll feel better if you eat something. It'll give you strength.'

'I just want to die tonight, I think I will.'

I wondered if she knew it would be tonight, as in those old tales of premonition or even sheer volition. She pushed away the sandwiches but eventually agreed to try a little tapioca.

'So you think I should eat a last meal, like a condemned man?' she asked me with a dry laugh. 'Well, I'll try.'

The trouble with moments of lucidity was that they tended to be like this, moments of all-too-rational despair. Dementia was often preferable. Many were described as 'depressed', as if it were a medical condition, when it was only a reasonable response to their plight.

Later that evening a young care assistant, vivacious Vicky, and I came back to wash and undress Minnie for bed. We got her hobbling and shuffling across the room to her bathroom on her wheeled Zimmer frame. She had an odd habit of referring to her stroke-paralysed left leg as Jane. 'Come on Jane', she would mutter to it under her breath. 'Come ON Jane!' urging it along. Vicky explained that Jane was the name of an old much-loved house-keeper Minnie once had. For some reason now in her mind the Jane of old had transmogrified into her bad left leg. 'Jane!' she would rebuke it in irritation when it failed to obey her. We manoeuvred Minnie on to the toilet, managed to wash her backside and started to get her going back towards her chair when she began to wobble badly and fall backwards.

'Stand up, stand up!' Vicky called out to her.

'I'm not doing it on purpose! It's Jane!' Minnie said.

'Quick!' Vicky said, flinging her arms around Minnie, hauling her upwards. 'Quick, get her legs or she'll fall!' Together we managed to lift her uncomfortably on to her bed. This went against all the rules of our induction but there seemed no alternative at the time. I said nothing but Vicky said, 'Look, we are not supposed to do that ever, but we do. I know I shouldn't be showing you the wrong ways, but that's how it is.' What should we have done? 'We should have let her fall slowly on to the bathroom floor, holding on to her as she went. Then we should go out and get the hoist, put the sling around her and hoist her up and on to the bed. But it would be worse for her. Falling is frightening for them. It would take a long time to do it that way and the hoist is not nice for them either. And anyway we have a lot more patients to get into bed tonight. It was the quick way.'

While we were undressing Minnie, Vicky said, 'You see, we get no sick pay here. If we pull our backs or arms so we can't work, and we do it from lifting patients, they pay us nothing at all. It is our fault. But sometimes you have to and that's that. Of course the managers know that we have to do it sometimes but it's not their responsibility.' Minnie's undignified and probably slightly painful method of getting to bed that night was at least better than a fall, a long wait and an elaborate hoist off the floor. In the next few days, if Sister wasn't looking, we lifted and hauled quite a few patients in unorthodox ways because it had to be done. But if there were any accidents, it would all be our fault, not the company's.

Coming in next morning, the first shift took a tour of all the bedrooms to check everyone was still breathing: never trust the previous shift, look at them for yourself, we were told. When we came to Minnie's room I held my breath. I thought (and hoped) she might have died quietly in her sleep as she had wished but she was as alive as ever. She was just gazing up at the ceiling. No doubt whichever night she does die – this year, next year, whenever – someone will say, 'The amazing thing is, she knew she was going that night!' She hoped she was going every night but her God was not merciful.

In another room Dora was curled up in a foetal position all day and night, her eyes always closed, her television always on in the vain hope it still gave her some contact with the outside world. Daft afternoon game shows and inanely chirpy presenters may have drifted somewhere into her consciousness, but if so there was no response. She had been in this state for at least three years, according to Vicky, but some of the carers remembered her from before that when she was not so bad. We rolled her over one way, changed her soiled pad, washed her all over, rolled her back the other way, changed her nightdress and left her still curled up and propped up on pillows. The only response she ever made to anything was when eating. She ate a lot, as much as you could shovel into her. Was eating her last remaining pleasure or was this just a reflex response to a spoon on her lips? There was no way of knowing, but however sorry you felt for her it was impossible not to ponder on this waste of everyone's time and energy, pouring food into her at one end and cleaning it up at the other day after day for a life that had long outlived any chance of happiness. You could only ever hope that she had no consciousness left. But those things were never said between us because once you started to think that way it could lead to callousness and I never saw any of that. If at times people were treated less than perfectly, it was always through lack of staff and time, never through unkindness.

In Dora's room when it came to washing and cleaning her, the pot of bedsore cream had run out, Care assistants were always pinching it from other rooms as there was never enough to round. On my first shift I had been puzzled when a kind assistant shoved a bundle of disposable rubber gloves and disposable wipes at me, warning me not to let go of them but to keep as many as I could fit into my pockets. There was always a shortage of wipes, cream, soap and gloves in most rooms. Also in the mornings clean sheets and towels often ran out. Yet these were the key tools of our trade, indispensable for all the wiping and washing of bodies and bottoms all day. Once Sister Davina caught a care assistant handing out a lot of gloves and wipes she had found in a store cupboard. Sister immediately demanded to have all boxes of these supplies brought to her. 'I have to keep control over them from now on!' she said sharply. 'We are issued with enough for the week every week, but if you people hoard them then there are not enough when we need them. You people go off duty leaving your little supplies in your lockers and secret places and we can't be having that!' She took command of the few remaining boxes in the store cupboard and kept them in her office. Could she order more? I asked. 'We are issued with enough' she said firmly and then added that it was difficult to get more because she would have to give special reasons to the admin offices downstairs. Petty meanness over essential equipment was something I encountered frequently in most of these jobs. Cheap labour does not deserve much spending on its tools.

Only a short while afterwards on the same day, Sister Davina and I were giving a bed bath to Edna, an almost totally paralysed woman with excruciatingly painful sores on her heels. She had been a nurse during the war but although she sounded superficially sensible, when I talked to her while feeding her lunch spoonful by spoonful, it was clear she remembered nothing very much. She was one of the many who just sat in their chair all day doing nothing. When it came to giving her a bed bath under Sister's supervision everything was done the right way as a demonstration of perfection. There was certainly no heaving people about with Sister watching. I fetched the hoist to lift Edna from her chair into the bed in the correct fashion, which took much time and indignity, then we wrapped her in towels, rolling her this way and that to wash her all over. I noted that Sister herself had no wipes or gloves and kept asking to share mine from my pockets, using wipe after wipe until I had none left. But she didn't offer to replenish my supply afterwards.

Most of the residents were touchingly endearing. There is something about dementia that is affecting – it is not just pity but a fascination with a condition that throws up memories, thoughts and feelings in random ways. There is the lack of inhibition, there are sudden surreal exclamations and snatches of long-ago conversations. Sometimes, among the grander residents, orders were given to unseen servants. 'George! George! Fetch me a packet, fetch me a packet!' one woman shouted repeatedly one morning. Childlike, yet sometimes sharply acute, they often surprised you. The care assistants were genuinely fond of most of them and I could see why.

Alice was a sad case. Dainty and thin, she wore her pearls most days with smart clothes, but she was profoundly depressed. She lay fully clothed on top of her bed all day unless you got her up, when sometimes she would wander up and down the corridors in a daze. 'So sweet', Vicky said, stroking her hands when she walked up to us, looking about with a vacant smile. Vicky said she had lost her mind with grief after her much-loved husband died. She had never recovered from the shock. She had no children, although other relatives visited her. 'Mrs Knightsbridge', Vicky called her, and she looked and sounded exactly like a lady shopping in Harrods. Her hair was done each week by the hairdresser and you could have taken here anywhere without anyone realising there was anything the matter with her. But all that was left were phrases and wishes. 'Oh, would you be most awfully kind . . . most awfully kind', she would say but forget what she wanted. When you tried to get her up to go for lunch she would say, 'Oh no, thank you so much. I don't think I will today . . . ' and you would have to swing her legs off the bed and urge her to her feet to lead her to the dining-room. On the first day I asked her which was her seat and she led me to the wrong table, a serious *faux pas*. I sat her down on the mostly more sensible table and everyone there looked quite affronted but they couldn't quite articulate what was wrong. She fidgeted and looked distressed until another care assistant hurried up to point out my mistake. It was very difficult to get her to move again; thrown into a muddle, she demanded to take all the cutlery with her to her own table. Later, walking her back into to her room, making polite conversation, I complemented her on an embroidered footstool she had propping open the door. 'Did you embroider it yourself?' I asked. 'Of course not, you silly woman!' she snapped, suddenly not so sweet. 'Why on earth would I do it myself!'

When it came to dressing and undressing her, I had to go down to the Sister's office to fetch the keys to Alice's cupboard. Her wardrobe was kept locked to stop her opening it and throwing everything on to the floor. Dressing her was a pleasure since, unlike some of the others, she had a plentiful supply of nice clothes to choose from, and she looked so smart when she was done. But she hated to be bathed. 'Oh no, I really don't think I'll take a bath today. Awfully kind, but not today, thank you so much', she would say emphatically. I could see why no one liked baths. In the bathroom, once she was naked, I would sit her on the chair attached to a hoist and winch her up, swing her over the bath and winch her down into the warm water full of bubble bath, wash her all over and winch her out again. However kindly we did it, it was not much fun and certainly not dignified. She had no memories left, or none she could communicate beyond the phrases she had used all her life, all politeness and refinement until she would shock you by blurting out, 'That's bollocks, all bollocks!' for no particular reason.

The mostly more sensible table in the dining-room didn't in fact make very much sense, although they looked like a cosy group of ladies chatting together in a tea shop. As I listened in, what looked convincingly like rational conversation was generally not, though there would be times when they all alighted together on the same subject. But usually the comments they made to one another were random, which made it difficult for them to catch one another's train of thought, though they tried. It was plain each thought the others dotty and they smiled indulgently at one another's foibles. Things went best when one of them held forth with a long story and the others listened, then added some unconnected story of their own. But on some tables they never spoke.

Mrs Knightsbridge was seated opposite Marina, a woman in a wheelchair whose mouth hung open all day, victim of a paralysing stroke. She could feed herself – just with a large bib and much splattering of food down her front and across the table, but Mrs Knightsbridge didn't seem to notice. Marina had a bigger room than the others with some fine paintings, including one huge eighteenth-century landscape that filled a wall and looked as if it had come from a big country house. Marina could not speak at all, but she frequently shouted out great 'Aaaaaah's', in a rhythmic modulated rise and fall that was distressing to hear going on and on for hours. I couldn't tell how much mind she had left. Sometimes in the morning she would sit reading *The Times* or the *Mail* for hours, turning the pages awkwardly but looking intently at them. Was she reading? Was her mind intact, trapped inside? The day I arrived there had been a loud shouter, a Lady Someone-or-other, who bellowed odd things like 'Your stomach is flatter, your stomach is flatter!', the same phrase all day long. She was due to be removed upstairs, a floor I never saw but assumed was a good deal worse than mine.

The residents' possessions were a dangerous problem. A couple of days earlier a very valuable necklace went missing. The woman's room was searched, everything was checked – the back of all seat cushions, under the mattress – but it was not found. We were told it was insured for £12,500 and there was a panic. But it turned up the next day. The resident smiled and took it out of a tiny reticule she had been clutching. It was decided that it should be returned to her relatives: her diamond rings had already been given back and the family had been encouraged to bring some valueless glass jewellery instead. 'You are responsible for all, I mean ALL their possessions.

If anything goes missing, it is down to you', Sister said firmly at the next hand-over meeting.

One old woman had died a few days before I arrived. Dorcas and I were sent to clear out her room and Michelle the cleaner came along to help. The relatives had said they didn't want any of her things returned, but here was a wardrobe full of grand clothes. 'It should all go to charity', Dorcas said. 'But I've seen what they do here. They throw it all in the bin downstairs. I've seen such good things go in there.' She was holding up a sequinned jacket and a silk embroidered blouse. 'She was such a lovely lady, she was so sweet', Dorcas said. 'She gave no trouble to anyone and always had a nice word for us. It was a shock when she went so suddenly like that, not expected. I miss her.' Michelle was superstitious and she shuddered. 'I don't know how you can touch a dead person's things!' she said. Cleaners were mainly women who couldn't face the caring work or the long hours involved. 'Nonsense, this should all go to charity if the family doesn't want it', Dorcas was saying, when Sister put her head round the door. 'You are not to take anything!' Sister said, rudely I thought, because Dorcas would never dream of taking anything that was not hers and Michelle wouldn't even touch it. 'It should go to a charity shop. I know they throw it out downstairs', Dorcas said. Sister replied tartly, 'That's none of our business, Dorcas. We obey the rules, that's all. The rules say we put it in bags and send it down to administration to do with it whatever they think fit. But I'm warning you, take nothing!' and she gave me a stern look as if I might pilfer. We packed it all away and sent it down.

Relatives were a frequent source of trouble. Dorcas and Vicky said. 'Maybe it is because they feel guilty. If they come here and give us a hard time it eases their conscience and they pretend they are doing something good for their relative.' Some relatives were pathetically grateful and nice to us, but others were demanding monsters, always complaining about small things, finding fault with trivia, keeping us on our toes, especially about possessions. I remember one marching into a room when we were trying to get a fallen patient off the floor, and demanding a vase, 'Right now, or these flowers will wilt!'

There were only two male residents on this ward. Alfred was completely paralysed from Parkinson's disease and just sat in his chair, dribbling on to a large bib. He too had *The Times* every day, and probably could read it and make sense of it, but he couldn't really speak. When Sister wasn't there, we heaved him into his wheelchair and on to the toilet several times a day and often he sat there too long, despite having a bell in his hand to pull. Once the toilet seat left a round red indentation on his skinny buttocks. He looked about sixty but I could glean little about his life, except for his hippie jacket over a chair, made of woven bright coloured ethnic stripes, and an embroidered purse on a string around his neck. The other man was a new arrival, a Major, who stayed in his room and watched television all day. All he really wanted were frequent cups of cocoa.

Only one or two of the residents were bad-tempered. Dolly had her own electric wheelchair, but its battery had broken down temporarily and it was a very heavy machine to push. She was sometimes full of complaints and would bark out in a sharp South London accent, 'I don't get what I want! I want what I want!' Other times she would cheer up and tell a string of dirty jokes that seemed to have lodged in her otherwise vague mind. She was allowed a tot of whisky at lunch and dinner, but she was no longer allowed to keep the bottle in her room as she had been drinking so much she fell out of her chair. Now she had to be wheeled to the Sister's office at mealtimes to have it measured out to her from a medicine cabinet. One or two others had a glass of wine at meals from their own bottles kept in the dining-room cupboard for them. 'They can have whatever they want', the Sister kept saying. 'This is their home.' But the wine didn't seem to add noticeable sunshine to the empty remains of these old ladies' days.

I was embarrassed when one or two relatives would automatically turn to me as the only white face with an unpleasantly conspiratorial air, implying we white folk had to stick together. Although I was by far the most junior and useless person on the floor, they just assumed I must be a figure of authority because of the colour of my skin. I would give them a frosty answer and refer them at once to Dorcas or Sister. The residents seemed to adore their carers, asking where they were each day, especially any day Dorcas was off duty. In this part of London, in many of the jobs I did, race was a marker for low pay. Wherever there are a lot of black faces, there the pay will be lowest, the work the hardest and the jobs the least desirable. I have not referred overmuch to race because that was just a feature of where I had chosen to base myself. In other parts of the country these jobs are all done by white women, wherever mothers need work and will take anything that they can fit around their lives.

The work here was hard, physically and emotionally, but at least it was never dull. There was Margaret, a tiny shrunken old lady with beaky, hawk like features who walked up and down the corridors all day. Everyone would smile at her and pat her hand as she passed and she always smiled back. She seemed to make reasonable sense, but you could never tell. I was dressing her one morning, chatting away to her about what she wanted to wear, discussing her wardrobe and where her clothes had come from. She didn't get things quite right, claiming she had worn this or that on her wedding day, but it didn't matter. She chose a blue dress but once I got it on her with a bit of a struggle (she was not good at working out where her arms should go), I found it had no buttons left. She was a compulsive button-puller. So I put a salmon-pink jumper on over the top to hide the button deficit, brushed her hair, and she smiled at herself in the mirror. I sat her in her chair where she took happily to shredding Kleenexes, which was her favourite occupation, while I made her bed and straightened the room. I was turning to walk out with a wave goodbye to her when Sister came in. 'Have you checked the bin?' she asked. I hadn't because the cleaners did bin emptying a bit later. 'Ah', she said. 'With Margaret, always check the bin.' I did and it was full of urine and Kleenex. 'She does that every night', Sister said as I emptied it and washed it out. 'Why don't we take away the bin if she gets confused at night, and maybe she'll find the toilet?' I asked. Sister said, 'Because her relatives don't like to come in here and find no bin. Everything in the room has to be just so. It's the rules.'

Relatives may often have been a nuisance to the care assistants, but the staff were more distressed by those residents who had no visitors or only very rare ones. In all closed institutions the constant watchfulness of outside eyes makes all the difference to standards. Nothing was allowed to slip, everything that happened here was on display, open to sharp eyes and noses. If some relatives grumbled and complained, it was not really about standards, it was about the general misery of the place. There was not much we could do about that, except be unnaturally cheerful and friendly, which most care assistants were persistently all day long, but beaming gets tiring too. I found the gloom oppressive however chirpy we were, due to the wretched condition of people who had outlived their bodies and their minds, for which we had no cure.

However well-managed this home was, some things would never go smoothly with residents such as these. One morning one of the room bells rang and I went off to answer it. Paula, a very large woman, was sitting in her chair. She seemed entirely rational, had a room full of books, mainly histories of the monarchy. She had an intellectual way of talking with a most convincing air. 'I know I must be a frightful nuisance, but I wonder if you could be awfully kind and just help me a bit?' She was struggling to get her large bulk out of her chair on to legs that plainly would not support her. I told her to stay sitting down while I did it for her. 'You see those books over there? They need straightening.' The books on the window sill were leaning very slightly to one side. 'I absolutely must have them straight!' Then she wanted various ornaments repositioned by a few inches this way and that. 'I am most awfully, dreadfully fussy, I know', she said. She was but I did it for her just as she requested with a smile, although we had pressing needs of other residents to see to at that busy hour. 'I have all these people coming today I think.' (Sadly, she was one of those with no visitors.) 'I'm not sure. I was thinking about, thinking about . . . ' but her thoughts petered out and she forgot what she was saying. With her, it was often difficult to gauge what was sensible and what was not.

I was just leaving her room when she said, 'I want, I want, you know, to go there.' Where? 'Oh, over there, over there!' She was pointing at the window. Vicky was passing by, looked in and asked bluntly, 'Do you want your commode, Paula?' Paula nodded yes. I didn't know if it was the remnants of embarrassment or just aphasia that had made her unable to find the right words. So we brought in the commode and between us managed to manoeuvre her on to it, a difficult job given her large size. No doubt it should have been done with a hoist, but we did it ourselves. 'Ring the bell when you've finished', Vicky said, putting the bell-string in her hand, and we went off to the Sister's office for a hand-over meeting.

The meeting went on a while, going through each patient's notes, describing what was happening or mostly not happening with each of them. As the time ticked by I worried about Paula sitting there on her commode, but her bell did not ring and I assumed Vicky knew better than me. Suddenly there was a big commotion out in the corridor. Paula had fallen off her commode, again. We hurried back to her room and there she was, her great baggy body sprawled on the floor, skirt above her head, the commode tipped up and a large pile of excrement and urine on the floor, stinking. Sister hurried in to supervise us and check that no harm was done. Paula seemed to be in one piece and in no particular pain. Her legs moved, her hips weren't broken, nor any other bones, and she just groaned a bit. 'Why didn't you ring the bell?' Sister asked her, but got no comprehensible reply. Getting her large frame off the floor with the Trixie hoist took a long time, putting the wide sling round and under her by rolling her one way, and then the other, attaching the sling to the hoist brackets at four points, strapping her in and slowly pressing the lift button so that she gradually swung upwards, dangling like a monstrous baby brought by the stork. We pushed and pulled and swung her over the bed, lowering her gently back down.

As there were no cleaners on duty in the afternoons we cleaned up the floor as best we could, but the smell remained overpowering until next morning when the cleaners came back on duty and shampooed it. Keeping smells at bay was a major part of our routine, obeying the rule that nothing must offend the visitors, and it worked. The stench of urine in geriatric wards or less well-run homes is a trademark of such places, but not here. Everything dirty or smelly we sealed in plastic bags immediately; everything was washed and wiped and a visitor might not guess almost all these residents were incontinent.

Sister explained to me later that some people considered Paula to be an attention-seeker who would fall on purpose to make people come running. 'But I don't think like that, and you must not either', she said sternly. 'These people are very confused and what they do is not to be considered in the same way as with normal people. They cannot help themselves', which was a kindly attitude. But the good intentions were not always matched by practice. Although I never heard any care assistants get angry with residents, insensitive treatment was sometimes inevitable with so much to be done by too few of us. People were often left too long on toilets or commodes. They often had to wait too long to be got out of bed in the mornings in rotation, or to be given breakfast. Hurrying past some rooms, you sometimes had to harden your heart to people who called out to be done next when you were half way through doing someone else. We were worked very hard, with no slack in the system. More staff would have allowed us more time and better care.

'Going the extra mile', 'Not good, not better, but the best!' just was not possible on many occasions. Most residents were remarkably patient and uncomplaining, but there was no way they could all be got into or out of bed, into and out of chairs and commodes, or have their food brought to them precisely when they wanted it. It must often have been insufferable for people whose lives had been reduced to basic things not to have small wants and needs dealt with quickly. Minor frustrations grew quickly to desperation among those who could not do the simplest things for themselves.

I don't know how the staffing ratio at Hazeldene compared with the average: this national information does not exist, according to Laing and Buisson, the care sector analysts. But Dorcas thought there were too few care assistants for so many residents and I trusted her experienced judgement. There were thirty-five residents on this floor and each shift had one care assistant assigned to a group of between six or seven residents, with one trained nurse (Sister) in overall charge. That felt like a very heavy load since so many of the residents were entirely helpless. Dorcas had worked in a small independent home in Tooting before moving to Hazeldene. She said in that home there had been three care assistants on duty every shift caring for just eleven patients with a Sister in charge as well – a ratio of more than 1:3 whereas it was 1:6 here.

All I know is the first shift that I was given six patients to myself was deeply alarming. I hurried yet I didn't want to hurry, since washing and dressing and chatting required time and patience to do it well with gentleness. Six people to get up, washed and dressed; six precisely correct breakfasts to be assembled – porridge or cornflakes, with or without sugar, prunes or All-Bran, eggs or bacon, toast with or without marmalade – all took time. For example, I spent a lot of time going in and out of Margaret's room, persuading her that her toast was for eating: 'This thing here is so strange', she kept saying, turning it upside down and pushing it about the increasingly sticky paper doily on her tray. 'I need to take time to decide what it is, don't you see? I can't quite understand it.' Sometimes she could be very articulate about what she could make no sense of. 'Is it something for my hands?' she kept saying as I tried to explain that it was toast and toast is for eating.

Time ticked by and my last resident was still not put of bed by 11 a.m. – and nor, I noted were some others, so it wasn't just my inexperience. Making up the beds, straightening the rooms, putting away their clothes, scurrying along to the sluice room two corridors away to dispose of soiled bags and dirty washing while trying to maintain an air of relaxed friendliness was not easy. Baths took a long time, hoisting and lowering people into the water, fearful of letting anyone slip, drying and powdering and rubbing their buttocks with cream, waiting while someone stopped for a long time half-way through putting on a dress, frozen as if suddenly struck by some far more important thought.

Nothing goes to rule. Just as you get one person finally settled and you start on someone else, the bell goes. Sister and everyone else could see when one of your residents was ringing, and you had to drop everything and hurry to answer it so that you could get the alarm switched off fast. It might be something easy – fetch me a drink – or it might be someone having an accident on the way to the toilet, which took a long time. You could never take the risk of ignoring those bells. No doubt if I'd stayed longer I would have got better at it. But I rarely saw the other have a minute's rest, except for the miserly fifteen-minute break we were given in every six-hour shift. I actually fell asleep in the staff room on a quarter-hour break one morning and had to be shaken awake by the others. Occasionally in the afternoons there was a little time just to sit and talk to residents, keeping them company in their rooms, but not often. The first day I had my own group to care for, one or two care assistants were off sick. One of ours was sent away to cover on another floor and her work was spread between everyone else. Management did not appear to budget for spare pairs of hands, nor was there any extra pay for care assistants working twice as hard to cover for others.

Laing and Buisson say local authorities are now paying about £100 a week too little for each patient they put into residential care. Many owners are abandoning the small nursing-home business before the government brings in rigorous new quality standards, requiring expensive new fire escapes and bigger rooms (the government has since relaxed standards because of this). At the same time the property price boom in the south-east reduces the incentives for care-home owners to work so hard turning a marginal profit when they can sell the place handsomely to developers and retire. The big companies have moved in everywhere as economies of scale make better profits, so they expand while the independents go to the wall. The government at the time of writing has yet to provide a staff/resident ratio guide, which is difficult to fix as it all depends on how feeble the residents are. As residents' dependency status keeps changing, usually for the worse, it makes it tricky to set hard-and-fast regulations. But Dorcas had told me she thought the work here was too hard and the staff far too few for such fragile patients.

According to Laing and Buisson, this company made some £3 million this year out of its 3200 beds nationwide. That means, says William Laing, they make around £1000 a bed per year clear profit after all capital and running costs. Those profits depend on keeping wages at rock-bottom. This, he said, is a growing company that does well out of building nursing homes in affluent areas and charging high prices to those who can pay, while also taking block contracts from the NHS, which pays more than local authorities to place its patients, because by definition NHS patients need more intensive care and the price for each can be negotiated individually. It is all a question of what it is worth a hospital to pay to unblock one of its acute beds by decanting a patient into a nursing home.

Dorcas complained vigorously about the low pay. She had to work forty-eight hours, including long twelve-hour shifts at the weekends, and it was still not a survivable wage. For reasons neither she nor I could understand, she got no overtime rate, no time-and-a-half or double-time for these terrible extra weekend hours. But at least here she could always work as many hours as she wanted when she needed to earn more, which is one reason some employers get away with low pay. Many jobs have no chance of extra hours, and many are now advertised for thirty hours or below with shifts to suit employers' heavy pressure times. This was taken to extremes in places like the Clement Atlee school kitchen, with its unpaid half-hour in the middle of a three-hour shift. Kinderquest's 'temporary' status was doing the same thing. I asked Dorcas if she had ever thought about joining a union, since unionised workplaces get better rates of pay. She nodded enthusiastically and said they had often thought about it. Once or twice people had suggested it and had tried to get something going, 'But it didn't happen. I don't know why. Of course there should be a union in here and the pay might improve. But the people who tried to organise it a few times, I don't know what happened to them. They don't work here any more. Maybe they walked away, I don't know.'

It is expecting a lot of people who already work so hard to take on the task of trying to organise union recognition in their workplace. It feels scary and dangerous, it is unknown territory, and in a 48-hour week with bad shift times and children, how was someone like Dorcas supposed to do it? I didn't suggest she should, though she nodded her head and said, 'Someone ought to. That would be a good thing.' It made me feel guilty. I should have stayed here a while, helped to organise a union ballot, tried to make things better. But staying any longer than strictly necessary for reporting purposes was more than I could bear. Dorcas said she often thought of leaving, but the trouble was that many jobs that paid more per hour, like her daughter's bus conducting, didn't offer enough hours' work to match her present total wage. Anyway, as I had already found, it is not so easy to change job without suffering several weeks without pay, leaving debts and rent arrears which someone like Dorcas would never countenance without fear.

I quit before the weekend, when I had been rotated to work two twelve-hour shifts, all day on both Saturday and Sunday in that claustrophobic place. Those three long windowless corridors where we worked, hardly seeing the light, were darkly oppressive. It was emotionally draining work, hurrying from drama to drama, from one suffering and demanding person to another, torn between pity, anxiety and irritation. It had its rewards when a resident smiled and expressed pleasure or gratitude, when you had the time to do something extra, to listen to them and talk a while. These were pleasures I saw all the carers take in their work from time to time, coming out of a room with an air of satisfaction after making someone more cheerful: they talked about the residents with affection and involvement. But I doubt this is work many would choose if they had a real choice, not at this low pay and low status. Nurses often have to do this same caring work and the same dirty work, but they are better paid (even if still not well-paid enough). They are professionals with ladders upwards if they want to take them and good qualifications to their name. They have general respect, even admiration, coming top of public esteem in opinion polls. Care assistants have none of that: health ancillaries feature nowhere in the national consciousness. Since I am lucky and I have the choice, I walked away from here with a sigh of relief.

I left Margaret, Minnie, Paula, Mrs Knightsbridge and all the rest, but they haunted me for weeks, daytime ghosts. It was more demanding work than the school kitchen, since the scrubbing of inanimate pots and pans was nothing compared to the washing of fragile old people with raw sores on their legs, who winced at the pain. The strain of engaging emotionally with all that misery was exhausting. The kindness and hard work of the care assistants here was worth far more than they were paid. But this is unseen, unmentionable labour, hidden away in these human oubliettes we would rather not think about. Considering directors' pay rises and weighing up the value of their work compared with the work of these women here, what is the scale of worth that puts care assistants at the bottom of every heap? Where do these values come from?

It is because caring is women's work. That attitude is embedded still in the values society apportions to the jobs people do. It is why there will never be equal pay until women's work is regarded with equal respect. There were no male care assistants here, only one or two male 'adaptation' nurses from abroad who were on their way upwards. Women's work is still treated as if it should be given almost free, a natural function. Any woman can do it because we are born to it, trained to it from infancy. Cleaning bottoms and being kind doesn't require qualification, only being a woman. At the heart of the low-pay problem lies the continuing low valuation of what are regarded as women's skills – caring, cleaning, cooking, teaching and nursing. Things your mother did for you she did freely out of love, and there is an unspoken expectation that all women at work should be society's mothers, virtually for free. The low value put on their labour springs from a deeply ingrained belief that they do these jobs because they love them. The gap between women's and men's pay will never be bridged until the value put on women's and men's work is re-balanced. Why does a mechanic cleaning sparking plugs rank higher than a care assistant cleaning old people? Companies like this rely on that gap to make their profits.

The standard week here was forty-two hours. That earned just £203.70. Of all the jobs I did, none made me so outraged at the pay. How could such good work be worth so shamefully little? Whenever anyone accuses me of naivety in imagining that these things can be changed, if anyone lectures me on the immutable laws of the market, I just ask them how they can justify paying £203.70 a week for work such as this?

A conversation with Mr Jones

Mr Jones, I shall call him. He is the chief executive in one of the larger care-home companies: it is a secretive sector and it is the policy of this company never to give on-the-record interviews. He is anyway better left anonymous as an archetype who could be speaking from any era down the ages. In Dickensian days he could have been in the flue-cleansing business, speaking of the economic disaster that would follow if chimney-sweeping were over-regulated and little boys were banned from fulfilling their economic destiny. As it happens he suited this part in appearance too: plumpish with small eyes and a bright pink silk tie.

We start off politely enough discussing the problems in the care-home industry. The government pays too little per patient, probably about £100–150 per resident per week too little in the south, driving some companies out of business. His own, he says, is among the most efficient and takes more private patients, which is why the Chairman's message in the company's annual report records 'profitability at a record high'. The introduction of the minimum wage, reports the Chairman, has had little impact on the company. (Which must be evidence the minimum wage was set too low, if even a low-pay, labour-intensive industry like this had no problem.)

Around two-thirds of Mr Jones's clients are government-funded residents. He wants the government not only to pay more for their care but also to force local authorities to close their remaining care homes and place their patients in the private sector. State-run homes are, he says, inefficient, badly run and their real costs are double private homes. I asked him why the few remaining local authority homes cost so much more to run.

'It's the usual, their staff are feather-bedded.'

'In what ways?'

'Oh, you know, the same as ever. They are very overstaffed by our standards and so feather-bedded.'

'How exactly?'

'All those pensions, holidays, sick pay, overtime pay and so forth.'

Those were all the things that were reduced to a bare minimum or non-existent for the staff at Hazeldene, as with agency staff and contracting companies everywhere. He is quite right that this is where the margins of profit and efficiency have been made in the private sector. I asked him what he pays ordinary care assistants.

'Around the £5 an hour mark', he said (though I discovered the 'around' meant it was 25p less).

'£5 is not a wage they can live on, especially in London', I said. Mr Jones gave me a beady look. 'They are working very hard', I continued. 'Most care assistants work forty-eight hours and even then they still can't make ends meet. Your business's success depends entirely on how well they do their job and how well they treat your clients, yet they can't afford to live on their pay.'

He sat up rather emphatically in his chair. 'We pay top-of-the-market rates and wages are our biggest cost', he said. I bit my tongue and said nothing. 'Look, we all work hard, don't we?' he said, leaning back in his chair. 'You and I, we use our heads. You and I work very hard and we sometimes we have to work until late at night, don't we?'

'But we don't work as hard as care assistants, nothing like.'

'Look, what exactly are you getting at?'

'OK, I'm not pinning this on you in particular or on your company. But care assistants aren't being paid enough to live on, not a living wage. We as a society, private or government-funded, are just not paying the going economic rate for having old people looked after. It should cost more. It should cost enough to pay carers a living wage, shouldn't it? Not just in this industry but wherever people are being paid less than they can survive on. If you and I eat in a restaurant where the kitchen staff can't live on what we pay for the meal, we're getting it too cheap. We are not paying the market price.'

'But the market price is whatever you can produce and sell something for.'

'No. It is a distorted market if it depends on sub-survivable wages. It is a below-market, fraudulent price, not the true price. The result is the government has to give out tax credits to subsidise low wages. The government subsidises every restaurant meal when they top up the pay for washing up our plates. Do you think that is acceptable? Why should the tax payer subsidise the services you and I purchase? Why subsidise a restaurant meal? But above all, how do you and I justify earning large salaries while these hard-working people struggle?'

Mr Jones pulls himself up to his full importance and leans across the desk to deliver the quintessential well-off man's reply. 'Look this is the way I see it. I believe this is a free country. I believe in this modern age that everyone has their opportunity. Everyone who really wants to reach their goal is free to do it. If making money is your thing, you can go for it and make it. If it's education you want, you can get educated. Otherwise, if you try to even everything out what do we get? We get soaring wages, soaring inflation and then soaring taxes to pay for it and then what? Communism? Is that it? Doesn't work.'

So he shall remain plain Mr Jones who is a middle-of-the-road chief executive of a middle-ranking company, nothing exceptional, with a very ordinary director's view of society to match his very ordinary director's salary. Checking his company's annual report, he earns £162,000 a year, plus his 387,100 shares in the company which, according to the report, will have yielded him another £85,162 in dividends. Although that gave him an income of £247,162 last year, it still puts Mr Jones at the low end of the scale for company directors. He probably does not regard himself as especially rich, certainly not as any kind of fat cat, since he compares himself with those in his own occupation, forgetting that he is still among the 0.5 per cent richest earners in the land. Instead of counting his blessings, Mr Jones will be looking up enviously at the median (not the top) earnings of directors of the FTSE 100, FTSE mid-250 and FTSE small-companies indexes, which he will find is nearly twice his salary at £416,000 and rising fast. The median, including small companies! It is rising meteorically, astronomically above the pay increases of their staff. Since 1994 directors' pay in these companies has risen by 107 per cent while the average salary of their collective employees rose by just 31 per cent. In other words, directors have had pay rises that outstrip their employees by a ration of 3:1.[1] The gap is not just widening, it is stretching out of sight. So Mr Jones at £247,162 per annum does not think he is a rich man.

Notes

Copyright (c) Polly Toynbee. From *Hard Work: Life in Low-pay Britain*, published in 2003 by Bloomsbury. Reproduced by permission of the author c/o Rogers, Coleridge & White Ltd., 20 Powis Mews, London W11 1JN.

1. *Empirical evidence on the ratio of CEO compensation to employee pay by* Professor Martin J. Conyon, the Wharton School, University of Pennsylvania, Hemmington Scott Publishing 2002, commissioned by the Trades Union Congress: www.tuc.org.uk/work_life/

13

Risky business: re-thinking the human in interactive service work

Sharon C. Bolton and Maeve Houlihan

The growing interest in front-line service work has revealed several recurrent, not to say paradoxical, themes. Close communication with customers requires that service workers present a desirable corporate image and create the profitable product of customer satisfaction. It is the emotional tone of the interaction between customer and service-provider that has become something of a talking point. Of particular interest to the current analysis are those front-line service workers who perform routine service interaction work whose design is mundane, tightly controlled and arguably low skilled. This 'emotional proletariat' (Macdonald and Sirianni, 1996) comprises the workers who make up the 'have-a-nice-day' culture where 'niceness' is routinely delivered: notionally faceless service workers dealing with faceless customers.

While the emotional proletariat come low in the status hierarchy of knowledge work, they are in fact a major means of a company differentiating in a highly competitive sector. Of course, 'quality service' is often cited as a main source of competitive advantage in an increasingly service-based economy and yet its qualitative features are very hard to define. The interaction between customer and service provider is often seen as the 'moment of truth' (Carlzon, 1987) and management exert considerable energy in trying to capture and routinely replicate that special moment through combinations of standardised processes, performance targets, surveillance mechanisms, recruitment and selection procedures and High Commitment Human Resource Management practices (Bowen and Lawler, 1992; Heskett, Sasser and Schlesinger, 1997; Houlihan, 2002; Kinnie, Hutchinson and Purcell, 2000; Pitt, Foreman and Bromfield, 1995; Schneider and Bowen, 1995). Though diverse in content, these studies suggest a concentration on the outcomes, rather than the processes, of production. Underlying the continued search for seemingly elusive but magical service quality is a persistent, if not over-anxious, reliance on the routinisation of service delivery via scripts, prompts and metrics (Fernie and Metcalfe, 1998; Ritzer, 1999; Taylor and Bain, 1999). The object of the exercise, it appears, is to replace the 'risk' of spontaneous/social interaction with something (supposedly) more predictable and reliable without ever really considering if this might actually represent 'quality customer service' (Bolton and Houlihan, 2005).

In this chapter, we argue that as important as the prevailing supporting mechanisms might be, enforced regulation of interaction between customer and service provider squeezes the human out and undermines the process of service production, thereby creating concerns over both service quality and workers' emotional health, and indeed, ultimately, the service itself. We propose that customer relations are better thought about as social relations and that service should not necessarily mean servitude. If the emotion work involved in providing customer service is viewed as a social accomplishment, front-line service workers can then be conceptualised as multi-skilled emotion managers (Bolton, 2000, 2001, 2003, 2005; Callaghan and Thompson, 2002) who are able to expertly judge what type and how much emotion work is required to maintain a stable and mutually satisfying order of interaction (Goffman, 1961, 1967). If the customer is understood as a *person* who is *also* a customer then customer service can be conceptualised as a form of social encounter that is not purely instrumentally motivated (Bolton and Houlihan, 2005; Goffman, 1967; Wray-Bliss, 2001, p. 53).

Utilising Goffman's (1959, 1961, 1967, 1974) insights into the 'interaction order' combined with qualitative data collected from telephone call centre workers we suggest that the ritual of every day social interaction is something of a feat, providing a remarkable level of consistency and certainty and offering 'ontological security' for those involved (Giddens, 1984). While constructed by managers as a risk-reducing activity, by binding service providers to scripts, imposed feeling and display rules of interaction and unachievable production targets, management are actually distorting and unbalancing this achievement. Workers are unable to calibrate their performances, the ceremonial order is disrupted, and irritation and disaffection are the result. We contend that by granting workers autonomy in what might be described as the emotional labour process, dignity will be restored to what is currently an unequal exchange and an alienating production process. This may well prove to be not such a risky business after all, with desirable outcomes for all involved.

Methodology

Call centres are telephone operations for the processing and management of routine customer communication by a centralised staff. Their interest lies in their attempt to resolve the pressing yet perennial organisational challenges of global/local, quantity/quality and control/responsiveness through the mechanisms of routinisation, standardisation and centralisation, facilitated by advanced information and communication technologies (ICTs). Their interest also lies in their use of restrictive work designs and intensive management strategies in the face of wider prescription towards more participative, knowledge developing, organic approaches. Our arguments in this chapter draw on a wider series of field studies of the experiences and performances of call centre workers, framed by a two-year ethnographic participation in the inbound sales and customer services department of a UK motor and home insurance call centre, *Quotes Direct*. Data in this chapter draws from direct participation in the work at *Quotes Direct* and close observation of work processes, and from the accounts of front-line customer service representatives (CSRs). Qualitative data such as this gives rare insight into how the organisation of customer service work impacts upon the day-to-day working lives of CSRs, their interactions with customers and each other. It thus offers a broad focus lens on what quality service might mean to the different parties involved in both its production and consumption.

The organisation of interaction in call centre work

The organisation of work in call centres seeks to resolve the often contradictory aims of quality and quantity. It is clear that 'a pervasive feature of the call centre is to regulate, and where possible standardise the performance of common interactional routines' (Cameron, 2000, p. 97).[1] The task of the CSR is to transform what is for the caller a relatively unique event, into a routine process with standardised features (Zimmerman, 1992). This logic introduces the possibility of controlling, optimising and predicting performance standards. Staff are given detailed scripts to perform,[2] the essential turns of which are embedded in the supporting ICT architecture. As an experienced call centre worker explains:

> [. . .] you've got to read your *information* when you are doing an inquiry or something, but other than that the system guides you and prompts you what to say and do . . . it's a dumb terminal, you know, the next move is *there* for

you. . . . You can't go any further until you put the information in. (Barbara, Centre Manager – *Housing Helpline*)

Whilst CSRs may have some discretion over actual words, the essential character of what must be said, when, and how is largely prescribed. This is not unusual in front-line service work but its impact in the context of voice-to-voice interaction is potentially far more constraining. To put this in context, here a CSR compares her customer services experiences in retail, to her work in the call centre. She makes the important point that while CSRs have many communication tasks, and much invested in their successful achievement, they have only one real communication channel available to affect them – their voice:

> It is so much different speaking to someone face-to-face. It is much easier to look them in the eye, and to express that you are listening, and you do understand, and that you are going to sort it out. To someone on the phone, they've had a million people from the gas to the electric, everyone has said 'yes I'll sort it out for you', and then they don't. Why should they believe me? They can't see me, and it frustrates me that I can't get the message across. I mean everybody can feign sincerity in their voice, but it is hard to feign it when you can see them face-to-face I'm not saying that I would do that but they think that I will, you know. And they won't listen to me, and it's so much harder to get their attention. (Anna, CSR – *Quotes Direct*)

Such scripting is designed to achieve process goals of sequencing, clarity, rapport building, and branding and task goals that include information gathering, information giving, information accuracy and sales – in other words, the process is painstakingly designed to provide an apparently risk free communication structure. And yet, a fixed work process becomes problematic when the script or job role invokes conflicting priorities or role expectations, such as customer service versus 'hard sell' imperatives. While scripts and job codification permeate the world of the call centre worker, this does not necessarily make the job of CSR easier, nor can scripts be 'blindly' followed. The impracticability of wholly 'working to rule' underscores the discretionary behaviour and tacit skills that are required from service workers. To manage this, training and coaching emphasises attitudes and values – the warmth of the voice, the sincerity of tone, the attitude of flexibility.

And yet at other times, CSRs may draw on the resource of withdrawal into the script, or 'going into robot-mode' both as a shield, and possibly to subtly punish the customer. The practice of 'depersonalisation' or 'cognitive distancing' to protect oneself from customer pressure or abuse (Hochschild, 1983; Leidner, 1993; Sturdy, 1998) is not automatically a form of resistance, and can be seen as a necessary form of skill and competence in customer service work.

> The good thing about the job is that when you walk out the door you don't think about it anymore, like driving a car. You don't have to think 'did I do that gear change really well? I must do it better next time' – you don't bother about that. Crunching gears, you know, its one of those things. And that's what the job is like – it's like driving a car. You know you can't do everything right all the time, but you know, because it is automated to a great extent you can't really control the things that are going right and wrong...[3] (Anna, CSR – *Quotes Direct*)

However, this is a delicate line to tread – the organisation seeks this sort of competence and pragmatism, yet it also discourages 'automatons'. Thus overall, CSRs are assessed in terms of their compliance to the 'rules', but also in terms of their personalisation and adaptation of them. Thus CSRs are in the position of at once enacting and mediating scripts, switching between stances of presenting their real selves and hiding themselves behind the scripts. They are required on one hand to enact 'positive' emotional autonomy and, on the other, to contain 'negative' emotional autonomy, thus to perform compensating emotion work.

This is troubling for the CSRs who endure it, but also for the organisation, as it spills over into the customer service relationship. The CSR is employed not as a machine (in which case surely a machine would be cheaper and more precise) but as a human representative, necessary to impart some of the non-replicable aspects of human connection and customer service – authenticity, professionalism, ability to inspire trust and rapport, ability to negotiate conflict and ability 'not take things personally' (Cameron, 2000, p. 117). And yet, such competencies are in many respects counter-values to the process of scripting interaction, which by implication suppresses, and even alienates natural responsiveness, instead introducing manufactured sincerity. To create a uniform standard, the authentic is rendered synthetic. Thus, as we argue throughout this chapter, highly restrictive practices actually introduce risk rather than proscribe it.

Customer relations as social relations – Goffman's interaction order

Goffman's insights are invaluable in aiding an understanding of how customer relations may be usefully reconceptualised as social relations. People involved in social encounters are highly effective social actors who are able to present themselves in certain ways according to the often implicit rules of the situation. Every social encounter is risky as there are moments of 'decision, of resistance and of feeling' but the social order of interaction is there to minimise the risk (Goffman, 1961; Schwabe, 1993, p. 337). Goffman describes this as the 'interaction order' and insists that it is an area of human activity worthy of independent study (Goffman, 1991).

People construct, absorb and deploy 'traffic rules of interaction' (Goffman, 1959) that ensure a routine compliance with the code of the prevailing emotional culture. Such is the efficacy of this process, most encounters pass without note: a stable, taken-for-granted achievement. People not only constantly monitor their own conduct but also the conduct of others, thus sustaining the predictability of much of day-to-day social life. The continuous monitoring and treatment of fellow interactants with 'ritual care' produces and reproduces what might be described as a moral order where the aim may be to save face, but the effect is to save the situation and the 'ritual structure of the self' (Goffman, 1967, p. 39). Even in a complex mass society where there appears to be no commitment to any particular 'rule-book' and the self must be fragmented in order to meet the challenge of diverse audiences this is the case (Schwabe, 1993).

The notion of 'traffic rules of interaction' should not suggest that the interaction order exists in a symbolic realm, rather the point is to emphasise that it requires a material stage for its production. The status of people in the interaction order will be a defining feature of how face-saving activity is to be distributed. For instance, it is notable that the codes of conduct which usually govern general social encounters, ensuring that everyone 'acts appropriately and receives his due' (Goffman, 1967, p. 55), do not apply to the exchange between service-provider and customer. Instead, how the rules of interaction are applied becomes unequal – consumers expect to be able to display dissatisfaction, yet the front-line service worker is expected to meet aggression with pleasantries, sympathy, or at worst, calm indifference, cast as they are in the role of deferent. As Hochschild states:

> Where the customer is king, unequal exchanges are normal, and from the beginning customer and client assume different rights to feeling and display. The ledger is supposedly evened by a wage. (1983, p. 86)

There can be little doubt that the economic interests that tightly control the interaction between service-provider and customer disrupt the balance of the interaction order that would normally serves to 'buffer the self from the direct ravages of inequality' (Schwabe, 1993, p. 342) and help to maintain an element of dignity for all involved. As an additional destabilising influence on the order of interaction, there is little recognition of the delicate processes involved and therefore little trust that any form of order can be maintained without management intervention (Callaghan and Thompson, 2002). The 'risk' of unpredictability (notably for the customer experience rather than the service provider) is instead (apparently) managed out through detailed surface prescription and scripting. Utilising Goffman's insights into the interaction order reveals these destabilising influences as the outcome of interaction is focused on a rather narrow conception of service quality and the humanity involved leading us to suggest that it is the neglect of the social embeddedness of the service encounter that leads to its violation.

Service quality

Despite extraordinary efforts to define and achieve 'quality' customer service there is little evidence of satisfaction with the results. The gap between customer expectations of service and perceptions of the service received continues to grow and, increasingly, concern is expressed about the detrimental effects upon workers in what can only be described as a no-win situation (Fernie and Metcalfe, 1998; Hochschild, 1983). Unsurprisingly, given the extent and range of emotion work involved, episodes of customer interaction are potentially fragile accomplishments, their success dependent upon the service worker meeting the expectations of the customer. Needless to say, interactions between customer and service-provider do not always proceed according to management prescription and both customers and workers are adversely affected by the experience. Diane, a *Quotes Direct* CSR here explains how repeated frustration with job restrictions caused her to change her normally highly customer service oriented attitude to one of 'not caring', but makes it clear that this is not an approach that sits comfortably with her:

> Yesterday I changed my attitude when I went into work. I thought 'right, I don't give a damn; I don't give a damn about any of them'. And I sat there and I argued with customers. And that is not me. And somebody gave me his postcode and I couldn't match it up with the number, so I said 'oh, I've typed your address in with the correct house number and it's actually given me a different post code'. 'Well that's wrong' he said. I said, 'well, it can't be wrong because it's been put in by the postcode people, but you can have more than one postcode in one street', and he said 'well I'm telling you it's wrong'. And I said 'well you go and ring the postcode people, mate, and tell them. I'm working with what I've got'. And my attitude was 'I don't give a damn if you hang up, I don't give a damn if you ring them up and give out about me'. And I got through yesterday a hell of a lot better, but that was not how I do my job.

Here frustration as a result of 'failed' social interaction is turned outwards as a means of survival, resulting evidently in negative effects for customers and company as well. Reconciling this dissonance becomes the responsibility of the CSR. Faced with a deeply demanding and contradictory system, CSRs experience the pain of conflicting emotions, and troubled self-concept, as indicated in what Diane goes on to say:

> That was not me operating the phone, doing my job. I'm *nice* to people, I want people to like *Quotes Direct*, I want people to think 'well yeah, it was twenty quid more expensive but. . . . ' I want people to think 'what nice people you speak to when you get through . . . what good service you get, how helpful'. You know, they're apologising because you are asking questions and you're saying 'don't worry about it! I will find out for you'. I will make you listen to that awful music while I find out, but I will find out for you and I'll do it now, because you are not an inconvenience, you are the reason for my job. Yesterday? Tough. 'What do you want? No, it's inconvenient – go away'. (Diane, CSR – *Quotes Direct*)

As Diane is clearly aware, the perspicacious customer expects to be satisfied and does not anticipate any 'leakage' that may intimate they are not receiving personalised service (Parasuraman, Berry and Zeithaml, 1991; Parkinson, 1991). Whilst apparently withdrawing from investing too much into her interactions with customers, Diane is clearly uncomfortable with the whole experience and is fully aware that the *customer* as a *person* will feel discomfited and alienated from the interaction. Most often such feelings of uneasiness concerning the 'misdemeanours' of CSRs are directed towards the service-provider at the expense of the customer's own sense of obligation to the encounter – as Diane explains when she claims that she does not care if the customer hangs up the phone. But Diane clearly does care, and so a cycle is created where uneasiness becomes a 'contagious disease' (Goffman, 1967, p. 126). This unease may materialise as open aggression, a sense of awkwardness or a vague sense of disquiet but, in whatever form, the social accomplishment that is the interaction ritual has been disturbed with very real consequences for those involved. This is not merely an isolated episode of poor quality service but a major disruption of our sense of self. Goffman usefully summarises the effects of such a 'failure':

> When the encounter fails to capture the attention of the participants, but does not release them from the obligation of involving themselves in it, then persons present are likely to feel uneasy; for them the interaction fails to come off. A person who chronically makes himself or others uneasy in conversation and perpetually kills encounters is a faulty interactant; he is likely to have such a baleful effect upon the social life around him that he may just as well be called a faulty person. (Goffman, 1961, p. 135)

The intricacies present in scripting thus introduce a series of dilemmas, which CSRs must manage. When the customer resists, or when the script is inappropriate or transparent, CSRs draw on a range of tacit skills to cajole, comfort or distract the customer, often necessarily in ways different from the idealised script. On most occasions, however, opportunities to carry out this 'balancing act' are limited due to the imposition of rigidly defined quantitative targets. Anna confirmed that her attitude to the work depends heavily on the conditions and regime at any moment in time. Anna conveys that there is a strong tendency to invoke the 'quantity' model, and when this is the case, the fundamental character of the work changes for her, as does her attitude towards it.

> If I feel that I've got to get so many [targets] in an hour, I've got to rush the *quantity* through well – then the customer starts to annoy me. I just want to know 'have you had an accident'? So they tell me about the other person, what they were wearing, what type of day it was. . . . Which is fine, and I understand, and I can do that, and I can enjoy that when I'm. . . . that doesn't bore me because I can build up a picture of them in my mind and I'm fine with them. But when it's *time* – I am thinking 'shut . . . your . . . mouth. . . . This is *my time* you are taking up. The answer to the question is *yes* or *no*'. That's what is going through my mind. When I've got that attitude, much as I am trying to disguise it, I know I can't possibly be disguising it. Because that is all I'm feeling. And it's not a nice feeling, and it's something that makes you not like yourself in a way. (Anna, CSR – *Quotes Direct*)

Humanity leaks out

Nevertheless, despite quantitative targets and scripted interaction, conversations with CSRs display how everyday forms of social interaction attempt to burst from the seams of prescribed customer interaction. The front-line worker develops many methods, often very subtle and barely detectable by management, of registering their refusal to be defined by organisational feeling rules. As Goffman (1967, p. 87) highlights:

> in scrupulously observing the proper form he may find that he is free to insinuate all kinds of disregard by carefully modifying intonation, pronunciation, pacing, and so forth.

Some episodes of 'misbehaviour' (Ackroyd and Thompson, 1999) may be classified as coping mechanisms others as acts of resistance and defiance against the obligatory rituals of deference that deny interactants the basic right to dignity (Hodson, 2001; Paules, 1996). This is in direct response to how CSRs through job design are in many ways constructed as school pupils or children, subjects without power or influence or dignity. Diane herself also invokes this image:

> I don't like being *treated like a school child* and being told you're not allowed to ring the underwriters to ask them things – I'm a grown-up and I've got a mortgage and a grown up daughter with her own house. I don't think I should have to go to somebody else and say 'please can you ring these people and ask them this question that I want to ask them but I'm not allowed to', which is a waste of everybody's time as far as I'm concerned. I'm an intelligent enough person to know what's relevant to ask somebody else and what isn't. (Diane, CSR – *Quotes Direct*)

It is important to note, however, that not all acts of defiance will have a detrimental effect upon the service encounter. On the contrary, a refusal to abide by a managerially imposed script has the potential to improve the quality of customer relations, though it may have negative connotations for the achievement of objective targets (Callaghan and Thompson, 2002; Korczynski *et al.*, 2000; Sutton, 1991; Wray-Bliss, 2001). Anna expresses this tension very well:

> Sometimes with the customers, when it's going how I like it, and *when it is 'quality' calls*, I can honestly say that I enjoy it, I really do. I can say I feel like I've done something for them, and they'll tell me that. When they call me by my name, and they are happy, and the customers will laugh at a joke that I make, and I can have a conversation with them. . . . Because I do enjoy speaking to people . . . that's what I do like about the job because I find I'm quite easy doing that . . . and if I get paid for doing that, that's brilliant. When it's going well. . . . I mean I don't mind it when it is *red button*.[4] Because if I'm giving a quality call, I'm dealing with one person and I totally enjoy it. But if I'm made to get *quantities* of calls through, then like I say, it upsets me. (Anna, CSR – *Quotes Direct*)

Under normal circumstances, the caller is a person to whom the CSR relates both socially and morally (Wray-Bliss, 2001), therefore, for both participants in the encounter the exchange of social niceties creates and sustains a 'moral order'. However, they are also aware of and frustrated by the elements of their work process that restrict or undermine these dynamics. Brenda captures something of the mixed feelings and emotion work involved in 'smiling, and not meaning it' (Sturdy, 1998):

> I'd like if you could build up more of a personal rapport with the customers. I don't tend to bother doing that as things are. I'm not interested in the weather; I'm not interested in the story that they have got to tell me. I'm quite good at being . . . sounding a bit interested . . . and then you come to the main point

which is me making my sale. . . . But I think I'd find the job more interesting if it was about really relating to people. (Brenda, CSR – *Quotes Direct*)

Brenda's tone here invokes a sense of ambivalence and weariness. Working within such a restrictive system and under continual pressure to achieve almost unachievable targets, she has learned not to engage. She has developed ways of interacting that avoid involvement and therefore, in her eyes, prevent the possibility of the 'cycle of unease' occurring. Brenda could be viewed as an automaton, not interested in her work or the customers; yet she is clearly wistful that it would be a more fulfilling work process if there was time and space to relate meaningfully. Ironically, the apparent order of customer interaction is actually an alienating form of disordered social interaction and Brenda is now unwittingly trapped in a perpetual 'cycle of unease' that adversely affects all involved.

Re-conceptualising customer service

It is misleading to view the recalcitrant, fragile or alienated worker, or even the obnoxious customer (du Gay, 1996; Hopfl, 2002) as the source of failure in service encounters. Rather, our focus should turn to the imposition of management controls upon the interaction between customer and service-provider that continually reproduce the concept of sovereign customer and subjugated service-worker. Interaction between customer and service-provider is essentially a social process that is violated by a control imperative that demands that emotion work be transformed into a profitable product. But what is the calibre of the communication that takes place – can customer service work truly be regarded as conversational? It would seem not when the continued emphasis on speedy transactions enhanced with routinised 'niceness' actually constitutes a form of 'misinvolvement' (Goffman, 1967, p. 117). The 'socialised trance' (Goffman, 1967, p. 113) of rhythmic interaction will never materialise as the imposed script deprives interactants of their involvement obligations.

Often this works very well, a straightforward query over the telephone dealt with in an effective manner without any obvious need for the spontaneous involvement of the social encounter. In fact, many workers are said to feel the benefit of this as they are able to offer 'empty performances' (Goffman, 1961), and previously in this chapter we have heard Barbara and Anna explaining how they use the script as a shield against personal involvement with customers (Leidner, 1996). However, even in these fleeting moments the customer is aware that the 'whole show is false' and the fragile order of the service encounter begins to be threatened:

> When the individual senses that others are insincere or affected he tends to feel they have taken unfair advantage of their communication position to promote their own interests; he feels they have broken the ground rules of interaction. (Goffman, 1967, p. 122)

As a call centre customer comments:

> I don't like to be called 'Mrs' or 'Miss'; I want to be called by my name. But call centres I speak to seem to insist that I must fall into one of those categories. Sometimes they are rude, or make assumptions and then sometimes I've found I've gotten into a human conversation and said – 'no I'm living with my partner' and the agent has said 'oh, right, me too, I shouldn't have assumed'. But it's like they insist that every one falls into these rigid categories, and that typifies the call centre experience to me. (Customer Story – *Elaine*)

And similarly, CSRs often voice unease about aspects of the script that require them to manipulate the customer, such as eliciting personal information or prompting a sale. As Brenda voices: 'it's not nice to be pushy'.[5] Yet pushing is intrinsically part of sales work, and customer service work is often and increasingly sales work in disguise. Here Anna illustrates the point, first in how she deals with herself and, secondly, in how she deals with customers.

> I used to get knots in my stomach when I asked people for their home number and dialling code. I really didn't like asking them for that because I know what it is for – cold calling purposes. I felt they used me because I had to ask it, but I also didn't want to upset [customers]. Because I wouldn't like to be asked in that way, I wouldn't like someone pushing me, you know. I've had to make myself change because it was making me ill. I didn't need to make myself feel that physically sick because I was asking that question: so I had to [learn to] say it without thinking about it. I had to just say the words, and pretend that I wasn't asking them this personal question. Because I had to think, 'why am I doing this to myself?' I was making myself feel sick about it. I had to start depersonalising it.

The service encounter is a minor event, one episode among many. However, in consumer capitalism it is an event that accounts for an increasing amount of day-to-day social interaction. When this interaction is perpetually experienced as dissatisfying or even distressing – when the interaction order is disrupted – both selves and society are at stake (Schwabe, 1993). As the call centre workers describe above, relating to customers is one of the most enjoyable aspects of their work and they lament their inability to interact with customers due to pressure of quantifiable targets and rigidly prescribed interaction. This is not to say they do not recognise the need to 'get the job done'; the voices of Anna, Brenda and Diane have all expressed an understanding of the essential 'sales' nature of their work. However, it becomes very clear that they also recognise that the job may be done in a different way with immediate and observable benefits for all involved. Anna echoes this when she says:

> When I get 'thank you very much for that love, you've explained a lot to me, and I think I've learned more about insurance speaking to you', which I've had, it makes me feel I've done something there . . . I'm not wasting my time. Because I am a human being as well. (Anna, CSR – *Quotes Direct*)

Some of these benefits may be described as improved quality service or increased job satisfaction but what they are in fact is the successful attainment of the interaction order which leads to a restoration of dignity and a protected sense of self. How could this not be an improvement on the empty, often alienating experience many come to associate with contemporary 'customer-service'? However, this state of affairs will not automatically materialise. As Goffman insightfully points out, systems and structures need to be in place in order to support the ceremony of successful social interaction;

> It is therefore important to see that the self is in part a ceremonial thing, a sacred object which must be treated with proper ritual care and in turn must be presented in a proper light to others. As a means through which this self is established, the individual acts with proper demeanour while in contact with others and is treated by others with deference. It is just as important to see that if the individual is playing this kind of sacred game, then the field must be suited to it. The environment must ensure that the individual will not pay too high a price for acting with good demeanour and that deference will be accorded him. Deference and demeanour practices must be institutionalised so that the individual will be able to project a viable, sacred self and stay in the game on a proper ritual basis. (Goffman, 1967, p. 91)

In other words we would suggest that, whilst recognising that consumer capitalism would find this an altogether far too risky proposition, service-workers should be granted some autonomy in how they deal with customers and offered the opportunity to restore any imbalance that may occur in customer interaction.

Conclusion

From the totality of our field data it is clear that active humanity persists in the call centre despite the most comprehensive attempts to 'manage it out'. Such actions included editing and shortcutting scripts, 'escape attempts' such as taking over-frequent toilet breaks, letting off steam 'off-stage', and game playing rituals with other colleagues. Staff also find ways to improve their performance and success as CSRs, for example through experimenting with and developing their customer service and sales techniques, responding to the coaching and development plans supervisors set for them, taking initiative and contributing constructive suggestions in team meetings, and carrying out informal coaching and mentoring work.

In all of these ways, it is clear that the work of the CSR involves extensive but under recognised discretionary skills in terms of constructively managing the call process and coping with the work. These skills take tangible forms of discretionary work effort such as dexterity in customer service handling, ability to use judgement, ability to tell stories, ability to multi-task and deal with large volumes of information and ability to sell and seduce. More opaquely, these skills take subtle forms of emotion work such as the ability to cope with complex and competing demands, the ability not to take things personally, the ability to manage one's own reactions and reinvent ways of seeing things, and the ability to absorb and yet decompress stress. These skills are unrecognised in the formal construction of call centre work, and yet they are well known within the micro-realm of that environment.

While the design of the call centre system itself and many of its managers and supervisors ignore the subtleties of these skills and focus instead on demanding and measuring performance outcomes, at *Quotes Direct* the more competent and involved team leaders and managers spend a great deal of time trying to elicit these skills and behaviours from their staff. However, despite these examples, the dominant character of work at *Quotes Direct* is 'putting up' and for all the uncertainty and stresses of the atmosphere in which they work, they get on with it. A brief dialogue overhead during a typical workday captures this alternative desperation and stoicism:

A: Only an hour to go.
B: I can't stand it another minute.
A: I bet you can. I'm going to sit here and watch you stand it like you always do.

But, we must ask: why should they stand it? This chapter serves to question the perceived benefits of enforced routinisation and regulation of communication. Whose interests do they serve?

Under the normative model, call centres are information handling organisations and the task of the CSR is to be the organisation's voice, rehearsing and performing the organisation's scripts. With scripting comes erosion of autonomy and creativity, and an associated message of low trust. The dominance of standardisation and codification begs a fundamental question: Is call centre work knowledge work or production work? Routinisation involves an abstracting process that necessarily standardises transactions and represses differentiation. Yet the task of capturing and inscribing tacit skills, in abstract performance scripts and guidelines, is highly problematic and tends towards idealised communication patterns and relational skills (Cameron, 2000). Thus CSRs and managers find themselves required to enact behaviour that is often out of sync with their intuitive or knowledgeable reactions, and often less than appropriate to the context. To compensate for these inadequacies, codification becomes more explicit and detailed, moving from words to behaviours, and increasingly to attitudes.

As the foregoing accounts have demonstrated this is clearly not the whole story. CSR work is a complex blend of knowing, sensing and rule applying – building on a largely unacknowledged set of personal skills and emotion work. However CSRs are cast with the notion of restricted skill repertoires and contained discretion. Non-routine activities and problems are diverted to supervisors and other functionaries, denying the CSR opportunities to learn from their experiences or feed this learning back into the system.

Data collected from the call centre field confirm other studies in their revelation that providing customer service for many front-line workers is actually viewed by them as 'working with people' or 'helping people' and is framed as a socially relevant activity with all the multiple interpretations and contradictions this brings (Callaghan and Thompson, 2002; Sturdy, 1998; Wray-Bliss, 2001). And yet, the human value of the interaction is negated via customer orientation programmes and scripted service encounters that cannot deal with the unpredictability and variability of the interaction order. If the service-encounter does not go according to the organisation's plan it leaves the service-worker little space for manoeuvre. What organisations appear not to have recognised is that such constraints actually have the reverse effect of imposing order and force the participants from the 'circle of the proper' into a cycle of 'unease' (Bolton and Houlihan, 2005; Goffman, 1967, p. 93).

Goffman stresses how important it is that the right balance be achieved during normal social encounters – that the people involved in the interaction be treated with 'proper ritual care' (Goffman, 1967) and we have seen from the CSRs' quotes here that they continually cite the need for their humanity to be recognised – that they are not mere machines. Quite clearly however, in the context of customer service, employees may not be treated with 'proper ritual care' according to general social feeling rules, but even exposed to verbal and physical abuse. In effect, there is no 'audience tact' or 'moral order' when the motive behind service encounters is not social ceremony (Goffman, 1961) but the creation of profit. The obnoxious customer can be a very real presence with which the service-provider has to deal but given the right to self-determination the employee can use various tactics to restore the ceremonial order. They may employ 'deferential stand-off arrangements' in order to deflect aggression and anger or various forms of humour to ease anxiety. Unsurprisingly, CSRs use break times and unofficial spaces as a cathartic space to share 'war stories', or use other means of catharsis such as putting difficult callers on speakerphone to that others could hear and mock what was being endured. Humour, via 'playful profanation', can also be used to make a serious point reminding the consumer of their obligations as an interactant (Emerson, 1973; Goffman, 1959, 1967; Taylor and Bain, 2003). And at all times, the service provider can choose whether to invest their performance with feeling or to offer a convincing but empty performance. In this way both service-provider and customer are reminded of the negotiative nature of interaction and its important role in the maintenance of the self as a sacred object:

> Whatever the activity and however profanely instrumental, it can afford many opportunities for minor ceremonies as long as other persons are present. Through these observances, guided by ceremonial obligations and expectations, a constant flow of indulgences is spread through society, with others who are present constantly reminding the individual that he must keep himself together as well as a demeaned person and affirm the sacred quality of these others. The gestures which we sometimes call empty are perhaps in fact the fullest things of all. (Goffman, 1967, p. 91)

In this chapter we suggest it is the human gestures of reciprocal social obligation that management prescription often misses in the attempt to manage out risk. Moreover, our field data suggest that in the attempt to control risk, new risks are introduced. By neglecting the socially embedded nature of the service encounter, it becomes a violated social interaction. We contend the necessity of re-imagining the service-provider and customer as 'creative composites' (Gabriel and Lang, 1995, p. 5) and customer service as a socially relevant activity. Only in this way will the business of quality customer service become less risky.

Notes

1. It is worth noting that in this sense the call centre is constructed using the root metaphor of 'machine'. As an alternative, what would the root metaphor 'conversation' look, feel and be like?

2. Scripting can be seen more generally to extend beyond the call structure itself to encompass the framing, abstracting and inscribing of input codes, product terms (insurance terms, jargon and acronyms for example), ACD (monitoring system) task classification codes, colloquial phrases such as 'going into idle' or 'managing the board' and all forms of organisational tools for the capture of local meaning.
3. This intriguing use of metaphor captures something of the acceptance/resignation that pervades Anna's relationship with her job. And yet, it does not really tell the full story for Anna, as she previously disclosed that she often leaves work worrying about the job she has done that day.
4. 'Red Button' is a colloquial term referring to times when service levels are falling behind and CSRs feel under pressure to rush calls to attend to the waiting queue of callers. An alert light on each CSR's ACD telephone monitor turns from green through amber and red, serving as a less than subtle prompt to 'speed up'.
5. Undoubtedly, this links into another discourse and domain about 'nice girls don't . . . [ask]' (Tannen, 1994).

References

Ackroyd, S. and Thompson, P. (1999) *Organizational (Mis) Behaviour*, London: Sage.

Bolton, S. (2000) 'Emotion Here, Emotion There, Emotional Organisations Everywhere', *Critical Perspectives on Accounting*, 11, 155–171.

Bolton, S. (2001) 'Changing Faces: Nurses as Emotional Jugglers', *Sociology of Health and Illness*, 23:1, 85–100.

Bolton, S. (2003) 'Multiple Roles: Nurses as Managers in the NHS' *International Journal of Public Sector Management*, 16:2, 122–130.

Bolton, S. (2005) *Emotion Management in the Workplace*, London: Palgrave.

Bolton, S. and Houlihan, M. (2005) 'The (mis)representation of customer service', *Work, Employment and Society*, 19:4, 685–703.

Bowen, D. and Lawler, E. (1992) 'The Empowerment of Service Workers', *Sloan Management Review*, Spring, 31–39.

Callaghan, G. and Thompson, P. (2002) 'We Recruit Attitude: The Selection and Shaping of Routine Call Centre Labour', *Journal Management Studies*, 39:2, 233–253.

Cameron, D. (2000) *Good to Talk?* London: Sage.

Carlzon, J. (1987) *The Moment of Truth*, Cambridge, MA: Ballinger.

du Gay, P. (1996) *Consumption and Identity at Work*, London: Sage.

Emerson, J. (1973) 'Negotiating the Serious Import of Humour', in Birenbaum, A. and Sagarin, E. (eds) *People in Places: The Sociology of the Familiar*, New York: Nelson, 269–280.

Fernie, S. and Metcalfe, D. (1998) '(Not) Hanging on the Telephone', *Centrepiece*, Centre For Economic Performance, London: London School Of Economics, 3:1, 6–11.

Gabriel, Y. and Lang, T. (1995) *The Unmanageable Consumer*, London: Sage.

Giddens, A. (1984) *The Constitution of Society*, Cambridge: Polity Press.

Goffman, E. (1959) *The Presentation of Self in Everyday Life*, London: Penguin Books.

Goffman, E. (1961) *Encounters*, New York: The Bobbs-Merrill Company Ltd.

Goffman, E. (1967) *Interaction Ritual: Essays in Face-to-Face Behaviour*, Chicago: Aldine Publishing Company.

Goffman, E. (1974) *Frame Analysis*, Boston: Northeastern University Press.

Goffman, E. (1991) 'The Interaction Order: American Sociological Association 1982 Presidential Address', in Plummer, K. (ed.) *Symbolic Interactionism: Contemporary Issues*, London: Edward Elgar Ltd.

Heskett, J., Sasser, W. and Schlesinger, L. (1997) *The Service Profit Chain*, New York: The Free Press.

Hochschild, A. (1983) *The Managed Heart: Commercialization of Human Feeling*, Berkeley: University of California Press.

Hodson, R. (2001) *Dignity at Work*, Cambridge: Cambridge University Press.

Hopfl, H. (2002) 'Playing the Part: Reflections of Aspects of Mere Performance in the Customer – Client Relationship', *Journal of Management Studies*, 39:2, 255–267.

Houlihan, M. (2002) 'Tensions and Variations in Call Centre Management Strategies', *Human Resource Management Journal*, 12:4, 67–86.

Kinnie, N., Hutchinson, S. and Purcell, J. (2000) 'Fun and Surveillance: The Paradox of High Commitment Management in Call Centres', *International Journal of Human Resource Management*, 11:5, 967–985.

Korczynski, M., Shire, K., Frenkel, S. and Tam, M. (2000) 'Service Work in Consumer Capitalism: Customers, Control and Contradictions', *Work, Employment and Society*, 14:4, 669–687.

Leidner, R. (1993) *Fast Food, Fast Talk: Service Work and the Routinization of Everyday Life*, Berkeley: University of California Press.

Leidner, R. (1996) 'Rethinking Questions of Control: Lessons from Mcdonald's', in Macdonald, C. and Sirianni, C. (eds) *Working in the Service Society*, Philadelphia: Temple University Press.

Macdonald, C. and Sirianni, C. (1996) (eds) *Working in the Service Society*, Philadelphia: Temple University Press.

Parasuraman, A., Berrry, L. and Zeithaml, V. (1991) 'Understanding Customer Expectations of Service', *Sloan Management Review*, 32:3, 39–48.

Parkinson, B. (1991) 'Emotional Stylists: Strategies of Expressive Management among Trainee Hairdressers', *Cognition and Emotion*, 5, 419–434.

Paules, G. (1996) 'Resisting the Symbolism of Service', in Macdonald, C. and Sirianni, C. (eds) *Working in the Service Society*, Philadelphia: Temple University Press.

Pitt, L., Foreman, S. and Bromfield, D. (1995) 'Organizational Commitment and Service Delivery: Evidence from an Industrial Setting in the UK', *International Journal of Human Resource Management*, 6:1, 389.

Ritzer, G. (1999) *The McDonalisation of Society* (2nd edn), California: Pine Forge Press.

Schneider, B. and Bowen, D. (1995) *Winning the Service Game*, Boston: Harvard Business School Press.

Schwabe, M. (1993) 'Goffman Against Postmodernism: Emotion and the Reality of the Self', *Symbolic Interaction*, 16:4, 333–350.

Sturdy, A. (1998) 'Customer Care in a Consumer Society: Smiling and Sometimes Meaning It?', *Organization*, 5:1, 27–53.

Sutton, R.I. (1991) 'Maintaining Norms about Expressed Emotions: The Case of Bill Collectors', *Administrative Science Quarterly*, 36, 245–268.

Tannen, D. (1994) *Talking from 9 to 5: Women and Men at Work; Language, Sex and Power*, New York: Virago.

Taylor, P. and Bain, P. (1999) 'An Assembly Line in the Head: The Call Centre Labour Process', *Industrial Relations Journal*, 30:2, 101–17.

Taylor, P. and Bain, P. (2003) 'Subterranean Worksick Blues: Humour as Subversion in Two Call Centres', *Organization Studies*, 29:4, 1487–1509.

Wray-Bliss, E. (2001) 'Representing Customer Service: Telephones and Texts', in Sturdy, A., Grugulis, I. and Willmott, H. (eds) *Customer Service*, London: Palgrave.

Zimmerman, D.H. (1992) 'The Interactional Organization of Calls for Emergency Assistance', in Drew, P. and Heritage, J. (eds) *Talk at Work*, New York: Cambridge University Press.

14

HRM is redundant?: professions, immaterial labour and the future of work

Gerard Hanlon

In the business school Human Resource Management (HRM) is perhaps the dominant lens through which we view the employment relationship and the future of work. However, if ever it was in touch with the changing nature of work, it certainly is not so today. In short I will argue that HRM should be made redundant. To make the case this chapter will examine a range of changes in work. It will suggest that although HRM makes a range of claims such as enhancing the human, enhancing the individual and the collective; enabling greater satisfaction and freedom at work and encouraging responsibility; satisfying customer and producer needs and allowing the space to improve and learn, in reality it misses some of the key points of change in the twenty-first century and certainly misses the human. The chapter will argue this by examining professional work and outlining some important aspects of transition within this arena. These areas of change concern marketisation, trust and rationality, and the shifting nature of work because of the expansion of immaterial labour as a form of production. It suggests that immaterial labour is the emerging work form and that increasingly work and products entail informational features and cultural activities that we do not usually associate with work, for example taste, aesthetics, sensuality, language, and so on. This chapter will argue such an alteration makes the quantification of performance which is key to HRM (see Fleetwood, this book, Chapter 3) increasingly problematic.

Why work, why Marx?

In a 1932 paper entitled 'The Meaning of Human Requirements where there is Private Property and under Socialism', Marx accuses political economy of being both a science of wealth and of denial because it downgrades the worker to the lowest possible status. He argues political economy reduces the individual to the general or the crowd and hence sees the individual and their particular needs as a cost to be whittled down and denied. Expressing it rather trenchantly he writes

> political economy, this science of *wealth*, is therefore simultaneously the science of *denial, of want, of thrift, of saving* – and it actually reaches the point where it spares the man the need of either fresh *air* or physical *exercise*. This science of marvellous industry is simultaneously the science of *asceticism*, and its true ideal is the *ascetic* but *extortionate* miser and *productive* slave. (Marx 1988, p. 118, emphasis in the original)

Marx bemoans the hold capitalist social relations in the form of money, profit, and commoditisation have over humanity because we work ever more for ever less. Subject to these prevailing social conditions, we receive ever less because our humanity, our needs, our desires, our sensuality are increasingly filtered through a profit and loss account. He rounds off this passage by suggesting that 'the worker may only have enough for him to want to live, and may only want to live in order to have [enough]' (Marx, 1988, p. 119). In short, the responsibility of the worker is to be an impoverished worker – emotionally, spiritually, intellectually, and so on; to be otherwise is a luxury that needs cropping.

As Marx also noted, the centrality of work in our society presents capital with something of a problem. Capital and the search for profit dominates our society; however, in order to produce and to continue to dominate, it – capital – is reliant on labour and this is its fundamental weakness. Hence, for example, the increasing refusal to work in the 1960s and 1970s through the growth of early retirement, university education, dropping out, the decline of the work ethic and so on, presented capital with a real dilemma (Bell, 1974, 1976). Workers, via their strategy of refusal (Tronti, 1980), were increasingly challenging capitalism's basis. Albeit somewhat subdued, these challenges to work continue today and are at the heart of the EU debates concerning retirement ages, 35-hour weeks, a 48-hour maximum working week, welfare reform, and more (Jordan, 1998). To cite two examples: one, Digby Jones, ex-head of the Confederation of British Industry, suggests that individuals should be allowed to work longer than the 48 hours put forward by the EU if they wish to – he uses a summer holiday as a reason why one should be allowed to do so; two, following the USA, the German state is attempting to increase the age of retirement (the UK is on a similar course). What Marx's work demonstrates is both the centrality of work to modern life and the homogenisation of humanity under capitalist private property. People are reduced to being workers and when not working they are seen as a depreciation of value or a loss in much the same way as machines left idle are seen as a loss. It is this reduction of the individual with all of his or her needs to the status of a worker, to being a general category whose needs are only to be met through labour and its rewards, and the simultaneous denial of that reduction via the argument that private property enables the satisfaction of wants and desires (for example, holidays), that Marx critiques.[1] Humans undergo massification by capitalism as they are turned into objects and things to be manipulated (Freire, 2003, p. 148).

In this world, humanity becomes living capital 'but the *worker* has the misfortune to be a living capital, and therefore a capital *with needs* – one which loses its interest, and hence its livelihood, every moment it is not working' (Marx, 1988, p. 85; emphasis in the original). Like any investment, for example machinery or shares, our individual and collective needs, desires, and wants are subordinate to the needs of capital and private property, that is to the needs of the investors. Work not leisure, responsibility not irresponsibility, training not education, the obligation but not the right to work[2] are the order of the day. These are the things people must excel at to be useful under capitalism. In contrast to this, Marx values our individuality but sees it coming from our collective and historic labour – what we as a species are is simply the product of our historic labour by which he means our engagement with and modification of nature in its broadest sense (Marx, 1988, pp. 104–105). However, the difficulty under capitalism is that this engagement with nature is based on capitalism's profit driven grounds and the subsequent rational instrumentalism which destroys a critical individuality (Adorno and Horkheimer, 1997; Held, 1980, pp. 223–246; Jameson, 1971, pp. 34–35). One must therefore argue that at the heart of a Marxist critique of work is a concern about capital's domination of production, of market forces, of objectivity and rationalisation, and the relationship between being an undistinguished part of a general mass and having real individuality.

Somewhat incongruously, human resource management also touches on some of these themes. Central to HRM are also a set of dichotomies: commitment and flexibility, individualism and co-operation, adaptability versus a stable organisational culture (Legge, 1989; Noon, 1992, p. 23). Unlike Marx however, HRM presents these dichotomies not as contradictory or fundamentally problematic but as things that will lead to universal benefits if managed correctly. But here is the rub, HRM's exponents also argue that management's right to manage represents an universal interest (Noon, 1992). By doing so of course, they empower some and not others. In this sense Redman and Wilkinson (2001, pp. 8–9) suggest HRM is aspirational because it seeks to wed the committed individual-worker ever more tightly to the capitalistic organisation and, as we shall see, such aspirations shape its engagement with professional labour.

Professional labour and professional ideology

Many writers from within and beyond management have argued that professional work has been undergoing a sustained period of change since the 1970s. This has come about via re-regulation by the state (Abel, 2004; Brazier *et al.*, 1993), the globalisation of both capital and the professional service firms that are a necessary part of this very process (Sassen, 1994; Sklair, 2001), the changing nature of organisations across a range of services – medicine (Kitchener, 1999), law (Abel, 2004; Muzio and Ackroyd, 2005), accountancy (Anderson-Gough *et al.*, 1998, 2000), science and education (O'Neill, 1998), and more. All of these alterations are currently reshaping the idea of professionalism, through an attempt to change values – the very normative variables that HRM often associates itself with (Redman and Wilkinson, 2001; Storey, 2001).

These changes fundamentally entail a hegemonic shift away from an embracing of a social democratic consensus that had loosely stressed need over ability to pay, an acceptance that there was a gap between the social good and market delivered self-interest, state-led growth of professional work over market-led growth and so on (Hanlon, 1999). The emergence of a social democratic state and monopoly capitalism, coming out of the strife of the nineteenth and twentieth centuries, led to a Fordist compromise which enabled state-led professional growth to be trumpeted as part of a wider package of reform which was deemed to be universally beneficial (at least in the major capitalist economies). This compromise brought with it a change in the nature of labour's social reproduction – thus how people's lives were reproduced in the 1920s was socially fundamentally different to the 1960s in areas as diverse as housing, education, healthcare, law, and so on. But just as importantly, it also delivered extra profitability and stability for capital (Aglietta, 2000; Hall and Schwarz, 1988).

As is well documented, key to these alterations were the development of the welfare state, the emergence of a dual labour market with an increasingly secure primary labour force, the agreed state goal of full employment and the right (of white males) to work, and so on – in short, a de-commodification of aspects of the labour market took place (Jordan, 1998, pp. 30–73). These alterations reversed both the polarisation of income in the inter-war period and intensified capitalist social relations by expanding wage society in terms of the numbers of individuals enmeshed within it (Aglietta 2000, pp. 94, 243). They also secured for professionals increasing power over more and more areas of social activity via a state dominated by expert labour (Perkin, 1989) and the growing need for expert labour in large capitalist organisations (Mills, 1951). In this world, what Marshall (1939) called 'social service professionalism' was presented as 'best practice' professionalism for a range of public and private sector professionals. Hence Marshall, Wilensky, Goode, Parsons, and others present accounts of professional labour in terms of it being shaped by non-self-interested, social service oriented professional values. This was the dominant view of professionals and professionalism until it is challenged by people such as Freidson, Larson, and Johnson, in the 1970s.

Despite the growing criticisms of social service professionalism, it seems fair to say that its ideology and its seeming concern for the lay person helped to both shape, and be shaped by, a set of institutional structures that locked the social service professional into non-market organisations and behaviours such as the UK's National Health Service or private sector driven (but publicly funded) growth such as legal aid. This helped to shift their working practices away from competition towards co-operation, organisational hierarchy, state-led growth, long-term client relationships, seniority-led careers, and so on (Hanlon, 2004). These institutional and working forms were then passed off as universally beneficial (Perkin, 1989, pp. 286–359). Such a transition was a necessary compromise in the move from what Perkin calls a time of crisis for class society to a more stable corporate society. This transition was based on a growth in profitability via the triumvirate of productivity increases, collectively negotiated wage increases, and increased consumption. This claim to universalism however could only be made good as long as Fordism – the name allocated to this era – was profitable.

Fordism's run of profitability began to decline in the 1960s and with its breakdown we have been experiencing a difficult period. This shift came about because the social reproduction of labour under Fordism generated rigidities, which led to a crisis in Western wage societies. The way out of these rigidities was to (1) spread wage society via globalisation and (2) deepen wage society via new products and services and the marketisation of previously non-marketed services and goods in an effort to recalibrate profitability (Aglietta, 2000, pp. 413–415). These routes to profitability entailed attacking collectivised labour, globalising production and consumption, undermining of the welfare state, holding down wages and the subsequent polarisation of incomes and working conditions[3] (Aglietta, 2000; Jessop, 1991).

HRM is both a result and a secondary casual factor in this process because it directly attempts to individualise wages and terms and conditions, to increase worker commitment to the organisation and smooth out the employment conflict foreground in the introduction of this collection (see Korczynski and Parker, this book, Chapters 6 and 8). That is, it is one of the tools in capital's arsenal to break the triumvirate of productivity increases, collectivised wages and mass consumption which had become dysfunctional to profitability. As such it is an outcome of this dysfunctionalism – one that reallocates social wealth differently to the past. Its importance as an active agent stems from its popularity as a nomenclature for a variety of different labour policies. Within this backdrop, professional labour are an interesting group to examine for two reasons one, they are important in terms of extending wage society via globalisation (Sklair, 2001) and two, they are key to intensifying wage society via marketisation or commercialisation (Hanlon, 1999). Given the emphasis of this chapter, I will only examine the second feature.

Professional labour and the intensification of wage society

Professional labour is undergoing something of a contradictory development. Although professionals such as lawyers, accountants, and medics increasingly work in co-operative and inter-professional teams they are evaluated more and more on an individualised basis. For example, in the large law and accountancy firms seniority-based models of payment for partners – often called the lockstep model – are being replaced by more individualised schemes wherein the amount of revenue generated is the key determinant in deciding promotion and salary. This 'eat what you kill' model has been designed to encourage staff to grow the firm and to develop new markets. It has also been accompanied by longer hierarchies and an elongation of the career path to partnership (Muzio and Ackroyd, 2005). This has helped to facilitate a huge amount of growth whilst simultaneously exposing firms to greater risk, to less organisational loyalty and more staff mobility. Greater risk has potentially been created because increasingly staff are promoted and rewarded on their ability to satisfy client needs, sell services and generate new revenue (Muzio and Ackroyd, 2005). Accountancy firms demonstrate this shift most obviously with the emphasis that emerged in the 1980s and 1990s on selling consultancy alongside auditing services – for example, Enron spent as much on consultancy fees with Arthur Andersen as it did on auditing. Thus the partner or staff member responsible for a particular client has to manage the tension between keeping the client happy or adhering to professional standards which historically stress a loyalty to some third party – the state, the citizen, shareholders, and so on.

In today's post-Fordist environment many professional organisations have shifted so that they emphasise an obligation to the paying client – seen as senior management, and one's career is judged on the variable over which this client has most say, for example fee growth (Hanlon, 2004). In this new institutional world professionals are altering their norms and ideology so that the paying client interest is presented as the universal interest. Thus today a commercialised professionalism is seen as the guarantor of this universalism because it supposedly stresses competitiveness in a globalised economy (an economy and a wage society that professionals have been crucial to developing – Sklair, 2001). However, this makes organisations vulnerable to their employees as both Enron and Barings testify. A further feature of this emerging institutional structure is greater staff mobility as individuals and teams move from one firm to another in pursuit of greater rewards. Although their experiences have been different, other professions – such as teachers, academics, medical professionals, and engineers, have also experienced shifts in similar directions.

What these changes represent is an undermining of the old institutional structures of professional labour and its social reproduction. This undermining directly challenges the previous norms and values of professional labour. As such, society's trust in professionals has supposedly altered. In the past the state and capital enabled social service professionals to dominate and manage large areas of social life through sectors and organisations such as medical services, education, and legal aid (Perkin, 1989). In particular, professional groups gained increasing control over key elements of the welfare state and they were central to setting the goals and labour processes of major areas of social activity. They did so oftentimes in decommoditised social spaces; hence they were not the raw 'living capital' described earlier and their needs were incorporated into the labour process because delivering professional services requires inter-subjective understanding. This is something the political right and HRM acknowledge and is reflected in their desire to use the market and consumers to break the 'producer' interests of the welfare state. However, replacing this 'producer' interest has oftentimes proved less appealing to the public than to the right because the public still tend to trust 'professionals' more than 'managers'. In the recent past the state also trusted professionals to manage large elements of social activity because professional values and corporatist social service norms were seen as universally benign under Fordism. With Fordism's demise, this is no longer the case. In light of this breakdown, professionalism and what it means are under threat. Groups in the private sector such as lawyers, accountants, and architects, have embraced commercialised or entrepreneurial professionalism whilst those in the public sector appear to be in a state of uncertainty as their old professional values and institutional structures are challenged (Hanlon, 1994, 1999). The values of professionals, especially in the public sector, are no longer seen as universal. Today, they and their ideology are partisan and not to be trusted – in Hayek's terms, professionals defend a partial and damaging producer interest because labour's needs are taken into consideration (Hayek, 1944, pp. 89–100).

Trust, rationality and professional labour

O'Neill (2002) has forcefully argued that trust in professional labour is currently being undermined by institutions such as the media and the state. However, she also comments that claiming that we trust less and actually demonstrating this are not the same thing. In her third Reith lecture she suggests that 'the experts and exponents of a crisis of trust are mainly sociologists and journalists: they tried to find out whom we do and don't trust, in particular whom we say we do and don't trust'. O'Neill (2002) questions these sentiments and goes on to argue that individual members of the public still trust medical consultants, teachers, the police, and so on in their daily actions. Drawing on Power's work *The Audit Society*, she claims that what we have is a crisis of accountability and a world of suspicion primarily driven by a managerialist state attempting to restructure welfare. I would argue that this crisis is based on the perceived need by capital and state elites to put the state on a post-Fordist footing of 'international competitiveness' (for an explicit statement of this distinction, see the changes made to legal aid, Lord Chancellor's Office, 1996). No longer are public (or indeed private) sector professionals simply to be trusted to manage and deliver services. Increasingly, they are 'living capital' only trusted if they exhibit a new commercialised professionalism which stresses cost, affordability, accountability, entrepreneurship, and more as the state and capital attempt to redistribute the cost of labour's social reproduction back to labour and to complete the transition to a new regime of accumulation (Aglietta, 2000; Liepitz, 1987). To sum up, they seek to make this professional and skilled labour into the 'productive slave' highlighted by Marx (1988). Strikingly, these norms appear to be what these elites value rather than the public hence the disjuncture concerning the seeming crisis of trust and support for public professionals, their values and the welfare state between elites and the general populace.

Today, the professional world is an increasingly bifurcating one as private sector professionals experience changes wherein they become significantly more entrepreneurial and public sector professionals are increasingly told to act like they were in private sector organisations. This implies that private sector values are predominant and offered up as universal on the basis that they will reverse the erosion of profit that took place from the mid-1960s under Fordism. The rationality of the market place is reshaping professional norms thereby giving it an entrepreneurial and/or managerialist tinge. In ways similar to the historic importance bureaucratic control had beyond the large organisations where it was housed (Edwards, 1979), the emergent commercialised professionalism of the private sector is challenging the organisation of professional labour in the public sector. This is especially so as private sector professional organisations actively engage in restructuring this public space (Hanlon, 2004). Indeed, opening up the public sector to 'market forces' is one of the big hoped for future markets for private sector interests (Cogman and Oppenheim, 2002). To return to the beginning, needs, desires, individuality, and so on are not important compared to time-keeping, accountability, quantification, and so on. In Marx's terms the individual with all her needs and desires is reduced and cropped into the mass category of worker.

Townley (2002) has suggested that management is based on an abstract rationality that aims for consistency and control.[4] This analysis of work is in direct conflict with many of the HRM theories of management which often emphasise flexibility, adaptability, individualised service quality, and self-actualised work. This is especially so in areas of professional labour. However, contrary to fashion, the evidence appears to support Townley's view of management. If we examine health care there is a wealth of data to suggest that formally rational programmes, work protocols, best practice, and so on are increasingly used to organise labour and to demand greater accountability and consistency from professionals. Berg (1997) argues that protocols, guidelines, standards and the like are increasingly being used as a management tool. He goes on to suggest that this undermines the individual, the hermeneutic, the affective, and so on. These control techniques prioritise the quantitative over the qualitative. The measurable becomes 'objective' and 'scientific' and that which cannot be measured, that is the qualitative, the hermeneutic, the aesthetic, is negatively rendered unscientific and subjective – quality is reduced to quantity.

Aspects of these processes can be seen in a variety of health professional occupations – general practitioner services (Berg, 1997), tele-medicine (Hanlon et al., 2005), occupational therapy and a range of other health services (Germov, 2006). This seemingly rational emphasis on measurement and objectivity belies the de-humanising and political nature of asserting rationality (Adorno and Horkheimer, 1997). For example, in NHS Direct – the UK's new tele-medicial service – this informatics-led, objective and rational, best practice view of objectivity is built into the technology and encourages nurses to prioritise the knowledge in the IT system over their own knowledge, experience and practice, over their interpretation of the health interaction and over the pooled knowledge of their colleagues. Hence the current structure of this innovative and new area of the health service in the UK actually resembles technical and bureaucratic control more than it does HRM. Indeed, where collegiality, individualised service, and the breakdown of demarcation does take place it often does so either against the rules (Hanlon et al., 2005) and/or because the humanity of health care workers encourages them to work beyond their remit – this latter factor is also true for other workers (Ehrenreich, 2002; Stacey, 2006).

What NHS Direct indicates is the political and normative nature of 'rationality' and 'objectivity' – the creation of winners and losers. These controls are presented as universal whereas in fact they are partial and organise production in ways that weaken labour in its relationship with management. Key in this process is the undermining of inter-subjective understandings in professional work (Apel, 1977). Inter-subjective understandings of health care, education, language, and so on are central to professions because they are fundamentally subjective not objective, especially when they deal with human issues such as cancer or value.[5] They are based on consensual agreement and shared rights at a variety of levels – individual, group, organisational, and societal, rather than a hierarchal view of management's right to manage in the name of objectivity. Shared rights could of course weaken capital's control (Marx, 1973a, p. 70) and acting in the universal interest. Yet management claims of objectivity enable it to appear as rational, trustworthy and to portray other groups as not these things (Berg, 1997; Townley, 2002). These claims are being used by the managerialist state in its bid to control public sector work and oftentimes it uses the language of HRM to do so.

Immaterial labour, value, and the future of work

These claims to rationality are even more undermining and redundant because as we move into a post-Fordist world, work is fundamentally changing (Hardt and Negri, 2000; Lazzarato, 1996; Virno, 2001, 2006). Increasingly, work is based on what autonomist Marxists call 'immaterial labour'. Building on Marx (1973b, pp. 706–708, the fragment on machines piece), these writers suggest that immaterial labour is based on two different aspects to work. First, it entails the informational elements of the commodity. These are based on communication within organisations of a vertical and horizontal nature via information technology systems. Secondly, this labour increasingly entails the input of cultural content from activities that have not historically been considered 'work' but are, nevertheless, as fundamental to our species being as our collective history and knowledge (Held, 1980, p. 243). Examples of this second form would include the development of taste, fashion, defining cultural standards, and consumer norms (Lazzarato, 1996).

One of the reasons for this shift is the mass intellectuality of the working class hence today they are knowledgeable and informed and develop opinions and subjectivities that were once the preserve of the bourgeois. Central to this change is the notion of the interface – workers increasingly interface between work teams, customers, hierarchies, functions, technology, and so on. Key features of this interfacing are (1) inter-individuality, that is the bringing together of existing individuals to produce products and services and (2) transindividuality wherein historically captured knowledge is based on a pre-individuality, that is the received historic and collective knowledge that we are born into and that allows us to become an individual within an existing collectivity. Thus Virno (2006, p. 38) comments:

> post-fordist labour has absorbed into itself the transindividuality of the collective as well: so much so that many productive operations seem like political actions, in that they demand the presence of others, and must contend with the possible and the unexpected. For all these reasons it seems that labour expands infinitely, to the point of comprehending that which, in terms of political economy, is not labour: passions, affects, language games, and so on.

For our purposes the most important features of immaterial labour are: (1) unlike traditional commodities it is not consumed in consumption but rather it is enlarged by it and (2) labour goes beyond traditional notions of labour. One way of thinking about this is the use of NHS Direct. A person rings to enquire about a pain in their throat and are asked to describe pain – something that is not easy to do but between the non-work-derived cultural and communicative skills of the nurse and the caller, an understanding of the problem is reached. Ideally, at this point knowledge and learning have taken place on both sides so that the traditional 'producer' – the nurse – has further developed communicative and cultural skills to elicit answers concerning pain from callers and the traditional 'consumer' has learned something about their health and, indeed, participated in the joint production of the healthcare which will enable them to describe pain better in the future amongst other things. Education provides another example wherein both the teacher and the taught – the producer and the consumer – add value to production and learn from it; open source software appears to behave in a similar fashion.

All three have been enlarged in Lazzarato's terms – the healthcare (or similar) has not been consumed in the sense of destroyed or obliterated – in this world consumption is productive because subjectivities and 'products' are enhanced. Immaterial labour 'gives form to and materialises needs, the imaginary, consumer tastes, and so forth, and these products in turn become powerful producers of needs, images and tastes' (Lazzarato, 1996, p. 137–138) – in short, we as workers and consumers continue to use and to develop products hence the interface is constantly innovative, constantly evolving, constantly beyond capital's control because to control it fully is to fossilise it. To return to the introduction, today it is the living part of Marx's living capital and it is the needs of living labour that enables production – these needs are no longer the excess, the drain – they are the value (on living labour as excess, see Marx, 1988, p. 85). Learning, knowledge, innovation, and value creation happen outside of capital because, in Marxist terms, it is based on mass intellectuality and species being.

This process of production, constant change, learning, innovation, evolution, and so on means that any measuring of labour's 'value' or productivity is made problematic – 'labour time is no longer the *true* measure of social wealth but continues to be the measure *in use*' (Virno, 2006, p. 41). Furthermore, because immaterial labour transforms its users, it presents first and foremost a social relationship and only then is this relationship given an economic value. Hence immaterial labour makes explicit capital as a social relationship that puts subjectivity to work because its generation and regeneration is a social event that is now valourised in ways that appear qualitatively different to the past (one need only think of the areas of emotional labour, designer employees, and so on that form an increasing part of employment in the West from trendy bars, to the media, to David Beckham's real life as media persona, to perceive this shift in work). But this is also political in that 'work' and 'non-work' merge and are subsumed into the form of the commodity. Again to take us back to the start of the chapter, the non-work of the worker as living capital is no longer simply losing its interest 'every moment it is not working', it is in fact adding interest to social wealth even if this cannot now be measured. Within all of this, immaterial labour presents capital with a challenge – how do you capture and value mass intellectuality? But it is also evidence of our further enmeshing within capitalist social relations because the market is reaching deeper and deeper into our social activity as taste, affect, desire, human-ness, language, ideas – non work – are increasingly commoditised. It is a moment of both exploitation and socialisation (see Negri, 1991, p. 33). However, if the legitimacy of this valuing is challenged, these social relations may come to be seen as an obstacle to value not a measurement of it, for example the public in the United Kingdom appear to reject attempts to put an economic value on medical interactions, law-abiding citizens seem happy, for example, to illegally download music from the Internet because they feel 'Bach' not EMI is the owner of the music and its value, and large parts of the world supported the rights of poor states to generic drugs for HIV – all of these are challenges to, or rejections of, property rights in one form or another and they seem to be increasing.

Immaterial labour is thus changing work because first, innovation stands outside of capital and capitalist organisations respond to this and try to control or manipulate it, for example fashion houses increasingly look to street fashion for design purposes. Secondly, manipulating taste, affect, emotion, desire, fashion, needs, and so on are becoming increasingly important as a labour activity thus labour and its management is ever more political and subjective. As a result management and capitalism may become open to potential challenge in terms of this management, this value and objectivity but also in terms of what the product, the work, the value actually is and who has the rights to it? For example, it may seem illegitimate that after modifying a strain of basmati rice, the US firm Ricetec Inc can now label its rice as basmati even if it is produced outside of North East India and the surrounding region simply because the US Patent Office has awarded it a patent to do so. Such an action could be construed as stealing away the generational knowledge, history, and culture that developed this rice strain in the first place and made the brand 'basmati' valuable (as well as putting rice farmers in this region at risk). Following from this second point, thirdly, measurement, productivity, consumption, production are all being complicated by the proposition that subjectivity, inter-subjectivity, communication, cultural knowledge and so on are central to this new form of labour hence making knowledge of what the product actually is *before* it is created more difficult. Finally, immaterial labour by its nature demands and provides an individualised service in ways that management theorists always aspire to but can never achieve. The very human and interactionist nature of this work is a diversified experience which is impossible to manage, control, standardise, and measure precisely because it facilitates a hermeneutic and phenomenological engagement between the producer and the consumer. As numerous interactionist studies of professional work in particular demonstrate, these features have always made controlling professional labour difficult for managers. In light of these challenges, HRM's claims to measure value, add value, assess productivity, be objective, and more, look spurious – they look so 1970s.

HRM is redundant?

This speculative chapter suggests that HRM is both irrelevant to the future of work and that it is incorrect in many of its claims for the present day experience of work. In its more idealistic moments, HRM posits work as liberating, as productive play and a route to a form of self-actualisation. Yet, it also has a contradictory performative streak wherein play needs to be measured, controlled, manipulated and, if the player disagrees, then the HRM manager needs to enforce the rules of the game. Productive play by all means, but only on HRM terms. It is therefore simultaneously a science (if one may use that term) of freedom and control with the emphasis firmly on the second. This tension is fundamental to its existence because as Marx so forcefully pointed out, the employment relationship is fundamentally confictual within capitalism.

This contradiction can be seen today in the current commercialisation of professional labour, the attempts at managerialism within the public sector combined with elements of more 'traditional' forms of control such as deskilling, bureaucratic control, and so on. However, damning as these criticisms might be, I believe the future of work presents HRM with an even bigger challenge. At the start of this chapter, I suggested that 'at the heart of a Marxist critique of work is a concern about capital's domination of production, of market forces, of objectivity and rationalisation, and the relationship between being an undistinguished part of a general mass and having real individuality'. Immaterial labour is potentially making this domination more open to debate. It makes our subjectivities, our non-working lives, our collective historic knowledge, our practices, our desires, wants, affect, and so on key to the future of production – these living needs are the things that increasingly create value whilst simultaneously making value harder to define and measure. We need to rethink early Marx's formulation that the excess outside of work is a drain on capitalism. Today, this is where value is increasingly generated and this may herald a point of transition from capitalism and its notions of value. Value creation takes place outside of the organisation because customers add to value, workers generate it in their 'personal' lives, and so on.

Think of open source software – it is productive play or what Negri calls (1991, p. 34) 'free planned activity' but it is beyond the organisation. It is a seemingly anarchic generation of value without profit. Think of education, or a good restaurant or bar. Think of many of the black and Hispanic health carers who look after, mainly white, elderly, ill people and 'add value' through their unpaid overtime caring for individuals they have formed a bond with, subsidising medicine from their own pockets, their 'use' of their personalities and subjectivities to ease someone's pain and/or fear and/or loneliness (Stacey, 2006). We can use labour time to measure this but we are not measuring value by doing so. Value is escaping HRM – and capital – in these examples. People may begin to ask the question what is value in these instances? What are we paying and being paid for and does this enhance or lessen us? It may encourage people to question exchange value and examine use value in the future. As may thinking about work that traditionally requires less immaterial labour. We can think of Wal-Mart's UK off shoot ASDA and its 250 g Brazilian sirloin for £2.96 – a steak coming from an animal which is reared for 18 months, slaughtered, refrigerated, shipped, and packaged to the UK for £2.44 less than it would cost to post a 250 g package from the United Kingdom to Brazil (Lanchester, 2006).

These examples highlight a moment wherein what people perceive as valuable, as worth something in their everyday lives – their practices – may lose its connection with market value or labour value as measured by time. Oddly enough in the time of 'bling' conspicuous consumption we may actually be able to see the disjuncture between market value, wages, and human worth more clearly – the real cost of a steak or healthcare for the producers, the worth of human succour, or the value of our subjectivities may not coincide with this market value thereby leading us to question it. This is not a prediction of what will happen – following Marx's (1973b) lead in the introduction to the 1857 Grundrisse, it is impossible to predict what future social relations will look like except through the prism of where you currently are. Thus future social conditions are unknowable in many ways. However, HRM has no answers to these possibilities except the tired answers of capitalism. At this point, suffice to say, the Marxists are asking much more interesting questions.

Notes

1. Incidentally, although he completely rejected Marx's ideas Keynes noted something similar when he commented that every capitalist is only ever interested in her employees as an expense to be reduced and yet they are interested in every other capitalist's employees as a potential consumer who is hopefully expensive as an employee and hence with lots of disposable income to buy goods and services. In short, as employees our needs, desires, wants are a hindrance to our employer.
2. A right which would challenge private property because our right to be employed regardless of profit would give labour power over capital (Marx, 1973a, p. 70).
3. In the USA, per capita GNP rose by 75 per cent between 1974–2004 while in constant dollars the wages per hour of the average male rose from $15.24 to $15.26 (Supiot, 2006).
4. For the purposes of this chapter, I will not examine issues concerning the spread of rationalisation and technical control of work in a host of non-professional arenas (see Ritzer, 2000). Nor will I examine the worsening pay and conditions of large swathes of the working population (Burchell *et al.*, 2002; Ehrenreich, 2002; Jordan, 1998).
5. Shared understandings often exist between private professional labour and its clients and one could argue these understandings facilitated the redistribution of wealth upwards over the past thirty years.

References

Abel, R. (2004). *English Lawyers Between Lawyers and the State*, Oxford: Oxford University Press.

Adorno, T. and Horkheimer, M. (1997). *The Dialectic of Enlightenment*, London: Verso.

Aglietta, M. (2000). *A Theory of Capitalist Regulation*, London: Verso.

Anderson-Gough, F., Grey, C., and Robson, K. (1998).'Work Hard, Play Hard: An Analysis of Organizational Cliché in Two Accountancy Practices', *Organization*, 5:4, 565–592.

Anderson-Gough, F., Grey, C., and Robson, K. (2000).'In the Name of the Client: The Service Ethic in Two Professional Services Firms', *Human Relations*, 53:9, 1151–1174.

Apel, K. O. (1977).'The a priori of Communication and the Foundation of the Humanities', in Dallmayr, F. R. and McCarthy, T. A. (eds) *Understanding and Social Inquiry*, London: University of Notre Damn Press.

Bell, D. (1974). *The Coming of Post-Industrial Society*, London: Heinneman.

Bell, D. (1976). *The Cultural Contradictions of Capitalism*, London: Heinneman.

Berg, M. (1997).'The Problems and Promises of the Protocol', *Social Science and Medicine*, 44, 1081–1088.

Brazier, M. Lovecy, J., Moran, M., and Potton, M. (1993).'Falling from a Tightrope: Doctors and Lawyers Between the Market and the State', *Policy Studies*, xli, 197–213.

Burchell, B., Ladipo, D., and Wilkinson, F. (2002). *Job Insecurity and Work Intensification*, London: Routledge.

Cogman, D. and Oppenheim, J. M. (2002).'Controversy Incorporated', *The McKinsey Quarterly*, 4.

Edwards, R. (1979). *Contested Terrain: The Transformation of the Workplace in the Twentieth Century*, New York: Basic Books.

Ehrenreich, B. (2002). *Nickel and Dimed: Undercover in Low-Wage USA*, London: Granta Books.

Freire, P. (2003). *Pedagogy of the Oppressed*, New York: Continuum International Publishing Group.

Germov, J. (2006).'Managerialism in the Australian Public Health Sector: Towards the Hyper-rationalisation of Professional Bureaucracies', in Pilnick, A. and Allen, D. (eds) *The Social Organisation of Healthcare Work*, London: Blackwell.

Hall, S. and Schwarz, B. (1988). 'State and Society 1880–1930', in S. Hall (ed.) *The Hard Road to Renewal – Thatcherism and the Crisis of the Left*, London: Verso.

Hanlon, G. (1994). *The Commercialisation of Accountancy: Flexible Accumulation and the Transformation of the Service Class*, Basingstoke: Macmillan.

Hanlon, G. (1999). *Lawyers, the State and the Market: Professionalism Revisited*, Basingstoke: Macmillan.

Hanlon, G. (2004).'Institutional Forms and Organizational Structures: Homology, Trust and Reputational Capital in Professional Service Firms', *Organization*, 11:2, 187–210.

Hanlon, G., Strangleman, T., Goode, J., Luff, D., O' Cathain, A., and Greatbatch, D. (2005). 'Knowledge, Technology and Nursing: The Case of NHS Direct', *Human Relations*, 58, 147–171.

Hardt, M. and Negri, A. (2000). *Empire*, Harvard: Harvard University Press.

Hayek, F. A. (1944). *The Road to Serfdom*, London: Routledge.

Held, D. (1980). *Introduction to Critical Theory: Horkheimer to Habermas*, Berkeley: University of California Press.

Jameson, F. (1971). *Marxism and Form*, New Jersey: Princeton University Press.

Jessop, B. (1991).'The Welfare State in the Transition from Fordism to Post-Fordism', in Jessop, B., Kastendiek, H., Nielsen, K., and Pedersen, O. K. (eds) *The Politics of Flexibility*, Hants: Edward Elgar.

Jordon, B. (1998). *The New Politics of Welfare*, London: Sage.

Kitchener, M. (1999). 'All fur Coat and No Knickers: Contemporary Organisational Change in United Kingdom Hospitals', in Brock, D., Powell, M., and Hinings, C. R. (eds) *Restructuring the Professional Organization: Accounting, Health Care and Law*, London: Routledge.

Lanchester, J. (2006).'The Price of Pickles', *London Review of Books*, 28:2, 3–6.

Lazzarato, M. (1996). 'Immaterial Labor', in Virno, P. and Hardt, M. (eds) *Radical Thought in Italy*, Minneapolis: University of Minnesota Press, pp. 133–147.

Legge, K. (1989).'Human Resource Management: A Critical Analysis', in J. Storey (ed.) *New Perspectives on Human Resource Management*, London: Routledge.

Liepitz, A. (1987). *Mirages and Miracles: The Crisis of Global Fordism*, London: Verso Publications.

Lord Chancellor's Office (1996). *Striking the Balance: The Future of Legal Aid in England and Wales*, London: Lord Chancellor's Department.

Marshall, T. H. (1950). 'The Recent History of Professionalism', *Canadian Journal of Economics and Political Science*, 5:3, 325–340.

Marx, K. (1973a). *Surveys from Exile*, London: Penguin Books.

Marx, K. (1973b). *Grundrisse: Foundations of the Critique of Political Economy*, London: Penguin Books.

Marx, K. (1988). *Economic and Political Manuscripts of 1844*, New York: Prometheus Books.

Mills, C. W. (1951). *White Collar*, New York: Oxford University Press.

Muzio, D. and Ackroyd, S. (2005). 'On the Consequences of Defensive Professionalism: The Transformation of the Legal Labour Process', *Journal of Law and Society*, 32:4, 615–642.

Negri, A. (1991). *Marx Beyond Marx: Lessons on the Grundrisse*, New York: Autonomedia.

Noon, M. (1992). 'HRM: A Map, Model or Theory?', in Blyton, P. and Turnball, P. (eds) *Reassessing HRM*, London: Sage.

O'Neill, J. (1998). *The Market: Ethics, Knowledge and Politics*, London: Routledge.

O'Neill, O. (2002). 'A Question of Trust', *Reith Lectures*, http://www.bbc.co.uk/radio4/reith2002/lectur3_text.shtml

Perkin, H. (1989). *The Rise of Professional Society*, London: Routledge.

Power, M. (1997). *The Audit Society; Rituals of Verification*, Oxford: Oxford University Press.

Redman, T. and Wilkinson, A. (2001).'In Search of Human Resource Management', in Redman, T. and Wilkinson, A. (eds) *Contemporary Human Resource Management: Text and Cases*, London: Pearson Education.

Ritzer, G. (2000). *The McDonaldization of Society*, Thousand Oaks, California: Pine Forge Press.

Sassen, S. (1994). *Cities in the World Economy*, Thousand Oaks, California: Pine Forge Press.

Sklair, L. (2001). *The Transnational Capitalist Class*, Oxford: Blackwell.

Stacey, C. L. (2006).'Finding Dignity in Dirty Work: The Constraints and Rewards of Low-Wage Home Care Labour', in Pilnick, A. and Allen, D. (eds) *The Social Organisation of Healthcare Work*, London: Blackwell.

Storey, J. (2001). *Human Resource Management: A Critical Introduction*, London: Thomson Learning.

Supiot, A. (2006). 'The Condition of France', *London Review of Books*, 28:11, 24–26.

Townley, B. (2002). 'Managing Modernity', *Organization*, 9:4, 549–573.

Tronti, M. (1980). 'Strategy of Refusal', *Semiotext(e)*, 3:3, 28–34.

Virno, P. (2001). *A Grammar of the Multitude*, New York: Semiotext(e).

Virno, P. (2006).'Reading Gilbert Simondon: Transindividuality, Technical Activity and Reification', *Radical Philosophy*, 136, March/April, 34–43.

15

Disrupting identity: trust and angst in management consulting

Joe O'Mahoney

In 1999, after finishing my PhD I joined fifteen other new hirees at Zantax, a management consultancy based in the Thames Valley. Whilst there, we all experienced the boom and bust of the DotCom era, worked in multi-million pound start-ups and saw far too little of our friends and families. By 2004, when I left, only five of those consultants remained in the profession. Some had left due to nervous breakdowns, stress and exhaustion, others due to disillusionment with the corporate world but all, including myself, were shocked by what they had become in such a short period of time. In the words of one colleague 'I didn't care about anyone... everything became about the project... I wasn't human any more'.

Introduction

What of the human in management consulting? And what about the management consultant as a human being? Management consulting has long been integral to both the theory and practice of HRM. As a peripheral labour force, consultants fit neatly with the vision of post-Fordist flexibility exhorted by most HR gurus, whilst the cycles of outsourcing, mergers and acquisitions, culture changes and delayering, provide a constant source of people-related issues which consultants are called in to 'solve'. Central to this depiction has been the portrait of consultants in the practitioner literature as an asocial 'resource' – geographically flexible, socially adaptive and intellectually objective, they are often depicted as independent outsiders – devoid of the social ties that 'get in the way' of economic efficiency and rational thought. The apotheosis of this image is the popular characterisation of the Anderson consultant as a 'cyborg'. The Fordist origins of the 'borg metaphor has been explored elsewhere (Grey, 1989; Wood, 1998) but for our purposes attention should be drawn to the ways in which social and psychological needs are seen as at best superfluous, and at worst damaging, to the performative ideal of the consultant. However, because consultants are humans and therefore require trust and ontological security, this depiction has always been more prescriptive than descriptive. It is argued here that the resulting tensions between what is expected of the consultant and what they can actually achieve manifest themselves in the disruption of the consultant's identity.

In contrast to many occupational groups, the identity of the management consultant has received little critical attention. Whilst in the popular literature the consultant is often caricatured as either a saint (providing intervention in ameliorating organisational woes) or a sinner (deploying rhetoric to trick managers into paying extortionate fees), it is only recently that serious consideration has been given to the social and political contradictions that underpin consulting work (Heller, 2002; Salaman, 2002; Collins, 2004; Alvesson and Robertson, 2006). Whilst these studies have made inroads into portraying consultants as more than a performative or managerial elite, few have attempted to relate the contradictions of their jobs to the difficulties consultants face when attempting to build secure identities.

This chapter attempts to illustrate the subjective experiences of management consultants under conditions that treat them as performative resources rather than human beings. It argues that this experience is characterised by an 'ontological insecurity' created through four destabilising aspects of the consulting relationship: the instabilities fundamental to consultants' flexible working practices, the uncertainty resulting from incomplete forms of learning, the low-trust relationships between consultant, client and employer, and, finally, the ways in which consultants distance themselves from the human and emotional aspects of their jobs. Using the author's experiences as a change management consultant from 1999 to 2004, the chapter argues that the insecurity experienced by consultants is directly related to their experience of low-trust relationships that contribute to what Giddens terms 'existential angst' (1990, p. 100): an ontological insecurity that involves the experience of meaninglessness at a fundamental level. From this perspective it is argued that the experiences of management consultants lack the ontological, moral and psychological anchors to support the basic identity stabilisers that many view as a basic human requirement (Laing, 1969). The dehumanisation sketched here is, therefore, less the impact that consultants have on their clients and more the pathology of their peculiar employment relationships on their own identities. In the pursuit of economic efficiency, this relationship, it is argued, strips away the anchors of trust that are so important to the formation of human identity. In illustrating this process, the chapter draws upon the notion of angst as explicated by Giddens and other existentialist writers to relate the way in which the destruction of trust is directly related to the experience of angst and the subsequent dehumanisation of the consultant.

Consulting identities

In contrast to the extensive literature investigating and theorising the exploitation of shopfloor workers and their subjective experiences, the study of the dehumanisation of management consultants has been virtually ignored by both practitioner and critical writers. Such an absence is perhaps understandable given the contradictory position of the profession in popular literature. On the one hand, consultants are portrayed as highly skilled knowledge workers focused on developing a 'helping relationship' (Schein, 1999) with their clients. From this perspective, management consultants form a critical part of the 'flexible firm', bringing in innovative practices that enable organisational learning (Turner, 1982; Nahapiet and Ghoshal, 1998). The vast number of practitioner guides to consulting take this perspective, but it is also commonly found in guru texts and journals such as the Harvard Business Review. On the other hand, consultants are portrayed as expensive parasites, feeding off the insecurities of hard-working managers, and providing services that could have been performed by core employees. An insight into populist attitudes towards management consulting can be gleaned from the titles of two recent books: *House of Lies: How Management Consultants Steal Your Watch Then Tell You the Time* (Kiln, 2005) and *Rip Off! The Scandalous Story of the Management Consulting Money Machine* (Craig, 2005).

For some time, the critical academic community has leaned towards the more negative of these caricatures, portraying the consultant as functionally, if not morally, defective in their interventions (Hilmer and Donaldson, 1996; Micklethwait and Wooldridge, 1997; Monbiot, 2001). These and other studies criticise both the process and outcomes of consulting interventions, suggesting that many projects undertaken by consultants were unnecessary and, in any event, were most likely to fail. Recent studies, however, have attempted to move the debate from castigation to critique, arguing against the caricaturing of both extremes and focusing upon the social, psychological and political aspects of the consulting relationship (Sturdy, 1997: Heller,

2002; Salaman, 2002; Collins, 2004). Such writers often appear to share a concern with Giddens (1991), Sennett (1998) and Jackall (1988) that in equating exploitation with low pay, traditional analyses of exploitation at work often marginalise white collar experiences that can be equally (albeit differently) manipulative.

One emergent theme in recent critical literature has focused on the construction of consulting identities by examining how consultants harness rhetorical and cultural devices to more effectively engage their clients (Robertson and Swan, 1998; Alvesson and Robertson, 2006). Such analyses, often drawing on post-structuralist thought, have emphasised the technologies of surveillance and control utilised by different programmes (e.g., HRM, BPR or TQM) and the rhetorical and discursive methods by which consultants legitimate their practices. Whilst this literature has done much to highlight the devices which consultants employ to persuade clients to buy their wares, the presentation of consultants as salesmen (Sturdy and Gabriel, 2000), magicians (Fincham, 2000), missionaries (Wright and Kitay, 2004) or preachers (Whittle, 2005) defines the consultant too strongly by their sales discourse and portrays clients as relatively impotent. As Clark and Salaman argue (1998, p. 156), 'they define the [client] manager as a passive, uncritical, vulnerable and exploited consumer of guru ideas' rather than representing client organisations as proactive and potent environments that may destabilise and challenge the identity construction of consultants themselves. This view of consultants too readily buys into the practitioner representation of the consultant as a performer and defines them by what they do rather than what they feel and experience. Thus, whilst much of the critical literature highlights the insecurities of management as a key reason for the use of management consultants (Jackall, 1988; Huczynski, 1993) 'there is little recognition of the pressures and insecurities experienced by consultants themselves' (Sturdy, 1997, p. 393).

It is easy to understand the absence of instability, insecurity and anxiety in studies of consultants as many writers might find it difficult to empathise with workers earning over £70,000 that routinely advise and implement the delayering of organisations. However, if a commitment to the humanisation of the workforce is to be taken seriously, then money cannot be the only measure of exploitation. The insecurities and stresses inherent in post-Fordist workplaces have increasingly been identified amongst professionals (Jackall, 1988; Sennett, 1998) and commented upon in the consulting literature (Berglund and Werr, 2000; Barley and Kunda, 2004). What for the moment remains under-theorised, is the emotional and psychological experiences of management consultants in relation to their clients: how the contradictions of the consulting role undermine the human need for secure identity and how the effects of this unstable relationship are reproduced in the workplace. In order to conceptualise these tensions inherent in the consulting relationship it is important to understand the dynamics between the experience of social instabilities and the subjective experience of individuals. Below, Giddens and others are drawn upon to argue that trust and its opposite, angst, are central to understanding how secure identities are created and destroyed in the workplace.

Angst, trust and identity in the workplace

Giddens (1991), Fukuyama (1995) and Misztal (1996) argue that organisations provide an anchor of trust for human identity in an increasingly unpredictable and changing world. Trust and knowledge, therefore, are key properties of institutions which allow humans to develop 'trust in impersonal principles, as well as in anonymous others' (Giddens, 1990, p. 113). Trust is inextricably entwined with the formation of secure identities that provide an ontological shelter against the insecurities of modern society:

> ontological security refers to the confidence that most human beings have in the continuity of their self-identity and in the constancy of the surrounding social and material environments of action. A sense of the reliability of persons and things, so central to the notion of trust, is basic to feelings of ontological security; hence the two are psychologically related. (Giddens 1990, p. 92)

It is important to recognise that the concept of trust, as Giddens uses it, also applies to distrust – distrust provides the individual with forms of knowledge that are fostered in habitual rules and social norms (Elster, 1989). Indeed, many workplace studies have also highlighted the effectiveness of *dis*trust in providing opportunities for individuals to develop stable identities: where organisations fail to achieve their goals of ideological or cultural forms of identity control, various forms of distrustful attitudes in employees have also been identified as forms of resistance. Thus in distrusting, workers adopt a recalcitrant identity defined by an oppositional stance that has variously been described as 'acting out' (Ogbonna and Wilkinson, 1990), 'role distancing' (Kunda, 1992, p. 163), 'dogged mimicry' (Hope and Hendry, 1995) and 'resistance through distance' (Collinson, 2003).

However, as many writers have pointed out (Berger and Luckman, 1976; Lewicki *et al.*, 1998) both trust and distrust are based upon forms of knowledge or, at least, habit. For a worker to decide that their organisation is trustworthy or otherwise they must first have knowledge of that organisation, either through information that is reflexively monitored or through habitual familiarity. It is for this reason that Schwartz suggests that (whether good or bad) 'social institutions... specifically work organisations, develop an ontological function' (1987, p. 329). However, this chapter attempts to challenge this notion by arguing that consultancies often actually *cause* ontological instability through the destruction of trust and as such have damaging consequences for individual identity. Giddens identifies the consequences of this process when he suggests that 'the antithesis of trust is thus a state of mind which could be best summed up as existential angst' (1990, p. 100).

The roots of 'angst' are to be found in the early twentieth century phenomenological reactions against the totalising discourses of Kant and Hegel. Existentialist philosophy stresses the *potential* freedom of humans from external forces such as religion, the heroic code or social norms whilst advocating the authenticity of being promoted by Heidegger's *Being and Time*. Whilst this chapter does not intend to use the entire ontological inheritance of existentialist thought,[1] the use of 'angst' is intended to reflect something more significant than mere anxiety. Angst differs from anxiety in that it is concerned with an *ontological* meaninglessness resulting from the inability (or refusal) to trust unreflexively in cultural identity-stabilisers. Anxiety, on the other hand, is a worry or concern, usually defined with regard to future uncertainties. Angst is generated through the (intentional or otherwise) rejection of habits that encourage an 'inauthentic' identity,[2] especially those formed by social stabilisers such as morality, religion, class or gender. As such, angst involves the rejection or disruption of what has come to be trusted: 'without the development of *basic* trust... people may experience existential anxiety, and lack of confidence in the continuity of their self-identity and the constancy of their environment' (Misztal, 1996, p. 91).

It is this concept that provides the basis for much of the existential thinking about workplace identities. Existential sociology is by no means a new project (Douglas and Johnson, 1977; Kotarba and Johnson, 2002). Several writers have drawn on existential thought when describing the identity-seeking behaviour of individuals in overcoming the ontological insecurity associated with consciousness, death and uncertainty (see, for example, much of the work of Knights and Willmott). These insecurities are not simply those economic and social changes identified by Sennett (1998) and Capelli (1999), but also the lived ambiguities experienced by all reflexive humans in the difference between the self as subject and as object. Contrary to Giddens, who argues organisations can provide identity stabilisers in an increasingly uncertain world, Knights and Willmott suggest that 'insecurity is an existential condition that cannot be avoided and attempts to do so are likely to be self-defeating' (Collinson, 2003, p. 533). This chapter follows a median point between the two approaches, suggesting that insecurity is contingent upon the social and structural formations of trust that humans find themselves occupying, being neither fundamental to the human condition nor simply avoidable through the occupancy of institutions or cultures. It suggests that the destruction of trust through the instabilities and contradictions of consulting work (Berglund and Werr, 2000; Alvesson, 2001; Whittle, 2005) can lead to the experience of angst and the subsequent destabilisation of the consultant's identity. This not only affects the consultant but also, it is argued, their relationships with those around them. Whilst much of the existing literature highlights the insecurities of management as a reason why management consultants are extensively used in modern corporations (Jackall, 1988; Huczynski, 1993), this paper agrees with Watson, who argues that 'consultants do not simply manipulate managerial insecurities, but experience similar anxieties derived in part from relationships with clients and their own labour process' (1994, p. 405).

Management consulting at Zantax

Personal reflections

The material presented below is not the result of a planned research project but a personal reflection on five years of my life which were immersed in the management consulting world. As such, a formal methodology would appear out of kilter with the rest of the chapter. Although the PhD I had previously undertaken primed me to notice interesting social and psychological tensions within the consulting world, there was no time to reflect upon and write up my thoughts in any detail. Instead, the research here draws upon a detailed diary I kept at the time (which was important for any consultant in case of legal wranglings with clients), meeting notes, emails and various documents that were circulated at the time. In some cases I later contacted relevant individuals to clarify any ambiguities in my recollections or to better understand why they acted the way they did.

The long hours, unstable conditions and instrumental relationships took their toll on me and many of those I worked with in consulting. It was common for young consultants to leave through exhaustion or nervous breakdowns. Whilst I avoided the extremes of some of my colleagues, the stress of the work and a deteriorating relationship led to a period on anti-depressants and an increasing detachment from those closest to me. It was an experience from which I have only recently recovered. Talking to other consultants, both at the time and now, indicates that my experience was not an unusual one. It was common, as one mentor had put it, for inexperienced hirees to be 'thrown in at the deep end to see if they would float'.

The research presented below does not attempt to provide a complete overview of the culture at Zantax. It attempts, instead, to illustrate the manner in which the destruction of trust at a personal level leads to an 'ontological insecurity' culminating in the experience of angst at an individual level. The chapter demonstrates the destruction of trust through four related themes: the ways in which 'flexible' working practices destroy routine, that incomplete forms of learning lead to uncertainty and stress, that performative ideals result in low-trust relationships between consultants, clients and employers, and, finally, that their experiences lead many consultants to distance themselves from the human and emotional aspects of their jobs. Through these processes it is argued that trust is destroyed and ontological insecurity is created thus both destabilising and dehumanising many management consultants.

Introduction to Zantax

I joined Zantax, one of the United Kingdom's largest consultancies, during the write-up of my PhD in 1999. I had been doing some simple contracting work since 1996 and believed consulting would be an excellent route to both repaying my student loans and getting useful experience and training. After sending my CV out to over 100 companies, I was called to interview by 12 consultancies and accepted by 10. Zantax offered the most, not just in terms of salary, but also in terms of the variety of companies they worked with. My interview with the Head of Department, Julie, was surprisingly brief and not particularly searching, though she made clear to me that my doctorate in management studies would enable a premium rate to be charged to clients. My hesitancy in pointing out that my (fairly theoretical) doctorate may not be the greatest use to Julie's clients was matched by her reluctance to feel that this should be a cause of concern. It also became clear at the interview that my recruitment was not prompted by a business need for more consultants but primarily because Julie's section was being merged with another company. Her recruitment of additional consultants would, she believed, give her 'a bigger slice of the cake' after the merger took place.

My induction to the company consisted of being pointed towards a 'hot desk' which I was told 'may, or may not, be free' – no-one, bar directors, had their own desks. The company induction was minimal, I was told, because I would not be spending much time there. True enough, within one year of arriving I had worked on projects with British American Tobacco (BAT), Energis, Royal Bank of Scotland (RBS), Barclays and a telecoms start-up called 'Three'. The department I was working for was called Maximus, which specialised in culture change, but would often get involved in e-business projects. My business cards simply named me as a 'consultant' so to provide an ambiguity that would allow maximum flexibility when it came to selling me into different roles. The team comprised around 30 consultants working under four different senior consultants who 'leased' us out to different account managers who ran the consulting projects.

The methodology of most projects followed the standard consulting cycle of introductions, proposals, signing a contract and then actually doing the work (usually defined as analysis, solution definition, implementation and evaluation). However, in reality, individuals would usually only be involved in part of the cycle, usually implementation. As standard practice, senior consultants sold and initiated projects and were then replaced with less experienced hirees as time passed. This provided Zantax with a way of improving efficiency (freeing up more experienced consultants to bring in more clients) and a method of providing free training (by allowing less experienced consultants to work on demanding projects). However, despite being a relatively inexperienced consultant, the research skills (ostensibly) developed during my doctorate allowed me to experience both ends of the consulting spectrum, bidding for contracts and implementing business 'solutions'.

Flexibility or instability?

Although many projects could last up to two years or more, most consultants were used for around four to six months before being moved on to other clients. This prevented consultants becoming too familiar with the routines of one client and allowed exposure to many different environments. Most projects were based in London and the Thames Valley but many were located abroad, where one would be provided with hotel accommodation or, if the projects were for more than three months, a flat (shared with other consultants). As a rule of thumb Zantax consultants were expected to be in by 8.30 a.m. and leave around 6.30 p.m. However, on a new or especially demanding project hours could be 7.30–7.30 and if deadlines were tight, we would often be called on to work through the night or at weekends. The travel, especially around London, could easily add another three or four hours to the day. We were encouraged to travel by plane and train because this meant we could work whilst travelling.

This geographical flexibility, whilst exciting for the first few months, was often cited by many consultants as their primary complaint about the work. Home, for many, became little more than an abstract notion. I was rarely home and even when I was there, I was generally asleep or working having eaten, exercised and socialised at the client site. However, this situation cannot simply be blamed on consulting work – the geographical flexibility mentioned above should also be seen against the backdrop of a life-style in which many young professionals move houses regularly, rarely know their local communities and neighbours and change jobs every 2–3 years. Relationships amongst these professional flexible workers were often strained to the point of breaking by the combination of absence, stress and long working hours. The vast majority of my (consulting) colleagues were male and unmarried and though this did change as they progressed up the hierarchy, it was always clear that time for family had to come second to the projects. Partners, including my own, were often from similarly stressful jobs, which often meant that there was no check to the excessive demands placed on individuals. The habit of being in new places for short periods of time meant that it was often impossible to build up routines that could provide a framework to an uncertain lifestyle. Correspondingly, it is important to note the extent to which such instabilities impinge upon one's ability to develop routines of identity. The consequences of this detachment are noted by Misztal: 'Without the development of *basic trust* (initially with parents, family, friends) people may experience existential anxiety, and lack of confidence in the continuity of their self-identity and the constancy of their environment' (1996, p. 91).

Unlike many workers who are surprised when they are made redundant or when their employers backtrack on promises made, most consultants are fully aware that their contract is a precarious one and the financial recompense for this instability would be high. For most of us, our dismissal was a question of when, not if. This meant that most consultants, especially in times of recession, were constantly applying for new jobs, testing the market and networking with key decision-makers. I checked the main consulting websites every week and usually had an application underway just in case I got the call from head-office. The meeting of colleagues at competitor's selection days was so frequent that it quickly became more humorous than embarrassing.

It was rare, however, to be fired whilst working at a client site – the most common scenario for dismissal was when one has been 'on the bench' for too long. As the 'rest' period 'between clients' when consultants were expected to work on 'internal projects' at home, the bench was both loved and loathed by consultants. Whilst it provided a much needed break for those exhausted by the pressures of travel, learning and long hours, it was also known as 'death row': a secure environment where, if you stayed for too long, you were likely to be dispatched. I was put on the bench twice as a consultant, but never for more than a fortnight. Although one was generally safe for a month or so (this depended on seniority, experience and the economic climate) those weeks were very disconcerting. Partly as a result of this insecurity, the first thing one does when put on the bench is to start looking for jobs outside the consultancy. This creates low trust relationships in two ways, first because one expects to be fired and second because Zantax is fully aware that you will be applying for jobs. Perhaps because of this, and perhaps because of the fear of guilt through association, many colleagues contact consultants less when they are on the bench making it both socially and professionally a disconcerting place to be.

For many, including myself, exhortations to temporal and geographic flexibility combined with high levels of insecurity did not just mean increased stress and less time with friends but also that it was impossible to build up a routine. The disruption of patterns of social interaction, habits and familiarity is integral to the failure of many consultants to be able to *trust* in personal, social and organisational structures that provide what Giddens calls 'identity stabilisers'. In existentialist terms: the 'system [of habit] is the basis of our action. If we do not know the nature of a danger, we make an assumption. Without such an assumption, we cannot act . . . man neither knows what he could nor what he should do' (Riezler, 1960, p. 152). Disruption to routine has long been accepted as a key contributor to stress, anxiety and psychiatric disorders (Schultz and Schultz, 1994; van Tilburg and Vingerhoets, 2005) but in consulting the performative ideal that is promoted by both employers and clients is one that embraces these instabilities rather than avoid them.

Limits to learning

In practitioner literature training is usually presented as a sign of good HR practice. The model of learning promoted by most professionals follows similar cycles of learning new skills, practicing the skills so they become habitual and then developing expertise through continuous improvement. The ultimate aim is to have become so proficient that the practice of 'excellence' is both instinctual and subconscious. However, in the consultancy world, the need to meet the varied demands of new projects often means that consultants have to learn skills excessively fast and never achieve proficiency, let alone expertise is any skill-set. It is suggested here that this practice is not only stressful but also leaves the individual in a state of uncertainty as partial learning leaves the consultant reliant upon the interventions of others and unable to trust their own knowledge.

Much of the work I undertook at Zantax was highly specialised and ranged from running training seminars and putting together 'culture change' proposals, to gathering requirements for new computing systems and designing web pages. The method of business development at Zantax was to bid for projects and then 'shoe-horn' existing resources into whatever skill sets were required rather than to propose projects based upon what skills their employees currently possessed. The short-term nature of many projects meant that many skills had to be learned from scratch in a short period of time. For the uninitiated, undertaking systems analysis, learning the nuances of different software packages or designing a corporate strategy proved both demanding and stressful, often pushing the brain further than it was capable. The effects of this were both exhaustion and a constant feeling of uncertainty (and guilt) as one's skills were rarely adequate to the task or indeed what the client had been told to expect.

A fairly typical example of learning on a new project was on Boxing Day, 2002. My (new) boss, Simon, phoned me close to midnight to tell me about a new client. The conversation contained the following exchange:

Boss: What do you know about 3G?
Me: Nothing, why?
Boss: You've got an interview tomorrow morning in Basingstoke with a
client starting a new 3G company. I'll email you some websites to read
tonight.

I was awake until 3.00 a.m. reading the relevant documents about 3G radio networks and then left at 6.00 a.m. to get to Basingstoke for my interview at 7.30 a.m. After the interview, Simon informed me that he had rewritten my CV to make it more 'amenable' to the interviewer. In effect, I had been sold into Three as a (senior) Business Analyst. Surprisingly, I got the job. Business Analysis requires a very specific skill set. At its simplest it involves the translation of the business needs of a project into technical structures for systems analysts and technical architects. As such, one needs to be able to communicate with product and marketing teams regarding costs, quality and usability and to turn this information into useful requirements for the IT department. Often complex computing languages and systems methodologies would have to be learned to communicate effectively with different parties and tools such as crash courses in metadata, class diagrams and systems requirements would need to be undertaken in one's own time. At the time I not only had no idea what these phrases meant but had also been placed in charge of two teams of employees who had been doing business analysis for some years. Regardless of the issues regarding integrity and honesty (which are discussed later), it was made clear to me by Simon that aside from the thirteen hour days (often six and seven days a week), I should also be undertaking a crash course in these disciplines.

The structural conditions that lead to such pressures come, in part, from the exposure of consultancies to economic cycles. During boom periods (such as from 1998–2003) consultancies cannot hire enough experienced people to meet demand and are forced to 'upsell' their relatively new hires into positions that they may not be prepared for. Many of my colleagues reported similar experiences: having to present proposals to clients having been given a days' preparation, having their CVs rewritten at short notice before an interview, or having to learn the language and skills necessary for the role whilst on the job. One of the first projects I worked on was the presentation of a communications proposal to the board of a major UK bank for a joint venture. For this project, I was being sold in as a 'communications consultant' and was working with a 'senior communications consultant' who was actually an expert in enterprise software. We had worked on the proposal for about a week previously which meant not only creating the presentation and handouts, but also learning what a 'communications proposal' looked like, the language that would be expected and the basic skills required, such as handling media enquiries, designing press releases and the foundations of libel law. As one of my first experiences, the presentation was embarrassing, awkward and unsettling. Although the presentation was reasonably successful (we were asked back a few weeks later) I felt duplicitous and completely out of my depth, not knowing either what to say nor understanding much of what was being discussed. This form of uncertainty, not being able to trust our own knowledge, was a constant feature of consulting for the first few years and one that caused many young colleagues of mine to leave the profession through disillusionment as well as stress.

Regardless of the time constraints and stress involved, learning new skills and keeping them up to date are essential for consultants given the job insecurity they are exposed to. As many writers have noticed, fashions change frequently in the consulting industry (Robertson and Swan, 1998; Collins,

2004) and it is vital for consultants to keep abreast with new developments. However, given the pressures of being a 'fee-earner', training as a consultant was much less frequent than many of us would have liked. The pressure to learn quickly and the incomplete nature of much learning left me frequently feeling undermined, not being able to trust in my own competence and constantly lacking the knowledge necessary for action. In existential terms, this insecurity of knowledge is fundamental to the inability to develop the levels of trust that are necessary for secure identities (Giddens, 1991). However, contrary to Giddens' arguments, the organisation (in this case) acts not to 're-embed' trust but instead to undermine it. The partial nature of the consulting performance did not simply undermine the consultants' trust in their own actions but also, as we discuss below, the trust between themselves and the client.

Trust and authenticity

These temporal and geographic forms of pressure not only affected consultants while at work but also disrupted the architecture of home life through more than simple absenteeism. The common practice for consultancies to provide employees with perks such as gym membership, discounted tickets and reductions off restaurants and bars near clients meant that any social time was monopolised by venues near the client organisation. This was especially so as consultants were required to socialise with clients both to develop an impression of *bonhomie* and to befriend decision-makers that might later be deciding upon their services. An example of this, in which I was involved, was in 2001 at BAT's stunning headquarters in Temple, London. Here, smoking was possible anywhere in the building as, at this time, the company was still denying the link between passive smoking and chronic disease.[3] As I had asthma, I asked my boss if I could be moved to another project or simply work from home on 'back office' duties. His refusal was not based upon the fact that my skills would be missed but that I had 'built up a great relationship with' one of the key stakeholders at BAT and that my absence might damage the relationship between Zantax and company.

These relationships are key to the structure of the consultant–client interaction. Whilst the textbooks rarely talk of the social aspect to contracting, it was seen as crucial by all consultancies I worked with. Consultancies would often go to extremes to befriend key decision-makers such as joining their local golf club, spending thousands on complimentary trips for their families and in one (possibly apocryphal) case renting a flat next door to their own. Whilst consultants often get criticised for such practice, what is rarely considered is the effect of the duplicity on the consultant involved. In existentialist literature, false personas and relationships lead to an experience of what existentialists term 'inauthenticity', an acting out of 'being' that results in one's dislocation from what one is feeling.

Due to the rapid movement between projects and the intense internal competition in consultancies, trust between consultants was minimal and relations were often artificial and inauthentic. I didn't trust other consultants with personal information and did not expect to be trusted myself. It was made clear to me by the Head of Department at Zantax that 'you are very much on your own out there . . . but you'll get paid for bringing the money in'. Success required that clients would keep me on when they were sacking others which in turn required me to compete with other consultants both in terms of performativity, politics and socialising. At the same time, I could hardly distrust information that was given to me by members of my own team, especially when it was necessary for operational decisions. I personally was, for some time, at a disadvantage at Three, knowing next to nothing about business systems but having to run teams that were responsible for them. This paradox of not trusting but being unable to completely distrust one's own colleagues made both personal relationships and operational 'normality' virtually impossible.

Low trust relationships were exacerbated with client employees who were suspicious (often rightly so) that consultants were being bought in to downsize the operation. There was also inevitably a certain amount of jealousy of people 'doing the same work for double the money' as one client employee told me. This, more often than not, meant that employees treated consultants badly. In one company, a re-engineering exercise I was involved with suffered badly from all the usual forms of sabotage from client employees towards consultants: information was withheld, software and hardware was lost or damaged, confidential documents were leaked and relevant meetings were not communicated. Whilst this behaviour was entirely understandable, the instinctual reaction of many consultants, including myself, was to react in kind. Trouble makers were identified and briefed on, processes were designed to minimise the power of awkward managers and useful information was hacked out of networked servers.

Clients also experience this 'angst' of not being able to trust but not being in the situation where they can distrust: clients usually call consultants in because they require expertise that they cannot find in-house. However, this lack of expertise places clients in a vulnerable situation in dealing with consultants as they are often in a weak position to judge the utility of the advice they are being offered. Of course, all clients know that consultants will attempt to sell as many services as possible; however, they do not necessarily know the implications of what they are buying for their future dependency on the consultancy. For example, it was common to be called into a client organisation to undertake some form of Business Process Re-engineering, only to inform the client that for this to be done effectively, some form of 'data cleaning' would need to take place to ensure that all forms of data are consistent. Following this, a consultant might suggest an Enterprise Resource Planning system such as SAP or Oracle which would automate and speed up operational processes. Naturally, the client is wary of consultants selling more than is strictly necessary (or the client can afford) but does not always have the skills to decide which services they need.

One of the first projects I worked on was researching the business case for the purchase of a 3G UK telecoms licence for a large company. I dutifully did the research which indicated that spending upwards of £14 bn on an unproven technology would be a significant risk that only a cash-rich and speculative investor should undertake (which the client was not). The eventual proposal that was presented by my manager, however, promoted the opposite point of view: that the purchase would make sense both strategically and financially. On questioning my manager it became clear that the reason for the change was not just that Zantax would be ideally placed to offer their services to support the new project but also that he personally would be ideal for a senior position rolling the project out. What surprised me most (at this early stage) was the complete disregard of any factors other than corporate and individual gain. Critical literature on consulting has consistently found this form of duplicity to be common in the consulting profession, however few writers have pointed out the effects on the *consultant* of being encouraged to become amoral in their working relationships. Authenticity and distrust is not just generated though the relationship with the client (as many observers have pointed out) but also because the consultant is acting out the role of a consultant rather than be honest both with themselves and with the client. The angst that many consultants experience is, I believe, a direct result of acting without the moral frameworks and trust that many workers take for granted.

Cycles of emotional damage

On first joining Zantax, it surprised me how dismissive and critical many of the consultants were of the client employees. Regardless of whether we were bought in to sack people or to train them, consultants held a derisory view of clients. Client employees were often described as 'Muppets' or 'monkeys' regardless of any knowledge consultants had of them. The assumption of many consultants was that the client had called us in simply because their people were not up to the job, rather than seeing our services as a specialism that most organisations had no need to maintain a permanent resource for. At British Airways, a colleague of mine got rebuked (by Zantax) for sending round a picture of massed ranks of zombies entitled 'BA training seminar 2002'.

Whilst in the first couple of companies I consulted at I was eager to please and fit in, this became less and less important as time went on. I noticed this change at the time and wrote in an email to a friend:

> After you've got up a 6.00 only to find that they [the client team] wander in at 9.30 you start to think: you deserve everything you get. But then you think 'well, if the boot was on the other foot' . . . but to be honest I'm too tired and too sick of this to care any more.

This attitude in me, and others around me worsened, not just because client employees were (unsurprisingly) often rude, aggressive and uncooperative with us but because I actually started to care less and less about the personal and emotional impact my actions were having on other people. I felt like I was being treated like a robot and became increasingly comfortable in treating people the same way.

The violence of the language used for these encounters was often expressed in sexual or military metaphors. When sacking people, the most common term consultants used was to 'fuck' them and it was not uncommon to walk in on a discussion of someone being 'shafted' or 'screwed' only to discover this referred to a particularly adept piece of politics on behalf of the consultant concerned. Similarly, expressions of 'annihilation', 'destruction' and 'slaughter' would be used, especially in reference to process re-engineering when entire departments would disappear under the direction of the consultant. Whilst the violence of consulting rhetoric has been noticed by other commentators (Grint and Case, 1998) who argue this rhetoric fits with nationalist discourse, from my perspective it is more a result of the dehumanisation of the consultants themselves who cease to see individuals as humans. This disrespect for client employees is part of a morally destructive dependency between consultants and clients. Clients need the consultant but cannot trust them to act ethically whilst the consultant needs the client, but is treated like a mere resource without the psychological, emotional or moral relationships necessary to live as a human. The result of this contradictory relationship is often that consultants respond by dehumanising those they work with.

This detachment to human concerns is a phenomenon noted in many professions requiring high levels of reflexivity and 'acting out' (Ogbonna and Wilkinson, 1990). In their study of consultants and contractors, Barley and

Kunda note that 'contractors learned to disassociate their definition of self from the immediate context of their technical practice . . . ' (2004, p. 217) and go on to illustrate some of the less human forms of this disassociation. Whilst this phenomenon is not normally identified as exploitation by organisational analysts, the detrimental affects on the humanity of the individual should not be underestimated: 'the identity protecting device of "cool alternation" [is] . . . a syndrome that is no less crippling in its impact upon human existence than doggish devotion to a deified individual' (Willmott, 1993, p. 539). However, this intensely emotional experience is rooted in a structural relationship that encourages the treatment of consultants as machines, devoid of emotional or social needs. The objectification of the consultant that results from the conditions of their employment necessarily results in their own objectification of those they work with as well as their own perception of themselves. It was remarkable the number of consultants who believed that it was they who had failed by not being able to match the performative ideals of both clients and consultancies.

Conclusion

In *The Myth of Sisyphus* Camus tells us of a man that 'had lost his daughter five years before and he had changed greatly since and that experience had "undermined" him. A more exact word cannot be imagined. Beginning to think is beginning to be undermined' (1955, p. 12). It is the undermining of trust through consulting work that this chapter argues results in the experience of ontological insecurity. At the core of the consulting relationship is a paradox that consultants experience in their day-to-day lives. They can neither be trusted by their own companies, their clients or their own colleagues, however, in order to function in any way they are forced to trust. This contradiction, I believe, produces angst which partially explains the high levels of stress and employee turnover in the profession. Contrary to Schwartz who suggests that work organisations perform an ontological function to keep the individual 'free from anxiety at the level of identity' (1987, p. 333), the consulting relationship produces both personal and institutional insecurity and anxiety. Neither clients nor consultants can afford or achieve the high-trust relationships that the HRM literature often argues characterises highly skilled professions. However, neither institution nor individual can afford to completely distrust those they are working with. The characteristics of consulting work serve only to support this inconsistency: the consulting engagement is so fleeting that by the time bad advice or duplicity has been discovered, the consultant will usually be working for a different client and possibly for a different consultancy.

Consultants must be inauthentic whilst appearing authentic. They must appear friendly whilst being instrumental and must appear competent whilst often being the opposite. They are encouraged to act instrumentally, without loyalty or morality and befriend clients so be harder to remove. Often these tensions produce an ambiguity and inconsistency that many writers have identified. However, unlike many jobs where some form of acting out or habit allows individuals to produce secure identities, the consultant is always insecure and incapable of trusting or being trusted. At worst, this not only produces a deep seated angst with regard to the consultant's own being but also powers a cycle of damage between consultant and client employees that dehumanises both.

A consequence of not being trusted and not trusting is the treatment of employees and colleagues as objects. The ideal of consulting practice is, perhaps necessarily, amoral and inhuman. To succeed, all forms of psychological and social relationships must be externally exploited and internally suppressed. Clients are deceived, colleagues are undermined and the employer can only be trusted to be untrustworthy. A common way of theorising this in the organisation studies literature is to use Goffman's front-stage/back-stage framework. However, this concept of a consulting performance (e.g., Clark and Salaman, 1996, p. 104) in some ways under-estimates how the front-stage pressures undermine and dehumanise the back-stage self. The existential model, however, places an emphasis on how 'human beings are required to make their own identity, yet lack access to the moral resources that are critical for fulfilling this requirement' Willmott (1993, p. 539). The geographical, social and psychological instability encountered by consultants on a daily basis provides them with little to trust in, but the extent of their individualisation does not give them the luxury of distrust either.

There is, of course, some irony in professing sympathy with workers who routinely earn over £70,000 and are in the profession voluntarily. However, two key points need to be made with respect to this charge. The first is that the profession of consultancy is highly addictive: one quickly gets accustomed not only to the money but to the reputation, the change and, in some cases, the stress. I personally had much difficulty in adjusting to the frameworks of morality and trust that are much stronger in the academic profession. Secondly, this raises a challenge for what academics term exploitation. In a world where organisational controls over identities, values and cultures are as common as those over time, motion and output, should we be seeking to move away from the identification of the wage as the key component in exploitative practice? The biggest threat to the new forms of labour prevalent in the brave new world of consulting is not, I believe, the lack of money but the absence of humanity.

Despite the rather pessimistic tone of this paper it should not be assumed that all consultants suffer from the existential conditions that have been described here. Many of my friends still in the industry love the job, thrive on the pressure and believe they are more than adequately compensated for the personal difficulties they face. The exposure I had at Zantax was more extreme than that faced by most consultants, many of whom will stay with clients for years, building up routines virtually indistinguishable from that of client employees. However, many admit that the experience has made them less trusting and more distanced from social relationships. Such an observation raises difficulties to finding an answer for the question of 'what should be done?' Unlike traditional accounts of exploitation where improvements to wages or basic working conditions can be recommended the consequences of interventions in such an industry might outweigh the symptoms identified in this paper. When graduate populations are higher than ever and competition for skilled jobs increasingly tight, it is difficult and perhaps unwise to convince debt-laden students that they should be more concerned with their identities than with their bank-balance. However, this is perhaps one of the emerging challenges of the post-industrial world.

Notes

1. This exclusion is not just for the sake of convenience. Existentialism was always a movement more united in culture than in dogma. Kierkegaard used angst to describe humanity's relationship and responsibility to God, a long way from its literary colonisation by Sartre and Camus. Associated definitions can be defined as 'abandonment' (Heidegger), 'despair' (Kierkegaard), 'absurdity' (Camus) and 'nausea' (Sartre).
2. Existential writers provide differing conceptions of 'authenticity'. Kierkegaard uses the concept to describe the potentialities of man's relationship to God, whereas Sartre equates the achievement of authenticity with freedom – the liberation from society's fetters.
3. 'The science on ETS and chronic diseases, such as lung cancer and heart disease, is in our view not definitive and at most suggests that if there is a risk from ETS exposure, it is too small to measure with any certainty': www.bat.com (March, 2006).

References

Alvesson, M. (2001) 'Knowledge Work: Ambiguity, Image and Identity', *Human Relations*, 54:7, 863–886.

Alvesson, M. and Robertson, M. (2006) 'The Best and the Brightest: The Construction, Significance and Effects of Elite Identities in Consulting Firms', *Organization*, 13:2, 195–224.

Barley, S. and Kunda, G. (2004) *Gurus, Hired Guns and Warm Bodies: Itinerant Experts in a Knowledge Economy*, Princeton: Princeton University Press.

Berger, P. and Luckman, T. (1976) *The Social Construction of Reality*, New York: Anchor Books.

Berglund, J. and Werr, A. (2000) 'The Invincible Character of Management Consulting Rhetorics', *Organization*, 7:4, 633–655.

Camus, A. (1955) *The Myth of Sisyphus*, Translated by Justin O'Brien. New York: Random House (Original work published 1942).

Capelli, P. (1999) *The New Deal at Work: Managing the Market-Driven Workplace*, Boston, MA: Harvard University Business School Press.

Clark, T. and Salaman, G. (1996) 'The Management Guru as Organizational Witchdoctor', *Organization*, 3:1, 85–107.

Clark, T. and Salaman, G. (1998) 'Telling Tales: Management Gurus' Narratives and the Construction of Managerial Identity', *Journal of Management Studies*, 35:2, 137–161.

Collins, D. (2004) 'Who Put the Con in Consultancy? Fads, Recipes and "Vodka Margarine" ', *Human Relations*, 57:5, 553–572.

Collinson, D. L. (2003) 'Identities and Insecurities: Selves at Work', *Organization*, 10:3, 527–547.

Craig, D. (2005) *Rip Off!: The Scandalous Story of the Management Consulting Money Machine*, London: Original Book Company.

Douglas, J. and Johnson, J. (1977) *Existential Sociology*, Cambridge: Cambridge University Press.

Elster, J. (1989) *The Cement of Society*, Cambridge: Cambridge University Press.

Fincham, R. (2000) 'Management as Magic: Re-engineering and the Search for Business Salvation', in H. Willmott and D. Knights (eds) *The Re-engineering Revolution: Critical Studies of Corporate Change*, London: Sage.

Fukuyama, F. (1995) *Trust: The Social Virtues and the Creation of Prosperity*, NY: Free Press.

Giddens, A. (1990) *The Consequences of Modernity*, California: Stanford University Press.

Giddens, A. (1991) *Modernity and Self-Identity: Self and Identity in the Late Modern Age*, Cambridge: Polity Press.

Grey, C. (1989) *Cyborg Worlds: The Military Information Society*, London: Free Associations.

Grint, K. and Case, P. (1998) 'The Violent Rhetoric of Business Process Reengineering: Management Consultancy on the Offensive', *Journal of Management Studies*, 35:5, 557–577.

Heller, F. (2002) 'What Next? More Critique of Consultants, Gurus and Management', in Clark, T. and Fincham, R. (eds) *Critical Consulting: New Perspectives on the Management Advice Industry*, Oxford: Blackwell.

Hilmer, F. and Donaldson, L. (1996) *Management Redeemed: Debunking the Fads that Undermine Our Corporations*, New York: Free Press.

Hope, V. and Hendry, J. (1995) 'Corporate Cultural Change – Is it Relevant for the Organisations of the 1990s?', *Human Resource Management Journal*, 5:4, 61–72.

Huczynski, A. (1993) *Management Gurus*, London: Routledge.

Jackall, R. (1988) *Moral Mazes: The World of Corporate Managers*, Oxford: OUP.

Kiln, M. (2005) *House of Lies: How Management Consultants Steal Your Watch Then Tell You the Time*, USA: Imported Little.

Kotarba, J. and Johnson, J. (2002) *Postmodern Existential Sociology*, Walnut Creek, CA: AltaMira Press.

Kunda, G. (1992) *Engineering Culture*, Philadelphia: Temple University Press.

Laing, R. (1969) *The Divided Self*, Harmondsworth: Penguin.

Lewicki, R., McAllister, D. and Bies, R. (1998) 'Trust and Distrust: New Relationships and Realities', *Academy of Management Review*, 23:3, 438–458.

Micklethwait, J. and Wooldridge, A. (1997) *The Witch Doctors*, London: Mandarin.

Misztal, B. A. (1996) *Trust in Modern Societies*, Cambridge: Polity Press.

Monbiot, G. (2001) *Captive State: The Corporate Takeover of Britain*, London: Pan.

Nahapiet, J. and Ghoshal, S. (1998) 'Social Capital, Intellectual Capital and the Organizational Advantage', *Academy of Management Review*, 23:2, 242–266.

Ogbonna, E. and Wilkinson, B. (1990) 'Corporate Strategy and Corporate Culture: The View from the Checkout', *Personnel Review*, 19:4, 9–15.

Riezler, K. (1960) 'The Social Psychology of Fear', in Stein, M., Vidich, A. and White, D. (eds) *Identity and Anxiety: Survival of the Person in Mass Society*, New York: The Free Press.

Robertson, M. and Swan, J. (1998) 'Modes of Organizing in an Expert Consultancy: A Case Study of Knowledge, Power and Egos', *Organization*, 5:4, 543–564.

Salaman, G. (2002) 'Understanding Advice: Towards a Sociology of Management Consultancy', in Clark, T. and Fincham, R. (eds) *Critical Consulting: New Perspectives on the Management Advice Industry*, Oxford: Blackwell.

Schein, E. (1999) *Process Consultation Revisited: Building the Helping Relationship*, Boston, MA: Addison-Wesley.

Schultz, D. P. and Schultz, S. E. (1994) *Psychology and Work today*, New York: Macmillan.

Schwartz, H. (1987) 'Anti-social Actions of Committed Organizational Participants: An Existential Psychoanalytic Perspective', *Organization Studies*, 8, 327–340.

Sennett, R. (1998) *The Corrosion of Character: The Personal Consequences of Work in the New Capitalism*, New York: W.W. Norton

Sturdy, A. (1997) 'The Consultancy Process – An Insecure Business', *Journal of Management Studies*, 34, 389–413.

Sturdy, A. and Gabriel, Y. (2000) 'Missionaries, Mercenaries or used Car Salesmen? Teaching MBA in Malaysia', *Journal of Management Studies*, 37:4, 979–1002.

Turner, A. (1982) 'Consulting is More than Giving Advice', *Harvard Business Review*, 60, 120–129.

van Tilburg, M. and Vingerhoets, J. (2005) (eds) *Psychological Aspects of Geographical Moves: Homesickness and Acculturation Stress*, Amsterdam: Amsterdam University Press.

Watson, T. (1994) *In Search of Management: Culture, Chaos and Control in Managerial Work*, London: Routledge.

Whittle, A. (2005) 'Preaching and Practising "Flexibility": Implications for Theory of Subjectivity at Work', *Human Relations*, 58:10, 1301–1322.

Willmott, H. (1993) ' "Strength is Ignorance; Slavery is Freedom": Managing Culture in Modern Organizations', *Journal of Management Studies*, 30:4, 515–552.

Wood, M. (1998) 'Agency and Organization: Towards a Cyborg-consciousness', *Human Relations*, 51:10, 1209–1226.

Wright, C. and Kitay, J. (2004) 'Spreading the Word: Gurus, Consultants and the Diffusion of the Employee Relations Paradigm in Australia', *Management Learning*, 35, 271–286.

Author index

Subject index